Louis Wolowski (1810-1876)

POLISH STUDIES

TRANSDISCIPLINARY PERSPECTIVES

Edited by Krzysztof Zajas / Jarosław Fazan

VOLUME 45

Rafał Dobek

Louis Wolowski (1810-1876)
A Biography

Translated by Ewa Dratwa

PETER LANG

Berlin - Bruxelles - Chennai - Lausanne - New York - Oxford

Bibliographic Information published by the Deutsche Nationalbibliothek
The Deutsche Nationalbibliothek lists this publication in the Deutsche Nationalbibliografie; detailed bibliographic data is available in the internet at http://dnb.d-nb.de.

Library of Congress Cataloging-in-Publication Data
A CIP catalog record for this book has been applied for at the Library of Congress.

The cover image courtesy of Benjamin ben Chaim.

Book written as a part of the project of the National Science Centre (Narodowe Centrum Nauki): „Życie i działalność Ludwika Wołowskiego (1810–1876)"[The life and activity of Ludwik Wołowski (1810–1876)], agreement no: UMO-2018/29/B/HS3/00523.

ISSN 2191-3293
ISBN 978-3-631-91094-8 (Print)
E-ISBN 978-3-631-91646-9 (E-PDF)
E-ISBN 978-3-631-91647-6 (E-PUB)
DOI 10.3726/b21670

Published by: Peter Lang GmbH, Berlin, Deutschland

info@peterlang.com http://www.peterlang.com/

This publication has been peer reviewed.

Contents

Introduction

After the defeat of 1831, some 6,000–7,000 Poles settled in France[1], among them twenty-one-year-old Louis Wolowski (in Polish: Ludwik Wołowski). However, he was not like the other emigrants: what made him different from most Poles on the Seine were, among others, his Jewish and Frankist roots. Indeed, the Wołowski family was one of the largest families of this 18th-century religious group. Louis was directly descended from Elisha Schor, a key supporter of Jacob Frank. While by the time Wolowski was born, the family had clearly severed ties with Frankist practices and traditions, some of them had had some influence on his life and thinking.

Wolowski's fate in exile was equally unusual. For all the years up to his death in 1876, he was associated with the Hotel Lambert and Polish institutions linked in one way or another to Adam Jerzy and Władysław Czartoryski, above all with the Polish school at Batignolles. He also played an important role at Czartoryski's side during the January Uprising. However, Wolowski differed in many respects from his friends from Île Saint-Louis. If we agree with Jerzy Zdrada, that "the emigrants dreamt of a victorious return to an independent Poland"[2], it can be assumed with a high degree of probability that Louis Wolowski did not believe it and did not think that he would ever return to Warsaw. It also seems doubtful whether he dreamt of it. For, unlike most emigrants, soon he applied for naturalisation in France, and was quickly granted it. What is more, Wolowski combined sincere attachment to Poland with undying French patriotism during his 45 years in exile.

Wolowski's great career in France was anything but typical. He completed his studies, started his own journal, began to publish economic works, and finally, at the age of 29, was given the prestigious chair of political economy at the Conservatoire des Arts et Métiers. By the 1840s, his position there was so strong that he was elected (by universal suffrage) to the revolutionary National Assembly in 1848, a success he repeated a year later.

Although his political career was interrupted by the coup d'état of Louis Napoleon Bonaparte in December 1851, Louis Wolowski was able to profit from this event too: in 1852, he obtained permission from the then Prince President to establish a bank. In time, this institution took the name Crédit Foncier and became one of the most important banks in France of the 19th and 20th centuries. Wolowski only headed it for the first two years but was associated with its management for the next nineteen years.

1 C. Mondonico-Torri *Les réfugiés en France sous la monarchie de juillet: l'impossible statut*, "Revue d'histoire moderne et contemporaine" no. 47 (4), 2000, p. 731.

2 J. Zdrada *Wielka Emigracja po Powstaniu Listopadowym*, Warszawa 1987, p. 75.

At the same time, his importance as an economist grew: he published dozens of books and brochures. In 1855, he became a member of the elite French Academy of Moral and Political Sciences and, through it, of the Institute of France. He took a prominent part in all the high-profile French economic debates of the era. His voice also influenced the subsequently adopted legal solutions.

He managed to return to politics after the fall of the Second Empire in 1871. He became first a deputy, then, a few months before his death, a senator for life. He belonged to a group of liberal deputies, former monarchists, who eventually built the Third Republic.

Wolowski was associated with the émigré Polish Literary Society, the Polish School in Paris, the Polish Bureau of the Hotel Lambert in 1861–1864, the Institute of Polish Ladies, the famous Parisian Conservatoire des Arts et Métiers, the Crédit Foncier, the Academy of Moral and Political Sciences, the Paris Society of Political Economy, the Free Trade Association, and finally with the French National Assembly during the Revolution of 1848 and after 1871. This needs to be topped with his intellectual activity, published books and articles. He left his own mark on all of these institutions through his activity.

At the same time, in the case of Wolowski, researchers are struck by another fact: he was never, in any of his fields of activity, an unambiguously leading figure. At the Hotel Lambert, at the Crédit Foncier, in parliament – he always remained in the shadow of others. And yet, as Iwona Pugacewicz put it, "all the doors of the most important institutions in Paris were open to his name"[3].

My intention, therefore, was to explain the phenomenon of this extraordinary man. A phenomenon which, in my opinion, is important for understanding 19th century French and Polish politics in general. To understand the mechanisms governing public life in the 19th century, it is necessary to look beyond the leading figures, beyond the best-known names. It is also necessary to recognise those who operated right behind the scenes of big politics. Wolowski was one of them. On the one hand, he was in many ways a typical representative of the French political and intellectual elite operating between the July Monarchy and the Third Republic. Tracing his political stance, its twists and turns and its evolution provides a better understanding of the events of the period. On the other hand, Wolowski, like few others, was able to bring together different people for different purposes and different ventures. Working behind the backs of the most important figures in French and Polish (émigré) political life, he created bridges between disparate communities. He acted like glue, sometimes weakly visible at first sight, but indispensable for the functioning of the state. Recognising this role of Wolowski allows for a better understanding of politics in general, not only 19th-century politics. In this sense, Wolowski's biography also differs from the major political figures of the

3 I.H. Pugacewicz *Batignolles 1842–1874. Edukacja Wielkiej Emigracji*, Warszawa 2017, p. 126.

period: Napoleon III, Czartoryski, Thiers, Guizot, Mac Mahon – to name but a few. Nor is it a biography of an average Polish émigré or an average French parliamentarian, economist, or politician. It sits, in my opinion, somewhere in between. This also makes it relevant and interesting.

What were Wolowski's sources of strength? What social or political strategies did he adopt? What constraints did he face? How did he resemble other French or Polish politicians of the period, what made him different? Finally, how far did his action in Paris reach, both in Polish and French affairs? These are the key questions that this work asks.

Questions, I should add, which historiography has so far failed to answer or has answered poorly. Louis Wolowski's name has been, of course, mentioned in Polish studies devoted to the Great Emigration, or French works on the political, parliamentary, or economic history of the 19th century. Two biographies of Wolowski and a monograph on his economic thought have been published in France. However, all these works date from the 19th century. A year after Louis Wolowski's death, Emile Levasseur published a 36-page brochure, *La vie et les travaux de Wolowski* (Paris, 1877). For years, Levasseur was the Pole's close friend and colleague, and the husband of his relative. The text therefore contains interesting personal recollections and some relevant information. Its shortcoming, apart from its brevity, is a lack of temporal and personal distance: Levasseur's work is understandably an apologia for Wolowski. Similar objections can be raised against another biography of the Polish French banker, written in 1880 by Antony Roulliet, a lawyer and economist, entitled *Wolowski. Sa vie et ses travaux*. Much more extensive than Levasseur's, Roulliet's biography is unfortunately equally apologetic. In both cases, the authors lacked access to Polish sources, which resulted in serious omissions and errors concerning the Polish part of Wolowski's biography or his family. Jules Rambaud's work *L'Oeuvre économique de L. Wolowski* (Paris, 1882) is simply a comprehensive compilation and summary of the subsequent economic studies of the Pole.

The most complete biography of Louis Wolowski to date has never been published. I mean the text of Patrice Markiewicz's 1994 doctoral thesis, *Louis Wolowski. Un intellectuel et un représentant du libéralisme en France au milieu du XIXe siècle* (Paris X – Nanterre, 1994). Markiewicz presented the French part of Wolowski's life best, while treating the Polish part too briefly. Leaving aside the otherwise understandable errors related to the complicated family colligations of the Wołowskis, in my opinion Markiewicz also made another important mistake – at times, his narrative resembled Wolowski's self-narration too much.

The Polish list of studies on Wolowski is incomparably shorter and contains only three short academic texts, one popular science text and two dictionary entries. The ambition of the present work is therefore to fill this gap.

My intention has been to describe Wolowski as a figure characteristic of France of his time, a representative of part of the elite educated during the July Monarchy, then struggling to find his feet in the Second Republic, collaborating with Napoleon III, and at the end of his life co-founding the Third Republic. At the same time, I wanted to show Wolowski as a man who often operated behind the scenes, very effectively linking different circles and different people, and thus influencing politics. He acted as a necessary link between Polish émigré politicians and the French political and economic elite; as the glue that united people from different ideological circles in one bank. Finally, as a liberal economist, a typical representative of the second generation of the French classical school. Understanding people like Wolowski, their official and behind-the-scenes role in 19th century France and among Polish émigrés will, in my view, allow for a better understanding of the mechanisms of French and Polish politics, economy, and finance in general, from the decline of Louis-Philippe's state, through the Revolution of 1848, the Second Empire, to the first years of the Third Republic.

For this purpose, I managed to access all or almost all the publications of the Polish French economist. Unfortunately, however, I found only a limited stock of his correspondence. The rest of it no longer exists, is in private hands unknown to me, or remains scattered in minor archives. I have only reached some of the Crédit Foncier materials, stored in the French Archives Nationales du Monde du Travail; access to them is still restricted and requires the owner's separate permission. The material that I have managed to obtain from the ANMT is included in this work. However, I have gathered the entire corpus of archival material from the French National Archives (Archives Nationales), the Archives of the French National Assembly (Archives de l'Assemblée Nationale), the Archives of Paris (Archives de Paris), the National Library of France (Bibliothèque Nationale de France), the Polish Library in Paris, the Adam Mickiewicz Museum in Paris, the Polish Central Archives of Historical Records, the National Library, the Archives of the City of Warsaw, the State Archives in Cracow, the Princes Czartoryski Library in Cracow, the Archives of the Polish Academy of Sciences and the Polish Academy of Arts and Sciences in Cracow, and the Ossolińskis National Institute in Wrocław.

The division of the book results in part from the turns of Louis Wolowski's life. Chapter I describes his family, its Frankist roots, the fate of Louis' mother and father, and their influence on their son. Chapter II (Youth in Poland) deals with his studies in Warsaw, his participation in the conspiracy movement and the November Uprising. In Chapter III, the readers learn about Wolowski's first years in exile, a time when he made the decision to naturalise and began to build the foundations of his career as an economist. Chapter IV is devoted to the Revolution of 1848 and its impact on Wolowski's political thinking, against the broad background of French politics. Chapter V tells the story of his involvement in the creation and operation of the Crédit Foncier, coupled with a broader picture of the entire change taking place in French banking in the 1850s and 1860s. Chapter VI depicts the 1850s and 1860s when Wolowski reached the apogee of his career, became a member of the Academy of Moral and Political Sciences, published the most, participated in key economic discussions in France, and experienced a series of turbulence and family changes. Chapter VII describes Wolowski's return to politics after the collapse of the Second Empire and his participation in the building of the Third Republic, against an extensive French background. The penultimate chapter is devoted entirely to Wolowski's economic thought, his research method, his economic liberalism, his advocacy of free trade, his vision of money, the banking system, etc. The final chapter of the work deals with the extremely important and diverse Polish émigré activities of Louis Wolowski. This classical division allows, in my view, for a thorough tracing of Wolowski's political career along with the evolution of his attitude over the years. It facilitates a comprehensive presentation of his Polish activities, as well as his banking career. Finally, it allows us to illustrate the development and transformation of his economic thought, its successive developments.

Behind every book is an author. Behind the author, however, are those who have assisted him, pointed out new leads, helped to eliminate shortcomings, to obtain materials for the work. Co-workers, friends, acquaintances without whom no book would be possible. I would like to express my sincere thanks to them. A word of great gratitude goes to Professor Jerzy Fiećko, who led me to new clues concerning Wolowski's relationship with Zygmunt Krasiński. I am also extremely grateful to Julia Słupska for her excellent biography of Ksawery Branicki, for her consultation on the relationship between Branicki and Wolowski and for the materials she sent me. I would also like to express my gratitude to Professors Eric Anceau and Dominique Barjot: I could always count on their assistance in French matters. For all the comments, words of encouragement and support, I sincerely thank the members of my home department at the Faculty of History of Adam Mickiewicz University in Poznań: Prof. Waldemar Łazuga, Prof. Damian Szymczak, Prof. Sebastian Paczos, Mariusz Menz, Ph.D. and Anna Chudzińska, Ph.D. I would also like to thank Piotr Kuligowski, Ph.D. and Stanisław Knapowski, for their comments and invaluable help.

Finally, this book would not have been possible without the endless patience and understanding of my beloved wife, Kamila. Thank you.

Chapter I: An Extraordinary Family

1. The Schors, disciples of Jacob Frank

In one of the last paragraphs of Olga Tokarczuk's *The Books of Jacob*, suspended between the world of the living and the world of the dead, Yenta, the readers' guide to the fate of the Frankists, looks at the Wołowski family:

> Nearly all its branches became ennobled, some under the Bawół coat of arms, others under Na Kaskach. A fabulous career was made by Franciszek, son of Isaac Wołowski, the boy whom Father Chmielowski had once called Jeremiah. Franciszek, born in 1786 in Brünn and raised in Offenbach, became one of the best lawyers and scholars of law of his era. Interestingly, when a proposal came before the Sejm to grant Polish citizenship to Jews, Franciszek, as a member of parliament, vehemently argued that it was not yet time to take such a step. First the Polish nation had to win its independence; only then they would be able to turn to such social reforms. When the November Uprising was put down, the grandson of another of the Wołowski sons, Ludwik, emigrated to France, where he, too, earned renown as a brilliant legal scholar, for which he was awarded the Légion d'Honneur.[4]

Ludwik Wołowski (Louis Wolowski) as seen by Yenta is the protagonist of this book. Indeed, an émigré and a lawyer; his brilliance is another thing. Indeed, he was also awarded the Legion of Honour in 1845[5] but for economic and political activities rather than legal. Yenta is also wrong in her description of the family connections: Franciszek Eliasz Wołowski, a lawyer and member of the Sejm (lower house of the Polish parliament) during the November Uprising, was Louis' father. However, most probably he was not born in Brünn but in Warsaw. Still, Yenta – Tokarczuk should not be blamed for these mistakes. Not only because it seems inappropriate to expect accuracy and historical precision in every detail from literature; also because of the exceptional complication of the fate and biographical data of the Wołowskis, extremely difficult for professional historians to interpret.

---

4 O. Tokarczuk *The Books of Jacob, or: A Fantastic Journey Across Seven Borders, Five Languages, and Three Major Religions, Not Counting the Minor Sects. Told by the Dead, Supplemented by the Author, Drawing from a Range of Books, and Aided by Imagination, the Which Bein g the Greatest Natural Gift of Any Person. That the Wise Might Have It for a Record, That My Compatriots Reflect, Laypersons Gain Some Understanding, and Melancholy Souls Obtain Some Slight Enjoyment*, Riverhead Books, New Yorks 2022, translation by Jennifer Croft, p. 17 (pages numbered backwards).

5 Dossier of the Legion of Honour of Louis Wolowski i: Archives Nationales, ref. LH// 2762/26.

The Wołowskis, baptised Frankists, maintained the customs characteristic of this group for several generations: they married among themselves and gave their children similar names. Louis Wolowski was therefore the son of Franciszek Wołowski and Tekla… née Wołowska. The name Ludwik (Louis) was a regular occurrence in the family, as was Franciszek, Michał, Jan and Józef[6]. In the light of the fact that many of them practised the same profession (lawyers) and the shortcomings following the destruction of the Polish archives during WWII, the confusions, and errors in the descriptions of the history of the Wołowskis are easier to understand.

The Wołowski family originated from Podolia, from Rabbi Schor Efraim Salomon ben Naftali, author of the acclaimed book *Tevuat Schor*, who died in 1633. The surname Schor probably derives from a Hebrew reflexive epithet meaning ox, and has biblical roots[7]. The most significant moment in the family's history came in the mid-18th century. A little earlier (it is not known exactly when), the Schors became involved with the Sabbatean movement[8]. Podolia

6 J.E. Utkin *Potomkowie kupca Wołowskiego – prawnicy, powstańcy w XIX stuleciu*, "Miscellanea Historico- Iuridica", vol. 18, part 2, 2019, pp. 71–74.

7 A. Trzciński *Składnik informacyjny w epitafiach ze starego cmentarza żydowskiego w Lublinie*, "Rocznik Lubelskiego Towarzystwa Genealogicznego", vol. VIII, 2016 (2017), p. 142.

8 The Sabbateans – Messianic heresy within Judaism. Its central figure was Sabbatai Zewi (1626–1676) who declared himself messiah in 1664. The Sabbateans would not have gained adherents, however, had it not been for Nathan of Gaza (1644–1680) who served as the Sabbatean chief theologian and prophet. According to the teachings of Sabbatai and Nathan, taken over from the earlier Kabbalah, the teachings of Abraham Cardoso (1626–1706) and Isaac Luria (1534–1572), a process of *tikkun* was taking place in the world: repairing the world by separating good from evil, freeing the *Shekhinah* (divine immanence) from the fetters. A key role in the end of this process was to be played by the messiah Sabbatai. His task was to raise with his power the divine sparks scattered in the world of evil. To this end, the messiah was to descend into the world of sin himself to smash it from within. The end of this process was to be the complete liberation of man from the bondage of evil, the full harmony of the worlds. This process of spiritual salvation was to be linked to the return of the Jews to Palestine which Sabbatai announced in 1666. In the same year, Sabbatai was forced to convert to Islam: Sabbatai, however, accepted it as part of his plan of salvation. Nathan described Sabbatai's betrayal precisely as a necessary descent into the valley of evil, to bring about all the more surely the release of the Shekhinah imprisoned in Islam. This was to be the "exile" of the messiah, who was henceforth to be the vessel of the Shekhinah. The conviction that the transformation of the world was taking place and had already been partly accomplished was accompanied among the Sabbateans by the thought that the old religious laws, including the Torah, also had to be changed. Sabbatai Zewi thus repeatedly behaved in clear contradiction to the precepts of traditional Judaism, outraging Jews.

became a mainstay of the Sabbateans during this period, and – according to Paweł Maciejko – the Schors were "probably the most important family" among the Sabbateans[9]. At the time, the family was headed by Elisha Schor (b. 1688) whose daughter Haia was perceived as a Sabbatean prophetess. The Schors also had family ties with the Sabbateans from across the region.

Although the "messiah" Sabbatai Zewi had died decades earlier, his followers secretly awaited the arrival of his next incarnation. This became Jacob Frank. He was born in 1726 in Podolia[10]. His father, Leib, was most likely a Sabbatean and probably had contacts with his fellow southern believers[11]. Perhaps it was the accusation of the Sabbatean affinity that contributed to Leib's departure from Poland with his family. They arrived in Bucharest where the young Jacob ended up as a shop assistance in training. He had most likely learned to read and write as a child, but his knowledge of the Talmud remained limited: he described himself much later as a "simpleton", an unlearned man. Jacob engaged in trade, and it was trade that took him all the way to Smyrna. While in Turkey, he became a "Frank": a European, a foreigner according to the local nomenclature[12]. In Smyrna, in 1750 he began his Kabbalistic studies and became more familiar with the Sabbatean doctrine. In 1752, he married Chana, the daughter of Yehuda Towa ha-Levi, a Sabbatean theologian.

The Sabbatean movement survived the death of its founder: its followers recognised that the messiah had "gone into hiding" and awaited his second coming. Some left Judaism altogether, some hid their beliefs carefully to avoid persecution by the rabbis. Some converted to Islam. It was a matter of time in this situation that further incarnations of the messiah appeared among the Sabbateans. Some (the so-called Dönmeh) saw him in Jacob Kerido (1661–1697), others ('Koniosos' from Thessaloniki) in Baruch Ruso. The latter were probably linked to the Sabbateans from Podolia. (G. Scholem *Mistycyzm żydowski i jego główne kierunki,* Warszawa 2020, pp. 459–512; A. Cała, H. Węgrzynek, G. Zalewska *Historia i kultura Żydów polskich. Słownik,* Warszawa 2000, pp. 294 and 328).

9 P. Maciejko *Wieloplemienny tłum. Jakub Frank i ruch frankistowski, 1755–1816,* Gdańsk 2014, p. 39.

10 The exact place of Frank's birth is uncertain. Marcin Soboń (*Od wspólnoty charyzmatycznej do grupy interesu: przypadek frankizmu,* „Czasy Nowożytne", no. 16, 2004, p. 92) and Jan Doktór (*Śladami Mesjasza-Apostaty. Żydowskie ruchy mesjańskie w XVII i XVIII wieku a problem konwersji,* Wrocław 1998, p. 141) mention in this context Korolówka, a village near Ternopil. However, Maciejko adds two other possibilities: a small village of Brchan or Buchach (*Wieloplemienny tłum...,* p. 32).

11 G. Scholem *Le mouvement sabbataïste en Pologne (troisième et dernier article),* "Revue de l'histoire des religions", no. 144 (1), 1953, p. 47.

12 H. Rosenthal, S.M. Dubnov *Frank Jacob and the Frankists,* [in:] *Jewish Encyclopedia,* https://www.jewishencyclopedia.com/articles/6279-frank-jacob-and-the-frankists (retrieved on 18.03.2022)

A short time later, he and his wife arrived in Thessaloniki. It was there that he probably recognised himself as the messiah[13].

In Smyrna and Thessaloniki, Frank may have encountered co-religionists arriving for trade or religion from Polish Podolia, some of whom may already have recognised his messianic message. It seems quite likely that Elisha Schor was among them. Meanwhile, the news from Podolia was not good, and the situation of the Polish Sabbateans, and therefore probably also of the Schors, began to complicate. The conflict between them and the Orthodox Jews was clearly escalating. In 1752, during a dispute [14] in Brody, Rabbi Natan ben Levi accused Rabbi Jonathan Aibeshits of the Sabbatean heresy[15]. The discussion around the Sabbateans and Aibeshits which initially ended with his exoneration, resurfaced in 1753 during a session of the Council of the Four Lands (centrall Jewish authority in Poland) in Yaroslav, where Aibeshits was again acquitted (although he was ordered to destroy the amulets he distributed among his pupils).[16]

Perhaps this is why Frank decided to return to Poland – summoned, as Doktór writes – by Schor and others[17]. Upon his arrival, the latter's sons Salomon and Natan also clearly recognised him as the leader of the Sabbatean community. Unfortunately, little is known of Frank's teaching. What we do know, however, is that an event took place of key importance to the history of all Frankists. On 27 January 1756, outraged Jews burst into the house in Lanckoroń on the Zbruch where Frank and his pupils were staying. They confiscated the writings found on the spot, and the Frankists were battered and arrested. Jewish witnesses later claimed that the Frankists sang and danced around the naked Haia Schor, kissing her breasts. Frank, on the other hand, argued that the ritual was limited to dancing and singing[18].

---

13 M. Soboń *Od wspólnoty charyzmatycznej...*, pp. 93–94; J. Doktór *Śladami Mesjasza-Apostaty...*, p. 143.

14 Soboń erroneously defines this dispute, probably following David Wurm (Z *dziejow żydostwa brodzkiego za czasów dawnej Rzeczypospolitej (do r.1722),* Brody 1935, pp. 55–56) referring to it as "rabbinic court", perhaps simultaneously confusing the dispute in question with the events of 1756 (M. Soboń *Od wspólnoty charyzmatycznej...*, pp. 94–95).

15 Jonathan Aibeshits, with a reputation as an exceptionally learned rabbi, was most likely indeed associated with the Sabbateans and Baruch Ruso (G. Scholem *Shabtai Zvi (1626–1676) The central figure of Shabbateanism, the messianic movement called after him*, http://www.radicaltorahthought.com/Bio Zvi_Frank.htm, (retrieved on 23.03.2022))

16 J. Burnell *Revivals in Eighteenth-Century Poland. Jonathan Edwards and the Conversion of Polish Jews,* [in:] R.S. Bezzant (ed.) *The Global Edwards. Papers from the Jonathan Edwards Congress held in Melbourne, August 2015,* Oregon 2017, p. 110

17 J. Doktór *Śladami Mesjasza-Apostaty...*, p. 144.

18 J. Doktór *Śladami Mesjasza-Apostaty...*, p. 153.

Frank was released rather quickly, as Turkish officials claimed him as a subject of the Sultan. Soon, he left the Republic and set off for Thessaloniki. However, a rabbinical court was convened in Brody, which accused him, his followers and the Sabbateans in general of offences against the Sabbath and dietary rules, heresy (including belief in the Trinity), sexual offences – extramarital relations, incestuous relations, "sexual hospitality" (giving one's wife or daughter to a guest staying at home)[19].

The rabbis sentenced the Frankists to fines or penance while they placed a curse on those who refused to renounce their beliefs. They also dissolved some Sabbatean marriages and declared their children illegitimate – effectively condemning them to a life of extreme poverty. Interestingly, these were exceptionally harsh punishments: a cherem (curse) meant being expelled from the community of believers. Jews were to break off all contact with the person under the curse which must have resulted in a total or partial loss of sources of livelihood. The cursed person also lost all other forms of support from the community. That person had no right to be buried in a Jewish cemetery[20]. In 18th-century Poland, this equalled expulsion from any community and no protection from it. Maciejko describes the case of Joseph of Rohatyn, almost certainly associated with the Schors, who had to publicly confess his sins and describe his deeds before the faithful gathered in the synagogue. Then a beating was administered to him, he was to fall on his face in front of the synagogue and the Jews coming out were allowed to tread on him. He also had to divorce his wife and declare his children bastards. He was excluded from the community of believers to "wander alone for the rest of his days"[21].

However, Maciejko makes an important remark in this context. Namely, the Frankists were somewhat saved by the fact that Mikołaj Dembowski, the Bishop of Kamieniec, joined the proceedings against them, most probably on the initiative of the rabbis who intended to accuse Frank of heresy[22]. Dembowski took the cherem off the Frankists and agreed to a debate between them and representatives of the rabbinate in Kamieniec. It began in June 1757 and quickly took a fatal turn for the

19 P. Maciejko *Wieloplemienny tłum...*, p. 57. Maciejko notes that the custom of giving a close woman away for the night to a stranger staying as a guest was indeed sometimes practised among the Sabbateans.

20 Z. Borzymińska, R. Żebrowski (eds.) *Polski słownik judaistyczny. Dzieje, kultura, religia, ludzie*, Warszawa 2003, pp. 284–285.

21 P. Maciejko *Wieloplemienny tłum...*, p. 58.

22 This was made possible by Innocent IV's 1254 bull *Apparatus*. In it, the Pope granted himself the right to judge Jews who invented "heresy against their own law". Another bull, John XXII's *Super Illius Specula*, made it possible to prosecute Jews for witchcraft and magic, qualified in this case also as heresy (H. Zaremska *Żydzi w średniowiecznej Polsce. Gmina krakowska*, Warszawa 2011, p. 490).

rabbis: it turned out that it was not the Jews who were accusing the Frankists, but the Frank disciples accused the Jews.

> 1. We believe whatever God in the Old Testament told us to believe and taught; 2. The Scriptures cannot be effectively comprehended by human reason without the Grace of God; 3. The Talmud, filled with unheard-of blasphemy against God, should and is to be rejected; There is one God and Creator of all things; 5. The same God is inseparable in nature in three persons; 6. It is possible for God to take upon Himself human flesh and to be subject to all passions except sin. 7. Jerusalem, the city according to prophecy, will not be built; 8. the Messiah promised in the Scriptures will not come; 9. God Himself will lift the curse of the first parents and all the people in it, and this is the true Messiah, God incarnate

- wrote the Frankists in a manifesto submitted to Dembowski. It bore the signatures of 21 of the most prominent among them, including Salomon (Shlomo) Schor. By contrast, it is not clear if Frank himself influenced this text in any way[23].

Its characteristic trait was a fierce attack on the Talmud – the Frankists, by the way, referred to themselves as "anti-Talmudists". As Maciejko mentions, they could not directly attack Judaism, the religion officially recognised in the Republic, so they tried to show that Talmudism was a distortion of it[24]. They were initially clearly successful. In October 1757, the clerical court not only exonerated them of all charges but allowed their doctrine to be propagated (in accordance with the confession of faith presented) and declared the Talmud to be a harmful book and ordered its copies to be publicly burned. The Sabbateans' joy was short-lived, however: less than a month after the verdict, Bishop Dembowski, their chief ecclesiastical protector, died. As a result, things returned to the state they had been in before the Kamieniec discussion: Frank's disciples continued to be persecuted, a dozen were probably killed, and some fled across the Turkish border.

There they met again the Master who had converted to Islam – presumably fearing for his own safety and considering the cause in Poland lost. In the meantime, however, August III granted him and his followers in the Polish-Lithuanian Commonwealth safe passage. The Polish authorities also agreed to another dispute with the rabbis, this time held in Lvov. As Doktór points out, negotiations on this issue were again led by, among others, Salomon Schor[25]. The latter probably succeeded his father, who had died in 1757, as leader of the Polish Frankists. The dispute finally began on 17 July 1759. The strength of the dislike or hatred between the rabbis and the Sabbateans is evidenced by the accusation made by the latter. Relying on Talmudic passages taken out of context, mistranslations,

23 A. Kraushar *Frank i frankiści polscy. 1726–1816. Monografia historyczna osnuta na źródłach archiwalnych i rękopiśmiennych* vol. I, Kraków 1895, p. 78.

24 P. Maciejko *Wieloplemienny tłum...*, p. 95.

25 J. Doktór *Śladami Mesjasza-Apostaty...*, p. 169.

or simple misrepresentations, Schor, Yehuda Leib Krysa and Moliwda (Antoni Kossakowski) – two of the main Frankist representatives besides him – accused Jews of committing ritual murder. The allegation was a deadly one for all Jews. Happily, it ultimately had no consequences. Instead, the dispute brought about a crucial change for the Frankists.

In fact, there had been talks about their conversion to Catholicism – the meeting in Lvov was dependent on it. Paradoxically, the baptism of the Frankists was also in the interest of the rabbis, who wished to rid their own ranks of a dangerous heresy once and for all. Conversion finally corresponded to Frank's own teaching, according to which the way to final salvation led precisely through the complete abandonment of Judaism. According to Charles Novak, "Christianity was the culmination and abolition of the Jewish Law, based on the Talmud and considered invalid"[26]. Another thing is that the Frankists also demanded during the baptismal negotiations the right to wear traditional Jewish dress, the right not to eat pork, to observe the Sabbath, to wear beards, to marry among themselves. And above all, they expected true autonomy and an area for settlement[27]. Notably, converts could also count on ennoblement in the Commonwealth (above all in Lithuania). It is therefore clear that they intended to form a separate community within Christianity, in terms of customs not essentially different from the followers of traditional Judaism.

However, all these demands were rejected by the Polish church hierarchy and magnates. The Frankists, on the other hand, had no choice: returning to the bosom of Judaism was impossible, and, from their point of view, the only solution remained baptism according to the rules imposed by the Polish party. Frank arrived in Lvov while the dispute was still in progress. Pressed by Father Szczepan Mikulski, Archdeacon of Lvov, on 17 September 1759 he finally decided to be baptised in Lvov in water. Later, in Warsaw, he was to be baptised with all the rites. Significantly, Salomon Schor was baptised on the same day (along thirty other Frankists). He took the name Franciszek, while his surname was changed to "Wołowski" – according to the translation of the noun "schor"[28]. Soon Elisha's other children followed suit. In early 1760, Natan Schor became Michał Józef Wołowski, Yehuda Schor became Jan Wołowski, and finally Isaac became Henryk Wołowski[29]. In

26 Ch. Novak *Jacob Frank, le faux Messie. Déviance de la kabbale ou théorie du complot,* Paris 2012, p. 65.

27 G. Pikulski *Złość żydowska Przeciwko Bogu y bliźniemu Prawdzie y Sumnieniu. Na objaśnienie Talmudystów. Na dowód ich zaślepienia y Religii dalekiey od prawa Boskiego przez Moyżesza danego,* Lviv 1760, pp. 149–151.

28 As Adam Kaźmierczyk wrote, the adoption, during or shortly after baptism, not only of a new name but also of a surname, was typical of Jewish converts in general, not only of Frankists. (A. Kaźmierczyk *Rodziłem się Żydem... konwersje Żydów w Rzeczpospolitej XVII-XVIII wieku,* Kraków 2015, p. 42).

29 A. Kraushar *Frank i frankiści polscy...,* vol. I, pp. 159 and 215.

addition to the brothers mentioned above, several more converts took the surname Wołowski, including Franciszek Józef, Michał, Feliks, Łukasz Franciszek, Jan Kanty[30]. It seems that they may have been related to Elisha – especially as, according to Kraushar, they were partly from Rohatyn, but the degree of this kinship is impossible to determine. Conversions of the Frankists continued for some time; their exact number is not known. Gershom Scholem estimates it at around 1,000, Doktór at around 2,000, and Soboń suggests a similar figure. Maciejko, on the other hand, mentions around 3,000[31]. This number certainly did not reflect the hopes of the Polish bishops; on the other hand, it represented the largest group conversion of Jews in the Republic of the 18th century.

However, this was not the end of this unusual religious group with which the Schor/Wołowski family was so strongly associated. Immediately after the baptism, suspicions arose about Frank's real intentions and the sincerity of his Christian beliefs and, consequently, the beliefs of his faithful followers. Admittedly, as Kraushar wrote, "After being baptised, the Frankists abandoned their Jewish robes, shaved off their beards and began to dress according to Christian fashion."[32]. However, this was clearly not enough to convince a sceptical section of the hierarchy with Archdeacon Mikulski in the lead. Frank has been fully baptised in Warsaw at the Royal Chapel in the Saxon Palace on 28 November 1759. At the same time, Father Pikulski was collecting testimonies in Lvov from newly baptised Frankists, including Franciszek Wołowski. Among other things, Wołowski recounted the light he allegedly saw over Frank at night, and his gift of prophecy. Together with several other Frankists, he was also alleged to have stated in Pikulski's presence that "Considering all these words [of Frank – RD], matters, and other circumstances, we have come to the understanding that Christ, Whom we believe in, is hidden in the Person of Frank Our Guide; because we have observed signs of the wounds of Christ expressed on his head and heart, even though he conceals them, making himself the most miserable of all"[33]. Perhaps these words were a testimony to the first Frankist rebellion against Frank, with the Wołowskis at the head. Jan Doktór suggests so, writing clearly that they diverged significantly from Frank's teaching at the time: "They seem to have wanted either to put him to the test or simply to get rid of a satrap who had lost their confidence, but they by no means intended to betray their Judeo-Christian, syncretic faith"[34]. Be that as it may, Pikulski then sent these confessions to Warsaw, from where they were forwarded to Rome. Frank and

---

30 A. Kraushar *Frank i frankiści polscy...*, vol. I, pp. 370–376.

31 G. Scholem *Le mouvement sabbataïste en Pologne...*, p. 68; J. Doktór *Śladami Mesjasza-Apostaty...*, p. 179; Soboń *Od wspólnoty charyzmatycznej...*, p. 103; P. Maciejko *Wieloplemienny tłum...*, p. 172.

32 A. Kraushar *Frank i frankiści polscy...*, vol. I, p. 175.

33 G. Pikulski *Złość żydowska Przeciwko Bogu ...*, pp. 330–332.

34 J. Doktór *Warszawscy frankiści*, "Kwartalnik Historii Żydów" 2001, no. 2 (198), p. 199.

his entourage were further accused of sexual and financial abuse.[35] It may also be, according to Maciejko, that it was only then that news of Frank's earlier conversion to Islam reached some of the bishops[36]. In any case, Frank was arrested on 7 January 1760, and less than three weeks later stood before a consistory court in Warsaw. It found him guilty of most of the charges and sent him to Częstochowa.

It may come as a surprise that the "Master" was the only one accused and convicted. For, in theory, the accusation of false baptism could have been extended to the entire sect, and certainly to Frank's closest disciples, including the Wołowski brothers. This, however, did not happen. Perhaps the Polish Church, as Doktór suggests, did not want to admit the failure of its missionary efforts towards the Jews[37]. Perhaps the judges felt that it was enough to hit the leader to get the entire group back on the righteous Catholic track.

In any case, the Wołowskis and other Frankists remained at large, while their leader was imprisoned. Jacob Frank was to spend the next 13 years in seclusion in the Jasna Góra monastery. Initially, he stayed there alone; the first disciples were only able to visit him in November 1760. Among them was Jan Wołowski; Franciszek, in turn, appeared in January 1761. While many of his followers left him immediately after his arrest, the Wołowskis remained with their "master". In fact, the brothers still belonged to his closest circle. In time, they settled in Częstochowa. The importance of the Wołowskis in this small group is also evidenced by the missions entrusted to them by Frank. In 1765, Franciszek and Jan Wołowski (and Paweł Pawłowski) were sent to Moscow, probably with a proposal to convert the Frankists to Orthodoxy – in exchange for the release of the "Master"[38]. As Maciejko writes, because of a rabbi residing in Moscow, the mission failed completely[39]. In 1768, Jan Wołowski set off for Moravia with a message calling on the Sabbateans to convert to Catholicism. In the same year, Henryk left with a similar message for Hungary[40], then he gave "all the true believers" an order to immediately move to Warsaw permanently[41]. However, there was another aspect of this close relationship with "the Lord", as the followers called Frank. For the religious rituals in the group sometimes contained surprising sexual elements. For example, one day "The lord ordered at that time that Mateuszewski, Pawłowski and Mateuszewski

35 A. Kraushar *Frank i frankiści polscy...*, vol. I, p. 181.

36 P. Maciejko *Wieloplemienny tłum...*, p. 216.

37 J. Doktór *Warszawscy frankiści...*, p. 201.

38 J. Doktór (ed.) *Księga Słów Panskich. Ezoteryczne wykłady Jakuba Franka*, vol. I, Warszawa 1997, p. 62. Doktór also pointed out elsewhere that the Wołowskis were clearly opposed to Frank's idea, as they "identified too strongly with the Polish Republic and the culture of the nobility." (J. Doktór *Warszawscy frankiści...*, p. 199).

39 P. Maciejko *Wieloplemienny tłum...*, p. 234.

40 A. Kraushar *Frank i frankiści polscy...*, vol. I, pp. 279–281.

41 J. Doktór *Warszawscy frankiści...*, p. 197.

Nadwornieński should be connected with the wife of Henryk Wołowski"[42]. On another occasion, Frank addressed the women in the following way:

> I have need of one great thing to bring forth, therefore I want you to choose one of your Sisters from among yourselves and give her to me: but it must be in love and harmony, in friendship, so that each one wishes her as well as if she herself were to go in her place. You will only give this Sister to me because *Eine Schwester ohne Brüder ist wie eine Schiff ohne Rüder*, and I will take her in, I will give her good food and drink, I will deal with her every night 7 times and 6 times during the day. This woman will become pregnant with my daughter (...) [the women] agreed among themselves and chose wife of Henryk Wołowski[43].

These practices were not new among the Frankists or Sabbateans, nor, it seems, did they affect the attitude of the disciples – including the Wołowski brothers – towards Frank.

Notably, the latter's teaching in Częstochowa changed somewhat. He presented himself no longer as God incarnate, the Messiah, but only as God's messenger. He also negated the divine nature of Sabbatai, who was merely preparing the way for him. Baptism, on the other hand, was intended to discover the saving truth found in Catholicism, in... the cult of the Holy Virgin. And the Virgin, combined with the notion of the Shekhinah, was to be sought by Frank in Częstochowa. It was no longer a question of combining Messiah and Shekhinah, as before, but of releasing the latter[44].

The Frankists witnessed the seizure of Częstochowa by the Bar Confederates and the defence of the monastery against Russian troops. It was the Russians who finally released them from captivity: after a conversation with General Alexander Ilyich Bibikov, Frank could leave the monastery, together with his family[45].

He then set off with his retinue to Brno because of an important group of Sabbateans residing in Moravia, headed by the Brno-based Dobruška family, with whom Frank was affiliated. Maciejko draws attention to the higher social position and better career opportunities of the converts in the Habsburg Empire than in Poland[46]. Frank may also have counted on the interest of Maria Theresa or Joseph II.

---

42 *Rozmaite adnotacje, przypadki czynnościowe i anegdoty Pańskie*, quoted from J. Doktór *Jakub Frank i jego nauka*, Warszawa 1991, p. 94.

43 *Rozmaite adnotacje, przypadki czynnościowe i anegdoty Pańskie...*, p. 99.

44 J. Doktór *Śladami Mesjasza-Apostaty...*, p. 183.

45 When in Częstochowa, Frank experienced two family tragedies. First, his son Jacob died in 1769, followed by his wife Chana in 1770. Still alive at that time were Frank's two sons Roch and Józef, and his beloved daughter Ewa (Avacha).

46 P. Maciejko *Wieloplemienny tłum...*, p. 251.

In any case, Elisha Schor's sons, who were probably in Warsaw at the time, did not accompany him[47]. However, he was in regular contact with them, as with the entire Warsaw Frankist community. The Wołowskis, moreover, continued to play a key role among the faithful. In 1774, Jan Wołowski was again one of the three deputies sent by Frank to Istanbul and, as before, without any significant results[48].

In 1775, Frank succeeded in obtaining an audience with the imperial couple. On 19 October he stood before Joseph II in Vienna, two days later before his mother. He was certainly accompanied on this trip by Michał Wołowski[49]. The Kaiser was clearly impressed by Frank's daughter Ewa. According to Novak who followed Scholem's claims, in Vienna Frank also held important political talks. Thus, he was to propose cooperation to the Habsburgs in the context of the impending war with Turkey. In return, he was to demand an independent territory carved out of the lands he had just conquered from the Turks. Novak adds that "In order to prove his loyalty, Frank sent emissaries to Istanbul, who made contact with the Dönmeh who held important positions in the Sublime Porte. We can thus assume that for a certain period, the Dönmeh and Frankist Sabbateans served as spy channels for Austria"[50]. If that was indeed the case, then Jan Wołowski, sent by "the Master" to Turkey on several occasions, was certainly involved in these activities[51]. However, they did not have the effect expected by Frank – he was not granted any land by Joseph II although they helped to support the "Master" and his court. In this context, Kraushar mentions the considerable sums brought by the Wołowskis from successive expeditions in 1784 and 1786[52].

The Wołowskis felt so connected to Frank that Franciszek was even said to have "shown sincere intentions" to marry his daughter Ewa. However, Frank or the woman concerned did not consider him worthy of such an honour[53].

Meanwhile, the entire company moved in 1786 to Offenbach, to a spacious palace purchased by Frank. "The Master" led a glamorous lifestyle. He used the title of Baron, with the tacit approval of Wolfgang Ernst II, Duke of Isenburg. Soon there were around a thousand Frankists in the small town, including the Wołowski brothers and their families. However, the cult was slowly dwindling in numbers. This was primarily due to the age and progressive illness of its founder. Over 60

47 A. Kraushar *Frank i frankiści polscy. 1726–1816. Monografia historyczna osnuta na źródłach archiwalnych i rękopiśmiennych* vol. II, Kraków 1895, pp. 5–6

48 A. Kraushar *Frank i frankiści polscy...*, vol. II, p. 11.

49 A. Kraushar *Frank i frankiści polscy...*, vol. II, p. 19.

50 Ch. Novak *Jacob Frank, le faux Messie...*, p. 93.

51 A. Kraushar *Frank i frankiści polscy...*, vol. II, p. 33. Interestingly, the same Jan Wołowski had been "bruised" by other members of the Warsaw commune a little earlier, on Frank's express orders, as punishment for some misdemeanour.

52 A. Kraushar *Frank i frankiści polscy...*, vol. II, pp. 85, 91.

53 A. Kraushar *Frank i frankiści polscy...*, vol. II, p. 52.

years old, Frank hardly left his rooms anymore. In 1788 he suffered his first attack of apoplexy, in 1789 another. Probably aware of the state of his health, he predicted his own imminent death on several occasions. He died on 10 December 1791.

He was succeeded by his daughter Ewa, who had been explicitly portrayed by Frank as a prophetess or a divine being, groomed for leadership. Ewa continued her father's extravagant lifestyle but no longer possessed his charisma or power of attraction. Shortly after the "Master's" death, most of the Frankists left Offenbach, most of them probably returning to Warsaw. The Wołowski brothers, on the other hand, most likely stayed with Ewa. Kraushar described three old men, among them (allegedly) Franciszek Wołowski, years later still lecturing on the "secret teachings" to the young[54]. The last clear trace of the Wołowskis' presence in Offenbach was the so-called "red letter" (from the colour of the ink). The letter, signed by Franciszek and Michał Wołowski and Jędrzej Dębowski, was addressed to the whole of Israel. It foretold disasters and misfortunes befalling all Jews. The only salvation from the apocalypse was to join "Edom" – to convert to Catholicism. Jacob Frank was presented in the text as the reincarnation of the patriarch Jacob. Ewa, a contemporary of Rachel, was also to play a key role in this salvation story[55]. Let me quote the opinion of Doktór who believes that the fact that it was the Wołowskis and Dębowski who signed the letter to all Jews (and not Ewa or her brothers) shows that they probably enjoyed much more authority than Frank's children[56].

Unfortunately, at this point, the trace of the Wołowskis is temporarily lost. They most probably returned to Warsaw, to join a significant part of the family. As I have noted earlier, the beginning of the Frankist community in Warsaw can be dated back precisely to 1768. It is likely that some members of the Wołowski family resided there continuously from that time onwards. The trouble is that, as Jan Doktór (a researcher perhaps best acquainted with the history of the Polish Frankists and the sources associated with them) writes, "the years 1760–1790 are almost a blank in the history of the Warsaw Frankists"[57]. Later information comes almost exclusively from anti-Frankist pasquils, texts that are in many respects questionable. When topped with the mentioned confusion regarding the repetition of names, professions, marriages between cousins and, finally, the usual gaps in the metric books, the resulting picture of this specific religious group is extremely difficult to capture and describe.

---

54 A. Kraushar *Frank i frankiści polscy...*, vol. II, p. 174.

55 The text of the letter: B.-Z. Wacholder *Jacob Frank and the Frankists Hebrew Zoharic Letters*, "Hebrew Union College Annual", vol. 53 (1982), pp. 271–274.

56 J. Doktór *Warszawscy frankiści...*, p. 206.

57 J. Doktór *Warszawscy frankiści...*, p. 201.

According to Mayor Witthoff's registry of 1780, quoted in one of the anti-Semitic pasquils, Warsaw was then supposed to be inhabited by around 6,000 converts[58]. Given the relatively high fertility rate in Frankist families, this figure seems likely. What is exaggerated, however, is the description from a similar pamphlet from the same period, according to which "There was a great multitude of these neophytes, so much so that on every street and in almost every house one could not pass without bumping into a neophyte."[59]. On the other hand, the list of professions of Warsaw converts, mentioned by the same author, seems plausible: "the neophytes made booze, strong and noble beer delivered from the villages, Hungarian, French wine, wine from Champagne, the Rhine region, etc. The neophytes sold all kinds of goods like cheese, butter, bacon, lard, meat, eggs, [...] sulphur, liquor, starch, litmus, pomade [...] various paints, threads, needles, silk, ribbons, you name it"[60].

Notably, although the neophytes were not only Frankists, and conversions from Judaism to Catholicism occurred both earlier and later[61], it was Frank's followers who were by far the largest, most cohesive, and longest-lasting distinct group. Undoubtedly, the Wołowski brothers played a key role among them since the very beginning. Not only because of their close contacts with Frank. As I have pointed out before, they were often his messengers, intermediaries between him and the outside world or other Sabbatean communities. However, there is every indication that they also enjoyed extraordinary authority among their fellow students in Warsaw. This was probably because they were among not only the "Master's" closest, but also the oldest disciples. As Doktór points out, their position in the Warsaw community was so strong that they were probably led the revolt against Frank's authority. Unfortunately, everything we know about the Wołowski brothers is linked to Frank. They did not leave behind any sources which would describe their family life or non-religious activities. Even the dates of death of Michał and Jan Wołowski remain uncertain – they must have died at the latest in the late 18th or the early 19th century, but the exact dates remain unknown.

---

58 Anonymous *Dwór Franka, czyli polityka nowochrzczeńców odkryta przez neofitę jednego dla poprawy rządu Roku 1790* [in:] A. Eisenbach, J. Michalski, E. Rostworowski, J. Woliński (eds.) *Materiały do dziejów Sejmu Czteroletniego*, vol. VI, Wrocław-Warszawa-Kraków 1969, p. 179.

59 Anonymous *List przyjaciela Polaka, niegdyś w Warszawie a teraz we Wrocławiu mieszkającego, do obywatela warszawskiego, wyjawiający sekreta neofitów, poprawy rządu wyciągające, pisany dnia 2 miesiąca kwietnia roku 1790*, [in:] *Materiały do dziejów Sejmu...*, p. 170.

60 Anonymous *Dwór Franka...*, p. 170.

61 See: A. Kaźmierczyk *Rodziłem się Żydem...*

2. The Wołowski family

Louis Wolowski was directly descended from Franciszek (Salomon/Shlomo) Wołowski through his mother. Tekla Wołowska, born in 1787 in Warsaw, was the daughter of Ludwik Wołowski and Elżbieta, née Lanckorońska[62], and by the same Ludwik, the granddaughter of Franciszek. Louis must have known his grandfather Ludwik, who died in 1832, at the age of 68, in Warsaw[63]. The Wołowskis were clearly keen to associate with the Lanckorońskis: both Ludwik's (grandfather's) wife and mother came from that family. However, a clear distinction must be made that this concerns the Lanckorońskis – Frankist converts, not the Lanckorońskis – Polish magnates. According to a theory put forward by Teodor Jeske-Choiński, the family was said to have originated from Lanckorona, its protoplast probably being Isaac Leibovitch and his wife Klara[64]. Kraushar also mentions the Lanckorońskis from Rohatyn[65]. Marianna Lanckorońska, wife of Franciszek and mother of Ludwik (grandfather), died probably shortly after her husband. She gave birth to four sons and a daughter, Agata Konstancja. The eldest child, Andrzej Wołowski, was born in the mid-18th century, most probably in Rohatyn[66]. He and his wife Teresa Matuszewska had four children: Wojciech (1772–1826), Stanisław Eliasz (1779–1836), Barbara (1783–1836) and Franciszek Ksawery (1785–1863).

The second-born son of the couple was Franciszek Ksawery Wołowski (1758–1839). The husband of Barbara, née Wołowska, is a somewhat better-known figure, largely due to his exceptionally talented daughter Maria and his granddaughter Celina's marriage to Adam Mickiewicz. Franciszek Ksawery was a popular Warsaw brewer, a representative of the local burghers. He and his wife had a total of ten children. Jan Ignacy, born around 1786, died in 1844[67]. Since 1809, he was a captain in the Duchy of Warsaw army, awarded the Virtuti Militari order in 1812, then a captain in the army of the Congress Kingdom of Poland, the head of the Krasnostaw district, ennobled in 1838[68]. He then received the coat of arms of

62 Marriage certificate of Tekla and Franciszek Wołowski: Warsaw ASC Division V, 54/1809, https://www.szukajwarchiwach.gov.pl/skan/-/skan/2f781b0c53e216f2cbc711e003bf06d037f09d54b81ecb6fb153140050636851 (retrieved 13.05.2022).

63 Death certificate of Ludwik Wołowski: Warsaw, St. Andrew, 16/1832, https://www.szukajwarchiwach.gov.pl/jednostka/-/jednostka/12478314?_Jednostka_delta=20&_Jednostka_resetCur=false&_Jednostka_cur=15&_Jednostka_id_jednostki=12478314 (retrieved 13.05.2022).

64 T. Jeske – Choiński *Neofici Polscy. Materyały historyczne*, Warszawa 1904, p. 85.

65 A. Kraushar *Frank i frankiści polscy...*, vol. I, p. 349.

66 T. Jeske – Choiński *Neofici Polscy...*, p. 100.

67 Obituary: T. Jeske – Choiński *Neofici Polscy...*, p. 389.

68 E. Sęczys (ed.) *Szlachta wylegitymowana w Królestwie Polskim w latach 1836–1861*, Warszawa 2000, p. 784.

Bawół II with the motto *Deum cole, regem serva* ("Worship God, serve the king")[69]. Julia was born in 1787 and died in Warsaw in 1873. Unmarried, blind since childhood (probably due to smallpox), she took care of the children of her sister Maria Szymanowska in her absence and ran her home in St. Petersburg. After Maria's death, she went to live with her parents in Warsaw[70]. Joanna was born in 1788 and died in 1871 in Warsaw. Her husband was Michał Brzeziński. Maria Agata was born in 1789 in Warsaw and died in 1831 in St. Petersburg. She married her closest cousin, Józef Szymanowski (a representative of another Frankist family). Under his name Maria gained fame as an accomplished pianist, giving concerts in Germany, France, England, Italy, the Netherlands, Switzerland, and Russia. The couple had three children: twins Helena (1811–1861) and Romuald (1811–1839), and Celina (1812–1855). However, the marriage was not successful, and ended in a divorce in 1820[71]. Teresa, another daughter of Franciszek Ksawery and Barbara, was born in1790[72] and died in 1862. Little is known about her, except that her husband was Roch Zawadzki, a beer producer in Solec, Warsaw. Equally little known is of her younger brother, Karol (1791–1863). The couple's other son, Stanisław, was born in 1796. He died in 1847 in Paris. He was a physician at the Holy Ghost Hospital in Warsaw. He took part in the November Uprising as a physician in Rybiński's corps, then chief physician of the General Staff, and was wounded at Grochów. In 1831, he emigrated to France. There he was a witness at the wedding of Celina and Adam Mickiewicz[73]. Aleksander Andrzej was born three years later and died in 1873[74]. Until 1838 he was an official of the Forestry Department of the Government Revenue and Treasury Commission, and a member of the Agricultural Society[75]. 1799 marked the birth of Kazimiera Fryderyka, future wife of Jan Tadeusz Wołowski[76].

69 T. Syga, S. Szenic *Maria Szymanowska i jej czasy*, Warszawa 1960, pp. 453–454.

70 T. Syga, S. Szenic *Maria Szymanowska...*, pp. 454–455.

71 T. Syga, S. Szenic *Maria Szymanowska...*, pp. 63–94.

72 Baptismal record: Warsaw Archdiocesan Archive, St Andrew's, 02.02.1791, https://metryki.genealodzy.pl/metryka.php?ar=8&zs=9159d&sy=101&kt=4&plik=str_170-171.jpg#zoom=1.5&x=980&y=105 (27.05.2022).

73 T. Syga, S. Szenic *Maria Szymanowska...*, p. 455; R. Gerber *Studenci Uniwersytetu Warszawskiego...*, p. 339.

74 Marriage certificate of Aleksander Andrzej Wołowski and Wiktoria Kubacka: Warsaw Archdiocesan Archive, Warsaw St. Andrew, year 1863, deed no. 238. https://www.szukajwarchiwach.gov.pl/skan/-/skan/fb19d2f4b8bd66c429b93fe0b6aaed7ac4910 0b00f6e2f67163a805f82ff8cec (retrieved 17.05.2022).

75 R. Gerber *Studenci Uniwersytetu Warszawskiego...*, p. 239.

76 Marriage certificate of Jan Tadeusz Wołowski and Kazimiera Fryderyka Wołowska: Warsaw Archdiocesan Archive, Warsaw, St. Andrew's, year 1835, deed no. 82. https://www.szukajwarchiwach.gov.pl/skan/-/skan/1c0fb78834f04d1cfe7a0c c1b07f8ccf476b293b92655378ccd3bb3cdf10724a (retrieved 17.05.2022).

He was her first cousin, and an accomplished lawyer[77]. Finally, in 1809, Teodor was born, a graduate of the Faculty of Law at Warsaw University in 1827, later secretary at the Ministry of State in Warsaw. In 1852, he became a councillor of state. He was ennobled, together with his brother Jan Ignacy, in 1838[78].

The third child of Franciszek "Shlomo" Wołowski was Agata Konstancja. The dates of her life are not precisely known. Bearing in mind her siblings and offspring, she must have been born around 1760. It is known that in 1783, she married Franciszek Szymanowski at St. Andrew's Parish in Warsaw[79]. The couple had numerous children. The first-born son was Józef Teofil Franciszek Szymanowski (1785–1832), the husband of Maria Szymanowska, née Wołowska. He was a leaseholder of an estate near Warsaw. After divorcing Maria, he married in 1822 Elżbieta Młodzianowska (who came from another Frankist family)[80]. His older three children remained with their mother at the time but Elżbieta gave birth to five more, three of whom lived to adulthood: Aniela (1824–1872), wife of Jan Nepomucen Leszczyński[81], Zofia (1825–1870) – a talented painter, poet, wife of another

77 Joanna Utkin suggests that Jan Tadeusz proposed to Kazimiera as early as in 1827 but was not accepted. According to Kazimiera's own words, in 1835 "he once again desired my hand, and it was my dying mother's wish that prompted me to accept him as my husband". (J.E. Utkin *Potomkowie kupca Wołowskiego...*, p. 75. About Jan Tadeusz Wołowski: R. Gerber *Studenci Uniwersytetu Warszawskiego...*, p. 240; K. Pędowski *Wołowski Jan Tadeusz,* [in:] *Słownik biograficzny adwokatów polskich S-Ż,* vol. I, Warszawa 1983, pp. 480–481. It is perhaps worth adding that when, in 1833, Piotr Wysocki, the young leader of the Polish conspiracy in 1830, named Jan Tadeusz as his defence counsel before the Russian Supreme Criminal Court, the latter asked the court to relieve him of this function because of an alleged collision with the defence of cadet Płaszkowski (T. Kędzierski *Proces „dyktatora Nocy Listopadowej" – Piotra Wysockiego,* "Palestra", no. 21/11(239), 1977, p. 49.).

78 T. Syga, S. Szenic *Maria Szymanowska...*, p. 456; R. Gerber *Studenci Uniwersytetu Warszawskiego...*, pp. 241–242.

79 Marriage certificate: Warsaw Archdiocesan Archive, Warsaw St. Andrew's, year 1783, deed no. 52.

80 Marriage certificate: Warsaw Archdiocesan Archive, Warsaw, St. Andrew's, year 1822, deed no. 125.

81 Jan Nepomucen Leszczyński (1806–1886) was an educator, owner, and head of a real school in Warsaw since 1843. He was among the first to introduce compulsory physical exercise at school and abandoned physical punishment (S. Konarski *Leszczyński Jan Nepomucen,* [in:] *Polski Słownik Biograficzny,* vol. XVII, Wrocław-Warszawa-Kraków-Gdańsk 1972, pp. 119–120). The son of Aniela and Jan Nepomucen, Stanisław Andrzej Leszczyński (1856–1914) a Warsaw lawyer, activist of the Warsaw Charity Society, the Warsaw Reading Society, co-founder of the Progressive Democratic Union in 1905 – also gained a biography in the PSB. (H. Kiepurska & S. Konarski *Leszczyński Stanisław Andrzej Wiktor,* [in:] *Polski Słownik Biograficzny,* vol. XVII...,

outstanding artist, Teofil Lenartowicz[82] and Leon Michał Szymanowski (1828–1916). Józef Teofil's slightly younger brother Adam, born in 1787 and "making his living by leasing the estate", died in 1809[83]. All we know about the next child, Anna, is that she was baptised while still in Offenbach[84]. Her younger sister, Marianna Kunegunda, was born in 1794, and died in 1858[85]. At the age of 17, she married Walenty Zawadzki (son of Marianna Wołowska), a Warsaw brewer[86]. The couple had six children, of whom four lived to adulthood: Cecylia (1818–1893), Aleksander (1822–1906), Helena Antonina (1826–1878) and Jan Kazimierz (1828–1894). Jakub

---

pp. 144–146; R. Łyczywek *Leszczyński Stanisław,* [in:*] Słownik biograficzny adwokatów polskich* G-Ł, vol. I, Warszawa 1981, pp. 213–215).

82 After her father's death, Zofia Szymanowska moved with her mother to Warsaw, where Elżbieta gave dance lessons. Since 1850, she stayed in Paris, caring for her sick stepsister Celina Mickiewicz and her offspring. During this time, she studied painting with Ary Scheffer. Zofia was also in Paris in 1855 at the time of Celina's death. Again, she took care of her nephews. She painted portraits of members of the Mickiewicz, Szymanowski and Młodzianowski families. In 1857, she went to Rome. In 1861, she married Lenartowicz, with whom she settled in Florence. The couple struggled with chronic deprivation; moreover, Szymanowska was suffering from tuberculosis. In 1870 she left for Poznań, hoping for new painting commissions. Seriously ill, she died on 8.7.1870 in the Mielżyński palace in Miłosław. (Z. Lewicka-Depta *Szymanowska (Szymanowska-Lenartowicz) Zofia,* [in:] *Polski Słownik Biograficzny,* vol. L/1, part 204, Warszawa – Kraków 2014, pp. 47–49. See also: J. Nowakowski *Lenartowicz Teofil Aleksander,* [in:] *Polski Słownik Biograficzny,* vol. XVII, Wrocław-Warszawa-Kraków-Gdańsk, 1972, pp. 39–43).

83 Death certificate: https://www.szukajwarchiwach.gov.pl/jednostka/-/jednostka/12481309?_Jednostka_delta=20&_Jednostka_resetCur=false&_Jednostka_cur=7&_Jednostka_id_jednostki=12481309 (retrieved 17.05.2022).

84 A complete list of Frankists and their children who were baptised (in an Evangelical parish) and died in Offenbach was published by Klaus Werner in an article *Versuch einer Quantifizierung des Frank'schen Gefolges in Offenbach am Main 1788–1818,* "Frankfurter Judaistische Beiträge", Heft 14, Frankfurt am Main, 1986, pp. 153–212. The list is also available in a text by Marek Jerzy Minakowski *Frankiści z Offenbachu i Warszawy,* https://minakowski.pl/frankisci-z-offenbachu-i-warszawy/ (retrieved 17.05.2022).

85 Death certificate: Warsaw Archdiocesan Archive, St John, 1858, no. 497, http://wielcy.pl/img/metrskan/z/3330681.jpg (retrieved 18.05.2022).

86 Marriage certificate: State Archive in Warsaw, ASC Division IV, 1812 no. 13 https://www.szukajwarchiwach.gov.pl/jednostka/-/jednostka/12481292 (retrieved 18.05.2022).

Szymanowski was born around 1795 and died in 1873.[87]. Jakub, leaseholder of Chruślin estate in Łowicz district, was married twice: first to Anna Zawadzka, who died in 1828, and then to Barbara, née Wołowska[88]. Anna gave him three children, including the well-known writer and journalist Wacław[89] and daughter Katarzyna Felicja (1825–1893). The second marriage produced one daughter, Józefa Teofila (1833–1875). Agata Konstancja's daughter was also the extremely talented Filipina Teofila Szymanowska[90]. In 1821, she married Franciszek Jakub Brzeziński;

---

87 Death certificate: State Archive in Warsaw, St Anthony, 1873, no. 34, https://metryki.genealodzy.pl/metryka.php?ar=1&zs=1218d&sy=1873&kt=3&plik=034-039.jpg#zoom=1&x=390&y=505 (retrieved 18.05.2022).

88 Marriage certificate: Warsaw Archdiocesan Archive, Warsaw, St. Andrew, 1832, deed no. 91, https://metryki.genealodzy.pl/metryka.php?ar=8&zs=9233d&sy=317&kt=2&skan=090-091.jpg#zoom=1&x=326&y=22 (retrieved 18.05.2022).

89 Born in 1821, Wacław Szymanowski was a poet, playwright, publicist, and translator. Since the time the newspaper was established in 1851, he was associated with "Dziennik Warszawski", where he ran a column section and a cultural chronicle. In "Dziennik" he was involved in humoresques, storytelling, novels, and translations. He was an excellent chronicler of Warsaw. Since 1855, he headed "Dziennik" together with Julian Bartoszewicz. Since 1856, they jointly ran "Kronika Wiadomości Krajowych i Zagranicznych" ["Chronicle of National and Foreign News"], replacing "Dziennik". He then began to write dramas – including *The Last Moments of Copernicus. A Dramatic Picture* (1855), and *Solomon* (1856). In 1859, he joined the editorial board of "Tygodnik Ilustrowany". In 1861, he wrote for Paris-based "La Presse" about events in Warsaw. As a result, the Russians exiled him from Warsaw to Biała Podlaska. On his return, he was briefly arrested in February 1862. He subsequently collaborated with several titles, and in 1868 took over the editorship of "Kurier Warszawski". Thanks to him, "Kurier" quickly achieved success in Warsaw, and in 1872 Szymanowski bought half of the paper's shares from his partners, becoming its owner. He also continued to manage it informally and to publish his own works. "It seems to me that at that time, apart from Szymanowski, there was no one in Warsaw who could organise a magazine in the fashion of both the local and the European, making it a specifically Warsaw organ, and one that reflected all the stronger rays of the West and the 'new' world," wrote Wiktor Gomulicki (*Warszawa wczorajsza,* Warszawa 1961, p. 284). Wacław Szymanowski died on 21 December 1886 in Warsaw (M. Kamela *Szymanowski Wacław,* [in:] *Polski Słownik Biograficzny,* vol. L..., pp. 102–106).

90 Filipina née Szymanowska Brzezińska (1800–1886) was a pianist and composer, primarily of religious songs. Her most famous work was the song *Nie opuszczaj nas* [Do not abandon us], with the lyrics written by Rev. Karol Antoniewicz (T. Ochlewski *Brzezińska Filipina,* [in:] *Polski Słownik Biograficzny,* vol. III, Kraków 1937, p. 36).

they had three children: Franciszek Teofil (1822–1881), Kazimierz (1824–1876)[91] and Teofila (1826–1907). The youngest child of Franciszek and Agata Konstancja was Jan Filip Szymanowski, born in 1802. On 10 February 1828 he married Teresa Gabriela Józefa Wołowska[92]; he died in 1846.

Ludwik Wołowski, the grandfather of this book's protagonist, was the fourth and penultimate child of Franciszek "Shlomo" Wołowski and Marianna, née Lanckorońska. He had a younger brother, Marcin. The only information about him comes from his death certificate: Marcin Wołowski died in 1810 at the age of 38. He was a merchant, leaving behind a widow, Ewa née Zielińska. Nothing is known about his children if any[93].

Finally, Ludwik (grandfather): he was born in 1764 and died in 1832[94]. In 1786, in Warsaw, he married Elżbieta Lanckorońska[95]. According to the marriage certificate of his daughter, Teofila, Ludwik was the owner of Żelazna, a village near Sobikowo in Mazovia. The couple, like almost all Frankists of the time, had many children. Their first-born was Tekla, mother of Louis, the subject of my interest. Another child was Julia Joanna Wołowska, born in 1790[96]. In 1812, Julia married Jan Zaleski (1784–1843), then "Knight Intendant of the Police Department of Cracow, aged twenty-eight, residing in Bracka Street in the city of Cracow"[97]. They lived together for 31 years[98] and had three children: Waleria Anna (1813–1878), Adolf

91 Kazimierz was a barrister, since 1860 at the Court of Appeal of the Congress Kingdom, since 1865 at the Senate (J. Różycki *Brzeziński Kazimierz,* [in:] Polski Słownik Biograficzny, vol. III..., p. 40; E. Dreżepolska *Brzeziński Kazimierz,* [in:] *Słownik biograficzny adwokatów polskich A-F,* vol. I, Warszawa 1980, pp. 43–44).

92 Marriage certificate: Warsaw Archdiocesan Archive, Warsaw, St. Andrew 1828, deed no. 22, https://www.szukajwarchiwach.gov.pl/skan/-/skan/a4375e2ee6d2e8031f3bb4e4797be7049edffd4cc180834eb480e1a65cc82870 (retrieved 18.05.2022).

93 Death certificate: State Archives in Warsaw, ASC Division IV, 1810, no. 84, https://www.szukajwarchiwach.gov.pl/jednostka/-/jednostka/12481354 (retrieved 18.05.2022).

94 Death certificate: State Archive in Warsaw, St. Andrew, 1832, no. 16. https://www.szukajwarchiwach.gov.pl/jednostka/-/jednostka/12478314?_Jednostka_delta=20&_Jednostka_resetCur=false&_Jednostka_cur=15&_Jednostka_id_jednostki=12478314

95 Marriage certificate: Warsaw Archdiocesan Archive, Warsaw, St. Andrew's, 1786, deed no. 129.

96 Baptismal record: Warsaw, St. Cross parish, baptismal register, 1790, no. 147.

97 Marriage certificate: Civil Registry Records of Sobików municipality, 1812, no. 9. https://metryki.genealodzy.pl/metryka.php?ar=2&zs=1452d&sy=1812&kt=2&plik=09a.jpg#zoom=1.75&x=0&y=0 (retrieved 27.05.2022).

98 Jan Zaleski's obituary: A. T. Tyszka (ed.) *Nekrologi „Kuriera Warszawskiego",* vol. I, *1821–1845,* Warszawa 2001, p. 372.

(1816–1882) and Aniela Paulina (1829–1880). Julia died in 1874[99]. In Offenbach, she was followed by Barbara Rozalia[100]. In 1817, she married Józef Łabęcki who came from another Frankist family, a former official of the Marijampole district[101]. She died in 1867[102], mother to two sons: Włodzimierz Szymon and Antoni Wincenty. Another daughter of Ludwik and Elżbieta was Teofila, born in 1798. In 1817, three months before her sister Barbara Rozalia, she married Dionizy Kazimierz Lanckoroński, a teacher at the Warsaw Lyceum (1787–1851)[103]. The couple most probably did not have any offspring. However, Teofila's younger brother, Adam Alfons Wołowski, had one daughter (Henrietta Teresa). Born in 1799 in Warsaw, he was a graduate of the Faculty of Law and Administration at Warsaw University, judge at the Civil Court of the Sandomierz District in Radom, and since 1844 judge at the Criminal Court of the Płock and Augustów Governorates, later of the Warsaw Governorate. Finally, since 1853, he was a judge of the Court of Appeal of the Congress Kingdom[104]. He died in 1861[105]. In 1832 he married Amelia, née Burghadt, in Radom[106]. A year later she gave birth to their only daughter. Paulina, the penultimate child of Ludwik and Elżbieta, was probably born between 1799

---

99 Inscription on the tombstone, https://cmentarze.um.warszawa.pl/pomnik.aspx?pom_id=2366 (retrieved 27.05.2022).

100 M.J. Minakowski *Frankiści z Offenbachu ...*

101 Marriage certificate: Civil Registry Records of Sobików municipality, 1817, no. 13 https://metryki.genealodzy.pl/metryka.php?ar=2&zs=1452d&sy=1817&kt=2&plik=k032.jpg#zoom=1.2139965297860034&x=2082&y=341 (retrieved 27.05.2022).

102 Death certificate: https://wielcy.pl/img/metrskan/z/9365695.jpg (retrieved 27.05.2022).

103 Marriage certificate: Civil Registry Records of Sobików municipality, 1817, no. 11, http://metryki.genealodzy.pl/metryka.php?ar=2&zs=1452d&sy=1817&kt=2&plik=k031.jpg#zoom=1.25&x=1666&y=1527 (retrieved 26.05.2022).

104 R. Gerber *Studenci Uniwersytetu Warszawskiego...*, p. 239. Gerber erroneously states in this short biography that Adam Alfons was a son of Tekla Wołowska (his sister) and Franciszek Wołowski. However, it is clear from the death certificate (see below) that his parents were Ludwik and Elżbieta née Lanckorońska.

105 Death certificate: State Archives in Warsaw, St. Andrew's, 1841, no. 759, https://metryki.genealodzy.pl/metryka.php?ar=1&zs=0159d&sy=1861&kt=3&plik=759-762.jpg#zoom=2.25&x=80&y=358 (retrieved 28.05.2022). Adam maintained contact with his eldest sister to the end of his life, as evidenced by Louis Wolowski's letter to Władysław Czartoryski of 9 January 1862, in which he wrote that his uncle, his mother's only brother, had died, causing her so much pain that her son had to spend a few days with her (Biblioteka Książąt Czartoryskich, ref. 7239 IV).

106 Marriage certificate: https://www.familysearch.org/ark:/61903/3:1:S3HT-XXC9-7ZL?referrer=FamilySearch&ipaddress=83.25.189.184&i=363&cc=1407440 (retrieved 28.05.2022).

and 1800, according to the certificate of marriage concluded in 1836 between her and Piotr Piasecki, a widower, obviously also of Frankist descent[107]. According to Piotr's death certificate, the couple remained childless or none of the children lived to adulthood[108]. Paulina outlived him and died over twenty years later, in 1882[109]. Finally, the youngest child of Ludwik and Elżbieta née Lanckorońska was Henrietta (or Henryka), born in 1801. At the age of 17, she married Józef Jeziorański, an official twice her age[110]. The couple did not have children and divorced (something that was nevertheless rare among the Frankists)[111]. Wołowska remarried, this time Jan Kanty Wołowski – unfortunately the date of the marriage is not known, but the marriage is confirmed by Henrietta's death certificate from 1860[112]. Jan Kanty Wołowski was a son of Paweł Wołowski (1778–1831), owner of a brewery in Warsaw. According to Jan Kanty's biographer, Paweł may have come from one of the lateral lines of the Wołowski family, possibly from one of the converts who adopted that surname together with Franciszek Shlomo Wołowski[113]. It is also possible that he descended directly from Elisha Schor. Family ties that go beyond kinship seem also to be evidenced by Jan Kanty's later relationship with the family of Louis, the protagonist of this book. In any case, Jan Kanty Wołowski joined the ranks of the family's lawyers. What is more, he became arguably its most eminent representative: he was first an assessor at the court in Warsaw, then a barrister at the Court of Appeal, since 1834 at the Court of the Supreme Instance in the Congress Kingdom, assistant to the chief prosecutor of the Ruling Senate (since 1842), and chief prosecutor (1847). In April 1861, Wołowski headed the Government

107 Marriage certificate: State Archive in Warsaw, Civil Status Records of the Roman Catholic Parish of St. John the Baptist in Warsaw,1836, marriage certificate no. 210. https://www.szukajwarchiwach.gov.pl/jednostka/-/jednostka/12478581?_Jednostka_delta=20&_Jednostka_resetCur=false&_Jednostka_cur=15&_Jednostka_id_jednostki=12478581 (retrieved 29.05.2022).

108 Death certificate of Piotr Piasecki: Warsaw, St. Andrew's parish, 1860, no. 561, http://wielcy.pl/img/metrskan/z/4931154.jpg (retrieved 29.05.2022).

109 Death certificate of Paulina Piasecka, née Wołowska: State Archive in Warsaw, St. Andrzej, 1882, no. 78, https://metryki.genealodzy.pl/metryka.php?ar=1&zs=0159d&sy=1882&kt=3&plik=077-078.jpg#zoom=1&x=462&y=2304 (retrieved 29.05.2022).

110 Marriage certificate: State Archives in Warsaw, ASC District VII, 1818, no. 64.

111 This is stated in Jeziorański's death certificate: State Archives in Warsaw, St. Andrew's church, 1853, no. 171, http://wielcy.pl/img/metrskan/z/4929559.jpg (retrieved 30.05.2022).

112 Death certificate: State Archives in Warsaw, St. Andrew's church, 1860, no. 3, https://metryki.genealodzy.pl/metryka.php?ar=1&zs=0159d&sy=1860&kt=3&plik=003-006.jpg#zoom=1.75&x=433&y=694 (retrieved 30.05.2022).

113 W. Witkowski *Aleksander This i Jan Kanty Wołowski, wybitni prawnicy Królestwa Polskiego*, Lublin 2001, pp. 42–43.

Commission of Justice of the Congress Kingdom[114]. However, he only served as Minister of Justice for a few days. According to Nikolai Berg, Wołowski, outraged by the Castle Square massacre on 08 April, resigned[115]. In 1862, he became the first dean of the Faculty of Law and Administration of the just-established Warsaw Central School. However, after a search of his flat by the tsarist authorities in early June 1863, he was arrested and exiled deep into Russia, to Penza where he died in 1864. Significantly, in Warsaw Jan Kanty's arrest was linked to his relationship with Louis Wolowski. Józef Kajetan Janowski, who misidentified Louis as Jan Kanty's brother, wrote, "it was even rumoured that some compromising correspondence between the brothers had been seized, and this was supposed to be the reason for the arrest and such a sudden deportation"[116]. This supposition seems even more likely as Louis Wolowski worked closely with Czartoryski at the time and may have used his family connections with the former minister for political purposes. He certainly maintained contact with Jan Kanty, as evidenced by Andrzej Edward Koźmian's letter to his family of 29 June 1862: "I had only a short time to go to dinner at Louis Wolowski's wife's with Jan Kanty Wołowski, who had come from Warsaw, an old friend of Margrave Wielopolski, but with whom his relations had cooled somewhat since he had refused to be minister after the April massacre"[117]. We also know from other sources that Laure, wife of Louis Wolowski, was in Warsaw in 1861[118].

It is therefore possible that Jan Kanty paid for these contacts with his life. His wife Henrietta, née Wołowska, who died four years before him, remained completely in his shadow during his lifetime. So much so that Wojciech Witkowski, in the work cited above, claims that Jan Kanty never married, and that Henrietta, who rests with him in one grave in Warsaw's Powązki cemetery, was "perhaps his sister", which, however, "cannot be established today"[119].

---

114 Correspondence between Gorchakov and Alexander II regarding the appointment of Wołowski: N. W. Berg *Zapiski o polskich spiskach i powstaniach*, vol. II, Warszawa 1906, p. 170.

115 N. W. Berg *Zapiski...*, p. 141.

116 J.K. Janowski *Pamiętniki o powstaniu styczniowem*, Warszawa 1925, p. 81.

117 A. Koźmian *Listy Andrzeja Edwarda Koźmiana*, vol. IV, *1860–1864*, Lvov 1896, p. 549.

118 A. Koźmian *Listy...*, p. 351. This stay is also mentioned by Eliza née Branicka Krasińska in a letter to Katarzyna Potocka from June 1861 (E. z Branickich Krasińska *Świadek epoki. Listy Elizy z Branickich Krasińskiej z lat 1835–1876*, vol. III, *Czerwiec 1853 – lipiec 1863*, Warszawa 1996, p. 353).

119 W. Witkowski *Aleksander This i Jan Kanty Wołowski...*, p. 228.

3. Tekla

Tekla, Henrietta's eldest sister and Louis' mother, shared that fate. Not only because she married a Wołowski but because her constant presence at the side of her husband and sons became almost imperceptible. Unfortunately, no family correspondence of the Wołowskis has survived. Another thing is that Tekla, her husband, and sons lived in the same town, so the correspondence was probably scarce. On the other hand, Wołowska appeared quite regularly in the life of Adam Mickiewicz, above all in letters written by Celina Mickiewicz. Tekla was a cousin of Maria Szymanowska, Celina's mother, and her closest relative in Paris. She turned out to be a tender and caring aunt. Celina lived with the Wołowskis before her marriage. Later they kept in regular contact, and during the days of Celina's illness, the Wołowskis (most likely Tekla herself) kept regular watch over her[120]. Adam and Celina's son, Władysław, described her as follows:

> Lady Tekla was the head of her large family. Once her husband fell ill, he said goodbye to his friends, assuring them that he would not see them again. When the danger passed, my father was allowed to visit Franciszek for a while, to whom he said: "See, you are not dead after all". The other one replied: "Tekla would not have it". In later years, she was the only one who stayed with my parents, because her children went their separate ways, getting rich and understanding less and less of Mickiewicz's aspirations and activities, and were bitter that concern for tomorrow played such a subordinate role in my mother's musings[121].

Tekla's letter to Mickiewicz from 1839 also testifies to close family relations in the Wołowski home thanks to the lady of the house: "As Franuś [Franciszek Wołowski] often mentions: why can't we play whist with Adam; it was so nice to quarrel sometimes. Of my attachment, be assured that it is most sincere and truly maternal"[122]. Another memoir by Władysław Mickiewicz mentions a strong bond between Tekla and her son Louis: "Accordingly, as her son and son-in-law changed their opinion of statesmen, she also changed hers. When she saw a portrait of one of the representatives of the provisional government in our living room, she could not hide her indignation; two weeks later, she was outraged again that the portrait had disappeared. Mother explained that the children, playing, had torn it up. Wolowski and Faucher, as adherents of the republic, rehabilitated Ledru-Rollin, and Blanc in Mrs Wołowski's eyes"[123]. It is also characteristic that in their

---

120 R. Koropeckyj *Adam Mickiewicz. Życie romantyka*, Warszawa 2013, p. 310.

121 W. Mickiewicz *Moja matka*, Kraków 1926, p. 31.

122 W. Mickiewicz *Moja matka...*, p. 31.

123 W. Mickiewicz *Pamiętniki*, Warszawa 2012, pp. 59–60. Tekla Wołowska's son-in-law was Léon Faucher (1803–1854), an economist, journalist and deputy associated with the July Monarchy, then a member of Parliament of the Second Republic, its Minister of the Interior between December 1848 and April 1849 and de facto Prime Minister

correspondence, Celina, and her eldest daughter Maria (Marynia) referred to Tekla Wołowska as "Granny". This clearly suggests that Wołowska acted as a substitute grandmother for Mickiewicz's children[124]. She also took care of Mickiewicz. "Hardly anyone visits us [...]. Grandmother sometimes comes to cook dinner for Papa and brings her delicacies," wrote Maria Mickiewicz in October 1854, during Celina's subsequent illness, to her aunt Zofia Szymanowska[125]. Tekla did not only take care of her own family, but she was involved in charity work, supporting her compatriots in need[126].

There is one unexpected element in this pleasant, if rather typical, portrait of a 19th century mother, grandmother, lady, and Pole, and Tekla Wołowska undoubtedly was it all. She was also the author of a *History of Poland*, a textbook published in 1860 in Paris[127]. Her book started with "The uncertain time in Polish history", namely a tale of the legendary Lech, Krak, Wanda and Popiel, and ended with the death of king Władysław III at Varna. The text testified to Wołowska's considerable historical reading; she quoted the chroniclers Wincenty Kadłubek, Jan Długosz, Marcin Kromer and historians as Joachim Lelewel or Adam Naruszewicz. It was also a work of popularisation, quite typical of mid-19th century historiography. Its purpose was obvious: to keep Poles' spirits up, to remind them of the greatness of their ancestors. So, according to Wołowska, the Poles adopted Christianity without resistance or compulsion, as a result of sincere conviction. Bolesław the Brave was portrayed as a near-perfect ruler, while Mieszko II was his "dull" and "despicable" contradiction[128]. Bolesław the Generous was, in turn, the archetype of the warrior king, at the same time a debauchee ultimately justly punished by Providence[129].

---

from April 1851 to October of the same year. Alexandre Ledru-Rollin (1807–1874) was a radical republican, after the Revolution of 1848, Minister of the Interior in the Provisional Government until May 1848. Louis Blanc (1811–1882) was a leftist thinker, the first ever socialist to be part of the government in 1848.

124 W. Mickiewicz *Moja matka...*, pp. 54 & 88.

125 Z. Makowiecka *Mickiewicz w Collège de France. Październik 1840-maj 1844*, Warszawa 1968, "Kronika życia i twórczości Mickiewicza" series, S. Pigoń (ed.), p. 349.

126 "Pielgrzym Polski" printed the following announcement on 05 February 1833: "Mr. Z..., an officer of the Polish Army, publicly declares his gratitude to the people who made it possible for him to bring his wife and four children, namely: Castellan Plater's wife, Mrs Wołowska, Roman Sołtyk, Major Adolf Krosnowski, MP Zwierkowski, Józef Straszewicz and doctor Wołowski."

127 T. Wołowska *Historya Polska*, vol. I, Paris 1860. The authorship of the work seemed doubtful to me for a long time, but it was confirmed by "Wiadomości Polskie" of 19 January 1861 (No. 3), which reported that Tekla Wołowska, Franciszek's widow, had donated thirty copies of her own work, entitled *The History of Poland*, to the reading room of Polish veterans at St Casimir's house.

128 T. Wołowska *Historya Polska*, pp. 40–48.

129 T. Wołowska *Historya Polska...*, pp. 70–76.

Bolesław Wrymouth equalled the virtues of Bolesław the Brave[130], while the heroic Władysław the Short "evoked good feelings even in the Germans settled on Polish soil"[131]. The most interesting passages in the *History*, however, related to the author's views. Such as, for example, the division into districts and the division of power: "Poland has long overlooked constitutional institutions for which many nations are still clamouring to this day, institutions designed to clash with power to guard against abuse"[132]. Or another, this time describing the Italian cities of the early Renaissance, but clearly referring to the present day: "The inhabitants saw their property secured, there was a love and encouragement of the sciences, fine arts and industry. The salutary institutions of education spread from Italy to the world, freedom endeared to the unassuming and respectable boroughs, and the way to honour and wealth was opened"[133]. In the light of *The History*, the "granny" of the little Mickiewiczes turned out to be a staunch opponent of feudalism, a supporter of the liberal rule of law, based on individual freedom, private property, and the separation of powers. And, equally important, separation of church and state[134]. As I will present it later, Tekla's views matched those of her husband and, to a large extent, her eldest son.

The collection of the National Museum in Cracow holds a miniature of Mrs Wołowska from the Warsaw period, painted by Stanisław Marszałkiewicz. The work, signed "Tekla Wołowska, wife of Franciszek Wołowski", is undated, but was probably painted in the 1820s. It shows a relatively young woman with her black hair tied up in a bun at the top and ringlets falling at the sides. She wears a green and white dress, tightly cinched at the waist and exposing her shoulders. Tekla looks at the viewer with a faint smile. She certainly is not pretty but her large, black, understanding eyes are mesmerising. She gives the impression of a warm, kind, and intelligent person. And independent – which she remained to the end. She outlived her husband by 27 years. On the day of her death on 09 May 1871, she was living in Paris, in her own flat, not far from her children yet independent[135].

---

130 T. Wołowska *Historya Polska...*, pp. 84–120.

131 T. Wołowska *Historya Polska...*, p. 287.

132 T. Wołowska *Historya Polska...*, p. 147.

133 T. Wołowska *Historya Polska...*, p. 316.

134 This is evidenced by a passage on Gregory VII, who wanted to show the papacy "the way of unlimited power". As a result, "the most terrible calamities have befallen mankind under the veil of faith. Proof of how the best and most sacred things can grow in the hands of man." (T. Wołowska *Historya Polska...*, p. 79).

135 Death certificate of Tekla Wołowska: Archives de Paris, reference V4E 3483 no. 6.

4. Franciszek

The fate of the Wołowski family on Louis' mother's side is therefore not straightforward, but it can be traced back to Elisha Schor. Franciszek Wołowski, father of this book's protagonist, also descended from Elisha. While Tekla was a descendant of his eldest son, Franciszek's grandfather was the younger Michał (Natan) Wołowski.

He and his wife Marianna, née Jeziorańska, had two daughters and one son. The eldest daughter, also Marianna, was probably born in 1771 in Kłobuck near Częstochowa, at the time of Frank's "captivity" in the monastery. She married Mikołaj Rudnicki; they had two daughters, Ludwika, and Barbara[136].

The younger – Barbara – was a late child, born ca. 1781[137]. In 1804 she married Eliasz Wołowski[138] and they had six children. Henrietta, born in 1808, died shortly after birth. Three years younger, Elisabeth Cecylia married Henryk Podowski, an eminent doctor, chief physician of St. Lazarus Hospital[139]. She died in 1907. Cornelius (1813–1886) and Marianna Wołowska (1814–1900) also survived into advanced age. Teofila (1816–1857) reached adulthood.

Louis Wolowski's grandfather was the eldest of three siblings. He was probably born in 1767, so perhaps also in the vicinity of Częstochowa. Characteristically, Louis Wolowski never mentioned his paternal grandparents, and he must have met them in his young years. Thus, the information concerning Michał Wołowski comes entirely from the death certificate, which is worth quoting at length: "[...] on the sixteenth day of the month of July this year [1826 – RD] at seven o'clock in the evening at Podwale Street, five hundred and eighteen, died of gangrene, the noble Michał Wołowski, supporting himself from his own property, aged fifty-nine, [leaving behind] a widowed wife and four children, namely: Franciszek aged thirty-nine, Ludwik aged twenty-four, Teofil aged twenty-three and Aleksander

136 Death certificate: Warsaw Archdiocesan Archives, Warsaw, St. Andrew's. 1844, deed no. 186 https://metryki.genealodzy.pl/index.php?op=pg&ar=1&zs=0159d&se=&sy=1844&kt=3&plik=183-186.jpg&x=2466&y=1938&zoom=1 (retrieved 02.01.2023).

137 Death certificate:https://metryki.genealodzy.pl/index.php?op=pg&ar=8&zs=9214d&se=&sy=508&kt=4&plik=0304-0309.jpg&x=2137&y=221&zoom=1 (retrieved 02.01.2023).

138 Marriage certificate: Parish Archives, Warsaw, St. Cross, 1804, k. 127 https://metryki.genealodzy.pl/metryka.php?ar=9&zs=9243d&sy=308&kt=1&skan=135.JPG (retrieved 02.01.2023).

139 Marriage certificate: Warsaw Archdiocese Archive, Warsaw, St. Alexander, 1832, deed no. 25. https://metryki.genealodzy.pl/index.php?op=pg&ar=8&zs=9214d&sy=301&kt=7&plik=025.jpg (retrieved 02.01.2023). Podowski's profile: T. Ostrowska *Henryk Podowski* [in:] *Polski Słownik Biograficzny* vol. XXVII, Wrocław – Warszawa – Kraków-Gdańsk – Lodz, 1982–1983, pp. 187–188. Notably, Podowski was also probably of Frankist descent, as he was the son of Maciej and Magdalena née Wołowska.

aged twenty-one, without a will he expired prematurely"[140]. Several elements are worth noting. Firstly, the "widowed wife" was Wiktoria née Rydecka (Radecka). She came from another Frankist family. According to her death certificate, she was the daughter of Ignacy and Anna Rydeckis and was probably born between 1768 and 1771[141]. We know nothing about her except that the last years of her life must have been exceptionally hard. Only two surviving sons, Franciszek, and Ludwik, appear in the same deed. The documents confirm the death of Teofil in 1831[142]; Aleksander's fate remains unknown.

Secondly, Podwale street where Michał Wołowski lived towards the end of his life testifies to the fact that he was probably a wealthy resident of the capital city. According to Eugeniusz Szwankowski, "In the time of the Congress Kingdom, Podwale was a street of taverns, hotels and inns"[143]. The former palaces stood next to newly built inns and beer halls. Furthermore the Wołowskis, as we shall see, could afford to send their eldest son to study abroad.

Thirdly, and finally, the term "noble" before the surname suggests nobility. The trouble is that there is no other proof of this title. As I will show further on, the coat of arms had been granted three years earlier to the son Franciszek mentioned in the text, but nothing entitled Michał to be treated as a nobleman. It is possible, however, that the parish priest of St. John's, who signed the document, used the phrase courteously, with a view precisely to the then already prominent figure of the younger Wołowski in Warsaw.

Wiktoria and Michał Wołowski had four grown-up sons, of whom, however, only two lived into their 30s. There was at least one more son who died immediately after birth[144].

140 Death certificate: State Archives in Warsaw, Civil Status Records of the Roman Catholic Parish of St. John the Baptist in Warsaw, 1826, no. 385 https://metryki.genealodzy.pl/index.php?op=pg&ar=1&zs=0161d&se=&sy=1826&kt=3&plik=382-387.jpg&x=2813&y=228&zoom=1 (retrieved 02.01.2023).

141 Death certificate: Warsaw Archdiocesan Archive, Parish of the Visitation of the Blessed Virgin Mary, 1832, no. 365 https://metryki.genealodzy.pl/index.php?op=pg&ar=1&zs=0160d&se=&sy=1832c&kt=3&plik=0364-0369.jpg&x=0&y=0&zoom=1.5 (retrieved 03.01,2023). The discrepancy between the possible dates of birth is due to the different entries on the death certificates of Michał Wołowski and Wiktoria Wołowska. According to the former, she was 55 years old in 1826; according to the latter, she was 64 at the time of her death in 1832. It seems, therefore, that her sons, reporting their parents' deaths in either case, did not know the exact date of their mother's birth – which was probably because she was not aware of it herself.

142 Death certificate: Warsaw Archdiocesan Archive, Warsaw, St. Andrew's 1831, deed no. 11 (inventory).

143 E. Szwankowski *Ulice i place Warszawy,* Warszawa 1970, p. 164.

144 Death certificate of Ksawery Michał Wołowski: St. Cross Parish Archive in Warsaw, *Liber mortuorum 1775–1801*, k. 218. https://metryki.genealodzy.pl/index.php?op=p

Unfortunately, nothing is known about Franciszek's only surviving brother, Ludwik Wołowski.

However, regardless of the fate of the uncle of this book's protagonist, the Wołowskis represented a remarkable clan, with a surprising number of extremely talented and distinguished members. Even Jeske – Choiński, clearly hostile to the Frankists, referred to them as "the most talented of the whole "bunch". A number of men, distinguished in various fields, came out of their blood. Even the women of this talented family were distinguished by uncommon abilities and civic virtues. All the Frankist homes into which a Wołowska entered as wife and mother produced people of ability"[145]. The family included prominent lawyers such as Jan Tadeusz Wołowski, Jan Kanty Wołowski and Kazimierz Brzeziński. Maria Szymanowska and Filipina Brzezińska, née Szymanowska, came to fame as pianists and composers. Wacław Szymanowski gained recognition as a journalist and writer, while Teofil Lenartowicz is still associated with Polish Romantic poetry.

Another worthy representative of this remarkable family was Franciszek Eliasz Wołowski, Louis' father. He was born in Warsaw in 1786. Information concerning his young years is extremely scarce, coming mainly from a biography published in Paris after his death, written down almost certainly based on information provided by his family[146].

It says that his parents had chosen a legal career for Franciszek and were therefore to send him to study law in Halle in 1803. He was to complete the three-year course in two years and then return to Poland[147]. The émigré author of the biography of Franciszek Wołowski mentions his involvement in financial operations involving enormous sums Polish landowners wed Prussia. Franciszek Wołowski was supposed to be the Prussian government's agent, and who "had a percentage allocated to himself from all the transactions, which he did not touch until the business had been arranged to the satisfaction of both parties". He was also to obtain "the most substantial part of his estate" in this way[148]. Although Wołowski's name does not appear in any study of these amounts due[149], his activity in this matter

g&ar=9&zs=9243d&se=&sy=515&kt=1&plik=224.jpg&x=2108&y=38&zoom=1 (retrieved 03.01.2023).

145 T. Jeske – Choiński *Neofici Polscy...*, pp. 100–101.

146 No author provided *Życie ś.p. Franciszka Wołowskiego deputowanego na Sejm Królestwa Polskiego: czytane na posiedzeniu Towarzystwa Literackiego Polskiego w Paryżu dnia 16 maja 1844 roku*, Paris 1844.

147 *Życie ś.p. Franciszka Wołowskiego...*, p. 5.

148 *Życie ś.p. Franciszka Wołowskiego...*, p. 6.

149 F. Skarbek *Dzieje Księstwa Warszawskiego,* vol. 2, Warszawa 1897; M. Handelsman *Konwencya bajońska 1808,* [in:] M. Handelsman *Pod znakiem Napoleona, Studya historyczne ser. II,* pp. 1–72, Warszawa 1913; T. Mencel *Sumy bajońskie,* "Roczniki historyczne", XIX, Poznań 1952, pp. 133–164.

was confirmed by himself in 1831 in a parliamentary rostrum. However, he did not mention any success. Rather, he said: "during my mandate and later after 1823, the Prussian government collected little by way of execution; indeed, during my stay in Berlin I presented to the Prussian minister the impossibility of executing these sums, that I would not undertake this task"[150]. Also, in his *Uprising of the Polish Nation in 1830 and 1831*, Maurycy Mochnacki quoted Wołowski's words of 1830, "that, having been formerly empowered by the Berlin bank to realise or surrender them to anyone, having recognised their undoubted bankruptcy, he had to send the files back to Berlin"[151].

F. Wołowski's primary occupation and source of income was therefore the practice of law. After 1807, he first became an assessor at the civil tribunal, and then an advocate at the Court of Appeal in Warsaw. After 1815, he was a counsel at the Court of the Supreme Instance of Congress Poland – that is, the highest civil tribunal of the state, definitively deciding disputes by way of cassation[152]. The elegiac description of the lawyer's work seems questionable (the author was, after all, writing down a eulogy):

> Wołowski owed his great fame not only to his talents but, what is less often, to his conscientious work, exemplary diligence, and noble selflessness. He was not in the habit of relying on young and inexperienced assistants to help him with his work; he did the smallest writing himself; he would devote himself to more important matters without interruption, without rest, renouncing the most necessary comforts of life. Sometimes, after working all night, he would be carried from the table to the bed, feeling faint. He never bargained for a reward, he did not even want to remind what was promised to him, he accepted from the rich what they gave him, he rescued the poor by paying the costs of their trial with his own money[153]

However, according to Tadeusz Burakowski, Wołowski must have enjoyed real popularity and recognition[154]. Jan Nepomucen Janowski later described the social evenings at Michał Brzeziński's house, attended by the Warsaw bourgeoisie, 30–40 people from the Frankist milieu, mostly brewers. "The evening meetings, as it were, were graced [...] by Franciszek Wołowski, an already famous and wealthy

150 *Dyaryusz Sejmu z r. 1830–1831*, vol. IV *Od 26 maja do 18 czerwca 1831*, Kraków 1910, p. 554.

151 M. Mochnacki *Powstanie narodu polskiego w roku 1830 i 1831.*, vol. II, Poznań 1863, p. 170.

152 M. Makuch *Organizacja sądownictwa cywilnego w Królestwie Polskim okresu konstytucyjnego (1815–1831)*, [in:] "Zeszyty Naukowe Instytutu Administracji AJD w Częstochowie", part 1 (13), Częstochowa 2016, p. 75.

153 *Życie ś.p. Franciszka Wołowskiego...*, pp. 5–6.

154 T. Burakowski *Wołowski Franciszek*, [in:] *Słownik biograficzny adwokatów polskich S-Ż*, p. 476.

patron [...]”[155]. For he had made a sum of money that allowed him to buy a landed estate in a short space of time, travel to Italy for a long time and send his son to study in Paris[156]. Another thing is that this puts some doubt on the “disinterestedness” and “accepting what they gave him”.

The wealth and position he enjoyed allowed Franciszek to get a wife. In 1809 he married, according to the Frankist custom, his cousin Tekla, née Wołowska[157]. The couple soon had children: in 1810, the eldest son, Louis was born, the hero of this book[158]. Two years later, the only daughter, Aleksandryna, was born[159], in 1813 – Kazimierz[160], and the youngest Feliks Franciszek in 1816[161].

As a lawyer, Franciszek remembered his closer and more distant relatives. The members of the Wołowski clan always stuck together and supported each other. In 1822, several Warsaw brewers, participants in the meetings at Brzeziński's, including Franciszek Wołowski (father of Maria Szymanowska), were arrested on the orders of Grand Duke Konstantin because of reports by the spy Henryk Mackrott. While Konstantin quickly released them, he had previously ordered them to sweep Saski Square. Mackrott later reported that the offended brewers had contacted lawyer Franciszek Wołowski, who was to prepare a complaint to the Tsar in secret. It probably had the desired effect: while staying briefly in Warsaw in January 1823, Alexander first danced at a ball with Szymanowska, then received her at a separate audience, clearly showing favour to the Wołowskis[162].

---

155 J.N. Janowski *Notatki autobiograficzne,* Wrocław 1950, p. 73.

156 Germain Sarrut and Benoit Saint-Edme, authors of another biography of Wołowski, written in 1836, estimated his fortune at the time at „one million Polish florins" (*Wolowski François,* [in:] *Biographies polonaises extraites de la Biographies des hommes du jour par G. Sarrut et B. Saint-Edme,* Paris 1836, p. 71).

157 Marriage certificate, Warsaw ASC Division V, 54/1809, https://www.szukajwarchiwach.gov.pl/skan/-/skan/2f781b0c53e216f2cbc711e003bf06d037f09d54b81ecb6fb153140050636851 (retrieved 13.05.2022).

158 Birth certificate: Warsaw, ASC District I, 1810 No131 https://metryki.genealodzy.pl/index.php?op=pg&ar=1&zs=183&se=&sy=1810a&kt=1&plik=129-131.jpg&x=2830&y=1812&zoom=1 (retrieved 12.01.2023).

159 Birth certificate: Warsaw ASC District I, 1810 No. 47 https://metryki.genealodzy.pl/index.php?op=pg&ar=1&zs=183&se=&sy=1812a&kt=1&plik=045-047.jpg&x=2201&y=1701&zoom=1 (retrieved 12.01.2023).

160 Baptismal record: Warsaw Archdiocesan Archive, St. Andrew's, 21.01.1814, https://metryki.genealodzy.pl/index.php?op=pg&ar=8&zs=9159d&se=&sy=104&kt=2&plik=str_0020-0021.jpg&x=1773&y=454&zoom=1 (retrieved 12.01.2023).

161 Baptismal record Archdiocesan Archives of Warsaw, St. Andrew, 18.03.1817 https://metryki.genealodzy.pl/index.php?op=pg&ar=8&zs=9159d&se=&sy=104&kt=5&plik=str_0312-0313.jpg&x=1619&y=1009&zoom=1 (retrieved 12.01.2023).

162 A. Młocki *Księga wspomnień Alfreda Młockiego,* Paryż 1884, pp. 11–12; T. Syga, S. Szenic *Maria Szymanowska...,* pp. 121–125.

Wołowski then came to Warsaw from his new landed estate. On 31 July 1822, he purchased by public auction "the estate of Kaski with the appurtenances of Jaktorów and other estates, for the purchase price of 710,000 zlotys"[163]. Kaski is today a village located near Błonie, just over 40 km west of Warsaw. According to the third volume of the famous Geographical Dictionary by Sulimierski, Chlebowski and Walewski, in 1827 Kaski alone had around 500 inhabitants[164]. Wołowski's estate, however, was much more extensive and included the farms of Regów, Baranów and Jaktorów, totalling some 8,000 ha. According to Witkowski, in an area where medium property (up to 900 ha) prevailed, "they were actually latifundial estates and some of the largest in the Warsaw area, more extensive than the estates of many aristocratic and landowning families"[165]. Franciszek Wołowski was therefore undoubtedly among the wealthier attorneys and residents of the capital city.

A court document sheds some light on Wołowski's management of the newly acquired estate. The peasants of Jaktorów had filed a lawsuit against the previous owners of the farm. Namely, citing a royal decree of 1701, they demanded to be recognised as free people, exempt from all services, and owners of cultivated land[166]. So, they had refused to perform serfdom, and to agree to Wołowski's proposed transition to tenancy. The lawyer first won the case twice in court, then evicted "a few who were a significant cause of disorder", and finally had them all evicted – agreeing only that they should remain in place until new premises could be found[167]. At the request of the citizens of Jaktorów, the General Prosecutor's Office was involved in the case, aiming to overturn the earlier verdicts – a letter from attorney Maciej Kostrzycki, representing Wołowski, was intended to prove the unfoundedness of these proceedings. Ultimately, the case was decided in his favour and Jaktorów remained part of his estate. The letter was also interesting in that it spoke of Wołowski's renting the peasants. He was to offer lease to the residents of some of his farms in return for an annual rent of 6 zlotys 7.5 gr. per morgen[168]; apart from the residents of Jaktorów, the majority agreed to the terms.

---

163 *Odpowiedź ze strony Franciszka Wołowskiego Dziedzica dóbr Kaski z przyległościami Jaktorów i innemi na skargę restytucyjną Prokuratoryi Jeneralney w imieniu włościan jaktorowskich podaną*, Biblioteka Narodowa, ref. 75.398 A; https://polona.pl/item/odpowiedz-ze-strony-franciszka-wolowskiego-dziedzica-dobr-kask-z-przyleglosciami,NjY4NDMwNTY/, p. 1.

164 *Kaski*, [in:] F. Sulimierski, B. Chlebowski, W. Walewski (eds.) *Słownik geograficzny Królestwa Polskiego i innych krajów słowiańskich*, vol. III, Warszawa 1882, p. 900.

165 W. Witkowski *Aleksander This i Jan Kanty Wołowski...*, p. 51.

166 *Odpowiedź ze strony Franciszka Wołowskiego...*, p. 9.

167 *Odpowiedź ze strony Franciszka Wołowskiego...*, p. 2

168 However, this only applied to part of the villages belonging to Wołowski. He "let others go on rent" in subsequent years. He mentioned this in the Sejm in 1831 (Dyaryusz...., vol. II *Od 9 lutego do 18 kwietnia 1831*, Kraków 1908, p. 524), and then in 1832 in "Kronika Emigracji Polskiej" (vol. I, Paris 1834, pp. 249–250).

Importantly, the rent proposed by Wołowski was neither unusually high nor low. It was comparable, for example, to the rent introduced a few years later in the Zamojski Landed Property, the largest complex of magnate estates in the Congress Kingdom[169]. Franciszek Wołowski the landowner was probably not significantly different from Franciszek Wołowski the lawyer. In both cases, he proved to be an efficient, hard-working man who managed a sizeable estate well. However, he was far from the friend of the poor described in his posthumous profile.

The purchase of the extensive landholdings had a significant impact on Franciszek's life. It enabled him to leave his profession, travel extensively in Italy and then get involved in politics. Above all, however, it contributed to Wołowski's ennoblement. Although Walery Przyborowski claims that the Wołowskis were ennobled as early as 1793, he does not provide any documents to support this thesis[170]. Finally, on 17 April 1823, Alexander I signed a decree in St. Petersburg, according to which, "Wishing to recognise the services rendered to the country by H.E. Franciszek Wołowski", he granted him "a coat of arms *na Kaskach*, that is: a black ox's head with a white stripe in the middle of the forehead on a shield with a gold rim in a blue field. Above the shield a crown of gold with five leaves in the midst of two helmets turned back towards it and decorated with three feathers, the middle one blue and the side ones red"[171]. Wołowski is likely to have settled the question of his own ennoblement on the occasion of the case of the Warsaw brewers. Be that as it may, from then on both he and his descendants could enjoy nobility.

The ennoblement and the fortune opened wide the gates to a political career, and Wołowski took advantage of it eagerly. In 1825, he became a deputy in the Warsaw constituency at the Sejm[172]. As Małgorzata Karpińska puts it, he was one of the MPs "clearly active at the time, and even attempting to mount an opposition"[173]. He was not the most famous oppositionist, and was probably far from the Niemojowski brothers, pillars of the liberal opposition, but he had made a name for himself, as evidenced by Janowski's words quoted above. His political talent, however, was not to be fully revealed until the November Uprising.

---

169 B. Tańska-Hus *Dzierżawa rolnicza w Polsce na przestrzeni* wieków, Wrocław 2009, p. 16.

170 Z. L. Sulima (W. Przyborowski) *Historia Franka i frankistów,* Sandomierz 2014 (reprint of the 1893 Kraków edition), p. 267. Przyborowski states that they received the "Bawół II" coat of arms. However, this coat of arms did not appear until 1838, and was granted to Jan Ignacy and Teodor Wołowski.

171 *Dziennik Praw Królestwa Polskiego,* vol. IX, no. 37, Warszawa 1824, pp. 57–59.

172 M. Karpińska *Senatorowie, posłowie i deputowani Księstwa Warszawskiego i Królestwa Polskiego,* Warszawa 2002, p. 95.

173 M. Karpińska *"Nie ma Mikołaja!" Starania o kształt sejmu w powstaniu listopadowym 1830-1831,* Warszawa 2007, p. 76.

Before that, Wołowski embarked on a Grand Tour. Initially, it had an explicitly therapeutic purpose. According to an 1844 text, the lawyer had already "fallen ill with a stone"[174]. In the 19th century, this ailment posed a potentially fatal threat; faced with the helplessness of domestic doctors, he decided to seek advice in Paris – incidentally, visiting his son. The French doctors, in turn, referred him further to Italy. "Still suffering, I heeded the advice of the doctors in Paris, and went to Italy to seek health in the company of my wife and seven-year-old son Feliks."

This quotation comes from Franciszek's only literary work – the memoirs of the *Journey to Switzerland and Italy begun in 1825*, published posthumously in Paris in 1845[175]. It was a travel book typical of the 19th century, a kind of guide to the Apennine Peninsula. In it, Wołowski presented a long series of descriptions of beautiful landscapes, successive architectural monuments, and masterpieces of art.

> Among the many villas that dot the shores of the lake, the Villa Pliniana is undoubtedly the most outstanding and most impressive. All the charms of nature entice there, even though the place is surrounded by villas, villages, lowlands, groves, meadows, rocks, waterfalls that are feast to the ear and eye so much that the thought is transported to distant times. Here, thousands of years ago, Pliny attended, and described a phenomenon of nature, as yet unexplained. One looks at the spring, which bubbles more every day at certain hours and fills up completely and disappears at others. We descended to the mouth of the spring, where it flows into the lake and forms a delicious cascade, two hundred feet high, from which it falls onto the rocky walls. In the grotto where the spring is, a letter engraved on the rock by Pliny explains that this place was the subject of his studies. Centuries pass, the mighty who ruled this land have disappeared, how many generations have not changed? The world has been transformed and the source grows and fades away every day. How, no one has figured out yet.

Here is a typical excerpt from the *Journey...* containing a description of the monuments and nature with accompanying historical and cultural facts – in this case the Villa Pliniana on Lake Como and the source described by Pliny the

174 *Życie ś.p. Franciszka Wołowskiego...*, p. 6.

175 Some of the text of the *Journey...*must have been written during the journey in 1825–1826 or later, on the basis of precise notes. This is evidenced, for example, by the detailed descriptions of certain monuments or cultural works. At the same time, however, in other parts Wołowski referred to texts published much later (e.g., on p. 314 to *Spirit from the Steppe* published by Józef Bohdan Zaleski as late as 1841). Fragments of the book must therefore have been written later. Interestingly, in the passage quoted above, Wołowski was clearly mistaken about the age of his youngest son: at the time of his departure, Feliks was nine years old, not seven.

Younger[176]. Wołowski's itinerary took him through Milan, Genoa, Siena, Pisa via Rome to Naples and back north to Rome, Perugia, Florence, and Bologna. Along the way, he admired works by Giotto, Raphael, Caravaggio, Michelangelo, Titian, Dürer, Giorgione, Leonardo, Thorvaldsen and Canova. The names of the authors he mentioned, testify to his classical, Enlightenment education and his Romantic readings. Ancient authors appear in various contexts on the pages of the *Journey...*, together with Grotius, Machiavelli, Montaigne, Vico, Montesquieu, Voltaire, Rousseau. There are also Poles: Niemcewicz, Zaleski and Mickiewicz. Characteristically, the *Journey...* contains practically no descriptions of meetings with Italians, as if the inhabitants of the lands cared the least about the author. This may come as a surprise in the case of a politician and later émigré, but there are no political references or comments on the situation in Italy after 1815. The only exceptions were the laudatory passages dedicated to Napoleon[177] and (marginally) to the French Revolution[178]. And lamentations over the fate of the Congress Kingdom – written, however, probably after Wołowski left Italy, between 1826 and 1830[179].

It is not known exactly when the Wołowskis returned from Italy; most likely it was the spring of 1826. Unfortunately, the place where they ended up in remains also unknown. The author of the Polish biography of 1836 clearly suggests France, from which they did not leave for Warsaw until 1830. A short passage from the *Journey...*, in which Wołowski wrote that "For the death of Emperor Alexander, it was necessary to shorten the stay in Italy to return to the country"[180] clearly indicates that he intended to reach the Vistula. But he may have changed his mind. The trouble is that Franciszek Wołowski then disappeared from the radar of history, only to resurface in 1830. Possibly, he was indeed in Paris, although it seems more likely that he simply returned to his estate in Kaski.

---

176 F. Wołowski *Podróż do Szwajcaryi i Włoch rozpoczęta w 1825 roku,* Paris 1845, p. 67.

177 For example, seeing the battlefields of Marengo, Wołowski recalled a time when "French arms spread liberties; at the slogan of freedom, peoples awoke from lethargy." (F. Wołowski *Podróż do Szwajcaryi...*, p. 70). Further on, he wrote of Bonaparte, "a ruler who distributed crowns, whose temples were crowned with immortal laurel [...] and whose victories and immense deeds may be placed by distant posterity in a row of fabulous novels." (F. Wołowski *Podróż do Szwajcaryi...*, p. 107).

178 When "the rotten, arbitrary abuses of the ruler's power were overthrown, France gained institutions based on laws in accordance with the will of the people". (F. Wołowski *Podróż do Szwajcaryi...*, p. 31).

179 Indeed, Wołowski wrote explicitly about the autocrats ruling Poland, "who think of the constitutional institutions as a burden" (F. Wołowski *Podróż do Szwajcaryi...*, p. 5).

180 F. Wołowski *Podróż do Szwajcaryi...*, p. 318.

In 1830, the Sejm reconvened, and Franciszek Wołowski again became a deputy from Warsaw. He quickly became one of the most important figures in the new Sejm, and one of the pillars of the Opposition. As late as in June 1830, when the government brought to the Sejm's deliberations its famous proposal to amend the divorce law, reducing the importance of the ordinary courts and strengthening the role of the Church[181], Wołowski took the floor, extremely suggestively at that: "he demonstrated the whole absurdity of the new law, he detected the false principles which want to set us back several centuries and, if they were adopted, would create the greatest mischief in life, in a word, incurable disasters. He concluded by saying that the present law should remain in force, while waiting for the next parliamentary session, during which a draft would be presented. His speech was so effective that a dozen or so MPs who had signed up to speak against the law declared that they were withdrawing their comments, as they had nothing more to say," recalled Tymoteusz Lipiński[182]. Wołowski, together with Joachim Lelewel, were ultimately instrumental in the rejection of the entire project[183].

In the summer of 1830, after the closing of the Sejm, Wołowski probably did not suppose that he would soon have to play a much more important parliamentary role. He probably did not participate in the conspiratorial activities preceding the November Uprising. He may have heard about them from his son, who had links with the conspirators – but it is not known what he thought of them.

In any case, on 18 December he appeared at the proceedings of the new, now insurgent Sejm. Since the very beginning, he was one of the most active MPs. He made himself known first and foremost as a staunch supporter of a limited constitutional monarchy. For, he said: "[...] a monarchy can be either constitutional or despotic. In the present law we declare ourselves in favour of a constitutional one. The throne can be either elective or successive. I expect that we, who owe our fall to royal elections, will declare ourselves in favour of the succession"[184]. Associated rather with the opposition [185], he stressed the

181 See A. Fastyn *Problem powstania i charakteru prawa małżeńskiego z 1836 roku,* [in:] "Czasopismo prawno-historyczne", vol. XLIV, 2012, part 2, p. 195.

182 T. Lipiński *Zapiski z lat 1825–1831,* Kraków 1883, p. 192.

183 M. Mochnacki *Powstanie narodu polskiego w roku 1830 i 1831...*, p. 299; similar account by Władysław Wężyk in *Kronika rodzinna,* Warszawa 1987, p. 237.

184 *Dyaryusz ...*, vol. I *Od 18 grudnia 1830 do 08 lutego 1831,* Kraków 1907, p. 490.

185 Karpińska emphasises that "People like Zwierkowski, Szaniecki, Wołowski and Tymowski were above all individuals, and undoubtedly played an outstanding role in the parliamentary arena, but they did not even form the nucleus of a unified party. It was only towards the end of the uprising that they met more systematically in the so-called Chłędowska Club." (M. Karpińska *„Nie ma Mikołaja! "...*, p. 128).

importance of the division and balance of powers [186], defended the principles of parliamentarianism [187], freedom of speech [188], the rule of law. Moreover, Wołowski also applied the principles of the constitutional rule of law in specific cases considered by the Sejm, for example during the discussion concerning the punishment that the House wanted to impose on Gen. Skrzynecki. He said: "The forms [i.e., laws – RD] are the guarantors of free, representative government; only despotism hates them, because they are opposed to it."[189]

In the context of the 1830–1831 insurrectionary Sejm, it is worth noting two more important discussions in which the Warsaw barrister took part. On 11 April 1831, he spoke before the combined Chambers on abolition of serfdom. His statement, moreover, seems quite characteristic of the 1831 Sejm. The owner of the Kaski estate was in favour of abolition of serfdom. On the other hand, he made it very clear that it could not be done in violation of the acquired rights, above all the right to property. During his speech, he also referred several times to the need to look after the interests of the treasury, if only through the administrative collection

---

186 On 22 January, as rapporteur of a constitutional motion granting the legislative initiative to the Chamber of Deputies and the Senate, Wołowski said: "It is already established by the principles of political law and by experience that there is no real freedom there, nor the necessary resilience to maintain national liberties in their entirety, where the legislative power is in one and the executive power in many hands. On the contrary, the law-making power should be distributed among the three political bodies, which, by maintaining a balance among themselves, should not allow any part to fall from its proper place: hence, in England and France, the two Houses and the veto, which serve the Government so that the legislature cannot make laws that would paralyse the executive in its actions." (*Dyaryusz ...*, vol. I, p. 116). At the same time, he acknowledged that, under insurrectionary conditions, the said veto should be suspended. A few days later, supplementing this statement, Wołowski mentioned four key authorities: legislative, ruling, or royal, executive, and judicial (*Dyaryusz ...*, vol. I, p. 277).

187 For instance, by demanding the presence of ministers at Sejm sessions (*Dyaryusz ...*, vol. I, p. 256), or protesting on 04 February 1831 against the possibility for the Sejm to be convened by the Marshal himself, bypassing both Chambers (Dyaryusz..., vol. II, p. 19). At the same time, he stressed that the next elections to the Sejm could be held only after the country had been completely liberated (Dyaryusz..., vol. III, *Od 19 kwietnia do 25 maja 1831*, Kraków 1909, pp. 363–366).

188 Dyaryusz..., vol. III, p. 109; *Dyaryusz...*, vol. V *Od 20 czerwca do 21 lipca 1831,* Kraków 1911, p. 464.

189 *Dyaryusz...*, vol. VI *Od 22 lipca do 23 września 1831*, Kraków 1912, p. 533. In the same speech, he noted that the Sejm wanted to impose on Skrzynecki – whom he did not hold in high esteem – a penalty not provided for by law. He considered this an unacceptable transgression of the rule of law (*Dyaryusz...*, vol. VI, pp. 531–532)

of abolition fees[190]. Above all, however, he was firmly opposed to granting any servitudes to the free peasants and to abolishing the right of propination laws. For "[...] one should wish that this law be abolished throughout the country. But now is not the time for that. We cannot diminish the treasury income in this way"[191]. In general, Wołowski's statements give the impression that, while supporting the idea of enfranchising the peasants in general, in practice he did everything to delay and limit it. For, as he emphasised in May 1831: "This is not the time to make trials, nor to use people, in part rightly discouraged, to defend the dearest liberties of the fatherland"[192].

Wołowski applied the same argument to the Jews, while discussing the reform of their status. Here, too, he emphasised that this was a necessary reform, but only after the victorious end of hostilities. In the end, he voted in favour of a law under which "Art. 2. The Jewish people in the Congress Kingdom were to be freed from personal military service by 1831. Art. 3. In place of personal military service, the said people were to pay a levy in 1831 to equal four times the recruitment tax"[193]. It seems that this altogether reluctant attitude of Wołowski towards the Jews cannot be considered in isolation from his background. Indeed, among the converts, memories, and stories of the former persecution of the Frankists by the rabbis were probably still vivid. Franciszek Wołowski fell into the category aptly described in the 20th century by Jean-Paul Sartre as "Jews through the gaze of others". Wołowski never mentioned his Jewish roots in public. Apart from his marriage, he no longer had anything to do with the doctrine of Frank. According to Ludwik Hass, since 1812 he belonged to the Masonic lodge "Temple of Isis", reaching the 3rd degree of the ritual in 1814 [194]. This information seems all the more likely as it corresponds to Wołowski's education and worldview. Franciszek Wołowski was a representative of the Enlightenment generation of Poles. He was a moderate Catholic: an undoubted believer in opposition to the Church's stronger role in the state. His religiosity was also discreet: in the *Journey...*, religious themes do not appear at all, although there was inevitably no shortage of opportunities for such reflections in Italy.

At the same time, the Polish milieu remembered his Jewish roots very well, and sometimes reminded him of them. Years later Władysław Wężyk recalled the senatorial elections of April 1831: "A number of MPs (however weary they all were of the several months' tribulations of the revolutionary state) applied for the senatorial chair. Among them was the particularly able and patriotic and (as a former

190 *Dyaryusz...*, vol. II, pp. 517–519.

191 *Dyaryusz...*, vol. II, p. 539.

192 *Dyaryusz...*, vol. IV, p. 17.

193 *Dyaryusz...*, vol. IV, pp. 71–72.

194 L. Hass Supplement to: S. Małachowski-Łempicki *Wykaz polskich lóż wolnomularskich oraz ich członków w latach 1738–1821*, Wielkpolska Bibliotek Cyfrowa, p. 155.

lawyer) very knowledgeable Franciszek Wołowski. But his eager applications did not have the desired effect, because as a neophyte ('ours' according to the nickname given to them) he was hesitant to present himself for this aristocratic function"[195]. These repeated anti-Semitic accusations against Wołowski may also have influenced his attitude towards Jews[196].

Recalling the parliamentary activities of Franciszek Wołowski, it is imperative to mention perhaps the most significant act to which he largely contributed, namely the dethronement of the Tsar. The Warsaw barrister was undoubtedly one of its initiators. On 24 January 1831, Wołowski appeared in the Sejm as rapporteur of a committee to normalise the relations between the commander-in-chief and the government. On this occasion, mentioning "the Russian self-rule, a descendant of the hateful memory of Catherine II [...] the perjurer king", he uttered the memorable sentence that "this dangerous Lord has already lost the right to rule over the Piast and Jagiellonian dominions"[197]. As Sebastian Ziółek points out, Wołowski has vociferously expressed many MPs thoughts[198]. On 25 January, he persuaded the Sejm to immediately strip Nicholas of his rights to the throne[199]. Along with 186 other representatives of the nation, on the same day he also signed the very act of dethronement.

The cited events of 24 and 25 January 1831 clearly testify to the political talent, persuasive power, and influence of the Schor descendant. He had an undoubted gift for eloquence. Karpińska cites the text of the "Polak Sumienny" of 10 June 1831: the paper, however reluctant towards Wołowski, admitted that, on the issue of reforming the government, "Wołowski's voice was the most decent and eloquent

195 W. Wężyk *Kronika rodzinna*, p. 299.

196 Wołowski was not the only target of the anti-Semitic campaign. Another representative of a well-known Frankist family, Dominik Krysiński, also sat in the Sejm. As Jan Nepomucen Janowski recalled, Krysiński was a great opponent and critic of Chłopicki's dictatorship, unlike Julian Ursyn Niemcewicz, the general's supporter. The men clashed with each other: "Niemcewicz, speaking of Krysiński, exclaimed: 'He's a Jew!' and pointed at him. Krysiński heard this and, repaying Niemcewicz in kind, snatched the stool with all speed and shouted: 'And you are an old sponge of the aristocracy!' and would probably have smashed his head or severely wounded him had he not been held back by Brodziński and, together with Brodziński, the stronger Bentkowski" (J.N. Janowski Notatki..., p. 189).

197 *Dyaryusz...*, vol. I, p. 165.

198 S. Ziółek *Sejm Królestwa Polskiego w okresie powstania listopadowego 1830–1831*, Warszawa 2007, p. 114.

199 After Wołowski's speech, Jan Ledóchowski raised the famous cry of "There's no Nicholas!", subsequently seized upon by part of the hall (S. Ziółek *Sejm Królestwa Polskiego...*, p. 243).

of the opposition"[200]. Added to this was his legal competence. According to Ziółek. he was "the best expert on legal issues in the entire Sejm"[201]. Similarly, Władysław Zajewski highlights his outstanding individuality in the 1830–1831 Chamber[202]. And indeed, the record of the 1831 Sejm debates seems to attest to these opinions. A case in point is this short passage from 31 May 1831: "Mr Wołowski drew the attention of the House to the fact that in the Senate, a similar allowance [proposed by the Speaker, according to which parliamentary committees were to be chaired by their members who had received the most votes at the time of their election to the committee – RD] could in no way be in force, because with this procedure the President could become the Castellan, where the Governor should be. After this explanation, the Marshal withdrew the addition"[203]. Wołowski spoke in the Sejm frequently and on almost every topic, regularly making use of elaborate legal arguments – which must have had an impact on his listeners and, on the other hand, made polemics more difficult for his possible opponents. Importantly, compared to other Sejm speakers, his speeches were relatively concise and precise, and he was irritated by the Sejm's verbosity. All this combined made Wołowski's voice one of the most important in the Sejm. Apart from the dethronement of Nicholas, there were many votes in which he significantly influenced the outcome. He played a key role, for example, in the discussion on the right of the Senate to nominate candidates for provincial governors[204], on the members of the National Government [205] and the prosecution of Mateusz Lubowidzki, former Deputy Mayor of Warsaw[206]. In June 1831, he spoke out clearly against reforming the government,

200 "Polak Sumienny" no. 166, 10.06.1831, p. 1. The newspaper devoted a separate article to Wołowski in issue no. 239 of 26 August 1831: "This honourable representative, both when the Romanov dynasty reigned in Poland and when the National Government was in power, gave undeniable evidence of an unbending soul, of pure patriotism, of an unwavering attachment to freedom and national liberties." And further on, "We can say that the greater part of the drafts for laws brought to the Sejm's deliberations are of Wołowski's editorship."; M. Karpińska *"Nie ma Mikołaja!"* ..., p. 120.

201 S. Ziółek *Sejm Królestwa Polskiego...*, p. 192.

202 W. Zajewski *Rola Sejmu w powstaniu listopadowym*, [in:] W. Zajewski (dir.) *Powstanie listopadowe 1830–1831. Dzieje wewnętrzne. Militaria. Europa wobec powstania*, Warszawa 1980, p. 114.

203 *Dyaryusz...*, t. IV, p. 103.

204 *Dyaryusz...*, t. III, p. 458.

205 Karpińska even writes that it was likely Wołowski who pushed through the candidacies of Wincenty Nemojowski and Teofil Morawski („*Nie ma Mikołaja!*"..., pp. 221–222).

206 Wołowski clearly demonstrated the lack of a legal basis for the charge, which the Chamber ultimately rejected (Z. Gołba *Rozwój władz Królestwa Polskiego w okresie powstania listopadowego*, Wrocław, Warszawa, Kraków, Gdańsk 1971, p. 157).

probably attracting many votes[207], and in August his vote was decisive in the adoption of new regulations defining the dependence of the commander-in-chief on the government[208]. The importance of Wołowski in the Sejm is perhaps best demonstrated by a scene in July 1831, when the House was debating a transfer to another place. The discussion was closed, the MPs, however, agreed to additionally listen to Wołowski alone. The Warsaw deputy uttered words that were soon to prove prophetic: "Should we – which we cannot expect or fear – have to choose between death in this place and a life dedicated to the sole purpose of rescuing our failing homeland, the country does not require us to die, but to leave our estates, wives, children, and at least to move the fiefdom of national representation to another part of the world and, wandering from country to country, everywhere to protest against the unlawful tearing apart of the hapless Poland and to demand the restoration of her independence"[209].

This is what actually happened. The Uprising collapsed, and Franciszek Wołowski went into exile with thousands of his compatriots. He had no choice: regardless of the interests of his homeland, with the threat of the repression, if only because of his role in the dethronement process, he had to leave the country. The destination must have been obvious from the start: Paris, for that is where his first-born son was. Franciszek left with Tekla Wołowska and their middle son, Kazimierz, a soldier in the Uprising[210].

Interestingly, the youngest Wołowski – Feliks – remained in Poland. Despite his young age, he too was an insurgent and a non-commissioned officer in the 4th uhlan regiment. After the battle of Siedlce, on 25 May 1831, he was awarded the silver *Virtuti Militari* Cross[211]. He was the only one who later used the title of count and the "Na Kaskach" coat of arms; he was also the owner of an estate in

---

207 M. Karpińska *„Nie ma Mikołaja!"...*, p. 219, 281–289.

208 *Dyaryusz...*, t. VI, pp. 402–410; W Zajewski *Walki wewnętrzne ugrupowań politycznych w powstaniu listopadowym 1830–1831,* Gdańsk 1967, p. 159.

209 W Zajewski *Walki wewnętrzne...*, pp. 18–19.

210 Michał Sokolnicki states that the Wołowskis arrived in Paris between 24 and 29 October 1831 (M. Sokolnicki *Les origines de l'émigration polonaise en France 1831–1831,* Paris 1910, p. 75).

211 B. Polak (ed.) *Virtuti Militari 1815–1831. Wybór źródeł,* vol. II, Koszalin 2001, p. 160; *Xięga pamiątkowa w 50-letnią rocznicę powstania roku 1830 zawierająca spis imienny dowódców i sztabs-oficerów tudzież oficerów, podoficerów i żołnierzy Armii Polskiej w tymże roku krzyżem wojskowy „Virtuti Militari" ozdobionych,* Lwów 1881, p. 116. According to the obituary contained in "Rocznik Towarzystwa Historyczno-Literackiego w Paryżu" (1873–1878, vol. II, Poznań 1879, p. 425) Kazimierz Wołowski was also "presented with the Virtuti Militari cross several times for his bravery". He did not receive it only because of "too limited a number of crosses intended for the regiment".

Osuchów (near Żyrardów) consisting of three farms (Osuchów, Wygnanka and Dęby)[212]. Here, in the mid-19th century he built a beautiful neo-classical palace and a neo-Gothic church. He was one of the most active members of the Agricultural Society[213]. He died in 1893[214]. Feliks obviously kept in touch with his family in exile, including his eldest brother. They met during stays at spa towns, and he certainly visited France. This is confirmed by the death certificate of his eldest Louis from Gisors in Normandy in 1876[215]. Feliks, perhaps summoned to France on hearing of Louis' deteriorating health, was by his side at the time of his death.

Indeed, the tsarist authorities did not forgive Franciszek Wołowski: his property was confiscated, while he was accused of involvement in the dethronement[216]. Finally, in 1834, he was sentenced in absentia "to the death penalty, by hanging on the gallows"[217].

Fortunately, the owner of Kaski had long been outside the Russian jurisdiction. The confiscation significantly affected his property status but did not prevent him from living a relatively prosperous life abroad with his family. In all probability, he managed to export at least part of his wealth in securities or cash. He may have enlisted the help of the Prussian bank he had previously represented, perhaps his family helped, as usual. The latter is supported by the fact that the confiscated Kaski estate was later bought out by Jan Kanty Wołowski, Franciszek's brother-in-law[218]. Given the mode of operation of the Wołowski clan, it seems unlikely that this move was not agreed. Franciszek could always also count on the financial

212 *Osuchów,* [in:] F. Sulimierski, B. Chlebowski, W. Walewski (eds.) *Słownik geograficzny Królestwa Polskiego...*, vol. VII, Warszawa 1886, p. 741.

213 This is evidenced by the minutes of the Society's meetings printed in "Roczniki Gospodarstwa Krajowego" (vol. XLIII, part 1, Warszawa 1861).

214 Death certificate: http://www.sejm-wielki.pl/img/metrskan/z/3563362.jpg (retrieved 23.07.2023); the date of death is also given on the gravestone of Feliks Wołowski in Osuchów.

215 The registrar in Gisors noted that Louis Paulin Passy, son-in-law of the deceased, and Feliks Wołowski "fifty-nine years old, landowner, brother of the deceased" appeared before him. (Death certificate: Gisors municipality, civil status records, 1876, no. 76, Wolowski Louis Michel Raymond).

216 Tsarist Manifesto of 20 October / 01 November 1831.

217 Bill of indictment: E.A. Poklękowski *Akt oskarżenia w sprawie przeciwko osobom oddanym pod Najwyższy Sąd Kryminalny w Królestwie Polskiem w zarzucie spełnienia zbrodni, wyłączonych od ogólnego przebaczenia,* Warszawa 1834, p. 138; tsar's decree confirming the death sentence: "Tygodnik Petersburski. Gazeta urzędowa Królestwa Polskiego", 1834, no. 84 & 89.

218 W. Witkowski *Aleksander This i Jan Kanty Wołowski...*, p. 51. In 1842 Jan Kanty sold Kaski to Aleksander Count Potocki.

assistance of Louis and his sister Aleksandryna. As we shall see later, he also probably managed to transfer a part of his Polish estate to his wife.

His moderate monarchist views corresponded to the political line of the Hotel Lambert: since the very beginning, Wołowski was one of the pillars of the party of prince Czartoryski[219], who finally settled in Paris in 1833. Prior to the constitution of the Conservative camp in exile, Wołowski had briefly been a member of the Provisional Committee of Polish Emigration[220]. On the other hand, he did not join its successor, Lelewel's Polish National Committee, established on 5 December 1831, and even signed a proclamation expressly opposing it. According to Lubomir Gadon, by that time Wołowski belonged to the core of the "moderate" (conservative) wing of the emigration, that was in the process of being formed[221].

In 1832, however, his name appeared among the founders of the National Committee of Polish Emigration (the so-called "Dwernicki Committee"). The organisation lasted not much longer than the previous one, as the Committee dissolved itself in early 1833. Wołowski did, however, manage to mark his presence there as a lawyer. As Aleksander Jełowicki, who also sat on it later, recalled: "One of the useful activities of this committee was a resolution on jury courts for migrants, composed by Franciszek Wołowski, one of the most eminent lawyers"[222]. Jełowicki went on to point out that, unfortunately, the resolution was never adopted. Another thing is that Franciszek Wołowski was partly responsible for the disintegration of the Dwernicki Committee: "21 January. Due to Hube's departure from Paris following the Minister's order, and to evade the obligation of Ledóchowski, Morawski, Wołowski and Plichta to sit on the Committee – the Committee dissolved," wrote another emigrant, Wojciech Darasz[223]. However, when Prince Adam Jerzy finally arrived in the French capital, Wołowski quickly and naturally found himself in his circle.

Perhaps the most important work, which – together with his older son – Wołowski co-created since the beginning, was not strictly political in nature, even though the same conservative émigré group was responsible for it. On April 29,

---

219 In a letter to Czartoryski on 24 December 1831, Gen. Karol Kniaziewicz described the conflicts emerging in the emigrant community at that time. He added: "Pac, Wołowskis, Zabiełło are on our side." (quote as in M. Sokolnicki *Les origines...*, p. 226).

220 Provisional Committee of Polish Emigration – formed on 06 November 1831, the first ephemeral organisation of Polish emigrants in France. It was headed by Bonawentura Niemojowski. The Committee dissolved after a month of functioning.

221 L. Gadon *Wielka Emigracja w pierwszych latach po powstaniu listopadowym*, Paris 1960, pp. 120–135.

222 A. Jełowicki *Moje wspomnienia*, Poznań 1877, p. 345. The aforementioned project by Wołowski can be found in the Biblioteka Polska w Paryżu (Biblioteka Polska w Paryżu, "Inventory of Members' Works 1832–1842", ref. BPP 1400).

223 W. Darasz *Pamiętnik Emigranta*, Wrocław 1953, p. 72.

1832, the Polish Literary Society was founded in Paris[224]. According to the statute published in the same year, the Society was to collect and publish texts related to the history of Poland, its present state and future[225]. According to the index of works by members of the Society from 1832 to 1842, the author of the *Journey to Switzerland and Italy...* produced a total of 32 texts during this period[226]. Half of them dealt with Poland's recent history, ten were of a purely legal nature and the rest were journalistic. In the historical texts, the former Polish deputy proved the right of Poles to the revolt in 1830 and 1831. In turn, their addressees were primarily French parliamentarians[227]. Thus, with his texts, Wołowski was part of the Hotel Lambert policy of strengthening pro-Polish sentiment among the French and the Polish faction in parliament, with the aim of ultimately influencing the foreign policy of King Louis-Philippe. His activity in this regard was not limited to the writing. When, at the turn of 1833 and 1834, Czartoryski was preparing for another address debate in the French Parliament[228], he visited all the members of

---

224 Founding Protocol of the Society – Biblioteka Polska w Paryżu, ref. BPP 1362. in addition to Franciszek and Louis Wolowski, it was signed by Józef Bem, Albert Grzymała, Alphonse d'Herbelot (French journalist from "Courrier Français"), Ludwik Jelski, Stanisław Kunatt, Teodor Morawski, Ludwik Plater, Andrzej Plichta, Jan Nepomucen Umiński and Alexandre Walewski. The assembled also recognised Prince Adam and Niemcewicz, who were in London, as co-founders of the Society. In 1854, already without Wołowski, the TLP changed its name to the Historical and Literary Society in Paris.

225 In 1834, he insisted that members of the Society fulfil their obligation to write and publish texts (Biblioteka Polska w Paryżu, ref. BPP 1360/37). Wołowski even stood as a candidate for vice-president at the second meeting of the Society. He was not elected (he received 2 votes out of 13), just as he was not elected editor-in-chief (he received 1 vote). In the latter case, the situation was all the more surprising as Louis Wolowski was also among those voting. This means that either Franciszek did not vote for himself, or his son did not do so. (Biblioteka Polska w Paryżu, ref. BPP 1371).

226 Biblioteka Polska w Paryżu, ref. BPP 1400.

227 See: F. Wołowski *L'Empereur Nicolas et la constitution polonaise de 1815,* Paris 1832 (As an example of the violation of constitutional principles by the authorities, Wołowski cited, among others, the arrest of Warsaw brewers); F. Wołowski, polemics with "Journal des Débats" of 1833 (Biblioteka Polska w Paryżu, ref. BPP 1402, p. 843; F. Wołowski *Dzień 25 stycznia 1831,* Biblioteka Polska w Paryżu, ref. BPP 1402, p. 849).

228 Once a year during the July Monarchy, the French Parliament issued an address to the King with the most important issues of domestic and foreign policy.

the address committee. He was assisted in this by, among others, Wołowski father and son[229].

As part of the Literary Society, Wołowski joined the Statistical Department, established in 1838. According to Lubomir Gadon, he was one of the most active members[230].

Franciszek also took an active part in the discussions and internal disputes of the emigration in the 1830s. His polemical fervour is reflected especially in the "Kronika Emigracji Polskiej" ["Chronicle of Polish Emigration"], to which he wrote regularly. He covered Poland in the future – republican or monarchical, depending on the nation's decision[231] where there was to be "the abolition of privileges, equality of all states, equality of rights"[232]. He was also against Polish participation in the conquest of Algeria[233] and supported the resumption of the Sejm in exile[234].

Wołowski also held passionate discussions in "Kronika". Particularly interesting was his polemic with Antoni Ostrowski, the author of the work *Pomysły o potrzebie reform towarzyskiéy w ogólności a mianowiciey co do Izraelitów w Polsce; przez założyciela miasta Tomaszowa Mazowieckiego* [Ideas on the need for social reform in general and namely as regards the Israelites in Poland; by the founder of the town of Tomaszów Mazowiecki] (Paris 1834). Ostrowski, while remaining at times highly critical of the Jews, nevertheless demanded that full citizenship rights be granted to those who would demonstrate moral and civilisational readiness. On the other hand, he blamed years of persecution, injustice, and lack of access to education for Jewish "sins". Wołowski received the book badly. In an extensive text published in "Kronika", he reproached Ostrowski for his failure to act on behalf of

229 H. H. Hahn *Dyplomacja bez listów uwierzytelniających. Polityka zagraniczna Adama Jerzego Czartoryskiego 1830–1840*, Warszawa 1987, p. 230. Władysław Zamoyski later recalled that the most effective in these endeavours was "Franciszek Wołowski, a former patron and state counsellor, a learned jurist, in demand among French lawyers, and perfectly fluent in French." (*Jenerał Zamoyski 1803–1868*, vol. III, *1832–1837*, Poznań 1914, p. 205). According to "Kronika Emigracji Polskiej", in the following years Wołowski also took part in the political endeavours around the address ("Kronika Emigracji Polskiej", vol. V, Paris 1837, p. 379)

230 The Statistical Division was to deal not only with statistics, but also with Polish geography, economic, administrative, and legal issues. The Division ceased to function in practice after Plater, President of the Division, left Paris and Franciszek Wołowski suspended his activities for health reasons (L. Gadon *Z życia Polaków we Francyi. Rzut oka na 50-letnie koleje Towarzystwa Historyczno-Literackiego w Paryżu, 1832–1882,* Paris 1883, p. 19).

231 "Kronika Emigracji Polskiej", vol. I, p. 185.

232 "Kronika Emigracji Polskiej", vol. I, p. 183.

233 "Kronika Emigracji Polskiej", vol. I, p. 179.

234 "Pielgrzym Polski: pismo polityce i literaturze narodowej poświęcone", 31.01.1833.

the Jews in 1831[235]. In this context, characteristic words were uttered, a diagnosis of the disease afflicting the entire emigration: "Emigration is a new kind of purgatory, in which everyone washes away past sins, not repenting but laying them on others."[236]. However, his words on the political weight of Judaism seem most interesting.

> The Jewish faith, as everyone knows, differs from the newer faiths in that it is a political knot. (...) In this phenomenon lies the reason why a nation concerned about its own well-being cannot unconditionally admit the Jews to political rights, if, like in Poland, they represent a nation within a nation, a state within a state, as long as they are guests and not inhabitants in it. Let the Polish Jews, as is the case in France, confine themselves to the pure-religious part of their faith, let them not resist complete mixing with the Polish nation, and that nation will surely accept them as its brothers, just as it accepted the Tartars and people of other faiths.[237]

Thus, Wołowski clearly regarded acculturation as the first condition for granting political rights. The second, he said, was to prepare the Polish public opinion for this step. On the other hand, he accused the Jews of favouring the stronger party, Russia, during the Uprising. It was also in this context that an interesting sentence was uttered: "No doubt, our ancestors did not give them great tokens of love; but less, apparently, than we deserved their allegiance did the Tsars, who threw them completely out of the bosom of their state"[238]. I am not concerned with historical facts, but with the words "our ancestors": they seem surprising when written by a descendant of the Schors. They may be indicative of the total assimilation of Wołowski and the recognition of the entire political and cultural Polish tradition as one's own. After all, they can also be part of an escape from one's own origins and a constant threat of anti-Semitism associated with it. The point, however, is that in the émigré environment of the 1830s and 1840s, this escape could not have succeeded. The Poles in Paris remembered very well the Frankist roots of the Wołowski family[239].

---

235 "Kronika Emigracji Polskiej", vol. II, Paris 1834, pp. 233 & 283.

236 "Kronika Emigracji Polskiej", vol. II, p. 234.

237 "Kronika Emigracji Polskiej", vol. II, pp. 285–286. On this occasion, Wołowski showed his complete ignorance when it comes to the United States. For to give an example of a misguided decision to grant political rights to an ethnic minority group, he wrote about the North American state of.... "Transylvania, which granted political rights to the liberated negroes." ("Kronika Emigracji Polskiej", vol. II, p. 286).

238 "Kronika Emigracji Polskiej", vol. II, p. 288.

239 This is evidenced, for example, by a fragment of Chopin's letter to Julian Fontana of 11.10.1841: "As for the sale of furniture, I would be a swindler, a Jew like Dr Wołowski, if I were to sell old junk". (B. E. Sydow (ed.) *Korespondencja Fryderyka Chopina,* vol. II, Warszawa 1955, p. 43). The "Dr Wołowski" mentioned was Stanislaw Wołowski, grandson of brewer Franciszek and Barbara.

Meanwhile, the family was expanding. Louis was the first to marry (I will expand on the wedding later). In 1837, Kazimierz Wołowski married Héloise Henriette Martin, a Frenchwoman[240]. Aleksandryna married Léon Faucher in the same year[241]. These marriages are worth noting. Firstly, the then youngest generation of Frankist descendants was slowly moving away from the custom of marrying within. Secondly, the family was thus reunited with Faucher – a promising young man with a rich journalistic past (between 1831 and 1834 he was editor-in-chief of the influential daily "Le Constitutionnel"). Moreover, he was a disciple and friend of two highly influential politicians of the July Monarchy: Odilon Barrot and Adolphe Thiers[242]. So, Faucher opened the door to great French politics for Wolowski[243].

Another marriage should be mentioned, this time within the broad Wołowski clan. On 22 July 1834, Celina Szymanowska, daughter of the late Maria, married in Paris Adam Mickiewicz. The news of Mickiewicz's marriage came as quite a surprise in Parisian circles. Although the poet had met Celina in 1824 in St. Petersburg, he had last seen her in 1829, when she was 17, and they had not kept in touch since[244]. The marriage was probably suggested to him by Stanisław Morawski, who visited him in the autumn of 1833, perhaps in consultation with Helena Szymanowska. Eustachy Januszkiewicz wrote years later that "it seems that the Wołowski family contributed most to this marriage"[245]. He was probably right. For Celina was staying in Warsaw with her grandparents on her mother's side, Franciszek and Barbara. What is more, after arriving in Paris in late June 1834, she stayed with the Wołowskis. Mickiewicz visited them regularly, spreading gossip among the emigrants. "Franciszek Wołowski, together with Stanislaw Wołowski,

240 Archives de Paris, ref. 5Mil/2094. Héloise's father was Jean Baptiste Martin, a retired Napoleonic officer, Chevalier of the Legion of Honour, "a noble remnant of the Grand Army" according to the inscription on his tomb (own information). Her mother was Anne-Marie Raphaël Bertolino, Jean Baptiste's wife.

241 L. Faucher *Léon Faucher. Biographie et correspondance*, Paris 1888, pp. XX & 69.

242 R. Lavollée *Léon Faucher*, "Le Correspondant", 10.10.1875.

243 For Mickiewicz, in turn, Faucher opened the door to the Collège de France. The poet took up the chair of Slavic literature in 1840, where he taught until 1844. According to Maria Dernałowicz: "The idea of a chair in Slavic literature at the Collège de France was born in the mind of Léon Faucher [...] Faucher was fascinated by Mickiewicz (a fascination that was to turn, in time, into a deep mutual dislike) and put considerable persistence into the realisation of his idea." (M. Dernałowicz *Avant que Mickiewicz n'entre au Collège de France...*, « Actes de la Société Historique et Littéraire Polonaise ", vol. IV, Paris 1998, p. 43).

244 R. Koropeckyj *Adam Mickiewicz...*, pp. 148 & 283–284.

245 E. Januszkiewicz *Notatki wspomnień z życia Adama Mickiewicza,* "Czas", no. 120, 25.05.1859.

Celina's close uncle, went to Mickiewicz to tell him about the delicate situation of the young woman he had brought,"[246] Aleksandryna Wołowska wrote. The intervention of the two elderly Wołowskis bore fruit and a wedding took place on 22 July. The wedding reception was held at the Wołowskis' home. Niemcewicz recalled "a truly Polish dinner" and "honest, hopeful young people". However, he added a characteristic passage: "The bride, née Szymanowska, daughter of a famous pianist, comes from Israel. Mickiewicz is a Lithuanian from the Niemen. This gave reason for someone to whisper to my ear: "This happens very seldom when the Niemen meets the Jordan""[247]. Another thing is that his marriage to Celina, as Jadwiga Maurer writes, further strengthened the already circulating rumours about Mickiewicz's Jewish roots[248].

After the marriage, the Wołowskis remained a strong presence in the life of the young Mickiewicz couple. They helped them to settle down in Paris[249], Tekla Wołowska became godmother to Maria, Celina's first-born daughter[250]. Maria herself described a somewhat later period:

> Every Sunday we usually had dinner at the home of Mr and Mrs Franciszek Wołowski, my mother's respectable relatives for whom my father had a great deal of friendship and respect [...] These Sunday dinners pleased me immensely, and to me, accustomed to my parents' modest table, they seemed a feast. In the evening, my father usually sat down to a game of whist with Mr and Mrs Wołowska and General Gawroński, who also sometimes gathered at our home for a game [...] When we returned home from the Wołowskis', it very often happened that [...] Mr. and Mrs. Faucher took me in for a couple of days, at whose home I spent my beloved, spoiled, happy days[251].

246 M. Dernałowicz *Paryż, Lozanna. Czerwiec 1834 – październik 1840,* Warszawa 1996, "Kronika życia i twórczości Mickiewicza", p. 22

247 J. U. Niemcewicz *Pamiętniki Juliana Ursyna Niemcewicza: dziennik pobytu za granicą od dnia 21 lipca 1831 r. do 20 maja 1841 r.: według autografu w Bibliotece Towarzystwa Historyczno-Literackiego w Paryżu,* vol. 2, Poznań 1877, p. 428. At the same time, Niemcewicz, remembering the origins of Franciszek Wołowski, counted him, along with Ostrowski, Sołtyk and others, among the "great men of our time". (J. U. Niemcewicz *Pamiętniki Juliana Ursyna Niemcewicza...,* vol. 2, p. 67).

248 Jadwiga Maurer„*Z matki obcej...*" *Szkice o powiązaniach Mickiewicza ze światem Żydów,* London 1990, p. 72.

249 E. Januszkiewicz, *Notatki...*

250 In a letter from 1861, Ignacy Domeyko recalled: "Niemcewicz was the godfather, Mrs Wołowska the mother, and I was in the second couple with Miss Wołowska." (I. Domeyko *Listy do Władysława Laskowicza,* Warszawa 1976, p. 269).

251 M. Gorecka *Wspomnienia o Adamie Mickiewiczu,* Kraków 1897, pp. 31–32. "The 'happy days' spent by Maria at the Fauchers" may have been due to the fact that the couple was childless.

Gorecka rightly emphasised her father's attachment to the Wołowskis, above all to Tekla. It is well reflected in Mickiewicz's letter to Tekla Wołowska of August 1841:

> Dear Madam, Mr Franciszek has left weak, please report to me of his health. [...] I greet you, my dear lady, and I ask you to keep in your motherly heart the word that I have told you. Believe me that your love for Poland, your bravery with which you sacrificed your children for the war, your bitter tears, with which you sometimes burst into in private when you saw how your compatriots despised so much love and sacrifice, these tears are already accepted by the Lord, that you will be rewarded beyond measure in the honour you will have with us, in your children and in their fate, and in the new children, that is, me and Celina, whom God has given you in your old age, and who will love you even more than the former ones. (...) Your loving son Adam Mickiewicz[252].

The Wołowskis also took care of Celina and her children during her days of illness in 1838 and 1839[253]. During Mickiewicz's stay in Switzerland, they corresponded. Mickiewicz arranged matters through Franciszek Wołowski after the late second Franciszek, Celina's grandfather[254]. Although these very warm relations cooled noticeably when Mickiewicz became involved with the Towiański group (sect), they were never severed and returned to normal after his departure from the cult. Only by that time, Franciszek Wołowski had already passed away.

Since the early 1840s, his political and social activity was visibly waning[255]. In 1841, in a letter to Czartoryski, he complained of feeling unwell[256]. Finally, on 10 December 1843, he sent a letter to the Literary Society announcing that due to his very poor health, which prevented him from participating in the work of the Society, he had decided to withdraw (interestingly, his two quite healthy sons left the Society with him, justifying this step with professional obligations)[257]. It remains unknown what led to this deterioration in health. We do know, however, that this time Franciszek Wołowski did not recover. He died on 12 February 1844[258].

---

252 *List do Tekli Wołowskiej, 08.08.1841,* [in:] A. Mickiewicz *Listy,* part II, *1830–1841,* (*Dzieła,* vol. XV), Warszawa 2003, pp. 635–636.

253 M. Dernałowicz *Paryż, Lozanna...,* pp. 398 & 440.

254 *List do Franciszka Wołowskiego, 28.03.1840,* [in:] A. Mickiewicz *Listy,* part II, pp. 538–539.

255 Wołowski's health was clearly failing. By 1835, his condition was so serious that Niemcewicz already said goodbye to him: "A pity, an expert lawyer and a good man," he wrote (M. Dernałowicz *Paryż, Lozanna...,* p. 120).

256 Biblioteka Polska w Paryżu, ref. BPP 1391/1.

257 The Society, recognising the merits of Franciszek Wołowski, then awarded him the honorary title of "retired member" ("Trzeci Maj", 18.05.1844).

258 Death certificate: Archives de Paris, ref. 5Mi1 1317.

He was "an exemplary husband, a caring father, an unfaltering friend, a kindly host, sweet and gentle in manner, generous to the poor, humane to his fellow men, he possessed all the qualities to win hearts and combat prejudice. He had one weakness [...], absentmindedness," wrote his biographer[259].

There are many indications that this anonymous biographer may have been the protagonist of this book, Franciszek's son Louis Wolowski. Not only because he knew elements of his father's biography not available to other authors in Paris. Not only because he had the talent to describe his father's life. And not just because he was probably most anxious for Franciszek to be well remembered. For Louis could, in many respects, see himself as the successor, the continuator of Franciszek's work. He could and probably did. He was also much more than that, a figure who played an important role on many levels of Polish and French history.

---

259 *Życie ś.p. Franciszka Wołowskiego...*, p. 22. Obituaries following Wołowski's death were posted by "Trzeci Maj" and "Dziennik Narodowy". Both were, in fact, somewhat... surprising. "Trzeci Maj" ["The Third of May"] "did not feel at liberty to strike down the symptom of the long and honest civic merits of the deceased", but clearly felt at liberty to reproach him for not having lately "paid any attention to the moral and political repair of the nation's mind, which is the task of the present moment, and which is already beginning to manifest itself around us." ("Trzeci Maj", 17.02.1844). "Dziennik", on the other hand, "did not know any more details of the life of the late Mr Wołowski", so it concentrated on criticising the lack of Polish speeches during the funeral ("Dziennik Narodowy", no. 150, 17.02.1844). The monument erected in May of the same year at the Père-Lachaise cemetery still bears the inscription "To the memory of the civic Polish merits of Fraciszek Wołowski, deceased in the thirteenth year of emigration, this stone has been laid by his compatriots and fellow immigrants".

Chapter II: Youth in Poland

1. Childhood

Raymond Michał Ludwik Franciszek (Raymond Michel Louis François) Wołowski (Wolowski) was born on 31 August 1810 in Warsaw, at his parents' home on Podwale Street, at around 5 p.m.[260] Unfortunately, we know next to nothing about his early childhood. Indeed, the young Louis did not appear in the archives until 1822, when he was 12. While Józef Bieliński claimed, and Marian Ptaszyk repeated the claim that Wolowski initially studied at the Warsaw Lyceum, Bieliński failed to provide any sources in his biographical note of Wolowski, while Wolowski himself never mentioned this fact[261]. The archives of the Warsaw Lyceum from the Congress Kingdom were mostly destroyed at the onset of WWII in September 1939. Assuming, therefore, that Wolowski indeed attended the school, it is impossible to ascertain when it was. The school accepted children of all ages. Back then it was located in the Kazimierzowski Palace. Founded in 1804, it had around 400 pupils in six classes[262]. All pupils at the Lyceum were taught religion, Polish, Latin, geography, arithmetic, and algebra, as well as natural history, physics, and chemistry. The younger pupils (grades 1–4) also studied calligraphy and drawing, while the older children (grades 2–6) studied French and German. From the fourth grade onwards, the pupils learnt Greek. The boys' curriculum had 32 hours of lessons a week[263]. In the early 1820s, when Louis could have attended the Lyceum, the teachers included Kazimierz Brodziński (a poet), Mikołaj Chopin (Frédéric's father), Karol Bogumił Diehl (later chairman of the General Consistory of Evangelical Denominations in Congress Poland), Jakub Falkowski (Piarist, founder of the Institute for the Deaf and Blind in Warsaw), Kajetan Garbiński (an insurgent minister), Ignacy Humnicki (a playwright), Aleksander Kokular (a painter), and Marek Antoni Pawłowicz (a mineralogist). The school was headed by Samuel Bogumił Linde, author of the famous Dictionary of the Polish Language[264]. Finally,

---

260 Birth certificate: Warsaw, ASC District I, 1810 No131 https://metryki.genealodzy.pl/index.php?op=pg&ar=1&zs=183&se=&sy=1810a&kt=1&plik=129-131.jpg&x=2830&y=1812&zoom=1 (retrieved 12.01.2023).

261 J. Bieliński *Królewski Uniwersytet Warszawski (1816–1831)*, vol. III, Warszawa 1912, p. 540; M. Ptaszyk *Liceum Warszawskie. 1804–1831*, Toruń 2020, p. 99.

262 L. Królikowski *Szkolnictwo dawnej Warszawy. Rzecz o korelacji pomiędzy rozwojem miasta a szkolnictwem (Od połowy XVII wieku do wybuchu drugiej wojny światowej)*, Warszawa 2008, pp. 219–220.

263 M. Ptaszyk *Liceum Warszawskie...*, p. 67; A. Winiarz *Szkolnictwo Księstwa Warszawskiego i Królestwa Polskiego (1807–1831)*, Lublin 2002, p. 230.

264 M. Ptaszyk *Liceum Warszawskie...*, pp. 121–130.

let me mention the specific atmosphere that prevailed in the early 1820s at the Lyceum and in Warsaw. It is well described by Ptaszyk: "The situation fuelled by the authorities' bans was very tense. In the early 1820, students and pupils began to wear the national costume which outraged Governor Zajączek who banned it. New uniforms were introduced, worn reluctantly by the Lyceum students (the Grand Duke's secret agent reported on 16 September 1821 that more than 20 students of the Lyceum left the school at midday dressed in civilian clothes). In April and May that year, ordinances banning pupils and students from congregating even in private homes, from frequenting public premises, proliferated"[265]. Pupils and students wrote texts and poems mocking the authorities, above all governor Józef Zajączek. Louis Wolowski was probably too young to have participated in these events, but he must have heard about them and witnessed them.

Unfortunately, we know almost nothing about his family home. Only one thing is certain, namely that it was in Warsaw. When his father bought Kaski, Louis was about to leave for Paris. Judging by Louis' later attachment to his parents and his cooperation with his father, we can assume that he had a happy childhood. Education must have played an important role in his family home, as was the case of all the Wołowskis. As I have indicated earlier, the family consistently secured its social position with education. It therefore seems very likely that Louis received his first lessons from private teachers, who probably taught him to read and write. Also, the home that Franciszek and Tekla built remained strongly connected to the entire Wołowski family in Warsaw, and probably to other families of Frankist origin. These ties survived for decades to come. At the same time, they represented the second important pillar of their social strategy. Louis Wolowski was well aware of this.

2. Paris, the first time

The decision, presumably taken by Franciszek, to take his son to France and choose a school in Paris had something of an ideological declaration about it. Firstly, France was a constitutional monarchy. Secondly, the school chosen by the Wołowskis had a specific recent history: before the Revolution, the school buildings belonged to the abbey of Canons Regular. Confiscated in 1790, five years later they were handed over by the state to the School of the Panthéon (École centrale du Panthéon). In 1804, as part of the Napoleonic educational reform, the school was renamed the Lycée Napoléon, in turn receiving Henry IV as its patron in 1815. Later, in 1848 Bonaparte returned as the patron, only to give way again in 1870, this time to Corneille. Finally, in 1873, Henry IV was reinstated, and has survived to this day. Franciszek Wołowski thus chose for his son a school with a distinctly revolutionary and imperial pedigree.

---

265 M. Ptaszyk *Liceum Warszawskie...*, p. 116.

He also chose an exceptionally beautiful school. The buildings were mostly built during the reign of Louis XIV. They included a beautiful rotunda, the Clovis Tower, monastery buildings with magnificent arcades and famous sundials, and a chapel. The famous St. Genevieve library is still a part of this complex, separated from the school.

We do not know what impression these monuments made on Louis, then aged 12. Unfortunately, his correspondence from the school years has not survived. So, there is no way to know how he endured separation from his family, how he perceived the new, big city, how he adapted to the new reality. The process was far from easy. According to Wolowski, he spent his first year of schooling in Paris at the Lycée Bourbon[266], to end up at the Lycée Henri IV, then headed by Jean Antoine Auvray[267]. The young Wolowski studied Latin, laboriously translating fragments of classical works, later Greek, rhetoric, philosophy, French, mathematics, the basics of geography and history, and to a limited extent zoology, botany, chemistry, and physics. Learning was not easy, and the expectations were high. The Henry IV Lyceum was one of the best schools in the country, one of the four famous royal lyceums in Paris[268].

Wolowski's schoolmates included many future celebrities of French politics and culture. In the school corridors, he would meet the future poet Alfred de Musset, Georges Eugène Haussmann (the prefect of Paris), Ferdinand de Lesseps (the builder of the Suez Canal), Eugène Emmanuel Viollet-le-Duc (an architect and restorer of medieval monuments), Gustave d'Eichthal (a writer and Hellenist). Undoubtedly, the most famous pupils were Ferdinand Philippe d'Orléans, Prince of Chartres, son of Louis-Philippe, later King of France, and his younger brothers Louis Charles, Prince of Nemours and François, Prince of Joinville. However, it seems doubtful that the young Wolowski would have been able to befriend them in any way: the princes were clearly isolated from the rest of the students[269]. Later, he skilfully exploited this distant "acquaintance" with Ferdinand Philippe when he applied for French citizenship[270].

---

266 This is what he wrote in his application to the Minister of Justice when he applied for French citizenship (*Dossier de naturalisation Wolowski, 1832*, Archives Nationales, ref. BB11/338, dossier 237x2).

267 The then *Collège Henry IV.* After 1815, the Napoleonic high schools were renamed "collèges" (grammar schools, secondary schools). However, they fulfilled the same role as before, preparing for the baccalaureate and study at elite universities.

268 These were: Bourbon Lyceum (today Condorcet), Charlemagne Lyceum, Louis the Great Lyceum and Henry IV Lyceum

269 A. Martin-Fugier *Louis-Philippe et sa famille 1830–1848*, Paris 2012, pp. 144–146.

270 In his correspondence with the Minister of Justice, while he did not directly refer to his acquaintance with Ferdinand Philippe, he quite clearly implied it (Dossier de naturalisation Wolowski...). Also, the alleged relationship with the prince was later referred to by many graduates of the Lyceum. For example, Haussmann, who

Unfortunately, Wolowski's school records have not survived, either. He was probably a good student, since in 1825 he was awarded first prize in the history section of a general competition[271]. Wolowski later reiterated that a few days before the competition, he had a dream that he was about to enter the competition and was asked a question about the Crusades. After waking up, he began to study the dreamed question diligently. On the day of the competition, to his delight, his topic was "The general effects of the Crusades"[272]. He also claimed later that he received awards at the end of every school year[273]. Similarly, many years later, the school achievements of the young Louis were described by his pupil and friend Levasseur, according to whom Wolowski was an excellent student. Levasseur stressed that the Pole had very good memories of his teachers: "Forty years later I heard him repeatedly eulogising his former history professor, whom he intended to induct into the Academy. The master, who probably did not know about it, died without having availed himself of the opportunity, but the former pupil treated the matter with the fervour with which he always returned favours"[274].

Be that as it may, Wolowski matriculated on 21 July 1827[275]. A short time later, he set off to return to Warsaw. Paris was then a troubled city, a political, ideological, and cultural melting pot, beginning to boil slowly. Since Charles X's seizure of power in 1824, the political situation steadily deteriorated. The royal coronation, conceived in medieval fashion, failed to make the desired impression on the public[276]. Clinging to a pre-revolutionary vision of the monarchy, the king introduced a succession of laws (the law of sacrilege, the law of the billion

---

later recalled that "During my stay at the Henry IV Lyceum, from the fourth year onwards, I was a fellow student of the Prince of Chartres – since then Prince of Orléans and heir to the throne – father of the Count of Paris. He was a very good student who usually finished the year among the top ten, on the 'bench of merit', where our affectionate personal relationships were formed." (G.E. Haussmann *Mémoires du Baron Haussmann* vol. I *Avant l'Hotel de Ville*, Paris 1890, p. 27). This entire section of Haussmann's memoirs, like several others, appears to have been fictionalised.

271 The general competition (concours général) is an extremely prestigious competition for students in the last two years of high school. It has been organised since 1747. It is held in French, history, geography, Latin, philosophy, and mathematics. The winners include the most prominent French cultural, scientific, and political figures. For example, during the period in question, the 2nd prize in the competition in the Latin section was won by Alfred de Musset.

272 *Concours Général, 1825,* Archives Nationales, ref. AJ16/638.

273 *Dossier de naturalisation Wolowski....*

274 E. Levasseur *La Vie et les travaux de Wolowski,* Paris 1877, p. 6.

275 A. Roulliet *Wolowski. Sa vie et ses travaux,* Paris 1880, p. 9.

276 J. Cabanis *Karol X. Król – ultras,* Warszawa 1981, pp. 270–279.

emigrants), which outraged the opposition and quite a few Parisians[277]. In 1827, he disbanded the national guard. He promoted ultra-conservative politicians, unpopular in the capital and other major French cities, like Jules de Polignac, whom he forced through as prime minister in 1829. As a result, opposition was growing in strength, most active in the "City of Lights" (as Parisians liked to call their capital). The moderate parliamentary opposition, united under the association "Aide-toi, le ciel t'aidera" ["Help yourself and the heavens will help you"], with several important newspapers, above all "Le Globe", was clearly successful in the 1827 elections, winning 10 times as many seats as four years earlier. Importantly, as Emmanuel de Waresquiel and Benoit Yvert note, almost all young people adopted an oppositional stance[278]. The opposition could also count on the support of the street. In 1825, a hundred thousand Parisians attended the funeral of Maximilien Foy, a Napoleonic general and liberal oppositionist[279]. In 1827, Parisians illuminated their flats and took to the streets again on the news of the opposition's parliamentary victory. They sang extremely popular songs by Pierre-Jean de Béranger, mercilessly criticising and ridiculing the authorities. Secret revolutionary organisations also proliferated; the most prominent of these, the Carbonari, probably had tens of thousands of members throughout France in the first half of the 1820s, of whom probably several thousand in Paris (in the second half of the decade their importance declined markedly)[280]. The city, like the French state as a whole, was slowly moving towards the revolution of 1830.

The emergence of new political doctrines and ideas were also of significance. Benjamin Constant warned against excess royal power and created his own liberal conception of freedom in his works: *Cours de politique constitutionnelle* (Paris 1818–1820), *De la liberté des Anciens comparée à celle des Modernes* (Paris, 1819), *De la religion...* (Paris 1824–1831).

François Guizot, in works both political (*Des moyens de gouvernement et d'opposition dans l'état actuel de la France*, Paris 1821) and historical (*Histoire générale*

277 The Sacrilege Act – a law passed in 1825, under which the penalty for sacrilege was forced labour and even the death penalty for profanation of the host. (R. Dobek *Sojusz tronu z ołtarzem we Francji w okresie Burbonów (1815–1830) i II cesarstwa (1852–1870),* [in:] P. Zając OMI (ed.) *Od Rewolucji Francuskiej do Nowej Ewangelizacji. Wokół osoby I charyzmtu św. Eugeniusza de Mazenoda (1782–1861) w 150 rocznicę śmierci,* Poznań 2012, pp. 72–73). The Billion Emigrants Act established huge reparations for representatives of the nobility who had lost land through revolutionary confiscations. A real fortune was recovered in this way by the later ruler Louis-Philippe d'Orléans (A. Castelot *Louis-Philippe le méconnu,* Paris 1994, p. 164).

278 E. de Waresquiel, B. Yvert *Histoire de la Restauration 1814–1830. Naissance de la France moderne,* Paris 2002, pp. 396–400.

279 E. de Waresquiel, B. Yvert *Histoire de la Restauration 1814–1830...*, p. 381.

280 S. Aprile *1815–1870. La Révolution inachevée,* Paris 2020, pp. 118–120.

de la civilisation en Europe, Paris 1828), extolled the virtues and achievements of the bourgeoisie and emphasised the importance of constitutional government. In the same years, Claude Henri de Saint-Simon shaped the foundations of his doctrine in publications like *Du système industriel* (Paris, 1822), *Catéchisme des industriels* (1823–1824) and *Nouveau christianisme* (1825). The first works (*Théorie de l'unité universelle*, vols. 1–4, Paris, 1822–1823; *Le Nouveau monde industriel et sociétaire*, Paris 1829), were also published by another thinker whose ideas underpinned left-wing doctrine, namely Charles Fourier. On the right, the sixty-year-old François-René de Chateaubriand was undoubtedly the most outstanding mind (*De la Monarchie selon la charte, Paris* 1816; *Voyages en Amérique et en Italie,* Paris 1827). Félicité de La Mennais began his long and surprising journey from the extreme conservative right to the revolutionary left (*De la religion considérée dans ses rapports avec l'ordre politique et civil*, Paris, 1825; *Des progrès de la révolution et de la guerre contre l'Église*, Paris 1829).

In parallel, another battle began. Its dividing lines were cultural, generational, and partly political, for Romanticism was taking France by storm. If even "the reign of sceptical rationalism over the souls of its readers" was undermined by Chateaubriand's *The Genius of Christianity* (*Génie du christianisme*, Paris 1802)"[281], the key decade was the 1820s. In 1820, Alphonse de Lamartine published the enthusiastically received volume *Méditations poétiques*:

> Thus ready to forsake life's outmost bound,
> Weeping my weary past of hope devoid,
> I turn me still with envious gaze around
> And view the blessings I have not enjoyed.
> Earth, sun, and valley – nature fair and bright,
> Beside my grave I breathe you each a sigh,

the 30-year-old wrote[282]. Two years later, Alfred de Vigny published a collection of *Poémes,* and Victor Hugo, only 20 years old, published *Odes et Ballades.* Hugo authored *Cromwell,* a drama staged in 1827, and *Hernani,* a play from 1830, in the preface to which the famous statement was made: "Romanticism, so often ill-defined, is only [...] liberalism in literature"[283].

---

281 J. Kowalski, A. i M. Loba, J. Prokop *Dzieje kultury francuskiej,* Warszawa 2007, p. 452.

282 A. de Lamartine *Autumn* (translated by Margaret Junkin), [in:] Southern literary messenger; devoted to every department of literature and the fine arts, University of Michigan: Humanities Text Initiative, Richmond 1851, p. 659.

283 V. Hugo *Author's preface to the first edition of Hernani, 1830* (translated by Frederick L. Slous), Newton Crossland, New York 1894, p. 16. The so-called "Battle of Hernani" also took place around the play. During performances of the play in February and March 1830, there were regular clashes over shouts, comments, booing and whistling between the generally young supporters of Romanticism and the more classically minded audience.

We do not know the extent to which the young Louis Wolowski participated in these social, political, and cultural changes in France in the 1820s. He was certainly not one of those "children of the century" who "drank with resignation the bitter chalice of your disdain" and, "to their satisfaction, gave themselves up to the intoxication of despair"[284]. Moreover, the Romantic "disease of the age" was completely incompatible with his rational mentality and disposition. Did he read the Romantics? This question remains unanswered. What we do know is that he later referred to the poetry of Hugo and Lamartine. However, he may have become familiar with it in the 1830s. Certainly, Wolowski – despite his links with Mickiewicz – was not a literary expert and did not particularly boast about his reading outside of work.

Instead, we can assume that the young Louis came into contact with at least some political literature, mainly liberal, in France in the 1820s. Benjamin Constant was among his favourite authors for the rest of his life, and in 1862 he even dedicated a separate pamphlet to him[285]. Later, he also frequently quoted Victor Cousin[286]. He may have also been familiar with the political and historical texts of Guizot, Pierre-Paul Royer-Collard and Prosper de Barante. To a large extent, these authors' parliamentarism and limited liberalism corresponded to the way of thinking of Franciszek Wołowski, otherwise in Paris for at least some time present alongside his son. Did Wolowski therefore participate in the political movement in the city? Almost certainly not, bearing in mind his young age, the absence of his name in the police archives and the absence of any mention of it in his application for naturalisation. It seems that if he could have boasted of any connection with the anti-royal opposition of the Bourbon Restoration period, he would not have failed to do so after 1830, when France was ruled by Louis-Philippe, elevated to the throne after the overthrow of the House of Bourbon.

Did the political and intellectual mood in Paris influence Louis Wolowski's activities in Warsaw? Unfortunately, in the absence of documents supporting any thesis, a historian is unable to provide a straight answer to this question. However, it seems probable. Undoubtedly, Wolowski came from a revolutionary European metropolis to a city that was incomparably smaller (Warsaw at the time had a population of less than 127,000, Paris about 800,000)[287], but equally restless, in which a revolt was also about to break out.

---

284 A. de Musset *The Confession of the Child of the Century*, Penguin Books 2013, pp. 119–120.

285 L. Wolowski *Mémoire sur le cours de politique constitutionnelle de Benjamin Constant, lu à l'Académie des Sciences Morales et Politiques*, Paris 1862.

286 He also knew Cousin personally, as evidenced by the latter's letter preserved in the State Archives in Cracow, ref. AKPot 3204.

287 *Tabella miast, wsi, osad, Królestwa Polskiego, z wyrażeniem ich położenia i ludności, alfabetycznie ułożona w Biórze Kommissyi Rządowćy Spraw Wewnętrznych i Policyi.*

3. The Royal University of Warsaw

If Bieliński and Ptaszyk are right, upon his return to Poland Wolowski had to pass once again his matriculation exam before the Commission of the Society for Elementary Books[288]. Having completed this formality, he initially attended lectures at the Faculty of Law of the University of Warsaw as an auditing student, and on 16 September 1828 he finally enrolled as a regular student[289]. In the first year, his curriculum included religion, general history, physics, applied chemistry, forestry, and political economy. In the second year: philosophy, administration and finance, church law, history of Polish law and Polish literature. Finally, in the third year (which Wolowski ultimately did not complete), he studied statistics, civil law, commercial law, criminal law, civil and criminal procedure[290]. The history of Polish law was taught by Jan Wincenty Bandtkie, dean of the faculty. "The major and most distinguished professors were Bandtkie, Szaniawski and Engelke, professors at the law school of the Duchy of Warsaw. Each was distinguished by the right qualities: Bandtkie attracted students with his extensive and thorough knowledge of the history and laws of old Poland. His lectures on Roman law, which he read in Latin, stood out with their clarity and systematic nature of teaching," recalled later Romuald Hube, another eminent jurist[291]. Father Franciszek Ksawery Szaniawski was responsible for civil and commercial law. "He made a general introduction to each matter, then read the individual articles, pointed out the union regulations and explained the ordinances from a practical side, breaking down the legal issue and quoting examples. His lecture was very simple and comprehensible, often interspersed with facetious words which he eagerly let slip between us," Hube wrote[292]. The last of the three, Alexander Engelke, dealt with criminal law. Of German origin, he spoke Polish with a distinct accent. He was said to be a very good lecturer, albeit an unprincipled one: he was notorious for being late for lectures and for cutting them short[293]. Engelke also turned out to be a tragic figure. According to Anna Rosner's account, his well-known loyalty to the authorities

---

vol. II, *M-Z*, Warszawa 1827, p. 255; L. Girard, *Nouvelle histoire de Paris. La Deuxième République et le Second Empire 1848–1870*, Paris 1981, p. 135.

288 J. Bieliński *Królewski Uniwersytet Warszawski...*, vol. III, p. 540; M. Ptaszyk *Liceum Warszawskie...*, p. 99.

289 J. Bieliński *Królewski Uniwersytet Warszawski...*, vol. III, p. 540

290 J. Bieliński *Królewski Uniwersytet Warszawski (1816–1831)*, vol. II, Warszawa 1911, p. 293.

291 R. Hube *Pisma*, vol. I, Warszawa 1905, p. XII.

292 R. Hube *Pisma*, vol. I,..., p. XII.

293 M. Mycielski *Uniwersytet Królewski 1816–1831*, [in:]. Kizwalter (ed.) *Dzieje Uniwersytetu Warszawskiego 1816–1915*, Warszawa 2016, p. 154

caused students to turn away from him in the late 1820s; he was also accused of collaborating with the secret police[294].

However, among the university professors, Fryderyk Skarbek proved a far more important figure for Louis Wolowski's further development. Skarbek, the only count and landowner among the professors, and a graduate of the university in Paris, taught political economy. His economic views are known from a work published in Paris in 1829, entitled *Théorie des richesses sociales suivie d'une bibliographie de l'économie politique*[295] . Skarbek largely adopted Adam Smith's theory for Polish purposes. Thus, he accepted the development of capitalism, free market principles, economic laissez-faire, and stressed the importance of individual entrepreneurship and the middle class. He postulated a gradual agricultural reform and transforming peasants into a group of smallholders. Finally, he was the first Polish scholar to deal with the problem of poverty, to which he devoted a separate work, *On Poverty and the Poor*, (Warsaw 1827). However, he believed that the best way to gradually alleviate poverty leads through the free market. Louis Wolowski, as an economist, later returned to these thoughts of Skarbek on many occasions. He also maintained contact with his former professor, as evidenced by two letters from Skarbek, from 1859 to 1864, respectively[296].

However, perhaps a more important teacher was Stanisław Kunatt, also an economist, who taught administration, commerce, and statistics. Kunatt was a follower of David Ricardo and translated into Polish *On the Principles of Political Economy and Taxation* (*O zasadach ekonomii politycznej i o podatku*, Warszawa, 1826–1827). After the November Uprising, he emigrated to France and, like Wolowski, became associated with the Hotel Lambert. The student and the professor also met during the former's wedding: Kunatt was Wolowski's best man.

In the context of Louis Wolowski, another of the University's professors is worth mentioning. At the time, general history was taught by Feliks Bentkowski, dean of the Faculty of Arts and Sciences. Wolowski knew him personally, and even visited him at home.[297]. He may have benefited from the professor's excellent

---

294 A. Rosner *Dzieje Wydziału Prawa i Administracji Uniwersytetu Warszawskiego w latach 1808–1831*, [in:] G. Bałtruszajtys (ed.) *Zarys dziejów Wydziału Prawa i Administracji Uniwersytetu Warszawskiego*, Warszawa 2016, p. 33.

295 Polish edition: *Ogólne zasady nauki gospodarstwa narodowego, czyli czysta teorya ekonomii politycznej*, Warszawa 1859.

296 Biblioteka Polska w Paryżu, ref. BPP 2339. In the first of them, Skarbek recommended to Wolowski a young Pole graduating in economics from St Petersburg, intending to continue his studies in Paris. In the second, written shortly before his death, he asked Wolowski for his opinion on the French version of his "History of the Duchy of Warsaw", which he wished to publish in Paris.

297 Bentkowski studied in Halle when Franciszek Wołowski was there. It therefore seems possible that he had already met Wolowski's father at that time, and later, through him, the son.

library. However, the professor was not popular among his students. This is how Kazimierz Wójcicki remembered him:

> Of good height, build athletic, he had a strong, loud voice, and a stern countenance. The students feared him, but did not love him, like Skrodzki and Brodziński, for his coarse demeanour, but they valued his lectures and teaching. In class, having targeted a freshman who had come from a provincial school, he asked in his booming voice: "Please tell me if the French Revolution was after or before the birth of Christ?" The student, recently arrived from the province, confused by his call, having only heard the professor's last words, replied in a trembling voice: "Before the birth of Christ!" General laughter resounded throughout the room. Bentkowski looked crossly at the freshman, to see if he had a mocking look on his face, but the latter, almost unconscious, slumped down on the bench. A murmur unfavourable to the professor followed, and these kinds of enquiries did not command the students' respect[298].

Some young people also took badly to the clerical and conservative content in the professor's teaching. Janowski wrote, for example, that during a lecture on general history, Bentkowski talked about the creation of the world on the basis of *Genesis*, quoting directly from it[299]. The antagonism between the students and Bentkowski is very well reflected in a story involving Wolowski. It was an incident that could have ended badly for him. On 19 November 1828, the professor made an official complaint to the rector about the students' unacceptable behaviour. One of them had, during a lecture a few days earlier, openly spoken to Louis Wolowski. When the lecture was over, Bentkowski decided to bring it to Wolowski's attention. The latter, in turn, was to reply that "I neither talked now nor was I admonished last year, and you, professor, should not admonish in public, like in school"[300]. Wolowski and the other students were annoyed by Bentkowski's manner of addressing them as "you", as if they were children. According to Wolowski, Bentkowski added insulting words such as "be quiet" and behaved "coarsely"[301]. As a result, the professor referred the student to Rector Szweykowski, who formally reprimanded him. This would have been the end of the matter, if the young law student's colleagues had not stood up for him. During the next lecture, the young people on the last benches decided to stomp at Bentkowski's sight. This in turn led to the formal complaint and investigation by a university committee. The immature behaviour of the honour-sensitive students and the professor's overreaction could have ended very badly for Louis: the University Council initially decided to expel him, along with his co-accused Leon Łubieński, by virtue of a verdict

---

298 Quote as in M. Mycielski *Uniwersytet Królewski 1816–1831...*, pp. 194–195.

299 J.N. Janowski *Notatki...*, p. 110.

300 J. Bieliński *Królewski Uniwersytet Warszawski (1816–1831)*, vol. I, Warszawa 1907, p. 301.

301 J. Bieliński *Królewski Uniwersytet Warszawski...*, p. 305.

of 22 November 1828. However, the defendants subsequently appeared before the rector and expressed remorse, vowing that similar incidents would never happen again. Bentkowski also wrote to the rector that the punishment was too harsh. As a result, the Council happily changed the sentence from expulsion to four days of detention[302]. Notably, we owe to Bieliński the knowledge of the commission's opinion on Wolowski: "Louis Wolowski, a first-year student. Up to the 14th day of this month, the inspectors had not noticed anything worth attention. It was only this year that they considered that he had a close relationship with Łubieński and others involved in this case"[303].

The Łubieński mentioned by the committee was Leon Count Łubieński, who soon left for Scotland to complete his studies. On his return to Poland, he worked at the Bank of Poland, and died in 1860. In the halls and corridors of the university, Wolowski could have made the acquaintance of Zygmunt Krasiński, incidentally also involved in the Bentkowski incident[304]. Patrice Markiewicz names the later author of *The Undivine Comedy* among Wolowski's student friends, including also Maurycy Mochnacki, Konstanty Gaszyński, Stanisław Egbert Koźmian, Dominik Magnuszewski and Chopin[305]. While in the case of Mochnacki he is clearly wrong, arguably also in the case of Krasiński[306], however, Gaszyński probably met Wolowski at the time, as did Koźmian[307]. Frédéric Chopin was probably also in his

302 J. Bieliński *Królewski Uniwersytet Warszawski...*, pp. 309–310.

303 J. Bieliński *Królewski Uniwersytet Warszawski...*, p. 307.

304 Józef Kallenbach recalls that Krasiński was then given two days of detention (J. Kallenbach *Zygmunt Krasiński. Życie i twórczość z lat młodych (1812–1838),* vol. I, Lvov 1904, p. 63.

305 P. Markiewicz *Louis Wolowski, un intellectuel et un représentant du libéralisme en France au milieu du 19 siècle,* Université Paris X Nanterre, U-E-R d'Histoire, Paris 1993 (typescript), p. 22.

306 In the 1930s, Maria Walewska, née Przezdziecka, described meetings with Wolowski from 1867 to 1869, during which he apparently mentioned his "great friendship with Zygmunt Krasiński." Asked about the poet's exceptional gift of foresight, he was to have replied, "Miss, the Romans used to call poets bards and they were right." (M. z Przeździeckich Walewska *Polacy w Paryżu, Florencji i Dreźnie. Sylwetki i wspomnienia,* Warszawa 1930, pp. 56–57). However, it seems that either the author or Wolowski himself distorted reality to some extent. In Krasiński's correspondence, Louis Wolowski does not appear at all (Z. Krasiński *Listy do różnych adresatów,* vol. I–II, Warszawa 1991) or sporadically (Z. Krasński *Listy do Augusta Cieszkowskiego, Edwarda Jaroszyńskiego, Bronisława Trentowskiego,* vol. I, Warszawa 1988). While it is certain that they knew each other, this acquaintance was most likely casual.

307 In 1864, Koźmian wrote in a letter to "dear Louis" Wolowski about their "old acquaintance professor Skarbek", evidently referring to their student years. At the end of the letter, he added: "May the memories of our happier youth at least shine

wide circle of acquaintances. However, judging by Chopin's correspondence[308] It was not a close friendship – which, incidentally, did not prevent Wolowski from speaking over the musician's grave on the first anniversary of his death[309]. Chopin knew his parents through his father back in Warsaw, and he visited Franciszek and Tekla in Paris[310]. Aleksandryna, Louis' sister, was one of the composer's first pupils[311].

One of the most poetic episodes in Louis Wolowski's life is connected with Gaszyński. Apparently, there was more to Warsaw students than education. Henriette Sontag, an outstanding German soprano, came to Poland's capital in May 1830. She gave 11 concerts, winning tremendous admiration[312]. Gaszyński clearly succumbed to this atmosphere, too and wrote a poem in her honour. The stanzas were subsequently translated into French by Louis Wolowski, and this Polish/French linguistic arrangement was printed in Warsaw.

> The notes that filled the air with zest,
> Could they escape a human chest,
> Or from another world they came?
> [...]
> Quel son mélodieux a fait vibrer les airs
> Est-ce la voix des anges aux celèstes concerts
> Est-ce une voix mortelle ?

---

through the darkness of the night [of the last period of the January Uprising]." (Biblioteka Polska w Paryżu, ref. BPP 2339, k. 21–22).

308 Z. Helman, Z. Skowron, H. Wróblewska – Straus *Korespondencja Fryderyka Chopina*, vol. I–II, Warszawa 2009–2017.

309 As "John Bull" said, "after the prayers had been said, Mr Wolowski, MP, attempted to make a speech, but was so moved that he only managed to say a few words." (quoted as in F. Niecks *Fryderyk Chopin jako człowiek i muzyk,* Warszawa 2011, p. 513).

310 This is evidenced, for example, by a somewhat malicious remark about Franciszek Wolowski, interjected into a letter to Julian Fontana from 1841: "Take comfort [!] in the fact that you do not have rheumatism or gout – or that you do not resemble old Wolowski, or that no similar misfortune has befallen you. – Console yourself with this – it is my only consolation too, although I am closer to Wolowski than you." (B. E. Sydow (ed.) *Korespondencja Fryderyka Chopina....*, pp. 24–25).

311 M. Tomaszewski *Chopin. Człowiek, dzieło, rezonans*, Kraków 2005, p. 60. Chopin dedicated to her the *Mazurka in B flat major*, inscribed in her album.

312 Clearly enchanted, Chopin referred to her in a letter as 'a divine messenger.'" (Z. Helman, Z. Skowron, H. Wróblewska – Straus *Korespondencja Fryderyka Chopina*, vol. I, p. 163). Also impressed by her talent was Mochnacki (M. Mochnacki *Panna Sonntag*, [in:] M. Mochnacki *Pisma krytyczne i polityczne*, Kraków 1996, vol. 1, pp. 375–377).

- so, the poets asked. And they answered:

> Sontag! The whole of Europe has
> Put on your head a laurel wreath.
> The future opens up the gate
> of immortality, your fate.
> [...]
> Sontag! Déjà l'Europe entière
> De lauriers merités a couronné ton front.
> L'avenir te découvre l'immortelle carrière,
> Et les siècles futurs vont répéter ton nom.[313].

It is difficult to judge Wolowski's poetic talent, arguably mediocre, on the basis of this translation. What can be said with certainty, however, is that he genuinely valued poetry to the end of his life. He would later read the Polish Romantics: Mickiewicz, Krasiński, Zaleski, as well as the French: Lamartine and Hugo. Moreover, the French text of the *Poem* proves that after his return from Paris he had an excellent command of the language. Soon it was to serve him in a much more serious matter.

4. The November Uprising

In 1830, Warsaw was like an awakening volcano.

> Such was the state of Warsaw at that time, open slavery, secret conspiracies in the army and in schools alike, under cloaks and habits. Warsaw was airless, as if before a great storm; everyone was expecting it, and no one knew where it would come from. In the meantime, everything was smart, splendid, and boisterous, as if in a day of merriment and happiness. In Kraków, the streets are empty, like during the plague, and when the carriage clatters, everyone goes to the windows to see this marvellous thing. Warsaw is filled with the incessant clatter of carriages and drums, there are people in the streets, in the gardens, in the suburbs. The atmosphere seems merry, but it is frightening; everyone is alert to see anyone eavesdropping or grabbing at the collar. And, as always and everywhere, there was the least fear among the students, the most eager bustle between them [...][314]

- Aleksander Jełowicki wrote later. Even if in 1830 the sentiment was not all-encompassing, it was typical of many young people, probably including Wolowski.

In mid-December 1828, Second Lieutenant Piotr Wysocki of the Infantry Cadet School in Warsaw set up a new clandestine organisation, later known as the Officer

313 K. Gaszyński *Wiersz do Henrjetty Sontag*, transl. L. Wołowski, Warszawa 1830, pp. 1–2.

314 A. Jełowicki *Moje wspomnienia...*, p. 68.

Cadet Conspiracy or Wysocki's Conspiracy. Of the three objectives adopted by the conspirators, only one was more general in nature: "to combine all endeavours, to sacrifice one's life, when necessary, in defence of a raped constitutional law"[315]. The young men intended to spark off an uprising by "propagating and spreading the good spirit in the army to a friendlier time"[316]. However, their plans did not go any further. They also accepted in advance that the power in the insurgent government would be assumed by more experienced politicians and commanders with national recognition. Nor did they develop any political or social programme. Despite this, the Conspiracy gradually developed. Its growth was aided by news of the July Revolution in France[317]. Several dozen young officers were involved[318], with a growing number of civilians, primarily students, since August.

It remains unknown exactly when Louis Wolowski joined them. He belonged to a circle of Jan Bartkowski, another law student[319]. It was probably the students who helped Wolowski find his way into the conspiracy. Unfortunately, the student fraternity was not cautious enough, and it was through them that Grand Duke Konstantin's secret police uncovered the conspiracy. In late September 1830, one of the Tsar's spies reported news of a conspiracy among students and mentioned three names from Bartkowski's group[320]. Ultimately it turned out that responsible for the denunciation was another student, Franciszek Kruszelnicki. On 10 November 1830, he reported to Mateusz Lubowidzki, the then deputy mayor of Warsaw, in charge of the municipal police, on the meetings held at Bartkowski's house[321].

315 P. Wysocki *Pamiętnik Piotra Wysockiego o powstaniu 29 listopada 1830 roku,* vol. II, Paris 1867, p. 12.

316 P. Wysocki *Pamiętnik Piotra Wysockiego o powstaniu...*, p. 15.

317 Zajewski quoted the words of Piotr Wysocki and Maurycy Mochnacki on 10 December 1830: "We, too, entertained a beautiful hope. The spreading enthusiasm in the army, then camped near Warsaw, convinced me of the agreement and unanimous will of almost all the officers. Everyone was talking about the French Revolution; everyone was discussing the events of July. As for our cause, we communicated more openly and with a greater disposition to raise arms, as long as someone was at the head of the army". He went on to say that, upon hearing of the victorious revolt in Paris, around 200 officers and students joined the Conspiracy (W. Zajewski *Wpływ rewolucji lipcowej na wybuch Powstania Listopadowego 1830 roku,* [in:] W. Zajewski (ed.) *Powstanie Listopadowe 1830–1831. Dzieje wewnętrzne. Militaria. Europa wobec powstania,* Warszawa 1980, p. 49).

318 Wacław Tokarz wrote that there were never more than 77 officers (W. Tokarz *Sprzysiężenie Wysockiego i Noc Listopadowa,* Warszawa 1980, p. 82).

319 W. Tokarz *Sprzysiężenie Wysockiego...*, p. 88; R. Bielecki *Belwederczycy i podchorążowie,* Warszawa 1989, p. 44.

320 W. Tokarz *Sprzysiężenie Wysockiego...*, p. 96.

321 Apparently, Kruszelnicki's motive was revenge. Insurgent and émigré Kazimierz Lewandowski later recalled that Kruszelnicki was said to have squandered in

Arrest ensued of Bartkowski, Wolowski, Stanisław Faliński, Leopold Giewartowski, Adam Bacewicz, Hipolit Rzewuski, Henryk Rychłowski, Aleksander Liedtke, Adam Piwowarski, Nicefor Wąsowicz, Maciej Kossowski, Ignacy Polichnowski, Kajetan Witkowski, Majeranowski, Leon Gorzeński, Seweryn Madan, Julian Łabędzki and Wiktor Józefowicz[322]. The defendants were initially incarcerated in university premises, then in the Warsaw Carmelite monastery in Leszno, a street in Warsaw. Bartkowski later recalled that they were treated relatively well; they were provided with books from the university's collection[323].

The interrogation of the arrested young men was conducted by a commission appointed by Grand Duke Konstantin himself[324]. The investigators' method was relatively simple: each of the accused was interrogated separately and then confronted with Kruszelnicki. The confrontation scene with Adam Piwowarski, Wolowski's departmental colleague, was described by Kazimierz Lewandowski:

> Informer: You will not deny that on the nth of October, when I stayed with you overnight, the twelve of you sat up until 2 a.m. and made plans to overthrow the Russian government.

Warsaw the money he needed to support himself and register at the University. In effect, he continued his studies thanks to the help and hospitality of his colleagues. One of them, however, after a dozen or so days, had enough of his guest and threw him out on the street. In revenge, he denounced his host and his guests. (K. Lewandowski *Pamiętnik wychodźca polskiego,* Warszawa 1977, p. 21). Maria Wawrykova, on the other hand, wrote in her history of the University that Kruszelnicki was accused by his colleagues of theft and immoral behaviour (M. Wawrykowa *Uniwersytet Warszawski w latach 1816–1831,* [in:] S. Kieniewicz (ed.) *Dzieje Uniwersytetu Warszawskiego 1807–1915,* Warszawa 1981, p. 183). Kruszelnicki himself was said to have testified in the investigation that the denunciation stemmed from a desire to avoid an assassination attempt on Konstantin (W. Tokarz *Sprzysiężenie Wysockiego...,* pp. 115–116). In general, the denunciation was also mentioned by another insurgent, Leon Dembowski (L. Dembowski *Moje wspomnienia,* vol. II, Petersburg 1898, pp. 9–10).

322 J. Harbut *Noc listopadowa w świetle i cieniach procesu przed Najwyższym Sądem Kryminalnym: (jeden z największych procesów politycznych w dziejach narodów),* Warszawa 1926, p. 45.

323 J. Bartkowski *Wspomnienia z 1830/31 roku (fragment),* Lvov 1898, pp. 11–12. However, it must be stressed that, years later, Bartkowski clearly whitewashed his role during the investigation.

324 It was headed by the curator of the University of Warsaw, Count Maksymilian Fredro, and also included rector Szweykowski, the deans of the various faculties, the inspector general of the University, Jan Kanty Krzyżanowski, generals Stanisław Potocki, Józef Rautenstrauch and Aleksander Rożniecki. (E.A. Poklękowski *Akt oskarżenia...,* p. 17).

> Defendant: Not true, we were studying, repeating chemistry and physics, and you were asleep and snoring, so you couldn't hear anything.
> I: I was snoring but not sleeping, and the other day I saw each of you bring concealed weapons under your clothes, and then some of you were casting bullets in the chimney and others were making loads at the table.
> D: This is not true, we had no weapons at all, apart from two small pistols, because there was going to be a duel (indeed the defendant was supposed to fight a duel which did not happen in the end).
> I: The other day, when you were sitting until dawn, I heard you say that you had relations with army officers and some young lawyers.
> D: I won't stand it, come over and I'll smack you!
> Hearing that, Bentkowski got up and said: Dear Mr. Piwowarski, you will not smack him here in our presence.
> Defendant: But Professor, he's lying so much I can't stand it.[325].

However, most of the interrogations were not as comical, nor did all the accused students withstand the pressure of the investigation. Above all, relatively extensive testimony was given by Bartkowski who admitted his intention to kill Konstantin and ratted on several colleagues[326]. Another arrested student conspiracy leader, Michał Szweycer, followed suit[327]. Tokarz also wrote in general terms: "They behaved badly in the investigation, they mentioned names, quoted details: Faliński, L. Giewartowski, A. Liedtke, M. Kosowski, K. Witkowski, S. Madan"[328].

In this context, the attitude of Louis Wolowski undoubtedly deserves recognition. Unfortunately, the minutes of Wolowski's interrogation have not survived, so we need to rely on the record of prosecutor Eugene Aleksandr Poklękowski: "Louis Wolowski, a student at the University, confesses that he used to visit Alexander Miączyński, and they learned English together, accompanied by Szymański; students: Alexander Mokronowski, Władysław Bielski, Stanisław Łubieński [...] He does not deny that in their circle they repeated the news spreading in Warsaw about the stirrings that were about to take place; but he claims that they deplored the ill effects that might result, and, on the contrary, did not discuss the means of orchestrating the revolt at all"[329]. Tokarz, who had an opportunity to review the full investigation files between the wars, wrote that Wolowski (questioned five times by the commission) spoke only about the secret police, its provocative activities. He also provided arguments that were embarrassing to the committee members. And sometimes, to avoid having to answer questions, he developed a

325 K. Lewandowski *Pamiętnik wychodźca polskiego...*, pp. 22–23.
326 E.A. Poklękowski *Akt oskarżenia...*, p. 22.
327 E.A. Poklękowski *Akt oskarżenia...*, pp. 24–25.
328 W. Tokarz *Sprzysiężenie Wysockiego...*, p. 121.
329 E.A. Poklękowski *Akt oskarżenia...*, p. 26.

broad view of the world and of life, which was also intended by default to protect him from participation in secret societies[330].

Unfortunately, in view of the testimony of his colleagues, the attitude of Wolowski himself was of relatively little significance. He faced the threat of long imprisonment or exile. Luckily, he was saved by the outbreak of the Uprising. The arrests forced Wysocki and the other leaders of the conspiracy into action. On the evening of 29 November 1830, a small group of conspirators (mostly students), led by Ludwik Nabielak, struck at the Belvedere with the intention of killing Grand Duke Konstantin. However, he managed to hide, and after a short time the conspirators moved towards the monument to king Sobieski on Agricola. In the meantime, Wysocki took command of the Infantry Cadet School. The cadets marched chaotically through the streets of Warsaw, occasionally clashing with Russian uhlans. Gradually, they were joined by the capital's residents. The swelling crowd found its way to the Arsenal, where the insurgents were joined by soldiers of the 2nd, 4th, and 5th infantry regiments. At around 9:00 pm, the Poles captured the Arsenal, while the rebellion began to spread spontaneously to the rest of the city. Poorly planned, almost unprepared, and exceptionally chaotic, the revolution broke out[331].

The Arsenal was relatively close to the Carmelite monastery. A group of insurgents, presumably enticed by students who remembered their colleagues left behind, moved towards the prison. The monastery was guarded by 24 Polish soldiers from the 4th Regiment, who, initially (probably unaware of the developments) did not intend to release the prisoners. There was a brief exchange of fire. The students were finally released when soldiers from the 5th Regiment turned up. "We ran to the Carmelites in Leszno, broke down the gate, disarmed the guard, dispersed the gendarmes and guards, broke down the doors to the prison cells and freed the poor people. Oh, the joy of it! There was no end to hugs and greetings. When we led the prisoners out onto the street, a huge cheer went up and we got into possession of several dozen bottles of wine, so that this greeting would not go unnoticed," Wiktor Feliks Szokalski, a scholar, recalled later [332]. Louis Wolowski was among them.

The young conspirator remembered that night very well. As it turned out, the danger was not entirely over. Forty years later, he told Józef Ignacy Kraszewski that, once the prison was opened, he rushed to the Arsenal to get weapons, and then ran out onto Krakowskie Przedmieście Street. On the way, he decided to stop by his parents' house in Mazowiecka Street. He could not find them, as they had

330 W. Tokarz *Sprzysiężenie Wysockiego...*, p. 120.

331 More: W. Tokarz *Sprzysiężenie Wysockiego...*, pp. 141–211; W. Bortnowski *Łuna nad Solcem 1830. Blaski i cienie nocy listopadowej*, Warszawa 1982, pp. 163–194; R. Bielecki *Belwederczycy i podchorążowie*, pp. 70–102.

332 W. F. Szokalski *Wspomnienia z przeszłości.* Vol. I. *1811–1837,* Wilno 1921, p. 201.

visited a sick relative in... Leszno Street. He decided to get through to them, so he set off with his old maid Teresa who would not let him go alone. Unfortunately, he was immediately stopped by Sergei Dmitrievich Bezobrazov, Konstantin's adjutant, who had known him. The Russian escorted him to the guardhouse; he was even said to have ordered a soldier "If he moves from his chair, thrust him with a bayonet". The next day, Wolowski, according to his own account, found himself in front of Konstantin who, enraged, allegedly shouted: "Are you going to tell me again that you are not conspiring!?" The Russians clearly did not know what to do with him and locked him up in the Old Orangery. Wolowski recalled later, that here he learnt "his first lesson in political economy". For the Russians had left him under guard but without food. The hungry young man "who only had a watch with him, worth five hundred francs, had to give it to a soldier for a piece of black bread". Happily, a messenger from the Grand Duke soon arrived at the Orangery and ordered his release. The justification was surprising: Konstantin was releasing Wolowski as... "the guiltiest", to silence the rumours spreading in Warsaw that he had ordered the captives to be shot. In response, Wolowski apparently insisted on the release of his fellow prisoners, to which the Russian eventually agreed[333].

It is difficult to say to what extent this story accurately depicts the actual course of events. Rumours indeed circulated in Warsaw. Although Wolowski was certainly not the "guiltiest", Konstantin really let the Polish prisoners go[334]. On the other hand, the statement that Wolowski had anything to do with it should probably be treated as a cock-and-bull story.

With his conspiratorial past behind him, Wolowski was far from any kind of revolutionary radicalism, as best demonstrated in Kraszewski's memoirs. He wrote that the young student had joined the newly formed academic guard. With the guard, he was to drive away "the first fervent clubs that came into being". This recollection by Wolowski is very much in keeping with the attitude of quite a few students at the time. It is extensively described by Maria Wawrykowa: the guard

---

333 J.I. Kraszewski *Ludwik Wołowski,* "Dziennik Poznański" no. 190, 22.08.1876. The same account appeared later in the "Yearbook of the Historical and Literary Society in Paris" ("Rocznik Towarzystwa Historyczno-Literackiego w Paryżu" 1873–1878, p. 427). "The Yearbook" added that Wolowski's co-prisoner in the Orangery was "a certain Mierosławski". Mierosławski was mentioned several times by Tokarz in a conspiratorial context. However, as Marian Żychowski wrote in his comprehensive biography of the future famous revolutionary Ludwik Mierosławski, it was most probably Hipolit Mierosławski, Ludwik's cousin (M. Żychowski *Ludwik Mierosławski 1814–1878,* Warszawa 1963, p. 45).

334 A. Barańska *Wymarsz korpusu Wielkiego Księcia Konstantego z Królestwa Polskiego w świetle wspomnień Nadieżdy Iwanowny Golicyny,* [in:] "Teka Komisji Historycznej" no. VIII, 2011, p. 20. A notable exception was Walerian Łukasiński, who remained a Russian captive.

was formed on 01 December 1830, numbered less than a thousand students, and was headed by Krystyn Lach Szyrma, a professor at the University of Warsaw. It had its own navy-blue uniforms with amaranth stripes. Initially, the formation oversaw policing activities in the city. It was also of distinctly conservative nature and supported the Provisional Government and Prince Adam Czartoryski. On 04 December 1830, the guards almost led to a lynching of Mochnacki, accused of insulting Niemcewicz. The academics viewed the Patriotic Society and all other "clubs" with extreme suspicion, seeing them as a manifestation of Polish disorderliness. Meanwhile, the Guard was transformed into Chłopicki's Guard of Honour (which also included Louis' brother, Kazimierz)[335] and the atmosphere grew more radical with criticism of the dictator gaining in strength. This eventually led to dissolution of the Guard in February 1831[336]. It seems that the mood among the academic youth was well reflected in a text written at the time by Louis Wolowski for the ephemeral magazine "Orzeł Biały" [White Eagle]. It exuded the enormous enthusiasm and hope characteristic of the first days of the Uprising. Wolowski emphasised the merit of the cadets and belvedere soldiers, the "heroes whose glory overshadows even the fame of Thermopylae". In the name of national unity, he called for the forgiveness of those who had remained loyal to Konstantin in the first days of the uprising, who "were later freed by us" and "were now tormented by the memory of their mistake". Like Franciszek Wołowski in the Sejm, Louis proved in writing that the Polish rebellion was legal, as the Tsar had violated the fundamental rights of the nation and the Constitution. In turn, he described the pre-November Kingdom as a time of "darkness and perversity, fettered feelings and thoughts, espionage, humiliation and widespread demoralisation". According to Wolowski, the key task was to maintain the unity of the nation. This was to be guaranteed by the dictatorship of a "MAN known to the world for his merits, talents and virtue, a worthy successor to Washington, [...] whose inherent virtues cannot even cause concern that he might abuse his power", i.e., Chłopicki. Wolowski called for unequivocal support for the dictator and the Sejm, which was soon to convene and unfailingly support him. Extremely important in this context were the historical elements mentioned by Wolowski which had previously doomed Poland: dissent, the freedom of the nobility combined with the enslavement of the rest of the nation, the weakness of the government, the clear excess of individual freedom over the effectiveness of the state. "Now all the forces are united," he went on, "for the victory of the dear liberties; all citizens equal in the face of the law, striving with equal zeal for the recovery of the liberty equally dear to each, and, learning from the past, are not restraining the strength of the whole in the Government imagined; on these foundations the scattered members of the great body will come together and the bulwark of European liberty will rise from

335 "Rocznik Towarzystwa Historyczno-Literackiego w Paryżu", 1873–1878, p. 425.

336 M. Wawrykowa *Uniwersytet Warszawski w latach 1816–1831...*, pp. 186–200.

the ruins"[337]. This concern for unity, and support for "the strength of everybody expressed in the Government", explained the reluctant attitude of Wolowski and other members of the Academic Guard in December 1830 towards the Patriotic Society and "other ardent clubs", which Wolowski was driving away. Interestingly, Louis' views were also fully in line with those of his father: Franciszek Wołowski was also unequivocally in favour of granting the dictatorship to Chłopicki on 20 December 1830[338].

Louis Wolowski's view of the Patriotic Society must have changed over time. It is not known exactly when this happened, perhaps at the moment described by Wawrykowa, in January-February 1831. One thing is certain – Louis Wolowski's name was on the list of the Society members since August 1831[339]. His activity in the Society is unknown – apart from the fact that, at the time of compiling the list, Wolowski was in Paris, unable to attend meetings.

In general, information concerning Wolowski between December 1830 and August 1831 is only fragmentary. Contrary to the memoirs written down by Kraszewski, it is known that in the Academic Guard he was a second lieutenant[340]. Then, probably promoted to captain, he became an aide-de-camp to Michał Radziwiłł and in this capacity fought in the Battle of Grochów[341]. However, as early as in February 1831, he left the army and ended up as a civil servant at the Ministry of Foreign Affairs, where he was promoted to secretary-treasurer in June that year. Interestingly, he was not paid for his work[342].

Louis was still politically active. It seems that he sometimes acted as an informal envoy of his father, with whom he shared opinions. This is clearly testified to by Kajetan Koźmian's reminiscences from the days preceding the act of dethronement:

> One evening young Wolowski, [...] barely a student out of school, came to see me, and, wishing to probe me as to what I thought of the present position of Poland after the news brought by Jezierski, he began to run through various means of giving what

337 L. Wołowski *Jedność, zapomnienie.*, "Orzeł Biały. Dziennik polityczny", no. 4, 14.12.1830, pp. 25–32.

338 *Dyaryusz...*, vol. I, p. 22.

339 Archiwum Głowne Akt Dawnych (Central Archives of Historical Records, Sejm and Senate of the Duchy of Warsaw and the Congress Kingdom, ref. 19, c. 19.

340 N. Jaruga *Formacje wojskowe akademików warszawskich w roku 1830 i 1831,* [in:] W. Tokarz (ed.) *Studia z dziejów Warszawy 1830–1831,* Warszawa 1937, p. 219. Antoni Ostrowski later wrote about Wołowski becoming a captain in the Warsaw national guard on 26 December – but it seems that he may have been referring to a different Wołowski (A. Ostrowski *Pamiętnik z czasów powstania listopadowego,* Wrocław – Warszawa – Kraków 1961, p. 206).

341 J.I. Kraszewski *Ludwik Wołowski....*

342 Archiwum Główne Akta Dawnych, Central Government of the Uprising 1830/31, ref. 648–658, c. 13.

> might be an auspicious direction to the revolution. But when he asked me if I would advise the nation, or rather its representation, to declare the throne *pro vacante*, I thought he was crazy, especially when he elaborated to me the reasons that as long as the Russian emperor sits on the throne, no one will volunteer as a candidate. When the throne is vacant, we will have plenty of competent people. I noticed that this crazy thought had not grown in his head alone, but he had borrowed it from someone and was only sent home to examine the elders. As I found it offensive, he fell silent, excusing himself, that it was only a thought which needed to be considered[343].

Given the role subsequently played on 25 January by Franciszek Wołowski, it seems very likely that Louis was sent to Koźmian precisely by no one else but his father.

Louis Wolowski's political activity in Warsaw ended abruptly in August 1831. At that time, he was appointed Secretary of the Polish diplomatic mission in Paris.

Apart from his excellent command of the language, which was not uncommon at the time, it is difficult to say what prompted the 20-year-old to travel to one of Europe's major capitals. We can only speculate – perhaps it was his father's influence, or an alleged acquaintance from his school years with the heir to the throne or other Frenchmen. In any case, on 16 August 1831, Louis Wolowski returned to Paris and took up a job at the local Polish mission[344]. It was headed by General Karol Kniaziewicz and Count Ludwik Plater, assisted by Teodor Morawski, Leonard Chodźko, Stanisław Plater and two French copyists[345]. The young Wolowski certainly played a secondary role. In the documents of the Polish mission preserved in the Polish Library in Paris, there is no trace of Wolowski's influence on the initiatives or discussions undertaken by Kniaziewicz and Plater. We do know, however, that he indeed performed strictly technical tasks: writing up minutes, copying documents, etc. The note in the "Yearbook of the Historical and Literary Society" also states that, with the help of the Prince of Orléans, he "established certain relations with the court". This seems doubtful, though not out of the question. Be that as it may, Kniaziewicz and Plater were satisfied with Wolowski's activities. When the mission's activities ended, they gave him a written testimonial in which, among other things, mention was made of his "exemplary attitude" and "zealous conduct", thanks to which he gained their recognition[346].

However, by the time Wolowski arrived in Paris, the Uprising was being suppressed. The military turning point was undoubtedly the defeat of the Polish army at Ostrołęka on 26 May 1831[347]. In mid-July the Russians crossed the Vistula,

---

343 K. Koźmian *Pamiętniki,* vol. III, Wrocław – Warszawa – Kraków – Gdańsk 1972, p. 300.

344 Biblioteka Polska w Paryżu, ref. BPP 360/1623.

345 I. Rusinowa *Generał Karol Otto Kniaziewicz,* Pułtusk-Warszawa 2019, p. 175

346 Biblioteka Polska w Paryżu, ref. BPP 360/361.

347 As Tokarz wrote of Ostrołęka, "It deprived not only Skrzynecki, but the entire Polish command of its final self-confidence." The Russian army, on the other hand, regained

and on 31 July they occupied Łowicz, approaching Warsaw from the west. The response of some of Warsaw's population was the events of 15–16 August 1831: a mutiny, extrajudicial punishment of some suspected "traitors", and the murder of 34 people[348]. As a result, on 17 August, the government of Prince Adam Czartoryski fell (he took refuge in Ołtarzewo), and the new one was headed by General Jan Krukowiecki. On 6 September, the Russians stormed Warsaw, and two days later the city capitulated. On 5 October, the remnants of the Polish army crossed the Prussian border and laid down their arms. Three days later, the fortress in Modlin fell, while on October 21, the last insurgent city – Zamość – surrendered.

Wolowski could only follow the events from afar. It is not known how he reacted to the news of the August hangings; we can assume that his reaction must have been similar to his father's, unambiguously negative[349]. In fact, never – including his later years in France – did he have any sympathy for revolutionary violence.

For the time being, the recent law student was probably taking diplomacy lessons alongside Kniaziewicz and Plater in a hopeless situation. Although the Poles met regularly with Foreign Minister Horace Sébastiani, absolutely nothing came of these meetings. They were unable to obtain an audience with King Louis-Philippe because, as Sébastiani stated, it would have been "against the relations we have with Russia"[350]. As late as in August 1831, Plater and Kniaziewicz were still presenting the military situation in Poland to the French in the brightest possible colours in order to induce Louis-Philippe's government to adopt a more proactive policy on the Polish issue. Unfortunately, the ministerial majority, headed by Prime Minister Casimir Périer, was strongly opposed to it. The latter, clearly the strongest figure on the French political scene, stated very emphatically during a parliamentary debate that France intended to abide by the Vienna Treaties and had no intention of interfering in Polish affairs, scaring deputies with the vision of another great European war[351]. This line, by the way, was also much to Sébastiani's liking. As Andrzej Zahorski writes, Warsaw's representatives remained in contact with the parliamentary opposition and hoped for the fall of a government

---

it, as well as the initiative on the ground. "It is becoming apparent to all that sooner or later its heavy machinery [...] will defeat the uprising just as it defeated us in 1792 and 1794." (W. Tokarz *Wojna polsko-rosyjska 1830 i 1831,* Warszawa 1994, p. 356).

348 T. Łepkowski *Warszawska rebelia sierpniowa 1831 r.,* [in:] W. Zajewski (ed.) *Powstanie Listopadowe...,* pp. 288–296.

349 Franciszek Wołowski, together with Aleksander Jełowicki, began to write the Sejm's proclamation to the people, condemning the Warsaw hangings. However, calm was fairly quickly restored in the city, so it was not published (A. Jełowicki *Moje wspomnienia...,* p. 312; *Życie ś.p. Franciszka Wołowskiego...,* p. 16).

350 Quoted from I. Rusinowa *Generał Karol Otto Kniaziewicz,* p. 174.

351 C. Périer *Opinions et discours de M. Casimir Périer,* vol. III, Paris 1838, pp. 410–411.

hostile to the Polish cause, but these hopes proved to be vain[352]. Moreover, Périer represented the mindset of many Frenchmen – otherwise sympathetic to the suffering Poles, but not inclined to participate in the wider conflict. The last important document and a kind of summary of all Polish diplomatic activity in Paris was the note handed over to Sébastiani on 3 September 1831 (the minutes of the meeting preceding its sending were drawn up by Wolowski). In it, Plater and Kniaziewicz once again presented to the Minister their actions, appeals and requests sent to the French Government, to conclude bitterly: "In spite of all these efforts on the part of the signatories [...], nothing, absolutely nothing, could influence the behaviour of the French Cabinet towards Poland". In the first paragraph, however, they emphasised: "from our side we spared no effort, neither pleas nor insistence, and it will not be our fault if [...] Poland, drenched in the blood of her brave sons, is once again lost to Europe and freedom"[353]. The last sentence also summed up the efforts of both the entire mission, which ended at the end of October 1831, and of Louis Wolowski himself. Thus, the Polish phase of his life was definitively coming to an end, and the French one was beginning.

352 A. Zahorski *Część I. Historia dyplomacji polskiej (1795–1831),* [in:] L. Bazylow (red.) *Historia dyplomacji polskiej*, vol. III, *1795–1918*, Warszawa 1982, pp. 197–199.

353 K. Kniaziewicz, L. Plater *Nota podana hr. Sebastjan dnia 3 września 1831 r.*, [in:] „Rocznik Towarzystwa Historyczno-Literackiego w Paryżu", r. 1866, Paryż 1867, pp. 70–74.

Chapter III: Immigrant, Lawyer, Professor

1. Immigrant choices

For Wolowski, since the very beginning staying in Paris must have been a completely obvious choice. He certainly had no reason to return to Poland. As a participant in Wysocki's conspiracy, he could expect from the Russian authorities only arrest if not capital punishment. The subsequent actions of the Russians confirmed this apprehension. The young Wolowski was accused of "inciting resistance", and eventually sentenced *in absentia* to ten years' heavy imprisonment[354].

Nor did he have anything or anyone to return to: he left no family behind, he was single, and his father with his mother, sister and brother Kazimierz were soon to join him in Paris. Lack of money was undoubtedly an inconvenience accompanying the emigration. As secretary of the Polish mission, on 19 October 1831, he asked Kniaziewicz for financial assistance[355]. Only that Wolowski could expect Russian repressions to extend to family assets (as it happened) – money was therefore not a factor attracting him to Poland, either.

Added to this was the obvious fact that Paris, with a population of about 800,000, the capital of a wealthy country, offered a lawyer with a command of French and knowledge of the local relations incomparably greater career opportunities than provincial, defeated Warsaw.

The decision to remain in Paris was probably taken very quickly. It is even possible that the family had considered it at the time of his departure for the City of Lights in early August 1831. It is an equally possible conjecture that the Wołowskis took into consideration the Uprising's defeat. After all, the return of the Russians posed a dire threat to Franciszek, while Louis' stay in France's capital offered a potentially convenient starting point. Perhaps, the thought of possible emigration had already occurred to the Wołowskis somewhat earlier.

---

354 The indictment: E.A. Poklękowski *Akt oskarżenia...*, p. 132; the sentence: "Tygodnik Petersburski. Gazeta urzędowa Królestwa Polskiego", 1834, no. 89.

355 Biblioteka Polska w Paryżu, ref. BPP 360, p. 23. In his letter, Wolowski mentioned that he did not receive any remuneration either in Warsaw or for two months of his activity in Paris. He also referred to a promise made by the Minister of Foreign Affairs that he would receive help if needed. Interestingly, the tone of the letter gave the impression that its author was ashamed of his own words: "This is the first time I have asked for something, please forgive me if I am getting on with it so clumsily," – he wrote (in French).

Another factor was probably at play: in France, no one knew about the family's origins. Franciszek's son must have heard about the anti-Semitic campaign launched against his father a few months earlier. Presumably, he was aware of all the informal constraints arising from the Frankist past. Meanwhile, in France, all these barriers were disappearing. Not least because no one in Paris was interested in the origin of the Wołowski family. Equally important was the attitude of the French towards Jews in general. According to Gilbert Roos, a historian of the Jewish community in France, the years of the July Monarchy were among the best in the diaspora's history. Catholicism ceased to be the state religion, which meant, among other things, that it was put on an equal footing with other faiths, including Judaism. This resulted, for example, in similar funding rules for all. Jews were also admitted to almost all professions. Apart from parts of Lorraine, Napoleon's so-called "disgraceful decree", according to which no Jew was allowed to trade without special permission from the prefect, ceased to apply. Although – and this is important in the context of Wolowski's later activities – Jews were traditionally still accused of usury, the economic and mental changes that were taking place changed the perception of usury into a simple loan. Roos adds that throughout this period, the sense of intolerance and rejection among French Jews, especially the urban elite, was clearly diminishing, replaced by attachment to France: by the late 1830s and the 1840s, the patriotism of French Jews was no longer doubtful. Characteristic was the mass appearance of tricolour illustrations on Jewish pennants[356]. Describing the history of the Jewish commune of Paris, François Lustman points out that after 1830, French public and intellectual life was enriched by an unprecedented number of eminently capable Jewish figures. They included bankers: brothers Isaac and Émile Pereire, Olinde Rodrigues; scientists like Michel Lévy, president of the Academy of Medicine since 1857 and, towards the end of his life, chief military physician of France and one of the first examples of a brilliant military career among French Jews; Léon Halévy, son of Élie, professor of literature and director at the Ministry of Education; Jacques Fromental Halévy, his brother, also a former professor and composer of opera. The most famous name in French theatre was Rachel, or Elisabeth Rachel Félix, a daughter

---

356 G. Roos *Les Juifs de France sous la Monarchie de Juillet*, Paris 2007. Roos admits that anti-Semitism did not disappear during Louis-Philippe's reign. It was largely linked to the anti-Orleans, traditionalist, and legitimist right wing. In 1840, during the Middle East crisis, it was the legitimist press that accused Rotschild of corrupting ministers and working against France. In Alsace, the hub of the French Jewish communities, anti-Semitic riots and tumults broke out from time to time; this old Alsatian anti-Semitism emerged again strongly in 1848. The historian stresses, however, that in the 1830s and 1840s, manifestations of violence against Jews were severely punished by the state, and the Jews could feel protected by the law and the apparatus of repression.

of Alsatian Jews. Adolphe (Isaac Jacob) Crémieux was a prominent politician and republican minister of justice in 1848. According to Lustman, at the end of the July Monarchy there were about 10,000 Jews living in Paris, in 1861 almost 15,000. From 1830 onwards, they faced no persecution or anti-Semitic excesses. In fact, the situation did not change until the first decade of the Third Republic[357].

It is not surprising that Louis Wolowski found his feet in France and in Paris. Nor is it surprising that he ultimately adopted a different strategy from his father in his dealings with Jews and issues related to his Jewish roots, Jews or Judaism. In 1831, Franciszek Wołowski clearly distanced himself from Jews. Louis Wolowski no longer had to. He simply did not take part in any discussions concerning Jews or Judaism. During my research for this book, I did not come across even a short mention or remark by Wolowski on this issue[358].

This silence had the effect probably desired by Wolowski – in none of the polemics or discussions, political or economic, in which he participated, was there an allusion to his origins. While the French remembered perfectly well that he was from Poland, they were apparently unaware of his family's roots. Nor did any of his 19th-century biographers mention the Wołowski ancestry[359].

On the other hand, his origin was well-remembered in Paris… by his compatriots, both close to him and immigrants completely unrelated to him. The former included Ksawery Branicki, a friend who worked closely with Louis Wolowski since the 1850s. Jadwiga Zamoyska later recalled that "Mr Ksawery Branicki used to say, because of the numerous tributes he [Wolowski] received: 'He does not care about what they say about him in Paris, but he must rejoice at what the Jews in

---

357 F. Lustman *De l'émancipation a l'antisémitisme: Histoire de la communauté juive de Paris 1789–1880*, Paris 2006.

358 The only text linking Wołowski in any way to the Jews is a short note from the *Allgemeine Zeitung des Judenthums*, No. 2, 04.01.1838, according to which he was to donate 24,000 francs to the Chief Rabbi of Paris, together with Mr Koreff, for the benefit of poor Jews. It is not known, however, which of the Wolowskis is mentioned. Moreover, the sum seems too high for Louis' financial capabilities at the time.

359 At the time in Warsaw, the memory of the Frankists was still vivid, both among Poles and Jews. This is evidenced by Adolf Jellinek's 1882 text *Nachkommen von Frankisten in Warschau* ("Das Judische Literaturblatt", no. 27, 05.07.1882). Based on an account by Ignatius Bernstein, a librarian, Jellinek described "significant and numerous families commonly known to be descended from Frankists". He listed the Brzezińskis, Jasińskis, Krysińskis, Majewskis, Piotrowskis and Wołowskis. Bernstein, however, argued that they had completely departed from the old customs and "no greater insult could be done to them than to remind them of their Jewish origin".

Nalewki Street in Warsaw are saying about him'"[360]. It should be noted, however, that Branicki was certainly not an anti-Semite; the words quoted by Zamoyska were probably only meant as a humorous reminder of Wolowski's background[361]. A background of which the regulars of the Mickiewicz couple were also necessarily aware. Józef Bohdan Zaleski, after a sojourn with Mickiewicz, wrote on 03 August 1851: "Interesting things [Mickiewicz] said about the Frankists, with whom he had the opportunity of coming into contact through his wife. They have strayed far from Frank, yet they carry on the tradition of his prophecies about Poland. The Rzewuskis are also of Israelite origin"[362]. The group of Frankists must have included above all Celina's closest Parisian relatives, the Wołowskis, who were otherwise well known to Zaleski.

Neither Zaleski nor Branicki, however, intended to reproach Louis his background. This was not, however, the rule. Józef Alfons Potrykowski, an emigrant completely unknown to Wolowski, who followed his activities in the press, noted in his diary with a distinct note of malice in July 1854: "'Le Siècle', 'La Presse' and other dailies advertise Mr Wolowski, a Polish representative [Potrykowski confused Louis with Franciszek – RD] and ex-Pole, a former French representative, ex-Jew, etc., etc."[363]. However, as I mentioned earlier, the memory of Wolowski's Jewish ancestors did not go beyond the émigré milieu.

Louis Wolowski's Frankist roots are inseparable from his faith and religious practices. Did the Wołowskis really, as Mickiewicz told Zaleski, "conceal the tradition of Frank's prophecies about Poland"? Did they retain any elements of Frankism? The answer to these questions seems simple: no, with one important caveat. Almost nothing in the life of Louis Wolowski or those closest to him points any longer to any links with the religious tradition of Frankism. The cult had clearly been in decline for some time. Maciejko is probably right that among the descendants of Jacob Frank's disciples, "The orgiastic elements were replaced by traditional Christian morality. The radical strands of Frank's teaching were

360 J. Zamoyska *Jadwiga Zamoyska między Londynem a Stambułem. Wspomnień część II*, Kórnik 2014, p. 90. „Nalewki" was the name of a commonly known Jewish street in Warsaw.

361 In her biography of Ksawery Branicki, Julia Słupska writes unequivocally that Branicki was a firm opponent of anti-Semitism and an advocate of equal rights for Jews with Poles (J. Słupska *Ksawery Branicki (1816–1879). Emigracja: polityka i finanse*, Warszawa 2008, p. 104).

362 J.B. Zaleski *Dzienniki Józefa Bohdana Zaleskiego z lat 1851–1857, 1859, 1861*, vol. I, *Dziennik z 1851 r.*, Biblioteka Jagiellońska, BJ Rkp. 9160 I vol. 1, p. 60; K. Kostenicz *Ostatnie lata Mickiewicza, styczeń 1850 – 26 listopada 1855*, Warszawa 1978, "Kronika życia i twórczości Mickiewicza", p. 115.

363 J. A. Potrykowski *Tułactwo Polaków we Francji. Dziennik emigranta*, vol. II, Kraków 1974, p. 83.

suppressed, and the group eventually turned into a kind of self-help society in which contacts made in the sect were used for business"[364]. This description fits Tekla and Franciszek Wołowski and their children very well. Tekla was undoubtedly a deeply religious person. This is evident even in her *History of Poland.* For example, in her surprisingly positive assessment of the Crusades: "The place where the Son of Mary redeemed the human race became once again the place of a new salvation, the religion of sincere worshippers of faith guided to the right path"[365]. In this context, I find it hard to agree with the reflections of Abraham Duker[366], and subsequently with Jadwiga Maurer[367]. Duker (and Maurer) attempt to convince readers that Celina Mickiewicz was a Frankist and, more broadly, so was the Wołowski clan. To confirm their theory, they cite the lack of Catholic references in Tekla Wołowska's correspondence. That is all very well but the quoted "correspondence" is limited to... one letter from Tekla to Celina from 1839. Duker also completely disregards the fact that the Wołowskis belonged to the Polish Catholic elite but at the same time, they were representatives of the late Enlightenment. This is reflected both in Franciszek's tests and speeches and in Tekla's *History...* Their way of thinking and communicating was not significantly different from other representatives of the same Enlightenment generation. Duker's other arguments – the alleged Frankist references in Celina's correspondence with Julia Wołowska – are equally unconvincing[368] as is the argument repeated by Maurer – the lack of specifically Christian expressions in Celina's letters[369]. Duker and Maurer adopted a rather arbitrary definition of what is or is not specifically Christian: references to God, the Most Holy, the Eternal, etc. in the absence of references to Christ or Mary are, in Duker and Maurer's view, Frankist indications. Similarly, the excerpt from Władysław Mickiewicz's 1861 memoirs from Warsaw, quoted by Duker as

---

364 P. Maciejko *Wieloplemienny tłum...*, p. 332.

365 T. Wołowska *Historya...*, p. 135.

366 A. Duker *Polish Frankism's Duration: From Cabbalistic Judaism to Roman Catholicism and from Jewishness to Polishness,* [in:] "Jewish Social Studies", no. 25 (4), 1963.

367 J. Maurer *Celina Szymanowska as a Frankist,* [in:] "The Polish Review", vol. XXXIV, no. 4, 1989; J. Maurer *"Z matki obcej..." Szkice o powiązaniach Mickiewicza ze światem Żydów,* London 1990.

368 J. Maurer *"Z matki obcej..."*, p. 323. The matter concerns the following excerpt from Celina's letter to her aunt, Julia Wołowska: "I sometimes bitterly reproach myself that I did not know how to judge you in the past, and that I was the cause of so much suffering and persecution for your true and quiet but sincere religion." (W. Mickiewicz Moja matka..., pp. 50–51). Duker perceives this "true and silent but sincere religion" as a reference to implicit Frankism. Meanwhile, this passage can be read as a description of Julia's specific piety.

369 J. Maurer *"Z matki obcej..."*, pp. 323–328; J. Maurer *Celina Szymanowska as a Frankist...*, p. 344.

further evidence of the memory of Frankist ideas among the Wołowskis, does not appeal to me. The poet's son wrote: "One aunt of mine [...] with a face as shiny as a freshly whitewashed and cleaned saucepan, suffered from an excess of sentimentality, to which I fell victim during my first stay with her. She took me by the hand, led me from the drawing-room to a side room, asked me in an emotional voice to remember her, and, kissing me gently, slipped a ring on my finger"[370]. In this case, the interested party's own interpretation indicating the old lady's sentimentality seems simpler and more accurate to me.

Ultimately, in my opinion, the Wołowskis appear as a fairly typical bourgeois family of the mid-19th century: believers but not zealots, critical of the political or legal demands of the Church. Suffice it to mention the attitude of Franciszek Wołowski towards the issue of divorce.

Moreover, Duker and Maurer completely disregarded Kazimierz Wołowski, Louis' brother. Meanwhile, he was an important figure in this context, as the author of *Méditations religieuses* [Religious Meditations][371]. Written after the death of his beloved wife, the book contained chapters on "the royal way of the Holy Cross", "the love of God", "the love of Jesus" and an appeal: "Let us submit ourselves to the teaching of the holy Catholic Church, which only communicates to us the truths given by Jesus Christ himself"[372]. It is, moreover, characteristic that this sentence found its way into the chapter on the relationship between faith and reason. In fact, Kazimierz, unlike his brother and father, subordinated reason to Revelation and the Church, in accordance with the teaching of Pius IX. If any member of the Wołowski clan was close to religious bigotry, it was probably him. On the other hand, he did not fit in at all with the thesis of the family's hidden Frankist sympathies.

In comparison to Kazimierz, Louis Wolowski's religiosity seemed exceptionally discreet. He made no direct mention of God, Christ, or salvation either in his works or the surviving correspondence. With a few minor exceptions, however, we can assume that he was a convinced Catholic. Wolowski undoubtedly sympathised with the Italian national movement during the Revolutions of 1848 and beyond. However, he was also in favour of maintaining the temporal power of the Pope. Indeed, as he wrote to Antonio Scialoja, a former minister in the revolutionary

370 W. Mickiewicz *Pamiętniki...*, p. 429.

371 C. Wolowski *Méditations religieuses,* Paris 1863.

372 C. Wolowski *Méditations religieuses...*, p. 219. At the same time, however, Kazimierz Wołowski sought to disassociate himself from religious intolerance and fanaticism, claiming that they were fundamentally non-Catholic: "As devout and fervent Catholics, we daily address our prayers to the Most High to convert the heretics and enlighten the infidels. We do not wish to persecute or oppress our opponents, whom we love as brothers. [...] The Holy Church, guardian of the teaching of the Gospel, rejects intolerance and fanaticism more than anyone."

government of Naples: "Please do not forget the respect due to the Holy Father and the ties that bind him to the hearts of the entire Catholic world. Thanks to the Pope, Italy still dominates the World, overthrowing his temporal power the country would abdicate itself, it would become a secondary power, because it is not matter but moral influence that ensures primacy, not even mentioning the duties indicated by religion"[373]. While still a deputy of the Second Republic, in 1849 Wolowski voted in favour of the so-called Rome expedition: the occupation of the then revolutionary Rome by the French army and the surrender of power in the city to the Pope[374]. At the same time, he remained an advocate of a clear separation of Church and State. In 1860, during a discussion at the Academy of Moral and Political Sciences, he criticised the pre-revolutionary French Church, which had, in his view, become an absolute organisation. Wolowski pointed out, that the discipline and morality of the Church were then clearly on a decline. Wolowski also claimed that in earlier times the kings, together with the French bishops and the Sorbonne, had defended the independence of the French Church against the pope's designs. This was supposedly due to the French mentality. The peculiarities of the French Reformation were also supposed to stem from it.

By contrast, according to Wolowski, the post-revolutionary Church was an entirely new organisation, rebuilt after the Concordat of 1801 on the ruins of the old one. In this new Church, however, the position of the Pope was much stronger and his influence on the souls of the French was also incomparably more significant. However, the concordat, which survived the fall of Napoleon, secured the independence of the royal power. At the time, Wolowski also conclusively acknowledged that the independence of power in temporal matters was one of the most important achievements of the modern age. At the same time, it also had to guarantee the freedom of the Church in relation to the state: in this context, Wolowski harshly criticised the Russian Orthodox Church which had "stooped to the role of a political instrument and become a blind helper of absolute power"[375]. Thus, although Louis Wolowski never publicly used Charles de Montalembert's famous words about a "free Church in a free State", this is in fact how he saw the relationship between religion and power.

---

373 J. I. Kraszewski *Korespondencja Józefa Ignacego Kraszewskiego. Seria III: Listy z lat 1844–1862,* vol. 23, Wo – Wy (Wojakowska – Wyziński), Biblioteka Jagiellońska, BJ Rkp. 6481 IV. The letter is not dated but the context suggests it must have been written in 1860.

374 A. Robert, E. Bourloton, E. Cougny *Dictionnaire des parlementaires français...: depuis le 1er mai 1789 jusqu'au 1er mai 1889...,* vol. V, *Pla-Zuy,* Paris 1891, p. 565.

375 L. Wolowski *Rapport verbal sur un ouvrage de M. Blüntschli intitulé: Dictionnaire politique,* "Séances et Travaux de l'Académie des Sciences Morales et Politiques", vol. I (LI), Paris 1860, pp. 296–298.

Adding to these thoughts is the fact that all Wolowski's children were baptised.

There is one more aspect of the decision to stay in Paris that is worth noting: apparently, since the beginning, Wolowski did not believe in a rapid return to Poland and did not consider it. In this respect, he differed significantly from most emigrants[376]. This was evidenced by his conduct.

Almost immediately after the fall of the Uprising, Wolowski returned to his law studies, interrupted in November 1830. He started them at the University of Warsaw and finished at the Sorbonne. Studying law in Paris subsequently opened the possibility of a brilliant career in France. The education was, moreover, slightly different, more modern as it seems, than in Warsaw. The Paris law faculty was divided into two sections, and studies took three years. Throughout this time, all future lawyers listened to lectures on the Civil Code, while students in each year group also studied natural law, the law of nations, Roman law, criminal law, administrative law, commercial law, civil procedure, and criminal procedure, as well as the history of philosophy[377]. Wolowski was credited with part of his studies from Warsaw[378], an accelerated procedure was also allowed, so that he eventually completed his bachelor's degree within a year. The defence of the bachelor's thesis took place on 30 August 1832 before a commission headed by Pierre-Paul Royer-Collard, a member of the French Academy, one of France's most famous politicians and thinkers at the time, and a leading figure of the conservative-liberal doctrinaire party. Wolowski's dissertation traditionally consisted of two parts. The first, 7 pages long and written in Latin, was entitled *Ius Romanum. De Pignoribus et Hypothecis* (Roman law. On liens and mortgages). The other part, more extensive and written in French, was devoted to mortgages in the light of the contemporary French law. It heralded Wolowski's later interests and work, and in part his banking activities. It began with a sentence that sums up Wolowski's economic thought throughout his life: "Credit is the most powerful source of society's prosperity"[379]. Wolowski went on to point out the weakness of the French credit system due to the flawed design of the loan security, namely the mortgage[380]. The dissertation, like the defence, was clearly to the committee's liking. The final exam was preceded by two previous exams; after each of them the committee members voted using

376 Sławomir Kalembka covers the belief of Poles in the possibility of returning to a free country and the associated reluctance to assimilate in France or England (*Wielka Emigracja 1831–1863,* Toruń 2003, pp. 245–248).

377 G. Antonetti *La Faculté de droit de Paris à l'époque où Boissonade y faisait ses études,* [in:] "Revue internationale de droit comparé", no. 43 (2), 1991, pp. 337–342.

378 A. Roulliet *Wolowski...,* p. 16.

379 L. Wolowski *Thèse pour la licence,* Paris 1832, p. 10.

380 L. Wolowski *Thèse pour la licence...,* pp. 15–32.

white, red, and black balls, signifying approval, abstention, and a negative vote, respectively. Roulliet wrote: "Although his examiners did not award him 'all the white balls', he was missing so little that it is not worth mentioning. Indeed, he received four white balls, with a commendation, in his first exam, four white balls and one red ball in his second exam and, finally, five white balls (a commendation) in his undergraduate exam." Reportedly, one of the examiners, having subsequently met the young undergraduate outside the faculty building, told him that he was passing at doctoral level[381]. In fact, according to the system of the time, Wolowski could have continued his studies and just finished with a doctorate. However, he chose not to do so. We can only assume that it was for financial reasons. Wolowski was probably keen to become independent of his family as quickly as possible and to earn his own income.

The title of Bachelor of Law enabled him to take up the practice of law. As early as in 1832, Wolowski took up a job at the law office of Désiré Dalloz, an eminent lawyer. Dalloz was a widely known figure, an advocate at the Paris Court of Cassation. In the 1820s, he was associated with the liberal opposition and took part in the July Revolution of 1830. He made a name for himself as a defender in political trials and (with his brother) as the creator and co-author of "Jurisprudence générale du royaume en matière civile, commerciale et criminelle", a key legal periodical, published since 1824. Later (1845) he also became the founder of a law publishing house bearing his name that has survived to this day[382]. Dalloz's law firm was one of the best in Paris and was certainly an excellent practice for a budding barrister. In a letter to the Minister of Justice, in 1834, Dalloz spoke highly of Wolowski's work. He wrote of his zeal, extensive education, superior intelligence and good knowledge of legislation and command of the German language. He also pointed out that "Mr Wolowski is one of my most outstanding colleagues"[383]. Unofficially, however, he also expressed a different opinion. In 1833, Joachim Lelewel wrote in one of his letters to Ostrowski: "The solicitor with whom Wolowski works came recently from Paris. [...] When the Governor [Ostrowski] sees his father Franciszek, he should thank him for recommending me well to the barrister and say that the barrister admires the aptitude of his son (supposedly Louis!) and is content with him, only has him a little too reckless and occupied by something else"[384]. However, it is easy to understand that in 1833, the young Wolowski

381 A. Roulliet *Wolowski...*, pp. 16–17.

382 More on the subject: T. Ravel (de) d'Esclapon *Désiré Dalloz – Vivre le droit,* Paris 2019.

383 Letter from D. Dalloz in support of Wolowski's naturalisation, Archives Nationales, ref. BB/11/338, dossier 237x2.

384 J. Lelewel *Listy emigracyjne Joachima Lelewela*, vol. V *Dodatek 1831–1860,* Kraków 1956, p. 94.

was occupied by "something else", namely his wedding and the beginnings of his married life.

Wolowski also intended to enrol himself on the Paris list of lawyers. However, the question of citizenship stood in the way: to become a lawyer in Paris, the Pole had to have full civil rights (in other words, take French citizenship)[385]. In early 1833, even if Wolowski obtained the right to reside in France, this proved insufficient. Finally, on 8 February 1834, he made an official request for naturalisation to the French authorities[386].

This is the second argument that clearly supports the thesis that Louis Wolowski had no thoughts of returning to Poland and may not have intended to do so at all. In fact, his naturalisation dossier contains some interesting information. Firstly, and this was a source of some confusion among French officials, Ludwik Wołowski became oficially Louis Wolowski. In fact, he explained this change in the spelling of his surname by the simple fact that the French generally read the Polish "ł" as a "t"[387]. Secondly, Wolowski asked the Minister of Justice to waive the administrative fees associated with the naturalisation procedure, justifying this with the limited resources available to him[388]. Thirdly, Wolowski was, of course, thoroughly vetted by the police before receiving his citizenship; they asked the opinion of the mayor of the 11th arrondissement of Paris where Wolowski was living at the time. The police report could read, among other things, that he resided at 39 Vaugirard Street and that "his moral and political conduct did not raise any objections"[389]. More interesting was the opinion of the mayor, who claimed, among other things, that

> He married a Frenchwoman who will soon make him a father. His family is one of the most prominent in Poland. His father was elected to the Sejm. Wolowski son, in turn, was secretary to the Polish embassy. Despite the sequestration imposed on paternal property, the family still owns property and Ms Wołowski, the petitioner's mother, has retained the right to dispose of her personal fortune, which is quite substantial. Mr Wolowski's conduct and morals are excellent. He combines an uncommon education with an exceptional spirit and character. His political views,

---

385 This is evident, among other things, from a letter from the Prefect of the Seine, Pierre-Marie Taillepied de Bondy, to the Minister of Justice, dated 26.10.1832, found in Wolowski's naturalisation dossier, Archives Nationales, ref. BB/11/338, dossier 237x2.

386 Letter from Wolowski to the Minister of Justice, 10.02.1834, Archives Nationales, ref. BB/11/338, dossier 237x2.

387 The Prefect's letter of 26.10.1832, Archives Nationales, ref. BB/11/338, dossier 237x2.

388 Letter from Wolowski to the Minister of Justice of 30 January 1835, Archives Nationales, ref. BB/11/338, dossier 237x2.

389 Letter from the inspector of police of the Luxembourg district to the mayor dated 20 February 1834, Archives de Paris, ref. VD6 624, dossier 9, p. 88.

like those of his entire family, are remarkably moderate. It seems, Mr Prefect, that no one more worthy of naturalisation than he is [...][390].

On 25 January 1833, Wolowski obtained the right to reside in France[391]. The citizenship he asked for was finally granted by royal decree on 19 December 1834[392]. Importantly, in no way was this act meant to erase Wolowski's Polish origin. He never turned his back on his compatriots, he never forgot his Polish roots. The speech he gave on the 17th anniversary of the outbreak of the November Uprising, on 29 November 1847, at the invitation of General Dwernicki, to a gathering of Polish émigrés and their French friends, reflects his attitude and national feeling. He spoke about himself and the children he raised on French soil. Finally, he added: "France has bestowed citizenship on me and, I can say it here, I am happy and proud of it, because she has allowed me to serve her in this way, and is not the service of France a continuation of the service of Poland? The same ideas, the same feelings, the same aspirations animate the spirit of both nations; the future of Poland is linked to the future of France for the happiness and freedom of the world"[393]. Wolowski's biography indicates that his words were sincere. He persisted in this attitude of attachment and devotion to his two homelands for the rest of his life[394].

Notably, this no longer applied to his daughter. She received French upbringing; Wolowski's assumption must have been that she would remain French. Andrzej Koźmian recalled in 1861: "Wolowski's wife and daughter, not speaking Polish, French women not Poles, returned from Warsaw fanatics of

390 Letter from the mayor of the 11th district to the prefect of Rambuteau, 21.02.1834, Archives de Paris, ref. Vbis6D2 25, file no. 18863. Tekla's "personal fortune", mentioned by the prefect, was probably another way to avoid Russian sanctions.

391 *Collection complète des lois, décrets, ordonnances, réglemens, et avis du Conseil-d'États*, vol. 33, Paris 1833, p. 9.

392 *Collection complète des lois, décrets, ordonnances, réglemens, et avis du Conseil-d'États*, vol. 34, Paris 1834, p. 302.

393 L. Wolowski *Discours prononcé au 17 anniversaire de la Révolution polonaise (29 novembre 1847)*, Paris 1848, p. 2.

394 According to Jerzy W. Borejsza, who repeated the argumentation of Armand Lévy, Mickiewicz's secretary, Wolowski's attitude affected the author of *Pan Tadeusz*. In Borejsza's words: "From the statements by Mickiewicz noted down by Lévy, one can conclude that the poet, when applying for French citizenship, was not only thinking about arranging his life in exile. His attitude does not lack that appreciation, veneration for France or conviction of its historic mission, which radiated from the activities of Ksawery Branicki, born and naturalised in Paris, and who was close to the poet, or from the Wołowski clan – the family of Celina Mickiewicz" (J. W. Borejsza *Armand Lévy i jego czasy 1827–1891*, Gdańsk 2005, p. 98).

Poland"[395]. There is also no indication that his only (surviving) daughter became involved in Polish affairs in any way.

Shortly after his naturalisation, Wolowski, a Pole and a Frenchman, enrolled on the Paris list of lawyers[396].

A little earlier, two more significant changes had taken place in his life. Both, in fact, could have contributed to the positive response of the authorities to his application for naturalisation. Firstly, as has already been mentioned several times, Wolowski got married. Secondly, he founded his own periodical.

Louis Wolowski's wedding is one of the more mysterious events in his life. Not only because, in view of the small number of surviving letters, we know nothing about Wolowski's agenda or the efforts preceding the marriage. Also, because the wedding was perhaps the only distinctly Frankist accent in his life. Although it is probably safe to assume that tradition was not the decisive factor in this case, for as we know, neither his sister nor his brother married descendants of Frankists a bit later. Louis chose a Frenchwoman, descended, after all, from the Frankists. Laure Marie Guérin was born on 14 February 1814 in Paris. Her father was Henri Guérin, inspector-general of the Grand Army's posts and commander of the national guard in Egypt[397]. Laure was therefore indeed French, as the mayor of the 11th arrondissement reported. What he did not know, however, was that her mother was Katarzyna Karolina Lanckorońska, descended from the Lanckorońskis, the Frankists, with whom the Wołowskis had already been associated on several occasions. Born on 11 June 1784, she died in 1871 in Warsaw. In addition to Laure, the couple had two sons, Adam Edouard (1810–1872) and Eugène Henri (1812–1853). Both were subsequently professors of French in Warsaw[398]. The latter, incidentally, married Laura Brzezińska, niece of Maria Szymanowska (daughter of her sister Joanna), also related to the Wołowskis[399]. Louis must have

---

395 A. Koźmian *Listy Andrzeja Edwarda Koźmiana...*, vol. IV, p. 351.

396 A. Roulliet *Wolowski...*, p. 22. Citing a letter from the president of the Bar Association at the Paris Court of Appeal in 1879, Roulliet gave a probably incorrect date of 16 December 1834. Wolowski probably made the entry in the last days of 1834, but after 19 December.

397 According to the inscription on the monument in the Powązki cemetery, Henri Guérin was probably born in 1773 and died in Warsaw in 1861. According to Szenic, in 1834 he moved with his sons to Warsaw (S. Szenic *Cmentarz powązkowski 1851–1890. Zmarli i ich rodziny*, Warszawa 1982, p. 128).

398 Marriage certificate of Adam Edouard: http://www.sejm-wielki.pl/img/metrskan/1542169.jpg (retrieved 20.02.2023); marriage certificate of Eugène Henri to Laura Brzezińska: https://metryki.genealodzy.pl/index.php?op=pg&ar=1&zs=0158d&se=&sy=1845&kt=2&plik=166-167.jpg&x=847&y=1390&zoom=1.25 (retrieved 20.02.2023).

399 Laura Brzezińska Guérin (1817–1883), however, was known above all as a teacher, owner of a renowned Warsaw school for girls, educating in the Christian spirit, also

met Laure in Paris earlier, probably during his stay in the 1820s. Unfortunately, we do not know their previous relation; the only small trace here is Kraszewski's remark that Wolowski was "married out of attachment rather than money"[400]. They both belonged to the same large family circle: this is evidenced by a brief entry by Helena Malewska, née Szymanowska, in her *Diary* of 19 February 1833: "I have had letters from Warsaw. They report to us that Ludek [little Louis] is marrying Laure Guérin"[401]. It seems almost certain that the family must have taken part in the pre-marriage negotiations, not least for financial reasons. Whatever the course of the negotiations, they were successful and on 21 March 1833 Louis Michel Raymond François Wolowski and Laure Marie Clara Guérin, having signed the relevant documents at the mayor's office of the 11th arrondissement, were married in the parish of Saint-Séverin. The groom's best men were doctor Stanisław Wołowski, mentioned here before, and Stanisław Kunatt, Wolowski's professor from Warsaw. The bride's best men included Ildefons Krysiński, a doctor, an émigré of Frankist origin, and a co-founder of the Literary Society (together with Kunatt), and Antoni Andrzej Plichta[402].

One thing is certain: Louis' marriage paid off, though not necessarly financially. It seems to have ultimately played an important role as an argument in the naturalisation process. It also brought him family stability and – as one might guess – a sense of being more firmly rooted in France. As the mayor of the 11th arrondissement wrote, the couple had children very quickly. On 30 May 1834, Elisabeth Victorine Sophie Henriette Wolowski was born[403], Charles François Henri Michel Louis on 29 October 1835[404] and, finally, the youngest Françoise Marie Catherine on 04 March 1845[405]. Unfortunately, the births of the children were also accompanied by deaths. The eldest, Elisabeth, lived less than 13 years and died on 17 March 1847[406]. Charles François died at the age

emphasising the social activities of the graduates. The school operated from 1838 to 1876, when it was closed by the Russian authorities. Laura also accompanied Celina Szymanowska on her trip to Paris in 1834. (K. Cybulska *Laura Guérin (1817–1883) – zapomniane tradycje oświaty dla kobiet,* [in:] "Piotrkowskie Zeszyty Historyczne", vol. 22, part 3, 2021, pp. 43–62; I. Łapinowa *Guérin Laura (1817–1883),* [in:] *Polski Słownik Biograficzny,* vol. IX, Wrocław-Warszawa-Kraków-Gdańsk 1972, p. 138).

400 J.I. Kraszewski *Ludwik Wołowski,* op. cit.

401 H. Szymanowska-Malewska *Dziennik,* Warszawa 1999, p. 299.

402 Marriage certificate: Archives de Paris, ref. 5Mi1 2072.

403 Marriage certificate: Archives de Paris, ref. 5Mi1 403, Baptismal certificate: Archives de Paris, ref. D.6J 2281, nr 217.

404 Baptismal certificate: Archives de Paris, ref. D.6J 2283, nr 29.

405 Birth certificate: Archives de Paris, ref. 5Mi1 573.

406 Death certificate: Archives de Paris, ref. 5Mi1 1353.

of 6 months[407]. Only Françoise Marie, known in the family as "Fanny", reached maturity[408].

2. "Revue Wolowski"

The second major change in Louis Wolowski's life was a magazine he founded in the late autumn of 1834 with three other lawyers, Paul Pont, Aimé Rodière and Jean-François Sacase. Wolowski's involvement, however, was strongest. As the quoted letter to the Minister of Justice of 1835 suggests (see note 388), it was a financial and personal commitment alike. Wolowski was editor in chief of the journal. The first issue of the "Revue de législation et de jurisprudence" ("Review of legislation and jurisprudence") was printed in March 1835. The journal soon began to be abbreviated as the "Revue Wolowski", thus distinguishing it from another legal periodical, the "Revue du droit français et étranger" ("Review of French and Foreign Law") by Jean-Jacques Foelix, established around the same time. Together with the latter, Wolowski contributed, in effect, to the renewal of French law writing and thought. Wolowski's periodical was devoted by default to the study of civil, commercial, criminal, and administrative law, as well as the history and philosophy of law, doctrines, the discussion of drafts of new laws, and – as is most evident in the case of Wolowski – political economy and its relationship to legislation. Importantly, since the very beginning Wolowski managed to attract a group of extremely capable collaborators and authors. These included François André Isambert, lawyer at the tribunal of cassation in Paris; Raymond Théodore Troplong, president of one of the chambers of the tribunal in Nancy; Charles Guillaume Hello, attorney-general in Rennes; Victor Foucher, attorney-general at the tribunal in Rennes; Pierre-Ambroise Plougoulm, deputy attorney-general in Paris; counsels of state: Charles Renouard and Alexandre François Vivien (former prefect of police); deputy Louis de Cormenin: law professors Hyacinthe Blondeau, Edouard Boitard, Pierre Claude Bravard, Julien-François Oudot, Charles Auguste Pellat, Henry Perreyve, François Frédéric Poncelet, Royer-Collard, Auguste Valette, Charles Demolombe, Emile-Victor Foucart; former University of Warsaw professors Hube and Kunatt; lawyers at the Court of Cassation: Toussaint-Ange Cotelle and Dalloz; also Charles Comte and Odilon Barrot, Pont, Sacase, Antoine

---

407 H. Zaworonko-Olejniczak, B. Kłosowicz-Krzywicka, A. Biernat *En terre d'exil: tombeaux polonais dans les cimetières de Paris et de Montmorency*, Paris 2011, p. 34.

408 Little Françoise almost did not survive either. In 1859, she fell ill with typhus. According to A. Koźmian's account, Louis was then to spend four weeks at his daughter's bedside (A. E. Koźmian Letter to his family of 16.09.1859, [in:] A.E. Koźmian *Listy Andrzeja Edwarda Koźmiana*, vol. III, *Część druga i ostatnia*, Lwow 1894, p. 378).

François Vatimesnil[409]. Franciszek Wołowski also published his articles in the magazine.

However, young people prevailed: most of the authors were between thirty and forty years of age, ambitious and on the brink of a professional position. As Firmin Laferrière, author of a summary of the journal published in 1860, later emphasised, many of them carved out for themselves great legal and political careers over time[410]. The magazine went out at varying rates, from 1 to 6 issues per year. By 1853, a total of 62 issues were to be published. In 1853, however, there was a merger with the much later established "Revue critique". As a result, a new title with a similar profile appeared at that time, the "Revue critique de législation et de jurisprudence" ("Critical review of legislation and jurisprudence") which Wolowski co-managed. The "Revue de législation et de jurisprudence" earned Wolowski quickly recognition in economic and legal circles. Laferrière, inspector general of all law faculties in France, wrote: "[Mr Wolowski's] Revue de législation has opened a wide and fruitful path for the philosophy and history of French law, for administrative law, for political economy in combination with civil and administrative law"[411].

Wolowski devoted considerable time to writing. This is how Levasseur, his close associate, described his mode of work:

> He had stamina, strength and ease of pen that astonished his friends. Having devoted the whole day to business, he was always ready to spend the evening in company, without a shadow of fatigue. He reserved part of the night for work; even when he returned late, he would take up his pen and spend long hours at his desk. However, he always stayed at his home when an issue of the "Revue..." came out. On such evenings, the young editors met in his small flat on rue des Beaux Arts and, since they could not afford to pay an assistant – they would write the addresses themselves [the magazine was sent by post to subscribers – RD]. Everyone did this joyfully, and [Wolowski's] young wife, who helped them, added to the charm of these moments.[412]

The "Revue..." was also a testimony to the young lawyer's professional reorientation. For it is not difficult to conclude, analysing the titles of his own articles, that over time, Wolowski was clearly moving away from law to political economy. While others covered strictly legal issues, he wrote about joint-stock companies, the issue of credit (repeatedly) and mortgages, child labour, customs, and industry.

---

409 "Revue de législation et de jurisprudence", vol. I, Paris 1835, editorial page.

410 F. Laferrière, *Introduction* to J.B.C Coin-Delisle, Ch. Million *Tables analytiques de la "Revue de législation" et de la "Revue critique de législation et de jurisprudence": précédées des tables de la "Thémis" et de la "Revue de droit français et étranger"*, Paris 1860, pp. XXXI–XXXII.

411 F. Laferrière, *Introduction...*, p. LXII.

412 E. Levasseur *La Vie et les travaux de Wolowski...*, p. 10.

Although he approached all these topics with reference to French legislation, the "Revue..." showed increasingly the economist that Wolowski was to become, at the expense of the lawyer he was slowly ceasing to be.

There is every indication that he was simply far less interested in the law. He still worked at Dalloz's law firm on pleadings, but, as Kraszewski later claimed, it was initially difficult for him to find clients because of his nationality. Ultimately, the first trial he won earned him 1,000 francs. But the second was already to alienate him from the profession: he defended young people accused of rape. He defended them successfully and they were acquitted. Confidentially, however, one of them later admitted to Wolowski that the rape had indeed taken place[413]. This fact was to shake him up and ultimately discourage from the legal profession which he then decided to abandon. However, he certainly still visited the court – if not as a lawyer, then as an employee of a law firm[414]. Finally, in 1853, he was struck off the list of lawyers at his own request. According to Roulliet, he wore the toga very rarely[415].

Edited from 1834 onwards, the "Revue..." admittedly brought Wolowski quick recognition in legal and economic circles[416] but it did not bring in the money. The magazine, which was clearly specialist in nature, was targeted at an influential and significant but clearly limited readership. The young spouse and father therefore had to earn a living. He was still working at Dalloz's law firm at the time, but apparently the income was not enough, and he may also have been encouraged by the success of the "Revue..." In any case, in 1836 Wolowski decided to produce the "Journal Général des Tribunaux" ("General Journal of the Tribunals"). "Devoted to judicial debates, jurisprudence and legislation", it was to be published daily; the annual subscription was to cost 40 francs. The newspaper's content was to consist mainly of reports from tribunals in Paris and outside the capital city, and court reports. Wolowski, who was to be the director of the "Journal", even set up

---

413 J.I. Kraszewski *Ludwik Wołowski...*

414 This is evidenced in the memoirs of William Nassau Sr, cited by Markiewicz. Nassau (1790–1864) was a British lawyer and economist who stayed in Paris during the Revolution of 1848 and was a friend of Wolowski's. He left behind his diaries, in which he described, among other things, how he was allowed by Wolowski on 14.05.1849 to take one of the privileged seats in court at the then famous trial (P. Markiewicz *Louis Wolowski...*, p. 66; W. Nassau Senior, *Journals kept in France and in Italy,* vol. I, London 1871, p. 131).

415 A. Roulliet *Wolowski...*, p. 216. Roulliet refers here again to the quoted letter of 1879 from the President of the Bar Association of the Paris Court of Appeal.

416 It is characteristic, for example, that Jules Michelet and Charles de Montalembert, two eminent French intellectuals, asked Wolowski by letter to publish a review of their books in the "Revue..." (both letters undated, State Archive in Kraków, ref. AKPot 3204).

a limited partnership to finance the paper[417]. On 1 November 1836, the first issue of the journal was published. After a few months, however, Wolowski's paper was absorbed by the competing, older and financially stronger "Le Droit"[418].

Louis Wolowski then began working with another well-known journalistic brand, "Le Siècle". Starting in 1837, for the next ten years he reported for the newspaper on the sittings of the two Houses. According to Roulliet, it was "a thankless job, very tiring then as now, bringing little profit and even less prestige as the author remained unknown"[419]. Wolowski therefore had to attend Chambers meetings regularly and maintain his concentration to the very end. It seems, however, that this work also brought him benefits. He gained parliamentary experience and insights into the work of the Chambers that proved of use to him later. He also had useful political connections such as his friend François Adolphe Chambolle, MP and director of "Le Siècle". It is characteristic that Wolowski, who in 1839 enjoyed a certain financial stability, did not give up his collaboration with "Le Siècle" for several more years. Apparently, it paid off for him after all.

3. Conservatoire (Royal) des Arts et Métiers

Financial stability came quite unexpectedly. In 1839, Wolowski became a professor at the Conservatoire Royal des Arts et Métiers (Royal Conservatory of Arts and Crafts)[420]. This was undoubtedly a huge success and promotion for the young Pole. The Conservatoire was a specific school. It was founded back during the Great Revolution and, since the beginning, it was predominantly technical and practical. Tuition was free of charge; the school was aimed mainly at workers, craftsmen and members of the petit bourgeoisie who were keen to improve their knowledge and skills. However, the school did not offer any diploma, so after completing the courses, the graduates did not become engineers, as was the case with the

417 Advertisement for "Journal Général des Tribunaux", *Le Charivari*, 08.10.1836.

418 According to Levasseur, Wolowski "would have continued to merge the newspaper with 'Le Droit,' had it not been for a misunderstanding at the time of the merger, which in 1837 resulted in someone else's hands taking over a property that was just beginning to bear fruit." (E. Levasseur *La Vie et les travaux de Wolowski...*, p. 10). Levasseur's account should, however, be approached with caution – for it is, as I have mentioned, clearly elegiac in nature. It seems more likely to conclude that Wolowski's journal simply did not hold up to the market.

419 A. Roulliet *Wolowski...*, p. 25. Roulliet noted, rather bitingly, that this function of the parliamentary rapporteur of "Le Siècle" forty years later, in a posthumous article, was overlooked... by "Le Siècle" itself.

420 *Ordonnance du 26 septembre 1839 relative au Conservatoire Royal des Arts et Métiers*; [in:] J. de Valserres *Manuel de droit rural et d'économie Agricole*, Paris 1847, pp. 875–876.

polytechnic. Rather, the aim was to further educate future workshop managers, foremen, small inventors, and entrepreneurs. Significantly, new faculties were established at the Conservatoire in 1819. It marked the evolution of the school towards tertiary education. Indeed, lectures were partly of this nature. Moreover, one of the faculties, industrial economics, was taken up by Jean-Baptiste Say. With Say's lectures, political economy entered the universities. The Conservatoire enjoyed considerable prestige from the outset, and taking up a chair, if only because of the small number of them, was regarded as the crowning achievement of a career rather than its beginning[421]. Wolowski himself, by the way, understood this perfectly – and regularly put his professorial title next to his name on all his writings.

And yet he was only 29 years old when he headed the faculty at the Conservatoire. According to his own story, which was later repeated by Levasseur, his academic achievements were crucial in this case. Indeed, he had published a short time earlier in his "Revue..." a text on joint-stock companies, which was to receive full attention at the time. He was then asked to give a lecture at the Academy of Moral and Political Sciences. To his surprise, after a lecture on the relationship between political economy and the economy, he received an invitation to dinner from Hippolyte Passy, Minister of Finance in Marshal Soult's second cabinet. During the meeting, Passy was to say: "I have heard your lecture, you are on the right track, dear sir; the science of economics which you are practising is a new and poorly known science; it can, however, do a great deal for the improvement of our laws and the progress of trade in France; you should therefore make an effort"[422]. According to Levasseur, these two elements: the article and the lecture, led to Wolowski heading the newly created faculty of industrial legislation at the Conservatoire in 1839. This narrative was later repeated by Roulliet and – at least in part – by Markiewicz[423]. However, Markiewicz added that the support of Wolowski's friends (Passy as well as Dalloz) was equally important as they had extensive political connections, coupled with the help of the well-known Italian economist Pellegrino Rossi. This is probably the key to this extraordinary personal success. Top Passy, Dalloz, Rossi with Wolowski's brother-in-law Faucher, and Chambolle – the director of "Le Siècle" – and you will come up with a substantial list of influential figures who could have lobbied for the Pole. Conservatoire historians Claudette Fontanon and André Grelon argue, moreover, that the key influence here was that of Dalloz[424].

421 More on the subject in A. Mercier *Un Conservatoire pour les Arts et Métiers*, Paris 1994.

422 E. Levasseur *La Vie et les travaux de Wolowski*, op. cit., p. 11.

423 A. Roulliet *Wolowski...*, pp. 28–29; P. Markiewicz *Louis Wolowski...*, p. 46.

424 C. Fontanon, A. Grelon *Introduction*, [in:] *Les professeurs du Conservatoire national des arts et métiers. Dictionnaire biographique 1794–1955*, vol. I, *A-K*, Paris 1994, p. 30.

1839 finally brought Wolowski financial and social stability. He earned at the Conservatoire about 5,000 francs a year (not monthly, as Markiewicz suggests)[425]. This income placed him among the 30,000 wealthier Parisians and allowed him to live a quiet life without worrying about the future, though without excess[426]. As a prelude to further considerations, I should add that Wolowski's fortunes improved over time. Between 1848 and 1849, as an MP, he received 25 francs a day during a parliamentary session, and between 1849 and 1851, an annual salary of 9,000 francs[427]. Between 1852 and 1854, as director of the Crédit Foncier, he drew a salary of 18,000 francs a year, then several thousand francs a year as a member of the bank's board of directors[428]. Since 1855, as a member of the Academy of Moral and Political Sciences, Wolowski earned 1,500 francs a year[429]. Last but not least, Louis Wolowski was also a stock market investor, as evidenced by his succession documents. Before his death, he held shares in Société Générale, Compagnie du Midi, Compagnie de l'Est, Société de Jarre et de Moselle, Société d'Orléans, Banque Hypothécaire d'Espagne, Guillaumin publishing house; shares in Société de Guano Dreyffer; Italian and Lombard bonds, Crédit Foncier securities. In total, his inheritance amounted to 942,000 francs[430]. It was a staggering sum, disproportionate, it seems, to his earnings. It may have been due in large part to his successful investments in securities – made possible, in turn, thanks to his many connections. Wolowski's share portfolio is a good indication of his caution: there were shares in railway companies (Orléans, Midi, Est), banks (Crédit Foncier, Banque Hypothécaire d'Espagne), and a sizable proportion of government bonds. Wolowski clearly did not like financial risk. This is in fact confirmed by Zaleski's correspondence. One day he asked Wolowski how to invest and this was his reply: "So, I prefer to say what I do myself when I have capital to deploy. I buy French railway bonds – guaranteed by the government – and charge safely 5%. I've also put some of my wealth in road stocks, which yield 6.5 – I shy away

425 *État du personnel du Conservatoire Royal des Arts et Métiers,* Archives Nationales, ref. F/12/5772; *Ordonnance du 26 septembre 1839 ...*, p. 876. In the 1860s, his salary increased to 7,500 francs (*État du personnel du Conservatoire Royal des Arts et Métiers,* Archives Nationales, ref. F/12/5771).

426 R. Dobek *Paryż, 1871,* Poznań 2013, p. 24.

427 F. Monier, Ch. Portalez. *Une norme démocratique? L'indemnité des élus en débats, de la Révolution française à la Grande Guerre.* 2019, https://shs.hal.science/halshs-02404207/document (retrieved 31.07.2023), pp. 12–15.

428 *Crédit Foncier de France. Registre des délibérations du conseil d'administration, séance du 02 juin 1852,* Archives Nationales du Monde du Travail, ref. 2001 26 1996.

429 *Institut de France. Personnel de l'Académie.* Archives Nationales, ref. F/17/3594.

430 Bequest of the Wolowski estate: Archives de Paris, ref. DQ7 12380 nr 362. However, the 300,000 francs of his daughter Françoise's dowry must be deducted from the said sum, according to the inventory.

from overseas funds, I have less confidence in them, and I look for safety before anything else"[431]. This attitude clearly worked. However, it should also be noted that Crédit Foncier was an extremely important player not only in the French but in the European financial market, with Wolowski as a member of its board for many years.

In the case of the Wołowskis, it was not only his personal wealth but that of the entire family. This, in turn also increased, as the Fauchers managed to recover some 60,000 francs from the Russian state on account of the mortgage imposed on the estate in Kaski[432]. Louis Wolowski's relative affluence is also evidenced by his successive Parisian addresses. Initially, the Wolowski couple lived on St. André Street, then moved to 9, rue des Beaux-Arts. Tekla and Franciszek Wołowski lived at number 11, which probably facilitated family contacts and the care of Louis's young children. In 1841 Laure and Louis moved to 3, rue St Fiacre. Three years later they moved to 21, rue Bergère, where they stayed until the early 1850s[433]. They then took up residence on rue de la Grange-Batelière, only to move again in 1857 to rue de la Victoire, and in 1864 to rue de Clichy 49[434]. This was the last address of the Wolowskis in Paris, where they spent the final 12 years of Louis's life.

These constant moves by the Wolowskis were probably partly linked to the gigantic rebuilding of Paris started in 1853 by Prefect Haussmann. However, they also indicate the significant mobility of Louis Wolowski and his wife. They are also an important indicator of their affluence. The last two addresses in particular attest to the family's wealth. Situated in the 9th arrondissement of Paris, de la Victoire Street was then, and still is, home to the great synagogue of Paris, the famous Beuharnais Hotel building (demolished in 1862) and the headquarters of the Hottinguer bank. On the other hand, in de Clichy Street, located in the same district, more or less at the same time as the Wolowskis, lived the super-rich Wendel family, owners of a large ironworks empire. Louis' other neighbours in the street included Victor Hugo (after 1874), and Ernest Feydeau – an archaeologist, writer,

431 J. B. Zaleski *Korespondencja Józefa Bohdana Zaleskiego z lat 1823–1886*. vol. 21 *Wodziński – Zaleska*,
Biblioteka Jagiellońska, BJ manuscript. 9215 III.

432 P. Markiewicz *Louis Wolowski...*, p. 40.

433 *Almanach des 25000 adresses des principaux habitants de Paris*, Paris :
1835, p. 582,
1841, p. 650,
1844, p. 634,
1848, p. 567.

434 *Almanach Impérial*, Paris:
1856, p. 877,
1857, p. 906,
1864, p. 900,

and journalist. The subsequent addresses on the map of Paris clearly indicate that, while initially living in the centre, the Wolowskis gradually moved to the north-west. This corresponded exactly to the migration of a large part of the wealthy Parisian bourgeoisie of the 1850s and 1860s. This is what Jacques Rougerie wrote about the demographic effects of Haussmann's great urban redevelopment: "The prefect's surgical cuts in old Paris, as well as the capital's prosperity attracting constant waves of immigrants, creating a dangerous housing problem, are contributing to an inexorable division in the city. While it was visible before, it was barely perceptible [...]. It is now alarmingly distinct. [...] The concentration of workers in the north, in the south and above all, unbelievably, in the east, can be evidenced. While the well-off remain for the most part in the centre, the rich (a well-known law) are settling more and more in the west [...]"[435]. The west of Paris, bourgeois, devoid of industry or major artisan workshops and therefore workers, with more beautiful and expensive townhouses, better aerated and sunny than the other districts, attracted the wealthier Parisians. Louis Wolowski was no exception.

Markiewicz draws attention to another element in the housing context: Wolowski would rent his flats until almost the very end of his life. He became the owner only of the last one, and not immediately either, but only in 1872[436]. Markiewicz fails to explain this otherwise intriguing fact. Unfortunately, the surviving documents and correspondence of Wolowski do not provide any explanation, either. Certainly, Wolowski could afford to buy not only a flat but a whole tenement house[437]. Clearly, he did not want to invest in real estate. We can only speculate as to why. Perhaps it was due to his nature, pushing him from one place to another? Perhaps from his emigration experiences and the loss of his parents' landed estate in Poland? We do not know.

What kind of lecturer was Louis Wolowski? The published text of his first lecture, which is also the programme text for the entire series, has survived. Wolowski's intention was to discuss legislation that would serve the development of the economy and industry. He stressed the importance of political economy in this process. Wolowski also made it very clear that the new laws, which were necessary, were also meant to preserve economic freedom. For "Freedom is not an endowment; it yields without difficulty to the rules of logic well received but rejects compulsion. Under the rule of wise and caring laws, the good organisation of industry will come of itself in time"[438]. Law and power were to play a supporting role

435 J. Rougerie, *Paris libre 1871,* Paris 2004, pp. 17–19.

436 P. Markiewicz *Louis Wolowski...*, p. 40.

437 In the second half of the 19th century, the average value of a townhouse in Paris was around 130,000 francs, around 250,000 francs in the wealthier neighbourhoods (G. d'Avenel *Le Prix et le Loyer des maisons en France depuis le moyen âge jusqu'à nos jours,* [in:] "Revue des Deux Mondes", no. 123, 1894, p. 826).

438 L. Wolowski *Cours de législation industrielle. Introduction. Discours prononcé à l'ouverture du cours, le 9 janvier 1840, par M.L. Wolowski, Avocat à la Cour Royale de*

in this movement. Wolowski believed that as a result of capitalism, the standard of living of the working classes had improved as never before. He stressed, addressing a working-class audience, that the improvement in the lives of workers could only be brought about by good legislation, morality, thrift, foresight, the ability to co-operate with others and the development of technology[439]. Wolowski therefore intended to devote his course to the general principles of classical political economy. As the lecture was open to all, newspaper advertisements appeared from time to time, announcing further topics during the year. In 1840 and 1841, Wolowski discussed, among other things, the relations between foremen and workers; workers' books; poorly arranged, unhealthy workshops; patent law[440]. In 1842, he spoke about the history of industrial legislation from the time of Colbert to the 19th century and about the organisation of labour in various European countries[441]. In 1843, in his lectures he covered the industrial legislation of the Great French Revolution, trademark law and child labour in factories[442]. In 1845, Wolowski discussed in general terms the principle of freedom of labour, the organisation of factories, the operation of labour courts[443]. Clearly, the topics of his lectures did not change significantly over the following years. In 1871 they covered "Productive forces – Labour – Intelligence – Land – Capital – Property – Population – Savings – Exchange – Factors determining production growth – Trade – Money – Co-operatives – Societies – Loan"[444]. The lectures were generally held twice a week, in the afternoon or evening.

We have two descriptions of the classes of courses taught at the Conservatoire by Wolowski. This is how Natalia Kicka, who attended them in the 1840s, kept the lecture theatre in her memory: "After working all day, at eight o'clock in the evening, the craftsmen sat in the huge Hall of the building called the Consevatoire des Arts et Métiers. Blue blouses, as far as the eye could see, filled the benches densely, the workers' weary hands resting on their knees, from factories and various establishments they ran to these courses drenched, smeared, but hungry for knowledge"[445].

Paris, Professeur de législation industrielle au Conservatoire des Arts et Métiers, Paris 1840, p. 15.

439 L. Wolowski *Cours de législation industrielle...*, p. 23.

440 "Journal des Débats Politiques et Littéraires", 07.01.1841. Identical advertisements appeared in other titles, including "La Presse" and "Le Siècle".

441 "Journal des Débats Politiques et Littéraires", 25.11.1842.

442 "Journal des Débats Politiques et Littéraires", 21.11.1843.

443 "Journal des Débats Politiques et Littéraires", 14.02.1845. The announcements were regularly read out by Potrykowski, previously mentioned, pointing out again maliciously to Wolowski that "propria laus sordet" (one's own praise stinks). J. A. Potrykowski *Tułactwo Polaków...*, pp. 83 and 133–134).

444 "Journal Officiel de la République Française", 04.11.1871, no. 306, p. 4294.

445 N. Kicka *Pamiętniki*, Warszawa 1972, p. 496.

Levasseur, who listened to them regularly and, towards the end of his life, often replaced Wolowski[446], wrote:

> He [Wolowski] was not looking for displays of oratory skills. He was fond of colloquial speech and was excellent at using it. His speech was easy, abundant, sometimes thrilling – especially when it came to demonstration, and the facts, arguments, anecdotes in his speech chased one after the other. He was not afraid to digress. Sometimes he would begin a lecture on a specific subject, with his notes in front of him, and during the speech something seemed unclear to him and worthy of explanation; he would then elaborate on this point, clarify all aspects, and the passage would become the whole lecture. He never tried to please the majority; after all, he had a good opinion of people and believed that they can improve themselves through education; so, he wanted to take the audience to his level, to his own thought, and therefore always spoke the truth, however hard it might be. The audience, on the other hand, listened slowly, as the kindness of the heart always shone through from beneath the stern speech; they felt that the professor, who understood the suffering of the working classes, was only warning them to improve their lot. Wolowski spoke as he wrote. [...] He was a man of action, so he always had a practical aim in mind; when he wrote an article, he usually thought of a necessary reform or a new institution; when he prepared a lecture, he usually had in mind a common error to be corrected or a superstition to be eradicated[447].

Levasseur went on to write that Wolowski gave his lectures almost continuously for 32 years. He suspended them during the Revolution of 1848, then again in 1871 when the Paris Commune briefly closed the Conservatoire. In 1864, the scope of Wolowski's faculty was changed slightly to political economy and industrial legislation[448]. This also involved a slight shift in emphasis in the teaching: industrial legislation receded clearly into the background, giving way to general principles and laws of political economy[449].

In mentioning Wolowski's teaching at the Conservatoire, another fact is worth noting. According to historian Lucette Le Van-Lemesle, in addition to the Conservatoire, lectures on political economy were also held at the Collège de France

446 "Journal Officiel de la République Française", 04.11.1872, no. 304, p. 6804.

447 E. Levasseur *La Vie et les travaux de Wolowski...*, pp. 13–14.

448 This change was linked to the death in 1854 of Adolphe Blanqui, Wolowski's friend and fellow Conservatoire professor. Indeed, Blanqui headed the faculty of industrial economics at the school, teaching largely political economy. After his death, this position was no longer filled and was effectively abolished. Louis Wolowski's course in political economy and industrial legislation was thus a combination of his earlier teaching and Blanqui's lecture.

449 E. Levasseur *L'enseignement de l'économie politique au Conservatoire des Arts et Métiers*, "Revue internationale de l'enseignement", no. 41, 1901, p. 216.

and the more technical École des Ponts et Chaussées. In the 1860s, elements of political economy also appeared in secondary -level teaching. All these faculties were staffed by classical liberal economists from one and the same circle, disciples of Jean-Baptiste Say. At the Conservatoire it was first Say himself, then Wolowski and Adolphe Blanqui; at the Collège de France Pellegrino Rossi (between 1833 and 1840) and Michel Chevalier (1840–1879), and Joseph Garnier at the École des Ponts et Chaussées. The gentlemen knew each other very well, were members of the same or similar societies, published in the same journals and publishing houses, and shared similar views in many respects. So, thanks, among others, to Wolowski, the classical liberal economic school completely dominated the teaching of political economy for several decades[450].

The previously mentioned topics of Louis Wolowski's lectures clearly indicate that he often used the comparative method, describing legislation, institutions and solutions adopted in France and confronting them with foreign ones. However, this method required frequent trips and journeys. In the case of the Warsaw-born economist, this was not a constraint but rather, an extra benefit of his profession. Wolowski liked to travel. After his death, his friend Louis Alexandre Foucher de Careil recounted: "He [Wolowski – RD] told me a few years ago that whenever he felt sick, tired, he would get on a train and travel several thousand kilometres"[451]. Even if travel did not necessarily act as a cure, Wolowski did indeed travel a lot. The historical moment for that was perfect: since the late reign of Louis-Philippe, France had more than 2,000 km of railway lines[452], 20,000 km in 1870. Louis Wolowski used them not only for academic purposes, but also for health-reasons. The meetings of Maria Walewska, née Przeździecka and Wolowski took place during health or leisure stays is spa resorts. Kraszewski also met him there; he later recalled: "Almost every day we met the late Wolowski who, with a vivacity peculiar to himself, almost without resting, had time to work, live and treat himself together with people. [...] almost every day he took long walks, attended meetings, made acquaintances, and never rested for a moment"[453].

Most important, however, were the academic trips. They were a part of a trend – in the 1830s and 1840s in which France sent many prominent individuals for scientific purposes: suffice to mention the trips of Michel Chevalier and Alexis de Tocqueville to America. These journeys were also possible because the state that was behind them. From 1842 onwards, the organisation of outer academic missions

---

450 L. Le Van-Lemesle*Le Juste ou le Riche. L'enseignement de l'économie politique 1815–1950*, Paris 2004, pp. 88–105.

451 *Société d'Économie politique, réunion du 5 septembre 1876*, "Journal des Economistes. Revue mensuelle de l'économie politique, des questions agricoles, manufacturières et commerciales", vol. XLIII, 1876, p. 428.

452 G. de Broglie *Guizot*, Paris 1990, p. 337.

453 J.I. Kraszewski *Ludwik Wołowski...*

was treated in Paris as "public service", one of the responsibilities of the state[454]. Perhaps Louis Wolowski made his contribution: shortly before, in 1841, he wrote a letter to the Minister of Education pointing out the need to organise study missions abroad for the professors of the Conservatoire des Arts et Métiers[455].

He intended to travel through the German states, the purpose of his peregrination being to familiarise himself with industrial legislation. Wolowski eventually managed to obtain the funding from another source, the Ministry of Agriculture. Laurent Cunin-Gridaine, Minister for Agriculture and Trade, agreed to pay for the trip, the books acquired, and to pay the professor an additional salary of 2,400 francs[456]. In 1841, Wolowski embarked on his first major academic journey. It is worth a close examination as it provided a good example of his *modus operandi* on similar trips. Wolowski visited Baden, Heidelberg, Frankfurt, Hanover, Brunswick, Prussia, Saxony, Bohemia, Bavaria, and Austria. In Karlsruhe he saw the local polytechnic, in Hanover the university of industry, in Brunswick the technical department of the Collegium Carolinum, in Berlin the university and business society. The scenario was repeated in Leipzig, Prague, Munich, and Vienna: Wolowski visited local industrial schools, polytechnics, and economic societies[457]. Following a ministerial order, he studied economic legislation, patent law, employer-employee relations, industrial and commercial education, the organisation of workers in manufactories. He purchased many studies by German economists and statistical works[458]. Perhaps more important than books were the acquaintances and friendships Wolowski developed in Germany. They included above all politicians

454 *Table générale des Archives des Missions Scientifiques et Littéraires comprenant les trois séries jusqu'au tome XV inclus*, Paris 1890, pp. I–II.

455 Archives Nationales, ref. F/12/2368.

456 Archives Nationales, ref. F/12/2368.

457 Archives Nationales, ref. F/12/2368.

458 A complete list of books acquired by Wolowski in Germany has survived. To a large extent, it reflects Wolowski's reading profile, including Merbach's *Theorie des Zunftzwanges* (Theory of the Guild), Georg Herold's *Die Rechte der Handwerker* (The Rights of Craftsmen), Schmitt's work on craftsmen's guilds [Wolowski's report only gives French translations of the titles, without the date of publication, sometimes misspelling the authors' names. This makes some of these works difficult to identify precisely – RD]; Bartenheim's 8 volumes on factories, Wildras and Krauss' book on factory legislation, Wolmar's book on savings banks, Moringer's *Statistik*, Mayer's essay on industrial development, Ziegler's *Über Gewerbefreiheit* (On freedom of labour), Wieck's *Die industriellen Zustände Sachsens* (On the industrial conditions of Saxony), Schiebe's *Universal-Lexikon der Handelswissenschaften* (Dictionary of Commerce), a compilation of Prussian legislation from 1806 to 1841, books on Prussian statistics and demography (*Mission commerciale de Wolowski en Allemagne*, Archives Nationales, ref. F/12/2368).

and economists: Karl Friedrich Nebenius, minister of Baden (author of the state constitution of 1818) and theoretician of the German Customs Union; Karl Bader – director of Karlsruhe Polytechnic; professors: Burs from Freiburg, Herman from Munich, Becker from Vienna, Karl Joseph Mittermaier from Heidelberg, Friedrich Bulau from Leipzig, the famous Robert von Mohl from Tübingen and Karl Friedrich Dieterici – economist and rector of the University of Berlin[459]. Wolowski spent a lot of time in the libraries of Frankfurt, Heidelberg, Berlin, and Vienna. He also visited, at the invitation of the owners, several manufactories and evening schools for workers.

The effects of his work are reflected, among other things, in letters sent from time to time to the Minister. In the last of them, sent from Dresden on 17 August 1841, Wolowski wrote: "Since I had the honour of writing to the Minister from Frankfurt, I have visited the whole of northern Germany. [...] I have dealt in particular with industrial and commercial training, patents, brands and trademarks and the organisation of work. [...] In all German cities I have only come across schools of industry, commercial education is only an add-on in them. [...] In contrast, child labour regulations are generally observed in Prussia. There are not yet any in Saxony, although six- or seven-year-old children work ten or twelve hours a day"[460]. These and similar observations from his travels, sometimes much more precise and in-depth, were then used by Wolowski in a work on his own doctrine and concepts concerning patents, the free market, shareholding companies, child labour and – above all – land credit.

Wolowski's subsequent – and numerous – journeys were largely reminiscent of the first one, and soon (in 1846) the Ministry of Agriculture and Trade sent him on a mission to Switzerland. This time his tasks, set by the ministry, included:

> 2. To collect all practical, relevant information on: – agriculture and industry in each of the cantons visited; – the mode of iron production, workshops and mines, consumption of raw materials; – agricultural and industrial goods for which cantons would be most interested in customs facilities abroad; general and unit prices of goods; – labour costs, wages, transport, etc. 3. Find out as much as possible about the agricultural and industrial technologies and procedures in use and the improvements already made or to be made, the progress of mechanisation, the number of workers employed in big industry, etc. 4. To examine if, in the event of Swiss cotton being subjected to a low duty, the Confederation could propose to France, in response, the reduction or abolition of internal duties primarily on goods such as beef, [...], Paris goods, wool, et al. 5. Examine the issue of transit, particularly in terms of the competition that the Swiss railways seem to have gone into in our Rhine transit, or, on the other hand, the impact that our new rail line from Marseille to Le Havre could have on Swiss interests. 6. Analyse the issue of smuggling from Switzerland to France, which is known to be well

459 *Mission commerciale de Wolowski en Allemagne*, Archives Nationales, ref. F/12/2368.
460 *Mission commerciale de Wolowski en Allemagne*, Archives Nationales, ref. F/12/2368.

> organised, above all when it comes to watchmaking and embroidery products. 7. Finally, it is necessary to investigate, based on information collected from Swiss factory owners and merchants, what they think of a more or less official project to change the customs regime or of the ideas [...] of a Swiss customs union with France[461].

Wolowski's trip to Switzerland included, in addition to his academic tasks, an informal diplomatic mission. This demonstrates the considerable confidence of the French authorities in the Polish émigré. This was all the more so because his mission also concerned issues of real importance to France. It is known, for example, that the extension of the railway lines in Switzerland and the Rhineland had raised genuine concerns in Paris about, among other things, a possible decline in transit on the Rhine. At the same time, he was certainly not commissioned with any strictly political tasks – even though Switzerland was in the midst of the Sonderbund crisis, slowly approaching a civil war. Unfortunately, the archives do not contain Wolowski's reports or information on how he fulfilled his mission. One thing is certain, however: again, he brought with him a considerable number of studies, reports and contacts. He also presented, at the invitation of the Academy of Moral and Political Sciences, a short report on the industrial exhibition in Zurich. Here, in passing, he also referred to the political situation in Switzerland, where everything, including exhibitions, was, in his view, cantonal, particularistic, and therefore limited. He noted in this context that "the other cantons have sent almost nothing [to Zurich]. [...] The rivalry and isolation that prevail among the residents have so far precluded the exchange of ideas and industrial products. I once asked Geneva why they did not send to Zurich some examples of excellent products created in the homeland of Jean-Jacques [Rousseau], the only answer I received was: 'Geneva is worthy of Zurich'"[462].

On his return from Switzerland, in 1847 Wolowski went to the Congress of Economists in Brussels. He then travelled several times across the Channel to London where he was received by, among others, members of the famous Athenaeum Club. In 1856, he appeared again for academic purposes in Vienna. On this occasion, according to a letter from Franciszek Wężyk, then president of the Cracow Scientific Society, he briefly visited Cracow[463]. In 1862 or 1863, he visited Wielkopolska and his old companion from his student years, Stanisław Egbert Koźmian, at his estate in Przylepki. He returned to Brussels, before moving on to the Netherlands in 1857 and then again to Germany. He repeatedly visited Wiesbaden, where he met, among others, Wolfgang Eras, an economist, and secretary

---

461 Dossier: *Wolowski: Suisse 1846,* Archives Nationales, ref. F/12/2593/C.

462 L. Wolowski *Communication sur la dernière exposition de l'industrie à Zurich,* [in:] "Séances et travaux de l'Académie des Sciences Morales et Politiques", vol. I (XI), Paris 1847, p. 390.

463 Letter from Franciszek Wężyk to Louis Wolowski, Biblioteka Polska w Paryżu, ref. BPP 2339, pp. 65–66.

of the chambers of commerce in Bielefeld and Breslau. In 1865 he spent several weeks in England studying the English banking system and preparing a book on banks in England and Scotland[464]. In the meantime, he had also been to Italy on several occasions.

Among all these journeys, a separate, specific category must be distinguished: international exhibitions. Since the very beginning, Wolowski participated in them with real enthusiasm. He saw the famous Crystal Palace in 1851 as a member of the French section of the jury of the London exhibition and vice-chairman of one of the committees. He returned to London for the third exhibition in 1862, again as a member of the French section. He also participated very actively in the international exhibitions held in Paris in both 1855 and 1867. Finally, in 1873, he spent the summer as chairman of the committee and member of the committee of chairmen of the international exhibition in Vienna.

His reports on successive exhibitions, written for the Academy of Moral and Political Sciences, were most often enthusiastic. Wolowski saw them above all as evidence of the progress of humanity, in which he firmly believed. It was also a clear affirmation that the free market, freedom of trade, freedom of work and choice of occupation best served this progress. On his return from London in 1862, Wolowski wrote: "The development of freedom of trade today brings nations closer to each other and allows each to share in the improvements emerging in each. If nations shake hands, it is most often not an empty gesture, for it contains the results of the power of production, which continues to grow – thanks to human intelligence and the application of science to industry and agriculture"[465]. In 1873, on his return from Vienna, he repeated: "we find that as civilisation advances, the human condition improves, and that better protected liberty and more respected property in all its forms: land, capital, intelligence, raise the powers to the highest level and improve the status of all"[466]. The exhibitions also naturally reinforced Wolowski's liberal, free-market pacifism. Unequivocally, as he repeatedly emphasised, they pointed to the advantage of cooperation and exchange between nations over conquest and annexation[467].

When analysing Wolowski's voyages and their significance for his economic and political thought, one fact draws attention. It is hard to resist the impression that, in essence, they brought relatively little new to his conception. If he brought back from Germany some comments on the Prussian credit system[468], these largely

464 L. Wolowski *La Banque d'Angleterre et les banques d'Ecosse*, Paris, 1867.

465 L. Wolowski *Communication verbale sur l'exposition de 1862. Extrait du compte-rendu de l'Académie des Sciences Morales et Politiques rédigé par M. Charles Verge. Sous la direction de M.le Secrétaire perpétuel de l'Académie*, Orléans, 1862, p. 10.

466 L. Wolowski *Rapport verbal sur l'exposition universelle de Vienne*, Paris, 1874, p. 18.

467 L. Wolowski *Rapport verbal sur l'exposition*, p. 19.

468 L. Wolowski *Réforme hypothécaire: organisation du crédit foncier*, Paris, 1844, pp. 25–26.

corresponded to his earlier views. Wolowski wrote about Prussian land credit societies back in 1839[469]. At the time, he also used the example of the Polish Land Credit estate manor and the loan taken out just for it. As early as in 1839, Wolowski saw the Prussian-Polish credit solution as a model for France to possibly follow. The trip to Germany did not change much in this respect, but rather strengthened his convictions. The timing of his trip to England in 1866 coincided with a fierce polemic among economists and politicians in France concerning the privileged position of the Banque de France in the country's banking system, the issuance of paper money and the possible monopoly of the Banque de France on such issuance. Across the Channel, Wolowski studied the events of the so-called English "Black Friday" of 1866 and the reaction to it by the British banking system[470]. He advocated money based solely on bullion, and therefore the exclusion or as wide a limitation as possible on the issue of paper money. This was his vision, for example, at a meeting of the Political Economy Club in London in 1866[471]. Only that, again, these ideas were not new for him; his stay in England did not change his views, which he published a year earlier in the work *Un chapitre de l'histoire financiere de l'Angleterre. La suspension des payements de la Banque et le bullion-report.* ("A chapter from the financial history of England. The suspension of the Bank's payments and the bullion-report").

The same observation applies to Wolowski's social and political views. Having settled in Paris, this former Warsaw conspirator became an opponent of revolutionary violence. The developments of 1848 further strengthened his conviction. Again, the observations collected abroad corroborated his views rather than changed them. In the report of his 1841 tour of Germany, he wrote admiringly of the Saxon workers: "The information I have obtained on Saxon industry shows clearly that the French workers are not, relatively speaking, the greatest wretches on the continent. However, the admirable patience and simplicity of the Saxon workers keep them from any complaints or disorder"[472]. In turn, ten years later, while in England, he visited a glassware factory. There he met "a large group of French workers who had been made unemployed by the revolution of 1848, and the English quickly employed them on very favourable terms". The Pole emphasised

---

469 L. Wolowski *De la mobilisation du crédit foncier*, [in:] "Revue de législation et de jurisprudence", vol. X, IV-IX.1839, p. 260.

470 "Black Friday" 11 May 1866 – the day on which panic broke out on the London Stock Exchange leading to a rapid loss of value in the securities of some banks and companies. It was linked to the bankruptcy of Overend, Gurney & Company, one of the most important English banks, arising in turn from many years of risky financial operations. The nascent financial crisis was, however, quickly quelled by the rapid, massive intervention of the Bank of England.

471 A. Roulliet *Wolowski. Sa vie...*, p. 304.

472 *Mission commerciale de Wolowski en Allemagne* Archives Nationales, ref. F/12/2368.

this with evident regret, once again stressing the disastrous consequences of ill-considered revolutions, the loss of financial and human capital. At the same time, however, he consoled the French: their compatriots across the Channel longed for their homeland, and above all for the uniquely French industrial atmosphere. For it was only in France, according to him, that industry and the economy were imbued with an atmosphere of art, through which they were "strengthened and ennobled"[473].

This conduct of Wolowski's, finding in fact in his travels abroad a confirmation of his earlier concepts and ideas, is related in part to the European intellectual circle in which he moved. People like Richard Cobden, Robert von Mohl, Pellegrino Rossi, Johann Caspar Bluntschli, Alexander von Humboldt (known to Wolowski from his travels in Berlin), Wilhelm Roscher, Leopold von Ranke and Józef Ignacy Kraszewski, as well as other economists, politicians, businessmen and bankers known to Wolowski, belonged (in different countries) to the same intellectual milieu. They were associated with the liberal economic school, by far the dominant one in European universities at the time. Louis Girard, an eminent historian, described this group in France in the following way (yet the passage fits all): "They refer to the English experience, but are above all disciples of Jean-Baptiste Say. They have inherited from him optimism, a belief in the value of entrepreneurship and progress [...]. Like their master, they want to end rationing and collective restrictions, to free the entrepreneur, to reduce deprivation through growth made possible by competition. [...] Influenced by England [...] they are fighting against protectionism and state regulation of the economy"[474]. Wolowski therefore read works revolving around these subjects, and met Englishmen, Austrians and Prussians in economic societies who thought this way.

When we look at the European peregrinations of this descendant of the Schors, one more element is striking: Wolowski mainly visited large cities, where he clearly spent a lot of time in libraries. He read a lot of reports, statistics, and economic works. As a result, Wolowski sometimes gave the impression that he knew mainly the theoretical side of reality. He visited factories, workshops, and schools for workers – but as part of demonstration visits, at the invitation of the owners. And there he inevitably saw mainly what they wanted to show him – the French glaziers, happy with their excellent pay conditions, or the "patient and simple" Saxons.

Finally, Wolowski's texts lack an in-depth sociological analysis: the influence of history, culture, and customs on economics or – so brilliantly described by Tocqueville at the time – of the links between economy and religion. Wolowski

---

473 L. Wolowski *XXVI Jury. Papiers de teinture, meubles etc.*, [in:] *Exposition universelle de 1851. Travaux de la Commission française sur l'industrie des nations: publiés par ordre de l'Empereur*, vol. VII, Paris1855, pp. 3–4.

474 L. Girard *Les libéraux français 1814–1875*, Paris 1985, p. 141.

saw equally rational individuals everywhere, willing to make rational and optimal decisions under conditions of economic freedom. All that was needed was to introduce this freedom.

Chapter IV: The Revolution of 1848 in Paris

1. The political ideas of Louis Wolowski

By 1848, Wolowski had not engaged directly in politics, partly because of his background and the need for acquiring citizenship, partly because of his age: Article 32 of the French constitutional charter set the minimum age of a deputy at 30. Of significance was the simple need of gaining social standing, of being popular enough to contemplate running for parliament. Finally, purely material considerations were at play: the need to provide for the family. Patrice Markiewicz is right that, while staying away from politics, Louis Wolowski operated within the broad elite of the Orléans Monarchy, which included all his allies and promoters: Royer-Collard, Passy, Cunin-Gridaine, Faucher, and Chambolle. According to Markiewicz, Wolowski was also close to the group of doctrinaires and Guizot[475]. However, this statement raises significant objections. Firstly, because the group in fact ceased to exist after 1830. Secondly, doctrinaires like Royer-Collard and Guizot placed fundamental emphasis on the political element of reality. Their intention was to reconcile pre-revolutionary and post-revolutionary France within a constitutional monarchy. While they were in favour of a strong and efficient royal power, it was clearly limited by law. Moreover, Reason was to be the overriding sovereign power, historically represented in France by the middle class. Its political agency, in turn, was the parliament, elected by census and cooperating smoothly with the ruler within the constitutional charter[476]. A side effect of this thinking was the acceptance of the free market as an arena for free action of rational individuals, at the same time testing their abilities and competences.

Interestingly, Louis Wolowski's vision of the political world was somewhat different. First, as Markiewicz notes, Wolowski did not perceive it as a uniform doctrine, a coherent system. Moreover, unlike the doctrinaires, he did not consider the question of who should govern of key importance. Much more significant was how a specific form of government protects freedom. In one of his early texts, Wolowski referred in this context to a state of nature, which he called "extra-state". In it,

---

475 P. Markiewicz *Louis Wolowski...*, p. 122.

476 B. Yvert *La Restauration. Les idées et les hommes*, Paris 2013, pp. 149–178. In doing so, Yvert clearly distinguishes between two generations of doctrinaires – an older one (Royer-Collard, Hercule de Serre, among others), strongly attached to the House of Bourbon and emphasising above all strong royal power, and a younger one (Guizot, Charles de Rémusat, Victor de Broglie and others) accepting the Bourbons but paying more attention to the constitution and parliament.

humans defended their own rights, were their own judges and repaired damage themselves, at their own discretion. According to Wolowski, in this state, injustice regularly triumphed. A state was therefore created to secure basic rights and for this purpose only. Its scope of action had to be clearly defined and limited. It had to guarantee the rights of the public (public law) and the rights arising from the relationships between individuals (private law). The police and criminal law were to ensure that public law was protected. Private law was to be protected by judicial processes. The state, in effect, also determined the procedural rights of the parties, the course of the trial, etc.[477]. Here, Wolowski clearly referred to John Locke's vision of the state of nature, ultimately drawing similar conclusions. Unlike the Englishman, however, he did not elaborate on this thought and did not return to it later.

Constant was a thinker most frequently referred to by Wolowski in his reflections on the state and its relations with the individual. In fact, in his text dedicated to the author of *On Constitutional Monarchy,* Wolowski most fully presented his own political thought. Above all, according to Wolowski, Constant was not attached to any form of government. And this was because, ultimately, "Liberty, order, and the happiness of peoples are the ends of human institutions, political organisms are merely the means."[478]. According to him, the key tools for securing freedom included representatives of the people freely (albeit not necessarily democratically) elected to control public expenditure, an independent judiciary, free press to keep an eye on the authorities, private property to secure freedom, and the freedom to dispose of one's own capabilities. Wolowski referred to this freedom as "genuine modern freedom". He also emphasised, following Constant, that political powers, though important, ultimately served only to secure it. They were only a tool to protect freedom, not freedom in itself[479].

In doing so, Wolowski seems to have overlooked some of Constant's scepticism about democracy and the popular vote. He would certainly have subscribed to the Lausanne-born thinker's statement on the sovereignty of the people: "When sovereignty is not limited, private individuals have no shield against governments. It is in vain that we pretend to submit governments to the popular will; governments will always dictate this will, and any remedy in this measure is a veritable delusion."[480]. Unlike him, however, Wolowski no longer questioned the principle of the popular vote. Constant did not completely reject it in the (undetermined) future,

---

477 L. Wolowski *Quelques observations sur le principe fondamental de la législation en matière de procédure civile et sur les conditions essentielles qui en dérivent,* "Revue de législation et de jurisprudence", vol. III, October 1835 – March 1836, pp. 30–39.

478 L. Wolowski *Mémoire sur le cours de politique constitutionnelle...,* p. 8.

479 L. Wolowski *Mémoire sur le cours de politique constitutionnelle...,* p. 19.

480 B. Constant *O Monarchii konstytucyjnej i rękojmiach publicznych,* Warszawa 2016, p. 72

but he remained committed to the idea of enlightened governance possible owing to a wealth census. Since the Revolution of 1848, Wolowski seemed to have accepted the popular vote. However, it is uncertain to what extent this was due to his genuine belief in the wisdom of the popular vote, or due to a conviction that the right to participate in elections, once granted to the poorer strata, could not be revoked, as the experience of 1848–1851 taught him. In his undoubted liberalism, Wolowski was perhaps a little more partial to the state than Constant. The former Polish insurgent argued that in his critique of the state, Constant went perhaps a little too far. He insisted that the state was not just necessary evil, as many liberals wanted it. Wolowski, subscribing to a school of thought known since the time of Plato and Aristotle, clearly emphasised that the human was a social being – thus, in his view, there was no human outside a community, outside a state. It was imperative, though, to clearly delimit its boundaries. The state had to guarantee the freedom of citizens, but it also had to take care of national freedom and external borders. The state was therefore responsible for the elements related to the common good that the individuals could not manage on their own: transport and communication, ports, education, administration. The state was responsible for the army, the navy, diplomacy, finance, the legislature, justice, the police, and public works. In doing so, the state could not replace individual activity, but only facilitate it. And it absolutely did not interfere in matters of faith, work performed, thought[481].

Louis Wolowski also referred in these reflections to another eminent Frenchman, Tocqueville[482]. The Pole was familiar with his works, and he knew Tocqueville personally (he was a friend of Faucher). It seems that a peculiar resignation in the face of inevitable democracy brought Wolowski closer to the author of *The Old Regime and the Revolution.* After all, in his excellent introduction to *Democracy in America,* Tocqueville wrote that "the gradual and progressive development of equality was at once their past and their future", and that to wish to arrest democracy "would then seem tantamount to a struggle against God himself".[483] Wolowski could certainly subscribe to this statement. He also shared with the Norman aristocrat a commitment to freedom. He saw his workers' lectures, after all, as part of what the Frenchman referred to as "education for freedom.". That, however, was where these (rather superficial) similarities ended. Tocqueville's thought was, above all, incomparably more profound than Wolowski's ideas. Even if we consider that Wolowski's scope of interest was much narrower, as he focussed on the economy, his outlook was also narrower. Wolowski failed to recognise, or recognised much less, the impact of democracy on a state's economy which Tocqueville covered

481 L. Wolowski *Mémoire sur le cours de politique constitutionnelle...*, pp. 30–31.

482 L. Wolowski *Mémoire sur le cours de politique constitutionnelle...*, p. 14.

483 A. de Tocqueville *Democracy in America,* translated by Arthur Goldhammer, New York 2004, p. 9.

primarily in Volume II of *Democracy in America.* As the following sections of this book show, Wolowski reduced the economy almost exclusively to the laws of free competition, while Tocqueville dealt with the impact of democracy and legal equality of citizens on wages, the change in relations between the capitalist and the worker, the mentality, and ambitions of workers. The descendant of the Polish Frankists steered clear of religious topics, while the Norman aristocrat described the importance of religion and religious pluralism in a state, including its importance for the development and self-control of capitalism.

The third important political thinker quoted by Wolowski was John Stuart Mill. Not least because he liked the Englishman's conception of freedom. The latter wrote:

> This conduct consists, first, in not injuring the interests of one another; or rather certain interests which, either by express legal provision or by tacit understanding, ought to be considered as rights; and secondly, in each person's bearing his share (to be fixed on some equitable principle) of the labours and sacrifices incurred for defending the society or its members from injury and molestation. These conditions society is justified in enforcing, at all costs to those who endeavour to withhold fulfilment [...] The acts of an individual may be hurtful to others, or wanting in due consideration for their welfare, without going the length of violating any of their constituted rights. The offender may then be justly punished by opinion though not by law. [...] But there is no room for entertaining any such question when a person's conduct affects the interests of no persons besides himself or needs not affect them unless they like.[484].

Wolowski took a similar negative view of individual freedom, limited only by the identical freedom of others. Like Mill, he linked freedom to individuals' responsibility for their own conduct, a responsibility of which no one could absolve them. Thus, like Mill, he did not allow restrictions on freedom arising from paternalistic motives, restrictions introduced for the good of the (adult) human being.

One more thing undoubtedly united them. In the work on Constant quoted above, Wolowski wrote: "Power over oneself is the first condition of freedom: it constitutes simultaneously its greatness as well as its dangers, for it requires strong habits and persevering effort. Strong enthusiasm is enough to win freedom, but to maintain it, personal, patient, unwearied work is necessary; everyone must cherish it within and against themselves, against fatigue, selfishness, mistakes, ambition, the desire to dominate."[485] These sentences were very reminiscent of Mill's thought: "Among the works of man, which human life is rightly employed in perfecting and beautifying, the first in importance surely is man himself. [...] Human nature is not a machine to be built after a model and set to do exactly the work prescribed for it, but a tree, which requires to grow and develop itself on

484 J.S. Mill *On Liberty*, London 1864, p. 135.

485 L. Wolowski *Mémoire sur le cours de politique constitutionnelle...*, pp. 15–16.

all sides, according to the tendency of the inward forces which make it a living thing."[486] Both shared a belief in the moral imperative of self-improvement and self-education for every human being. Hence, Wolowski's unquestionable emphasis on education including, in addition to lectures at the Conservatoire, courses for workers and activities associated with the Polish school at Batignolles.

There was, of course, much that Wolowski and Mill did not share. The Pole's thoughts on freedom were essentially much more secondary, following Constant as they still revolved around the danger of the tyranny of power. Arguably, Wolowski's Polish experience was also relevant. Mill went much further in pointing out, for example, the dangers of the omnipotence of public opinion. The two authors also differed markedly in their attitude to women. Mill opened his famous work *The Subjection of Women* with the all-encompassing sentence: "That the principle which regulates the existing social relations between the two sexes – the legal subordination of one sex to the other – is wrong in itself, and now one of the chief hindrances to human improvement; and that it ought to be replaced by a principle of perfect equality, admitting no power or privilege on the one side, nor disability on the other."[487] Mill's view of women's rights was clearly beyond his era, while Wolowski was still firmly rooted in it. In fact, he never explicitly commented on women's rights, but the issue appeared incidentally in his writings. In 1873, he said when reflecting on women and child labour: "Let us not forget, when we speak of women's freedom, that their condition is not equal to that of men. I am not one of those who would like to make them equal, nor am I in favour of systems which, by granting the same rights, wish to switch the sexes." He went on during a parliamentary discussion: "We now dispose of women without getting them involved, we dispose of women without granting them any rights; we act as their guardians. Let us exercise this guardianship in a generous and beneficial way for the fair sex."[488] This approach meant, for example, that women's work had to be reduced – Wolowski justified this primarily on moral grounds and in the interests of the family (as he emphasised, shortening women's work was also to bring an important gain in the form of… the man's home rest[489]). It also meant a specific view of marriage; according to Wolowski, the fullness of humanity was realised precisely in marriage. As he wrote back in the 1830s: "If a man and a woman have been endowed with different qualities, the ideal of marriage is realised through the full union of the spouses, in every respect; in this way the first and noblest friendship in the world is formed, according to Vico's expression. Neither spouse

486 J.S. Mill *On Liberty…*, p. 107.

487 J.S. Mill *The Subjection of Women*, New Delhi 2015, p. 5.

488 *Assemblée nationale, séances des mardi 4 et mercredi 5 février 1873 Projet de loi sur le travail des enfants dans les manufactures. Art. 3.*, "Journal Officiel de la République Française", 05.02.1873, no. 35.

489 L. Wolowski *Le Travail des enfants dans les manufactures*, Paris 1868, p. 24.

should have anything exclusive to themselves, everything between them should be shared."[490] Wolowski saw marriage as part of the destiny of both man and woman. However, his words about the full commonality of all the goods of husband and wife in the concrete legal context of France must have meant total subordination of woman to man[491].

Louis Wolowski's view on divorce was characteristic in the context of marriage. The right to divorce, included in the Napoleonic Code, was abolished in France by the Bourbons in 1816, while Wolowski fully accepted and even supported this ban. A little later, in 1850, he said: "When the right to divorce was abolished in France, it could have been argued that it was a reactionary measure, driven by the party spirit. This abolition, sanctioned today by the Constituent Assembly, this abolition is, I believe, definitive: divorce has been banished from our laws."[492] Indeed, Wolowski saw the family as the foundation of all morality. Referring to ancient Rome, he argued that the permissibility of divorce had been one of the factors responsible for the decline of morality in general. This argumentation may come as a bit of a surprise in the light his fathers' attitude during a debate on the divorce law in 1830. The difference in views between the older and younger Wolowski, however, seems smaller than it might seem. For the latter clearly viewed marriage as a social good. Instead, he rejected religious arguments against divorce, reminding that religion is always a private and individual matter[493].

---

490 L. Wolowski *De la société conjugale. Introduction*, "Revue de législation et de jurisprudence", vol. I, 1846, p. 173.

491 According to the Code Napoleon, still in force at the time, a woman was completely subordinate to a man. The famous article 213 of the Code stated: "The husband owes protection to his wife, the wife obedience to her husband" (*The Code Napoleon*, London 2015 p. 25). In turn, 1421 article of the Code said: "The husband alone administers the property of the community" (*The Code Napoleon...*, p. 164). A woman could not enter any legal or financial obligations without her husband's consent, sign contracts, earn her own money, practice any profession or even testify in court. As Florence Rochefort put it: "Even if, in many cases, many women circumvented the prohibitions quite easily thanks to their agreement with their husbands, the social arrangement of marriage remained patriarchal and many dramatic or absurd situations showed that in the event of conflict, abandonment or simply a long-term absence of the husband, the woman was left out of action." (F. Rochefort *Laïcisation des moeurs et équilibres de genres. Le débat sur la capacité civile de la femme mariée*, "Vingtième Siècle. Revue d'histoire", no. 3 (87), 2005, p. 130). The only exception to this was any property brought by the woman into the marriage by way of a dowry, over which she had little control. Wolowski's proposal was essentially aimed at eliminating even this scrap of a woman's financial freedom.

492 "Moniteur Universel. Journal Officiel de la République Française", Paris 1850, p. 2151.

493 L. Wolowski *De la société conjugale...*, pp. 180–187.

In this context, Franciszek Wołowski does not appear by accident. For it seems that his influence on Louis' political attitudes and views was considerable, if not crucial. Although Louis never directly quoted his father in political or economic writings, he did encourage him to contribute to his "Revue...". As I have mentioned, father and son had collaborated in 1830/31, and continued this collaboration in Paris until Franciszek's death in 1844. Clearly the father played a leading role in this family political partnership, which also included his younger son Kazimierz. Echoes of the former Warsaw deputy's thoughts are also reflected in Louis' political concepts. He strongly defended freedom of speech as necessary for the control of power. In turn, control of power had to involve freedom of the press: "When you stifle [the press] everything dies." According to Wolowski, the movers and shakers were also in need of freedom of speech, if only to get a true picture of the country and the world. Wolowski wrote that without freedom of speech in newspapers, even those wielding the highest power in the state could be misled by others (ministers, prefects, officials, etc.). According to him, however, freedom of the press must also have meant full responsibility of journalists for their words. The state had the right to punish texts encouraging violence, insulting, lying, and slandering political opponents. But, he stressed, these were always ex post punishments; preventive censorship was completely unacceptable[494]. Thirty years earlier, Franciszek Wołowski had argued in the Sejm that "We need to defend it, to insist that we do not violate it, because freedom of printing is a pillar of representative governance". The same observation applies to the principle of the rule of law: both Wolowskis were ardent supporters and defenders of it. They both shared Constant's view: as complete equality of all (including representatives of the authorities) before the law. Franciszek justified the right of Poles to revolt in 1830 by abandoning it, while Louis based much of his economic theory on it. They also placed similar emphasis on the parliament and its crucial importance in the state.

Louis Wolowski thus drew the foundations of his political thinking from Western European liberal thought in the broadest sense (to which his father also referred earlier). He represented the same liberal generation as Tocqueville (born in 1805) and Mill (1806). Significantly, representatives of this generation, unlike the slightly older Constant (1761) or Royer-Collard (1763), were prepared to accept democracy – provided the rule of law and fundamental freedoms were preserved. Just as they accepted a monarchy operating on the same principles.

This explains why Wolowski so calmly accepted the successive political transformations taking place in Paris. He was a supporter of the House of Orléans but in 1848, he very quickly came to terms with its fall and the birth of the Second Republic. When this failed to live up to his hopes, he bid it farewell in 1851 with clearly no regrets. Politically, he was undoubtedly furthest from the authoritarian Second Empire, but he was able to take advantage of the economic freedom

494 L. Wolowski *Mémoire sur le cours de politique constitutionnelle...*, pp. 22–24.

offered by Napoleon III. Finally, in 1871, Wolowski quickly and without hesitation supported the nascent conservative and anti-revolutionary Third Republic.

2. Representative of the people

However, Louis Wolowski's first unequivocal political involvement came during the Revolution of 1848. Not only did Wolowski become a parliamentarian: he was also heavily involved in the ideological and economic conflict with the emerging socialist doctrines. The February Revolution of 1848 probably came as a surprise to him as well as to most of the political staff of the July Monarchy, headed by the omnipotent Prime Minister Guizot[495]. Namely, in late 1847, amid the most acute economic crisis in years[496], and the long-lasting political crisis of Louis-Philippe's monarchy[497], the opposition organised a campaign of banquets[498]. The last of them was to take place on 22 February 1848 in Paris' 12th arrondissement. While the authorities banned it, some participants did turn up, so the would-be banquet

495 The exception was Tocqueville; on 27 January, he said in the Chamber of Deputies: "It is said that there is no unrest, therefore there is no danger; it is said that since there is no turmoil on the surface of society, revolutions remain a remote thing. Let me tell you, in all honesty, I think you are wrong. Indeed, there is no confusion in the facts, but it has penetrated deep into the souls. [...] This, gentlemen, is my strong conviction; I think that we are sleeping on a volcano; I am deeply convinced of this." (https://www2.assemblee-nationale.fr/decouvrir-l-assemblee/histoire/grands-discours-parlementaires/alexis-de-tocqueville-27-janvier-1848, accessed on 04 March 2023). The revolution was also expected by Pierre-Joseph Proudhon as he noted on 15 February: "A banquet has been announced for one of the days of the week: it is as if the people had been told: to arms!". (P.-J. Proudhon *Carnets,* Dijon 2004, p. 777).

496 For example, in 1847 potatoes were five times more expensive than three years earlier, wheat twice as expensive. The price of bread in 1847 reached 5 francs, while the average daily earnings of a Parisian worker were less than 5 francs (E. Labrousse (ed.) *Aspects de la crise et de la dépression de l'économie française au milieu du XIX siècle 1846–1851,* La Roche sur Yon, 1956, pp. VII–IX).

497 Several factors contributed to the political and moral crisis of the House of Orléans. The most important, undoubtedly, included the high property censuses linked to the system of "official candidacies" (i.e. supported by the state) in elections, resulting in the weak legitimacy of power and its inability to self-reform; the successive moral and corruption scandals linked to the power elite, the declining popularity of the ageing king, accompanied by his rejection of any concept of change (more on the subject in: G. de Broglie *La monarchie de Juillet,* Paris 2011, pp. 381–392).

498 While typical political meetings and demonstrations were forbidden, banquets were a form of circumventing this ban.

turned into a demonstration, followed by the first clashes with the army. The following day, barricades were put up in Paris; the revolutionaries were supported by part of the National Guard, the most significant armed force in the capital city. In response, Louis-Philippe decided to dismiss Guizot which seemingly calmed the public. However, in the evening of the same day, there was a shootout between an army unit and the demonstrators, with some 20 people killed in the process. So, on 24 February, barricades were formed in Paris yet again, but this time the rebels demanded the abdication of the monarch himself. Around midday, Louis-Philippe signed a document to this effect[499].

Later the same day, a republican Provisional Government was formed, headed by the old Jacques Charles Dupont de l'Eure, a veteran of the Great Revolution. The Ministry of Foreign Affairs was taken over by the poet Alphonse de Lamartine who was in fact the central figure of the government. Alexandre Ledru-Rollin oversaw home affairs; Adolphe Crémieux was given the justice ministry, François Arago the navy, and Pierre Marie the public works. The ranks also included Louis Blanc, the first ever socialist in the government, and Alexandre Martin, a worker commonly known as Albert.

The new government promptly issued a series of decrees. On 26 February, it removed the death penalty for political offences; on 4 March, it abolished slavery in the colonies, and introduced complete freedom of assembly; on 6 March, complete freedom of the press was secured, followed by religious freedom on 10 March. In addition, on 2 March, the principle of universal suffrage was established, a decree resulting in elections. Initially, they were to be held on 9 April 1848[500].

Wolowski's writings of 1846 and 1847 do not include any revolutionary predictions or concerns whatsoever. Nor did he deal with socialist doctrines of the time, of which he was presumably unaware. It is known for a fact that he had previously met Proudhon in person[501]. However, he did not seem to have paid attention to Proudhon's works. It was only the revolution and the events following it that prompted him to engage in polemics with revolutionary thinkers. Nor is there any indication of the Pole's involvement in the turbulent days of 22–24 February 1848. If André Lavertujon, author of a posthumous text on Wolowski in "Le Temps", is to be believed, he became active in March, that is when the February Revolution had broken out[502]. It was a time of complete freedom of speech in Paris, with political

---

499 More on the subject in: S. Charléty *Histoire de la monarchie de Juillet 1830–1848,* Paris 2018, pp. 535–554.

500 Ph. Vigier *La Seconde République,* Paris 1967, pp. 5–10.

501 P.-J. Proudhon *Carnets...*, p. 18.

502 A. Lavertujon *M. Wolowski,* [in:] "Le Temps", no. 5601, 17 Aug. 1876. Markiewicz, referring to the same text, is slightly wrong stating that "During the February riots, he took part in clubs and street assemblies, denouncing social revolutionaries." (P. Markiewicz *Louis Wolowski...*, p. 124).

clubs mushrooming. Gustave Flaubert left a picturesque description of these clubs in his *Sentimental Education*: "They visited them, or nearly all, the red and the blue, the furious and the tranquil, the puritanical and the licentious, the mystical and the intemperate, those that had voted for the death of kings, and those in which the frauds in the grocery trade had been denounced; and everywhere the tenants cursed the landlords; the blouse was full of spite against broadcloth; and the rich conspired against the poor. Many wanted indemnities on the ground that they had formerly been martyrs of the police; others appealed for money in order to carry out certain inventions, or else there were plans of phalansteria, projects for cantonal bazaars, systems of public felicity; then, here and there a flash of genius amid these clouds of folly, sudden as splashes, the law formulated by an oath, and flowers of eloquence on the lips of some soldier-boy, with a shoulder-belt strapped over his bare, shirtless chest. Sometimes, too, a gentleman made his appearance – an aristocrat of humble demeanour, talking in a plebeian strain, and with his hands unwashed, to make them look hard. A patriot recognised him; the most virtuous mobbed him; and he went off with rage in his soul. On the pretext of good sense, it was desirable to be always disparaging the advocates, and to make use as often as possible of these expressions: 'To carry his stone to the building,' 'social problem,' 'workshop'."[503]. Flaubert admittedly presented a somewhat distorted picture of the clubs[504], which nevertheless reflected the atmosphere, or at least how it was perceived by a large part of the bourgeoisie. This is a good moment to quote an excerpt from Tocqueville's memoirs of the spring of 1848, as it also explains, in part, Wolowski's later attitude. "I beheld, therefore, an universal endeavour to make the best of the new state of things and to win over the new master. The great landlords were glad to remember that they had always been hostile to the middle class and always favoured the people; the *bourgeois* themselves remembered with a certain pride that their fathers had been working men, and when they were unable, owing to inevitable obscurity of their pedigrees, to trace back their descent to a labourer who had worked with his hands, they at least strove to discover a plebeian ancestor who had been the architect of his own fortune. They took as great pains to make a display of the latter as, not long before, they would have taken to conceal his existence: so true it is that human vanity, without changing

503 G. Flaubert *Sentimental Education; Or, The History of a Young Man,* New York, and London, 1904, pp. 134–135.

504 Daniel Stern wrote more extensively and thoroughly about the clubs in her memoirs (real name Marie d'Agoult, *Histoire de la révolution de 1848*, Paris 1869, pp. 230–238). The general tenor of d'Agoult's description, however, is like Flaubert's. A slightly different view of the clubs is taken by Samuel Hayat, a contemporary French historian, and an excellent expert on the popular history of 1848, who sees them as part of a popular, grassroots version of republic and democracy (S. Hayat *Quand la République était révolutionnaire. Citoyenneté et représentationn en 1848,* Paris 2014).

its nature, can show itself under the most diverse aspects. It has an obverse and a reverse side, but it is always the same medal. As there is no longer a genuine feeling left save that of fear, far from breaking with those of his relations who had thrown themselves into the Revolution, each strove to get closer to them"[505]. The key word here falls in the last sentence: fear. Fear of chaos, fear of a society temporarily deprived of power and hierarchy, fear of the armed workers, the "aliens", the "barbarians" who have overrun the city[506]. This fear, which peaked during the June workers' uprising of 1848, otherwise understandable (understanding not to be confused with justification) was evident in Wolowski's own recollections of the time between March and June 1848, and in contemporary descriptions of his activities. When, in the mid-fifties, Wolowski recalled the Revolution of 1848, he referred to a "volcano from which we had just emerged", to the many dangers lurking in the midst of heated debates, to the "great services rendered at the time by people like Léon Faucher, Michel Chevalier, Blanqui and many others who enlightened public opinion and put a dam against the doctrines of social upheaval", to the "historic merit" of Faucher polemising in April 1848 with the doctrines of Louis Blanc[507]. Wolowski's account of the economic discussions taking place at the time resembled an account of a battle whose participants, especially representing one ("reasonable and rational") side, were exposed to innumerable dangers. Lavertujon gave a similar account of Wolowski:

> All of today's fifty-year-olds remember the struggle that Mr Wolowski, a liberal imbued with the true spirit of the Revolution, and a trained economist at that, undertook against the socialist systems, then much appreciated, in March 1848 in the Parisian clubs. [...] The malady, widespread even in milieus once completely unaware

---

505 A. de Tocqueville *The Recollections of Alexis de Tocqueville*, New York 1896, pp. 103–104.

506 This alienation, mental, cultural, and social barrier between the bourgeoisie and the working classes, is brilliantly analysed in the now classic work by Louis Chevalier. In summarising his description of the relations and mutual perceptions of the bourgeoisie and the working classes in Paris in the first half of the 19th century, Chevalier wrote: "Beyond the class conflicts and independently of the progress of class awareness, there appears in these years [of the July Monarchy] a purely Parisian problem: a population which, unsuccessfully, tries to find a place for itself in a hostile environment and which subjects itself to hatred, violence, rape. A class struggle, yes, but complemented by a struggle that the contemporaries described as a conflict of races: a conflict between two populations different in every respect, above all in body, not only socially but biologically." (L. Chevalier *Classes laborieuses et classes dangereuses à Paris pendant la première moitié du XIX siècle*, Paris 2007, p. 553)

507 L. Wolowski *Introduction,* [in:] L. Faucher *Mélanges d'économie politique et de finances. Histoire financière*, Paris 1856, pp. I-XIX.

> of it, was all the more dangerous. Its source was extraordinary ignorance of the most basic truths of political economy; no wonder then that it wreaked havoc among the working masses, suddenly granted with the freedom of assembly. It took no small amount of courage to go to these prejudiced and passionate, agitated assemblies, to combat the fashionable utopias. Wolowski demonstrated boldness and, perhaps more importantly, a sense of humour. Although he made no concessions to mistakes, his frank and open nature, his clear vocabulary, appealed to this volatile audience. The success was enormous.[508]

In a similar vein, Levasseur described Wolowski's activities at the time[509]. Unfortunately, we do not have the reports of these club meetings or street gatherings, and the 'enormous success' of Wolowski is doubtful. What we do know, however, is that in March, Wolowski appeared at the deliberations of the so-called Luxembourg Commission. As early as on 25 February, the Provisional Government issued a decree pledging to "guarantee every citizen a job"[510]. On 28 February, the first major workers' demonstration took place, demanding the establishment of a separate Ministry of Labour within the government. Also advocating this solution was Louis Blanc, the incumbent of the Provisional Government, albeit without portfolio. Lamartine was immediately against it, and with him most of the ministers. Blanc threatened to resign; to avoid this, his fellow government members proposed that he set up a special government commission with workers in mind. Blanc initially resisted, but eventually gave in[511]. The commission was formally established on the same day with a sole purpose of improving the lot of workers, with Blanc as chairman, Albert as vice-chairman[512]. The commission was seated in the Luxembourg Palace, from which it subsequently took its name. It consisted of one hundred and several dozen delegates elected by various professional corporations[513]. As Blanc later wrote, the commission invited as

---

508 A. Lavertujon *M. Wolowski...*.

509 E. Levasseur *La Vie et les travaux de Wolowski...*, p. 15.

510 *République Française, Paris, le 25 février 1848. Le Gouvernement de la République Française s'engage à garantir l'existence de l'Ouvrier par le travail*, poster, Musée Carnavalet, inv. no. AFF2652.

511 Years later, Blanc wrote: "Instead of a ministry equipped with offices, officials, a budget, administrative resources, real power, implementation capacities, ways of working, what was I was offered? The establishment of a tumultuous university where I was to lecture on hunger before a starved populace!" (L. Blanc *Histoire de la Révolution de 1848*, vol. I, Paris 1880, p. 134).

512 L. Blanc *Histoire de la Révolution de 1848...*, pp. 136–137.

513 *Procès-verbal de la Commission de Gouvernement pour les travailleurs, 2 mars 1848*: [in:] *Le droit au travail au Luxembourg età l'Assemblée Nationale*, Paris 1849, p. 5. François Bruand showed well that the representativeness of the Commission's workers was problematic: firstly, because workshop owners were also elected, and

members "competent people, regardless of the school represented; these included Charles Duveyrier, [Pierre] Cazeaux, Jean Reynaud, [Alphonse] Toussenel, Victor Considérant, Wolowski, [...] Pierre Leroux, [...] [François] Vidal [...], [Constantin] Pecqueur".[514] The experts mentioned by Blanc represented very different points of view indeed. Duveyrier, Cazeaux and Reynaud had a Saint-Simonist background. Toussenel and Considérant were Fourierists. Leroux and Pecqueur, author of *New theories of social and political economy*[515], were also socialists. Wolowski was thus the only representative of the liberal school in this group. However, as he later recalled, his main opponent was the chairman of the committee, Louis Blanc.

The Pole spoke on 20 March, during the first substantive debate. At that time, Blanc proposed a systemic economic reform, a system of national workshops of his own design. The workshops were to be taken over voluntarily from entrepreneurs by the state, with compensation, and then handed over to workers' co-operatives. The workers were to manage them and set their own wages, but Blanc was clearly in favour of their equality. The system of associations was also to involve all the workshops in a specific industry: they were to jointly set the prices of their products and the ranges within which wages would evolve, depending on the needs of the various regions. The final agreement would be that between the various industries, wages in all the branches would be guaranteed and an insurance fund would be built up in case of difficulties. The whole system was to be entirely voluntary[516]. Wolowski accused Blanc's system of completely abandoning the individual in favour of the common interest. He stressed that this would probably result in a decline in production rather than growth. He also disagreed with top-down wage regulation, sticking to the principle of supply and demand. Interestingly, in doing so, he referred to the revolutionary principle of economic freedom and the triad of liberty, equality, and fraternity. However, he stressed that Blanc's system would ultimately be the end of freedom. In addition to Blanc, Toussenel, Vidal and others took part in the discussion, all more or less opposed to Wolowski. They accused him predominantly of equating freedom with chaos and of depriving the working masses of their freedom[517]. The deliberations ended without any decision being

secondly some minority groups of workers were poorly or not at all represented. The absence of women was conspicuous. A separate issue was the actual role of the workers in the Commission, sometimes reduced to listening to successive speeches (F. Bruand *La Commission du Luxembourg en 1848,* [in:] F. Démier (dir.) *Louis Blanc. Un socialiste en république*, Paris 2005, pp. 107–131).

514 L. Blanc *Histoire de la Révolution de 1848...*, pp. 171–172.

515 C. Pecqueur *Théorie nouvelle d'Économie sociale et politique ou Études sur l'organisation des sociétés*, Paris 1842.

516 *Commission de Gouvernement pour les travailleurs. Projet d'organisation du travail. Séance du 20 mars 1848,* [in:] *Le droit au travail au Luxembourg...*, pp. 65–69.

517 *Commission de Gouvernement pour les travailleurs. Projet d'organisation du travail. Séance du 20 mars 1848,* [in:] *Le droit au travail au Luxembourg...*, pp. 70–80.

taken. While Wolowski single-handedly defended the principles of the free market, there is no sign of physical threat to him in the meeting minutes. It is also difficult to see his "tremendous success", reminisced later. On the other hand, his argumentation deserves a credit: it was quite simple, clear, common-sense, and tailored to a working-class audience. Hence probably the recurring references to the Great Revolution.

Wolowski reprised the views presented during the committee's deliberations in a separate text in *Le Siècle* where he explicitly disagreed with Blanc, again emphasising the importance of individual initiative in the economy. He also mentioned national workshops, in his view an auxiliary tool but absolutely useless in replacing private property, and certainly not through coercion. He accused the socialist minister of being detached from humanity. "We believe completely," he wrote, "in the future of the associative movement; in our view an association is not a mechanism, it is above all a sense. It requires enlightenment and virtues – without them we will build on sand. We must be able to create them, they cannot be decreed." It also seems that these words were not entirely honest: to a historian, his nods to workers' associations and co-operatives seem forced by political circumstances. Interestingly, further in the text Wolowski admitted that the state should not only be a "night watchman" in the economy; it should also act as a driving force of action, a lever pushing private economy forward[518]. These words largely corresponded to Louis Napoleon Bonaparte's later economic programme.

Louis Wolowski must have presented the same views at the République Nouvelle ('New Republic') club, founded in April 1848, and based in the Palais National (former Palais Royal). Auguste Barbier, a poet, and playwright, was its founder and president while Wolowski became one of the vice-presidents. The club clearly had an anti-socialist bias. "When envy, greed, hatred and all sorts of bad feelings were let off the chain against the most sacred institutions, [...] the president of the République Nouvelle club held the banner of civilisation with a sure hand; he was seconded in this by the superbly respectable figures with whom he surrounded himself," wrote a contemporary (conservative) witness[519].

Wolowski's presence at the Luxembourg Palace, and later in *Le Siècle*, is an indication that his name in Paris was becoming familiar not only to a narrow circle of economists, lawyers, and "Revue..." readers. The text published in *Le Siècle* was probably a part of his election campaign. Indeed, he decided to stand for parliamentary elections. Initially announced for 09 April 1848, at the request of a delegation of radicals led by Louis Auguste Blanqui[520] the elections were postponed

518 L. Wolowski *De l'organisation du travail,* "Le Siècle", 09.04.1848.

519 A. Lucas *Les clubs et les clubistes: histoire complète critique et anecdotique des clubs et des comités électoraux fondés à Paris depuis la révolution de 1848,* Paris 1851, p. 223.

520 Louis Auguste Blanqui (1805–1881), a radical revolutionary, was the younger brother of Adolphe, the economist and friend of Wolowski's.

by the government on 17 March by two weeks. Blanqui, fearing a Conservative victory in the popular vote, tried to postpone the elections for at least a year. They were finally held on 23 April[521].

In a proclamation to voters, Louis Wolowski portrayed himself as a child of Poland as well as France: "for Poland is, after all, the France of the north". He also emphasised his attachment to the republic, which he saw as "free from all excesses, strong in virtue, generous as in the first days after the victory when it abolished the death penalty, based on respect for family and property, called upon to solve the greatest problem of modern times, the problem of improving the moral, material and intellectual condition of the working people." This republican credo gives the impression of being not entirely sincere, forced by the revolutionary mood of the time. As I pointed out earlier in the part of the book devoted to his political thought, Wolowski was not an opponent of the republic by conviction, but neither was he an ardent supporter of it. Probably more sincere was his declaration of devotion to family and property and the following words about the importance of economic freedom or education creating "moral capital and intellectual capital, the first sources of wealth, happiness, and human dignity."[522]. Wolowski appeared as a typical representative of a group later referred to as the "republicans of tomorrow", mostly members of Louis-Philippe's former monarchical elite. More or less willingly, they came to terms with the republic the day after the February Revolution. However, they did not intend to accept any significant social concessions. For, in essence, Wolowski's programme defended the economic and social status quo while accepting political change.

Paris elected 34 parliamentarians at the time. Wolowski scored 22nd, with 132,333 votes cast in his favour[523]. It is, however, difficult to judge clearly to what extent this should be attributed to his popularity and to what extent it was linked to voting for specific lists. As the then Minister of Finance Louis-Antoine Garnier-Pagès wrote with regret: "In Paris, the number of nominations exceeded all predictions. It was estimated at two thousand, probably far below the actual number. It is no longer possible to describe the din today. A constant turmoil without a moment's rest. Streams of words flooded by more streams. [...] Every evening, new declarations of principle resounded from the five hundred stands. [...] Not being able to hear everything or read everything, the voter was forced to trust the lists drawn up by the committees, which thus became the supreme arbiters of elections."[524] Wolowski's name was included on several such lists of moderate or conservative candidates, most of them sharing his views. The lists

521 M. Agulhon *1848 ou l'apprentissage de la République, 1848–1852,* Paris 1992, pp. 56–57.

522 L. Wolowski *Aux citoyens électeurs du département de la Seine,* Paris 1848.

523 "Journal des Débats Politiques et Littéraires", 29.04.1848.

524 L.A. Garnier-Pagès *Histoire de la Révolution de 1848,* vol. V, 3, Paris 1866, pp. 229–230.

were subsequently reprinted by influential press[525]. In addition, Wolowski could count on the support of Chambolle and *Le Siècle*, a newspaper enjoying the largest circulation at the time.

Be that as it may, Louis Wolowski became a member of the first French parliament elected by universal (albeit exclusively male) suffrage in April 1848. It was a Chamber very different from that under the July Monarchy, not only because of its composition. The nomenclature also changed; the electors were no longer "deputies" but "representatives of the people". There were also more of them, some 900 in total (the Second Republic discreetly followed the pattern of the first, Jacobin period). Among them, Wolowski was undoubtedly a member of the moderate republican and conservative majority[526].

Wolowski suspended his lectures at the Conservatoire des Arts et Métiers and devoted himself entirely to parliamentary activity. Right at the very beginning, he unexpectedly found himself in the epicentre of a real political turmoil, completely against his intentions. The issue at hand was the Polish cause. On 20th March 1848, upon hearing of the revolution in Berlin[527], a National Committee, later transformed into the Central National Committee, was established in Poznań. The Committee also set up a military department. Since early April, there were clashes between the forming Polish troops and the Prussian army. On 11 April, a settlement was signed in Jarosławiec, according to which part of Wielkopolska was to be granted autonomy. In return, the insurgent troops were to be limited to 3,200 men. However, the Prussian authorities quickly broke the agreement, and further fighting ensued. On 29 April, Wielkopolska troops suffered defeat at Książ, but the next day triumphed over the Prussians at Miłosław. The advantage of the latter was enormous: on 30 April the National Committee dissolved, on 09 May the

---

525 E.g. "Journal des Débats Politiques et Littéraires", 22.04.1848; "Le Constitutionnel " 22.04.1848, " Le Siècle " 22.04.1848.

526 Due to the difficulty of indicating a specific political affinity of some of the representatives, the figures vary. Maurice Agulhon suggests 500 moderate republicans, 250 monarchists and about 150 radical republicans, close to socialism (M. Agulhon *1848 ou l'apprentissage de la République...*, p. 66). Philippe Vigier mentions 500 republicans (some 280 of them "authentic", the rest being mainly former notables of the July Monarchy), 300 conservative monarchists and a hundred radicals (Ph. Vigier *La Seconde République...*, p. 33). Sylvie Aprile, on the other hand, mentions moderate republicans "some of whom are in fact monarchists", 200 Orleanists, 50 legitimists (supporters of the House of Bourbon) and 200 radical republicans (S. Aprile *1815–1870 La Révolution inachevée...*, p. 310).

527 In another text, I point out that the Paris February Revolution also contributed to the growing tensions in the capital of Wielkopolska. See: R. Dobek *Paris and Poznań in 1848*, [in:] P. Matusik (ed.) *A Polish, European city: studies in the history of Poznań*, Poznań 2022, pp. 149–166.

main insurgent troops capitulated in Bardo, by mid-May 1848 the uprising finally collapsed[528]. These events were followed closely in France. Polish émigrés decided to take advantage of this so, on 10 May 1848, Wolowski presented to Parliament a petition signed by Józef Wysocki, Wincenty Tyszkiewicz and Ryszard Berwiński, representatives of the three partitions. In elevated words, they addressed the French: "People of France! The empty declarations of your ex-king of the last seventeen years about us fill you with noble and holy indignation. Today, when God has given you your independence back, you will not allow your Polish brothers, your former comrades in glory, to be cowardly murdered."[529] Given Wolowski's links with the Hotel Lambert, it seems almost certain that the speech was agreed in advance with Prince Czartoryski[530]. However, there was no response for a while. After Wolowski's words, at Lamartine's request, further debate was postponed to the following Monday, 15 May 1848[531].

The first to speak that day was again the Polish representative of the people. Wolowski tried to convince the other members of the Assembly that they should not consider doing anything for Poland, only *what* it would be. He also protested the words of Lamartine (biased against Poles) who had earlier portrayed them as a nation perpetually at odds and incapable of maintaining a state. Finally, he stressed

---

528 More on the subject: S. Kieniewicz *Społeczeństwo polskie w powstaniu poznańskim 1848 roku,* Warszawa 1960, pp. 144–392; M. Rezler *Wielkopolska Wiosna Ludów 1848,* Poznań 1993, pp. 56–243; A. Wojtkowski *Powstanie wielkopolskie roku 1848,* Poznań 1938; M. Zgórniak *Za Waszą i naszą wolność,* Warszawa 1987, pp. 23–31.

529 "Moniteur Universel...", Paris 1848, p. 1007.

530 In the same days, the Prince sent a letter to Lamartine, a letter subsequently published by the "Journal des Débats Politiques et Littéraires", May 08, 1848. In it, Czartoryski warned of a Prussian reaction and referred directly to the National Assembly.

531 Interestingly, Joachim Lelewel reacted negatively to this speech. On 26 May 1848, he wrote to Stanisław Worcell from Brussels (asking him also to forward the letter to Wolowski):

> The Polish cause raised in an unfortunate way. It was not Wolowski's responsibility but a Frenchman's, was there none? [...] Why talk about the nationalité [nationality] of Louis-Philippe? We have long since denounced it in exile. Why grumble about an ex-roi [ex-king]? La nation francaise [the French nation] spoke par l'organe des Chambres [through the Chambers], not Louis-Philippe. It is not what must be exhibited, that blood is pouring, but that when they do not give our element support, a threatening reaction rears its head. It is necessary to enumerate what has not been done, so that they comprehend what, in their own interest, they can and should do.

(J. Lelewel *Listy emigracyjne Joachima Lelewela,* vol. III, 1842–1848, Kraków 1952, pp. 438–439).

that without an independent Poland, Europe would never know a lasting and just peace. He even mentioned the French army, although he did not seem to have been thinking of war. The beginning of Wolowski's speech was clearly at odds with the Provisional Government's foreign policy line, led by Lamartine. This was best described in a circular published by French newspapers on 05 March, in which the poet declared very clearly the peaceful intentions of the Second Republic (thus dissociating himself from the martial traditions of the First Republic), while at the same time clearly delineating France's sphere of influence, which traditionally included Italy, Switzerland, Belgium, and Spain, but certainly not Poland[532].

This was only the beginning of Wolowski's speech, and it is unclear how it was to continue because he did not finish his train of thoughts. In the transcripts of the House meeting, in this passage there are repeated references to "an uproar outside", "shouting outside the chamber", etc.[533]. After a while, a crowd of people burst into the room and the meeting was adjourned. Charles de Rémusat, a key Orléanist politician, former Minister of the Interior and later Minister of Foreign Affairs, recalled: "Wolowski began his speech, rigid as usual, which this time, however, at least gave the impression of courage, when we heard an indefinable noise from outside. I went out immediately and, from the northern peristyle, I saw a long procession of people, dressed differently but above all workers, walking in an extended line from the Madeleine area and the Louis XV Bridge. [...] Soon, the entire hall was filled with a crowd in which it was difficult to move. The attackers mingled with us and sat on our benches wherever they could find room"[534].

Consequently, Louis Wolowski became an unwitting perpetrator and witness of an attempted coup, for that was precisely the point. Aware of the impending Polish debate in Parliament, the representatives of the radical, revolutionary left: Louis Auguste Blanqui, Armand Barbès, Aloysius Huber and François-Vincent Raspail, decided to seize the opportunity to undermine what they saw as a reactionary Assembly and the new government – the so-called Executive Commission[535]. They were aware of the agitation caused in Paris by the news of the defeat of the Wielkopolska Uprising. Earlier, moreover, Blanqui said that "The word Poland is magical and incites the people of Paris"[536]. Wolowski's intervention thus became

532 A. de Lamartine *Circulaire du ministre des affaires étrangères aux agens diplomatiques de la Républque française*, "Le National" 05.III.1848.

533 "Moniteur Universel...", Paris 1848, p. 1053.

534 Ch. De Rémusat *Mémoires de ma vie*, vol. IV, *Les dernières années de la monarchie. La Révolution de 1848. La Seconde République (1841–1851)*, Paris 1958, p. 300.

535 On 09 May 1848, the Assembly (including Wolowski) appointed the Executive Commission, or a new government. It consisted of Arago, Garnier-Pagès, Lamartine, Ledru-Rollin, and Marie. Clearly, the Assembly just removed from the government the two most left-wing members, Blanc, and Albert.

536 Ph. Vigier *La Seconde République...*, p. 36. Similarly, Lamartine later wrote: "The Poles, an expatriate nation which has adopted the world as its homeland, and which

a convenient pretext for organising a huge demonstration in defence of Poland. Only that the aim of the demonstration, of which the vast majority of participants were initially unaware, was to bring about a change of power not on the Vistula or Warta, but on the Seine.

At first it seemed that the goal of the revolutionaries would be achieved. Indeed, some 100,000–150,000 people took to the streets, ready to support the dying Poles. The demonstrators broke into the National Assembly building. Let Rémusat speak again:

> Having read out his petition in favour of Poland, which was neither offensive nor threatening, but contained a conclusion in the form of a war for Polish independence, Raspail tried to persuade the crowd to withdraw. [...] But Blanqui was spot on; for him it was not enough. I have not seen him since July [the July Revolution of 1830 – RD] in the editorial office of the *Globe*. Weary, worn out by passion, he grew old in his sense of hatred; in a sharp, properly morbid tone he added to the address in favour of Poland the expressions of discontent and the demands of the workers. [...] The crowd and its leaders hesitated. They were the masters of the Assembly; they only came to intimidate them, now they held them in the palm of their hand. They did not know what to do. To retreat without taking advantage of such a victory would have meant passing up an excellent opportunity. They had to take a step further or retreat. Huber, one of the leaders of the movement, came up with the idea of allowing the people to march through the Assembly. [...] Barbès immediately supported this idea and decreed the march of the army towards the borders and a tax of one billion on the rich[537].

Finally, Huber announced the dissolution of the Assembly and ordered, in accordance with the revolutionary tradition of Paris, a march towards the Hotel de Ville – the building where the new state system was usually announced. It turned out, however, that the radicals had lost too much time, for in the meantime, the demonstrators, not keen on overthrowing the government, began to disperse to their homes. In turn, the National Guard troops, loyal to the government, arrived on the scene. The remnants of the demonstration were quickly dispersed, Blanqui, Raspail, Barbès – arrested. It all lasted just a few hours. Notably, once again these hours among the members of the Assembly were accompanied by fear. This time real, direct fear for his own life, about which Rémusat also wrote directly.[538] Wolowski probably shared that fear. The fear, and the humiliation associated with it, makes one partially understand the subsequent votes and behaviour of the people's representatives.

---

brings to all its adoptive homelands all the virtues and defects of this great and unhappy nation: heroism, unruliness and anarchy, moved the people of Paris to madness." (A. de Lamartine *Mémoires politiques*, Paris 1863, p. 141).

537 Ch. De Rémusat *Mémoires de ma vie*, vol. IV..., p. 302.

538 Ch. De Rémusat *Mémoires de ma vie*, vol. IV..., p. 303.

The events of 15 May were perhaps most aptly commented on by Tocqueville; according to him "[...] it was at least one of those equivocal enterprises which so frequently occur in times of popular excitement, in which the promoters themselves are careful not to trace or define precisely their plan or their aim, so as to remain free to limit themselves to a peaceful demonstration or force on a revolution."[539].

For the time being, the danger passed. So did the Polish moment in the Assembly. After the defeat of the Wielkopolska uprising, interest in Polish issues inevitably declined. Moreover, after the revolutionary attempt in May, it was better not to raise them for some time.

In France, a lot was still going on, and Wolowski also had a lot of work to do as a parliamentarian. In most cases, he voted in line with the moderate conservative parliamentary majority. Thus, on 26 May, he voted in favour of expelling the Orléans family from France. As Markiewicz notes, he severed the last ties with the recently fallen dynasty. Contrary to Markiewicz, who argues that Wolowski was "deeply aware of the irresponsibility" of the Orléans[540], I would rather be inclined to regard this vote as pure opportunism. It is also difficult to ignore the fact that apparently, by 1848, he no longer remembered Ferdinand Philippe d'Orléans, a "schoolmate" who died in 1842.

He also took part in the key political and economic discussion of May-June 1848, a dispute over the national workshops. As early as in late February 1848, the Provisional Government established the national workshops. This was a response to the workers' growing demands of actual implementation of the labour decree of 25 February. The workshops had nothing to do with Blanc's vision. The authors of the finally implemented concept were the minister Pierre Marie and the young engineer Emile Thomas. Unlike the idea of the President of the Luxembourg Commission, the national workshops were top-down, highly centralised, and hierarchical entities. The workers were employed in the Paris districts. They were organised in squads of 11, which then formed brigades, which in turn were part of the district governorates. They were paid 2 francs for a day's work, 1.5 francs for readiness for work on a day when work was lacking. By design, the employees of the national workshops were to work primarily on major investments, public works, and railway construction. According to Mark Traugott, the workshops also had a political dimension – their task was to pacify the workers and draw them away from the radical revolutionaries. Taugott, citing Donald McKay's book *The National Workshops*[541], emphasises that in this political (and only political sense), they were successful until June 1848: workers employed in the national workshops

539 A. de Tocqueville *Recollections...*, p. 157.

540 P. Markiewicz *Louis Wolowski...*, p. 125.

541 D.C. McKay *The National Workshops. A study in the French Revolution of 1848*, Cambridge, MA 1933.

took little part in anti-government demonstrations. Only the government did not see this at all.

From an economic point of view, the workshops were a complete fiasco. Primarily because the government could not or would not guarantee enough jobs. Moreover, in March Marie and Thomas assumed that the workshops would employ a maximum of 10,000 people. After three months, there were more than ten times as many workers; the workshops also attracted visitors from the province with no work during the crisis. As a result, as Taugott acknowledges after McKay, the workshops became a crippling financial burden that the state had to bear in times of an economic crisis[542].

In late May 1848, therefore, a debate heated up in parliament about the workshops. A large majority of the parliamentarians called for their immediate closure and for the workers to be sent back to wherever they came from. To them, the workshops were an epitome of laziness and indolence at best, an army of revolutionary bandits ready to turn against the Assembly at any time, like on 15 May, in the worst-case scenario. Thomas, the greatest defender of the workshops, was dismissed, immediately arrested, and sent out of Paris.

Louis Wolowski also spoke out. As late as on 10 May, he suggested the establishment of a special parliamentary committee to deal with improving the lot of workers[543]. In his view, however, this improvement could only come about through the application of free market principles. He was also concerned about the influence of leftist or socialist thinkers in the working-class world[544]. Hence his unequivocally negative opinion of state-controlled and state-paid workshops. He defended the idea of sending workers outside the capital on 31 May in the Assembly in the name of free-market principles. For it was not, as he claimed, about depriving them of work, but about sending them to where the market needed them. He had a very negative opinion of the workshops: "their efforts are completely sterile,

---

542 M. Taugott *Les ateliers nationaux en 1848,* [in:] J.L. Mayaud (dir.) *1848: actes du colloque international du cent cinquantenaire, tenu à l'Assemblée nationale à Paris, les 23-25 février 1998,* Paris 2002, pp. 185–202.

543 "Moniteur Universel...", Paris 1848, p. 1009.

544 Rémusat recalled that he met Wolowski one day, who told him about his trip to Lyon and his meeting with the local workers. According to Wolowski, they had already established beliefs, acquired through regular meetings in cafés or reading rooms. They read mainly democratic literature and listened to golden-mouthed populist speakers. Left to their own devices by the authorities, they found themselves primarily influenced by Proudhon's theories. Wolowski claimed that the Lyon workers were also keen to listen to his arguments. The trouble, he argued, was that "The whole population of Lyon is imbued with socialism. It wants education very much at the same time, but it receives none. I pointed this out to the authorities, but they did not listen to me." (Ch. De Rémusat *Mémoires de ma vie,* vol. IV..., pp. 165–166)

they also entail an enormous loss for the country, even if we limit ourselves to the 140,000 or 150,000 francs paid in the workshops every day in wages, but we should count twice or three times this sum, because we lose the useful work that these arms could have given to the country; this work is completely lost; this loss is all the greater in that it may entail the loss of part of their ability and, in some cases, of their morality."[545] Wolowski's speech featured a typical element of the time, a vision of demoralised workers ready to attack the people's representatives. Wolowski also overlooked the obvious fact that there was a shortage of work outside Paris as much as in the city itself. He failed to see the evident contradiction in his own words: the forced relocation of workers was completely incompatible with the principles of the free market. Finally, taking away sources of livelihood from more than a hundred thousand people overnight simply condemned some of them and their families to starvation. It seems, however, that after 15 May, the entire Assembly (Wolowski included), horrified by the events, completely lost whatever empathy they felt for the poorest.

In the end, the Executive Commission, pressed by the Assembly[546], decided to immediately expel the workers from Paris. On 21 June 1848, a decree was published in the "Moniteur", the republic's official newspaper, according to which workers aged 18–25, employed in the national workshops, were to report immediately to the army or prepare to leave Paris quickly[547]. In the evening, the first demonstrations took place. The next morning a delegation of workers was unceremoniously dismissed by Minister Marie. On the evening of 22 June, the first barricades were erected in the working-class neighbourhoods. The next morning, more barricades were set up. The government forces were headed by General Louis-Eugène Cavaignac, Minister of War since 17 May. The revolt spread to the entire north and east of the city, with the first clashes taking place on the afternoon of 23 June. The advantage of the government side was crushing: Cavaignac had at his disposal not only regular troops, but also a part of the bourgeois National

---

545 "Moniteur Universel...", Paris 1848, p. 1216.

546 Lamartine later recalled: "The newspapers of the monarchist parties kept repeating that the people of the Provisional Government had paid this army of paupers [the national workshops] to put pressure on the Assembly, to intimidate it and, by a clear threat, to subject it to their will to domination. The Assembly was ready to believe these calumnies. While the government neglected no effort, no caution, no preparation to dismiss without bloodshed this militia, whose existence it deplored and whose offences it restricted, the Assembly saw in the most important members of this government the accomplices of the revolt." (A. de Lamartine *Mémoires politiques...*, p. 402). As this passage suggests, the Executive Commission also intended to dissolve the national workshops, presumably somewhat later, in a way less violent for the workers.

547 D. Stern *Histoire de la révolution...*, p. 421.

Guard and volunteers from the provinces. The insurgents were also virtually devoid of artillery. The last shots were fired on 26 June, when the workers' suburb of Saint-Antoine fell. As Michèle Riot-Sarcey and Maurizio Gribaudi write in the conclusion of a book largely devoted to the June events, the exact number of victims on the workers' side is virtually impossible to indicate. Official figures from an investigation carried out in the Assembly in July that year mentioned approx. 1,000 dead. Contemporary historians estimate the number at around 5–6,000, including a significant group of individuals shot after the fighting. This should be topped with 1,500 soldiers and guards killed, and several thousand workers imprisoned, most of them later deported[548].

Incidentally, the Executive Commission became also a kind of victim of the revolution. On 24 June, an overwhelming majority of the Assembly voted to impose a state of emergency in Paris, thereby forcing the Commission to resign, and immediately appointing Cavaignac as President of the Executive of the Republic, and Prime Minister. Wolowski did not take part in this vote due to his absence; however, given his views and subsequent support for Cavaignac, it appears that he would have voted in line with the majority. Again, it seems this vote was primarily the result of horror. Many deputies felt that they were witnessing a clash between civilisation and barbarism, order and chaos, good and evil. Even Victor Hugo, a man otherwise sensitive to the wrongs of the people, described June 1848 in the following way: "Nothing could be more chilling and more sombre. It is a hideous thing this heroism of abjection in which bursts forth all that weakness has of strength; this civilization attacked by cynicism and defending itself by barbarity. On one side the despair of the people, on the other the despair of society."[549]. In turn, the defence of civilisation and humanity justified all actions. Wolowski was of a similar opinion. He voted on 25 August in favour of the arrest of Blanc and Marc Caussidière (prefect of police of the Provisional Government). Both were accused of complicity in the May coup, Caussidière also of the June events. There was no shadow of evidence of any revolutionary action by either of them, but the case of a socialist and a radical republican was lost because of their convictions. Again, Hugo quoted a characteristic story; he sat next to a journalist from *Le Siècle*, Wolowski's favourite title. As Blanc was about to ascend the stand to defend himself, the man shouted: "We don't give a damn about you! Say what you like!"[550]. Caussidière, one of the involved individuals, recalled the same event as follows: "The faces of many representatives showed a complete lack of interest in the words of citizen Louis Blanc. Each of them seemed to think 'You can tell the

548 M. Gribaudi, M. Riot-Sarcey *1848, la révolution oubliée*, Paris 2009, pp. 198–257.
549 V. Hugo *Choses vues. Souvenirs, journaux, cahiers*, Paris 2002, p. 567.
550 V. Hugo *Choses vues...*, p. 578.

smartest stories; you'll still be convicted.'"[551]. We can assume that Wolowski's attitude was similar....

However, Wolowski could also speak out against the majority on important issues in the name of basic humanitarian values. This was the case, for example, in September 1848, during a debate on the new state constitution (republican France still lacked basic law at the time). The Assembly adopted Article 5 of the new constitution without much reservation: "The death penalty for political crimes has been abolished."[552]. In passing, however, there were also proposals to abolish the death penalty in general. On 15 September, a famous speech against the death penalty was delivered by Hugo: "Gentlemen, three kinds of things belong to God and do not belong to man: irrevocable things, irremediable things, and irresolvable things. Woe to man if he brings them into his laws!"[553]. Three days later, Wolowski also tried to speak on the subject. He was, of course, far less eloquent than the famous poet. In fact, he only managed to utter a single sentence, calling for the total abolition of the death penalty because of past experiences. The assembly, however, interrupted him and ordered the discussion to be closed[554]. It rejected all the amendments by 498 votes to 216.

Wolowski presented his arguments against the death penalty outside the Chamber, in a letter addressed to the editors of *Le Siècle* and reprinted in his *Revue...* The abolition of the death penalty should be a natural consequence of the introduction of the republic, he wrote. Since France became a republic, the country reached a degree of moral development sufficient to abolish the death penalty. Indeed, the moral development of society depended on respecting basic norms, including the inviolability of human life. French society was, he went on to point out, strong enough not to have to use this punishment as a form of defence. Wolowski rejected the argument referring to the universality of this form of punishment: for in the same way, for example, extracting confessions through torture had been commonplace until recently. Wolowski also described well the clash between the finality of the punishment and the ambiguities accompanying any sentence: the death penalty was, according to its proponents, to apply only to incorrigible enemies of society. But how to define the "incorrigibility" of an

---

551 M. Caussidière *Mémoires de Caussidière, ex-préfet de police et représentant du peuple*, vol. II, Paris 1849, p. 254.

552 The Constitution of 1848: https://www.conseil-constitutionnel.fr/les-constitutions-dans-l-histoire/constitution-de-1848-iie-republique, (retrieved 11.03.2023).

553 https://www2.assemblee-nationale.fr/decouvrir-l-assemblee/histoire/grands-discours-parlementaires/victor-hugo-15-septembre-1848, (retrieved 11.03.2023). Hugo authored the novel *The Last Day of a Condemned Man*, written as early as in 1829, an extraordinarily poignant and still highly relevant literary statement against the death penalty.

554 "Moniteur Universel...", Paris 1848, p. 2493.

individual in this context? – Wolowski asked. Who would dare to say that it was final, that an individual could not improve? He also referred to the divine commandment "thou shalt not kill" which also applied to society as a whole. Finally, he rejected the thesis that death at the hands of the executioner was a means of protecting society: for society's power, he insisted, was so overwhelming in the face of the individual that it could apply a whole range of other measures, like life imprisonment[555].

Incidentally, in the Assembly, Wolowski's speech was cut off by closing the discussion more often. This was also the case during a discussion extremely important for him, on the organisation of land credit, that took place in October 1848[556]. This was probably because his parliamentary speeches were reminiscent of academic lectures and were therefore too long and tedious for the listeners. In this respect, Louis was nothing like his father Franciszek who would speak competently and concisely. This was humorously expressed by Honoré Daumier in his *Album Comique*, published at the time, with caricatures of the most famous parliamentarians. The image of Wolowski (with a characteristic Polish cap on his head) was captioned: "Wolouski (sic!) is a professor of political economics, commercial economics, social economics, etc, etc.- yet there is no economy on his own words."[557] Armand Marrast, president of the National Assembly from July 1848 to May 1849, was to say that "Wolowski is a Polish word for closing [the proceedings]"[558].

In this respect, the parliamentary debate of 14 August 1848, concerning the right of workers to form "coalitions": associations or agreements intending to improve working conditions or wages, including by strike, was also characteristic. Shortly after Wolowski started his speech, somewhere in the hall there was a hoot of laughter: "Watch it, a lecture in progress!". Clearly irritated, Wolowski replied that he did not intend to lecture. He went on to defend the workers' right to self-organisation, as long as it did not violate the rights of third parties (like property rights or the freedom of others to work). He also emphasised the workers' right to defend their own wages. Incidentally, he was again in the minority[559].

The issue of workers' coalitions was to return to the House as late as in November 1849. At that time, Wolowski also defended the right of workers to fight for their own wages through coalitions. This time, however, he placed more emphasis

555 L. Wolowski *De la peine de mort,* "Revue de législation et de jurisprudence", vol. 3, September–October 1848, pp. 111–119.

556 "Moniteur Universel...", Paris 1848, p. 2804.

557 H. Daumier *Album comique,* vol. II, *Les représentants représentés,* Paris. The misspelling of the surname Wolowski was quite typical. The French often distorted it, spelling it Wolousky, Woloski, Wolowsky, etc.

558 "Ateneum: pismo naukowe i literackie", vol. 3 (3), part 9, Warszawa 1876, p. 637.

559 "Moniteur Universel...", Paris 1848, pp. 2022–2023.

on the negative effects. Above all, he stressed, he did not believe that employers could undercut workers' wages of their own accord. In doing so, he referred to the traditional theory of the positive action of the free market: lowering wages would mean lowering the costs of the entire industry, thus increasing profits, resulting in an influx of new entrepreneurs, increased competition for the worker and a necessary increase in wages. Workers' coalitions potentially only distorted this positive market mechanism and were therefore, on balance, disadvantageous to employers and workers alike.

At the same time, Wolowski the economist pointed out that not every worker's agreement and work stoppage should have been punished. What was at stake, in his view, were above all situations striking at the constitutionally guaranteed freedom of labour and freedom of industry. He therefore proposed the following definition: "Any agreement between employers or between workers to restrict the freedom of labour and industry constitutes a [punishable] coalition." According to Wolowski, in practice this meant a fight against the agreements of employers or workers that went beyond one enterprise and covered, for example, some part of the national territory. In effect, he told the Chamber: "as long as [...] the workers of one workshop discuss wages with the factory owner without coercion or violence, the law should not intervene. The debate on wages should remain free, the guarantee of this freedom, which you cannot deny the workers, even if they represent the whole of the workforce... is the right to stop working together in a factory where they do not receive the wages to which, in their own opinion, they are entitled". The situation was different, however, when there was a broad agreement of workers between factories, and this should no longer have been allowed by law. Just as it could not permit similar agreements, concerning workers' wages, between employers[560]. Wolowski, however, lost again: the Assembly rejected his labour-friendly provisions and adopted the text of an amendment to the Penal Code punishing all workers' agreements[561].

Speaking of workers' associations Wolowski, the people's representative, took an intermediate position, at least in part on the side of the people; the situation changed during the next discussion of a social nature. In late August 1848, the Assembly considered the issue of the length of the working day. As late as in March that year, the Provisional Government, under pressure from the Luxembourg Commission, limited the length of the working day to 10 hours in Paris and 11 hours outside the capital[562]. The House deliberated in August on the abolition of the said decree. Wolowski spoke out clearly against the 10 hours. He justified it

560 "Moniteur Universel...", Paris 1849, pp. 3716 & 3818.

561 "Journal du Palais. Lois, décrets, règlements et instructions d'intérêt général suivis d'annotations", Paris 1848, p. 675.

562 Announcement poster for shortened working day: https://gallica.bnf.fr/ark:/12148/btv1b530143001.image (retrieved 12.03.2023)

on the grounds of the good of the workers who would lose money following this restriction. He also highlighted the inequality between Paris and the provinces. In the end, although he allowed for state intervention on the working hours, it was only in the case of women and children[563]. This time, Louis Wolowski's vote connected with the will of the majority of parliament where, notably, only a dozen workers and craftsmen sat out of 800 elected. On 09 September 1848, the decree was revoked. Bearing in mind the date, it is difficult not to see this as an act of revenge for the June uprising.

The conservative Assembly was also fast to erase other achievements of the February Revolution of 1848. This included the Provisional Government's decree of 09 March 1848 abolishing imprisonment for debt[564]. Supporters of this solution argued that, modelled on Roman law, it was salutary to commerce, that without the threat of possible imprisonment some debtors would, by definition, not repay their loans. Wolowski protested these claims in a lengthy parliamentary speech delivered on 01 September 1848. Above all, he stressed, freedom was not an object of commerce. He also rejected the historical argument, recalling the obvious fact that Rome was a slave state. He referred to family rights and family ties, stronger than creditors' rights. Finally, he cited data according to which it was often not the debtors themselves who were imprisoned for debt, but people who were accidentally involved in the relationship between debtor and creditor. In short, he used extremely well-prepared, elaborate and stylistically refined arguments[565]. However, they were of little use. By an overwhelming majority, the decree of 9 March was revoked[566].

One other parliamentary debate in which Wolowski took part in 1848 is worth mentioning, a debate in which, in his case, personal and public motives probably mixed. The matter concerned the chair of political economy at the Collège de France[567] where Michel Chevalier previously lectured. In the spring, Education Minister Hippolyte Carnot abolished the chair. Officially, the move was justified by setting up a new central school of administration. However, during an address to the Assembly, Carnot's colleague, Jean Reynaud, explicitly pointed to the real reason as the very nature of political economy as a subject. Reynaud, a

563 "Moniteur Universel...", Paris 1848, pp. 2230–2231.

564 Text of the Decree: H. Durand *Commentaire de la loi du 13 décembre 1848 sur la contrainte par corps et du tarif du 24 mars 1849*, Paris 1850, pp. 1–2.

565 H. Durand *Commentaire...*, pp. 40–51.

566 H. Durand *Commentaire...*, p. 109.

567 The Collège de France has been one of France's most prestigious educational institutions, dating back to 1530. At the time, teaching was provided on a similar basis to the Conservatoire des Arts et Métiers: free of charge and without a diploma. The chairs at the Collège de France have enjoyed extraordinary prestige. As a rule, teaching has been of a similar standard to that of a university.

former disciple of Saint-Simon, referred to a "monarchical" economy that had to be contrasted with a more republican one. The fact is that Michel Chevalier, also a former Saint-Simonist, was certainly not a supporter of the republic[568]. Reynaud, however, clearly had the liberal and free-market nature of his thought in mind. During the budget debate in November 1848, Wolowski sharply criticised this decision. Instead, he defended the independence of the Collège de France, whose professors were elected by their peers. He emphasised the republican nature of the teaching, referring above all to the history of the chair of political economy set up during the Great Revolution. It was clear that this teaching had to be liberal and revolve around the free market. According to Wolowski, all other doctrines were mere errors or utopias, threatening disaster at the first attempt at implementation[569]. We do not know to what extent this speech by a Polish French economist influenced the Assembly: arguably more important was the attitude of the representatives towards the reforms of the Provisional Government and the Executive Commission. In any case, the chair of political economy was reinstated with Michel Chevalier at the head; he taught until 1879.

Louis Wolowski was undoubtedly a very active parliamentarian. In 1848, he became a member of a standing committee on labour and the committee on agriculture and land credit[570]. He was a member of ad hoc committees in the Chamber: the accounting committee[571], considering the draft law on primary education[572], dealing with the prison labour project[573], developing the law on public aid[574], considering the remuneration of representatives[575], dealing with the

568 Carnot was also associated with the Saint-Simon movement in his youth. Indeed, Carnot, Reynaud and Chevalier on the other hand, well represented the rupture that had occurred between democracy and socialism among the then Saint-Simonists. More on the movement in K. Popowicz *Saint-Simon i saint-simoniści – od rewolucji do kolonizacji. Historia pewnej religii (1803–1870),* Warszawa 2018.

569 "Moniteur Universel...", Paris 1848, p. 3209.

570 Unfortunately, with a few exceptions, the minutes of parliamentary committee meetings have not survived.

571 Assemblée Nationale Constituante 1848–1849 *Feuilletons*, vol. XVIII, Paris 1849, no. 7, p. 4.

572 Assemblée Nationale Constituante 1848–1849 *Feuilletons*, vol. XVIII, Paris 1849, no. 61, p. 3.

573 Assemblée Nationale Constituante 1848–1849 *Feuilletons*, vol. XVIII, Paris 1849, no. 94, p. 3.

574 Assemblée Nationale Constituante 1848–1849 *Feuilletons*, vol. XIX, Paris 1849, no. 181, p. 4.

575 Assemblée Nationale Constituante 1848–1849 *Feuilletons*, vol. XIX, Paris 1849, no. 218, p. 3.

Versailles – Chartres railway line[576], preparing a list of candidates for the Council of State for the Assembly[577].

In contrast, Wolowski had relatively little involvement in the most important political discussion of August and September 1848, the constitutional debate. As I have mentioned, he spoke out against the death penalty. Later, he did not comment on constitutional issues, but we know how he voted: generally, in line with the conservative, pro-government majority. So, he was against introducing the right to work in the constitution. On 25 September 1848 he supported a provision ruling out the possibility of a progressive tax, later voted against the prohibition of combining a parliamentary seat with a paid public office, for the possibility (extremely unfair) of buying up substitutes in military service[578]. He also supported perhaps the most widely debated provision at the time, introducing the function of president of the republic elected by popular vote. Finally, on 04 November 1848, he was one of 739 representatives voting in favour of the constitution (with only 30 votes against)[579].

The text was a peculiar combination of models from the revolutionary period (one chamber of parliament) and the American experience (the office of president). The constitution was undoubtedly democratic: its article 25 explicitly stated that all Frenchmen (with the emphasis placed on males) over the age of 21 had the right to vote. At the level of fundamental values, it combined democratism with a moderately conservative approach. Point IV of the preamble stated that the principles of the constitution were "Liberty, Equality and Fraternity. It is based on the Family, Work, Property, Public Order". The guarantor of the latter was to be a strong president at the head of the executive. It was the president who appointed and dismissed ministers, prefects, army commanders (Article 64) and judges (Article 85)[580]. He had the right of legislative initiative (Article 49). However, his power was limited by two provisions: he could not dissolve the Assembly (Art. 68) and, at the end of his 4-year term, he could not stand for re-election for four consecutive years (Art. 45)[581]. According to Philippe Vigier, the constitution reflected the belief of a sizable

---

576 Assemblée Nationale Constituante 1848–1849 *Feuilletons*, vol. XIX, Paris 1849, no. 255, p. 3.

577 Assemblée Nationale Constituante 1848–1849 *Feuilletons*, vol. XIX, Paris 1849, no. 259, p. 3.

578 In France, from 1798 onwards, a draw was made within each vintage of conscripts. Only those who drew the "wrong" numbers were eventually sent to the army. However, if they were wealthy enough, they could pay for a replacement. This system was repeatedly criticised as immoral and unfair but was not changed until 1872.

579 Wolowski's key parliamentary votes: A. Robert, E. Bourloton, E. Cougny *Dictionnaire des parlementaires français...*, p. 565.

580 This provision was introduced into the constitution thanks to Wolowski ("Journal des Débats Politiques et Littéraires", 15.10.1848).

581 The Constitution of 1848....

part of the Assembly, including arguably Wolowski (who voted for universal presidential suffrage) in the power and rationality of the people's vote, which ultimately legitimised both the executive and the legislature[582]. A belief which was soon to be shaken. Maurice Agulhon, on the other hand, rightly observes that a moderate section of the Assembly, of which Wolowski was certainly a part, was clearly dreaming of a French Washington, who would build up to the end and consolidate the republican institutions, and then, like a modern-day Cincinnatus or, indeed, the first President of the United States, would relinquish power and retreat as a private person[583]. Moderate supporters of the republic, including presumably Wolowski, saw in this role General Cavaignac, genuinely committed to republican ideals[584]. There are many indications that Wolowski supported Cavaignac in the presidential election of December 1848. Although I have not found a direct statement of his support for the head of government (or any other candidate), this seems most likely. Wolowski was part of the parliamentary majority which, on 25 November, decreed that the general "served the republic well". A close associate of Cavaignac, Minister Marie, knew Wolowski well from the "Revue...". He was also backed by Chambolle and *Le Siècle*. The only argument against Wolowski's support for the general's presidential candidacy was Faucher's attitude, clearly averse to it. Faucher was associated with the so-called "committee of the rue de Poitiers", uniting conservative monarchists and Bonapartists reluctant to the republic. Members of the committee included the legitimist leader Pierre-Antoine Berryer, the liberal Catholic Montalembert, the Orléanists Victor de Broglie, Cousin, Thiers, Rémusat, Barrot or Mathieu Molé, and the Bonapartists Charles de Morny and Victor de Persigny. The committee, led by the legitimists and the Orléanists, was unable to agree on a common monarchist presidential candidate in 1848. In the end, it decided to support Louis Napoleon Bonaparte. This explains the attitude of Faucher, who wrote

---

582 Ph. Vigier *La Seconde République...*, p. 52.

583 M. Agulhon *1848 ou l'apprentissage de la République...*, p. 93.

584 Cavaignac came from a family with a long republican tradition. His father was a member of the Convention and voted in 1792 in favour of the King's death. His elder brother Godefroi was a key figure in the republican party during the July Monarchy. The general himself, according to Nicolas Texier, was one of the few genuinely republican officers in 1848. This is also evidenced by his conduct: he did not attempt to introduce a military dictatorship, when undoubtedly in a position to do so, but he also insisted on holding presidential elections as soon as possible (N. Texier *Louis-Eugène Cavaignac*, [in:] E. Ebel (dir.) *Les Ministres de la guerre, 1792–1870*, Paris 2018, pp. 375–383). Odilon Barrot recalled that Cavaignac, having been assured of victory if the president was appointed by the National Assembly, made a very clear case for universal suffrage during the constitutional discussion – which essentially closed the discussion (O. Barrot *Mémoires posthumes*, vol. II. Paris 1875, p. 395).

to a friend at the time: "It is very likely that I will vote for Louis Napoleon. [...] The decisive fact is that the most illustrious men of the country, whatever opinion they share, agree that Louis Napoleon is the lifeline which Providence is sending us during a catastrophe. Yes, Messrs Berryer, Montalembert, Molé, Thiers, Odilon Barrot stand in line with the peasants and the army. Some do it out of reflection, others instinctively; in both cases, however, wisdom speaks"[585]. Faucher was only partly correct in this description, but it is interesting that among the "most illustrious men" he did not mention his brother-in-law, which further seems to indicate that the latter supported Cavaignac.

The presidential election finally took place on 10 December 1848, with Lamartine, the radical democrat Alexandre Ledru-Rollin, Raspail, representing the revolutionary left, and General Nicolas Changarnier, designated by a section of the legitimists, running in addition to Louis Napoleon Bonaparte and Cavaignac. Changarnier was a candidate against his own will – less than 5,000 people who voted for him did so despite his express resignation (voters could write any name of their choice on the ballot).

Louis Napoleon Bonaparte clinched a crushing victory. Out of just under 7,500,000 votes cast, he received more than 5,500,000 (almost 75%). The second runner-up, Cavaignac, was supported by 1,500,000 Frenchmen (4 million fewer). 380,000 people voted for Ledru-Rollin, 37,000 for Raspail, 21,000 for Lamartine, so popular in the spring of 1848[586].

In the letter quoted above, Faucher described the first ever president of the French Republic in the following way: "Louis Napoleon is certainly not the ridiculous creature depicted by the slanderers. He conspired just as republicans conspired, and people always laugh at failed conspiracies. Coincidence or choice has placed him in the Assembly room just behind me; we often talk, and he then shows a sound judgment of things, an extensive education, and the noblest feelings. He is an outstanding man, as is Cavaignac; the latter's superiority on the parliamentary tribune is offset by the former's thoughtfulness and cabinet deliberations. One and the other were initially poorly acquainted with people and political issues, but Louis Napoleon knows Europe well, which is a great asset in France when one is to participate in the affairs of government"[587].

Bonaparte was indeed a relatively new figure in politics. The French may have associated him mainly with criminal and social chronicles. Born in 1808, the son of Hortense and Louis Bonaparte had a history of involvement in the Italian Revolution of 1830–1831 and two failed coup attempts, in 1836 and 1840. The latter,

585 L. Faucher *Letter to Mr Perche, notary,* 26.11.1848, [in:] L. Faucher *Correspondance,* vol. I, Paris 1867, pp. 235 and 236.

586 Report presented to the National Assembly by the electoral commission rapporteur René Waldeck- Rousseau, "Journal des Débats Politiques et Littéraires", 21.12.1848.

587 L. Faucher *Letter to Mr. Perche...*, pp. 235–236.

in Boulogne, ended in discredit and the arrest of most of the conspirators (as mentioned by Faucher). Napoleon I's nephew was then sent to Ham prison, from which he escaped in 1846[588]. As a result, some revolutionary politicians initially treated him with mild disdain. Even Faucher approached him with indulgence reflected in the quoted text. In a letter to Henry Reeve in mid-December 1848, he wrote that Bonaparte previously had surrounded himself with the wrong people but that he now "desired the good, understood political necessity and appreciated wise counsel".[589] Of course, this "wise counsel" was to be given to him by Faucher's political friends.

Franciszek Wołowski's son-in-law, as it was soon to transpire, was mistaken in his assessment of Louis Napoleon Bonaparte's character. On the other hand, he had correctly recognised his electoral chances. The prince's growing popularity in the country had been palpable for some time. On 4 June 1848 in Paris, during the Assembly by-election, he received more than 80,000 votes[590]. The election was accompanied by multi-tiered demonstrations by Bonaparte supporters. Quite a few republicans, however, did not yet see them as a threat. They were probably misled (as was Faucher) by the personality of the imperial nephew, whose natural reticence and caution were mistaken for shyness or even stupidity[591]. Jules Favre, later one of Bonaparte's greatest political opponents, defending his right to sit in the Assembly, said: "As far as I am concerned [...], I am firmly convinced that as a result of excessive zeal and a certain misunderstanding, the Executive Commission unnecessarily exaggerated the personality of citizen Louis Bonaparte and gave the impression that the state of the French people could be overthrown by a pygmy blast"[592]. Louis Wolowski probably shared this conviction to a greater or lesser extent and did not yet give in to any special threat from Bonaparte, for he voted to approve his mandate. A mandate which Louis Napoleon eventually relinquished.

---

588 P. Milza *Napoléon III,* Paris 2006, pp. 59–159.

589 L. Faucher *Letter to H. Reeve,* 17.12.1848, [in:] L. Faucher *Correspondance...*, pp. 239–241.

590 Bonaparte appeared in Paris immediately after the overthrow of the Orléans, in late February 1848. He pledged his allegiance to the revolutionary Republic but was "politely asked" by the Provisional Government to leave French territory, which he did. As Louis Blanc later noted, this February sojourn of the future Emperor of the French in their capital went almost unnoticed (L. Blanc *Histoire de la Révolution de 1848...*, p. 97).

591 After his first meeting with Louis Napoleon, Victor Hugo noted: "The prince in his salon gave the impression of being shy and uncomfortable. He strolled from one group to another like a slightly intimidated stranger rather than a master of the house. Apart from that, however, he spoke reasonably, sometimes even with evident intelligence." (V. Hugo *Choses vues...*, p. 630).

592 "Journal des Débats Politiques et Littéraires ", 14.06.1848.

It turned out, incidentally, that this move also paid off for him – Bonaparte thus avoided any involvement in the June workers' uprising. Meanwhile, his popularity in almost all social classes was growing. In mid-September, in another by-election, Louis Napoleon won a total of more than 300,000 votes in five departments[593]. It was therefore quite clear that the political phenomenon was increasing. This time, moreover, no one questioned his right to sit in the Assembly anymore.

Some republican politicians were beginning to fear him. When Jules Grévy tabled a constitutional amendment whereby the function of President of the Republic was to be replaced by a head of government designated by the Assembly – it was directly aimed at Bonaparte, "a descendant of one of those families that ruled France, who never gave up his rights". Lamartine replied to him "you can poison a glass of water; you cannot poison a whole river". Apparently, he did not see in this river (society) the Bonaparte slowly hijacking everything. As I have mentioned, Cavaignac probably did not either, just like Wolowski: together with the parliamentary majority, he voted against the Grévy amendment.

He must have realised his mistake quickly. According to Louis Girard, a great expert on the period, in early December 1848 the French political class predicted Bonaparte's victory. All social classes voted for him: peasants, workers, bourgeoisie, landowners. The peasants, previously on the outskirts of events, rejected the Second Republic because of the taxes it imposed. The workers remembered the unfulfilled social promises of the Republicans, and Cavaignac's role in the bloodily suppressed June uprising. The bourgeoisie saw Louis Napoleon as the guarantor of order. Moreover, as Girard writes, the French people, in a kind of plebiscite, voted *en masse* in favour of the magical, historical name "Bonaparte"[594]. However, it was also a vote against the Republic of 1848. As the historian points out, "The Revolution of 1848, an 'unexpected revolution', plunged the nation into such confusion that, no longer trusting in any classical remedies, it placed its hopes in a miracle-working saviour"[595].

If even Louis Napoleon was not quite the candidate of the parliamentary majority or Louis Wolowski's, the representatives of the people aligned themselves quite quickly with the "Prince President". In the case of Wolowski, it was all the simpler because Faucher, a member of the family, entered the government. On 20 December, he was given the portfolio of Minister of Public Works, which he

---

593 P. Milza *Napoléon III...*, p. 178.

594 Haussmann, who was in the Bordeaux area at the time, later recalled meeting a peasant. Asked about his candidate, the man replied that he would vote for the emperor. When – to his amazement – he learned that Napoleon I had been dead for 27 years, he was ready to vote for his son. When he too turned out to be dead, he finally chose his nephew (G.E. Haussmann *Mémoires du Baron Haussmann* vol. I...., p. 279).

595 L. Girard *Napoléon III*, Paris 1986, p. 96.

swapped on 29 December for Internal Affairs. In addition to Faucher, there were other Conservatives from the rue de Poitiers in the government. They were headed by Odilon Barrot, another Orléanist. Passy, well known to Wolowski, became the minister of finance. Alfred de Falloux, a legitimist, was responsible for education. It was therefore a cabinet exceptionally close to Wolowski in terms of the composition. At the same time, it was the most conservative and monarchist (not necessarily Bonapartist) of the Second Republic cabinets, the first without a single Republican minister.

At the time, Wolowski seemed to remain somewhere halfway between conservatives and republicans. The anonymous author of a pamphlet containing a biography of Wolowski, an excerpt of which only survives in the Crédit Foncier papers at the Archives Nationales du Monde du Travail, wrote that he "became a devoted and useful aide to his brother-in-law."[596] Indeed, on most occasions, although not always, Wolowski voted in line with the government. When the Republicans proposed abolishing the salt tax, a tax particularly vexatious for rural people, Wolowski voted against it (and lost). In March 1849, he voted jointly with the Conservatives to ban political clubs. Back in January, the Republicans prepared a proposal for the so-called Organic Laws. These consisted of 10 peri-constitutional laws designed to bring existing legislation into line with the new basic law. In practice, this meant an extension of the Assembly's constitutional activities, while the Conservative government, expecting an electoral victory, sought to dissolve it. And this time Wolowski sided with the ruling party. However, when the pro-government representative Jean-Pierre Rateau presented a draft resolution to shorten the Assembly's term of office, on 29 January 1849 Wolowski voted against it. In this case he was in the minority: the Assembly was dissolved, and new elections were to be held on 13 and 14 May 1849. Wolowski also took an active part in the discussion of the new electoral law. When a proposal was put forward to restrict the right to vote in the case of, say, civil servants, Wolowski spoke out clearly against it[597]. Ultimately, his comments were rejected by the majority. The new law, while again granting active suffrage to all French people over 21 (subject to residence in the municipality for a minimum of six months), listed a long list of those who could not be elected. This included bishops and archbishops (ordinary priests were not excluded though), presidents of tribunals, prefects and sub-prefects, senior civil servants, commanders of military districts. The restriction also applied to businessmen receiving government contracts and railway directors[598]. The Republicans, who won a majority in this case, were clearly concerned to limit

596 No author provided, *Louis Wolowski 1810–1876,* p. 171, Archives Nationales du Monde du Travail, ref. no. PI471.

597 "Moniteur Universel. Journal Officiel de la République Française", Paris 1849, p. 799.

598 *Loi électorale en date des 8 et 28 février et 15 mars 1849,* "Bulletin officiel du Ministère de l'intérieur", n.3, Paris 1849, pp. 73–91.

the government's ability to put direct pressure on members of parliament. This, moreover, stemmed from the bad experience of the July Monarchy. Wolowski clearly sided with the government.

At the time, Wolowski seems to have shifted consistently to the conservative side, eventually taking a position on the republican right. This is also evidenced by his 1849 proclamation to voters. Although it still contained the word "republic", much more emphasis was placed on "order". 1848 was a year of threat and defence of order, and "France passed its hardest test; through its courage and reason it managed to defeat rebellion and stop utopias." As a result, only the newly elected Legislature was to make key positive changes to the country. Wolowski highlighted three: the need to expand education, above all primary and vocational; credits for agriculture; and social welfare. This last notion was, in fact, rather vague, as Wolowski mentioned that rather than be a handout, it should "supply energy and enhance human dignity". However, he did not specify how this could be achieved, which made the whole passage devoted to social aid seem like an electoral platitude[599].

During the election campaign, Wolowski was included both on moderately republican lists – for example, a list promoted by *Le Siècle* with Victor Hugo, General Cavaignac, Dupont de l'Eure (former president of the Provisional Government) and Odilon Barrot alongside him[600]; as well as on the decidedly more conservative ones, like the list of the "Union électorale", supported by the Orleanist "Journal des Débats Politiques et Littéraires". On the latter, Wolowski's name appeared alongside Passy, Faucher, Thiers, and Marie[601]. Moreover, his name was also among the personalities promoted by the most important Catholic and legitimist periodical of the era, *L'Univers*[602]. Clearly, Wolowski was accepted by the republican centre-right and the monarchist right of the French political scene. This was partly due to his social and economic views, and probably also partly because Wolowski did not speak in the most turbulent political debates – so he did not make many enemies. He was not the leader of any of the informal parties and was therefore acceptable to a relatively broad political spectrum (except for the radical left). In these circumstances, his re-election seemed in principle a foregone conclusion; and indeed, on 13 May 1849, Louis Wolowski was re-elected to the National Legislative Assembly (Legislature) with 110,630 votes[603].

599 L. Wolowski *Aux électeurs du département de la Seine,* Paris 1849.
600 "Le Siècle", 12.05.1849.
601 "Journal des Débats Politiques et Littéraires", 12.05.1849.
602 "L'Univers", 12.05.1849.
603 "Journal des Débats Politiques et Littéraires", 19.05.1849.

3. Deputy of 1849

This was undoubtedly his personal success. In doing so, he was one of less than 30% of the 1848 House representatives re-elected in 1849.This was partly due to a slight reduction in the number of representatives (to 750), again called deputies and elected for three years. Above all, however, moderate republicans suffered defeat. A few dozen were left in the House, with Lamartine and Marie outside parliament. The "party of order", as the right was collectively called, received a little over 50% of the vote and 450–500 seats[604]. Wolowski was undoubtedly among them. Interestingly, the Conservatives were not at all delighted with the election result. On the contrary, they were highly concerned, if not horrified. In a letter from Bonn, on 23 May 1849 Tocqueville wrote to Gustave de Beaumont: "the newspapers provide me with all too much news of the full gravity of the situation. It is enormous and imposes huge responsibilities which I hope each of us will be able to meet." He continued: "I have never been more moved or felt more anxious".[605]. The source of this anxiety was the electoral result of the radical left: 2,300,000 votes (35% of the total) and some 200 seats. What puzzled Tocqueville, Rémusat, Thiers and other leaders of the party of order, however, was the geographical distribution of these votes. An important part of the departments of central and eastern France voted for the Democratic Socialists. This meant that for the first time, the revolutionary parties went beyond the big cities and managed to attract some of the rural population.

The political situation was therefore extremely tense since the very beginning of the new Legislature. All the more so because, according to François Furet, the two sides of the political barricade treated each other with enormous distrust and hostility. For the right, the Mountaineers (members of the "Mountain" – as the representatives of the left callled themselves, referrinf to the Great Revolution) were, regardless of their actual views, "reds", bloody heirs, and continuators of the Jacobins, while socially they were supporters of the plundering of the rich in favour of the poor.

The fear of the economic and social ideas of the left, fought against by Wolowski in the Luxembourg Commission, was conveyed by the untranslatable word "partageux": an advocate of dividing the property of the more affluent. Of relevance to the right were the memories of May and June 1848.

The perception of reality on the right side of the then political scene is well reflected in a text by Faucher from 1851, of relevance to this book as it was probably close to Wolowski's thinking:

> As usual, Paris is the source from which anarchic ideas spill over into the whole of France. [...] In Paris, among the lower classes, there is a sizable population deprived of work, of income, people left to depravity and poverty, representing a kind of reserve

604 Ph. Vigier *La Seconde République...*, pp. 62–63.

605 A. de Tocqueville *Listy*, Kraków, Warszawa 1999, p. 237.

> army of the enemies of civilisation and law. This anarchic element is strong, relentless; it can only be silenced by force, the authorities in Paris must therefore be constantly on guard. [...] [Outside Paris] the anarchists work with unbearable perseverance to stir up hatred and war between the poor and the rich; while the working classes and peasants willingly listen to these doctrines that bait them with capricious happiness. They see themselves as the helots whom the bourgeois classes have condemned to perpetual labour and poverty, and dream of "liberation", which, however, would have to mean destroying the foundations of the whole of society.[606]

Characteristic of this passage is the undoubted awareness of the poverty of a large part of the French population, combined, however, with the conviction that it is somewhat inevitable, and that an attempt to radically change the situation would lead to the collapse of civilisation. In essence, speaking of the necessary aid for workers and the disastrous utopias prevalent in the poor classes, Wolowski was thinking very much along the same lines.

On the other side, for the left, the "men of order", were *en bloc* monarchists, just waiting for an opportunity to put the republic to death, deprive the people of their influence on power and put a representative of one of the old dynasties on the throne[607].

The relatively minor importance of Bonapartism in the 1849 elections is noteworthy. The Bonapartists did not play an independent role in this election but a large group of them was on the electoral lists of the "party of order". Persigny, Morny, Eugène Rouher and Prince Napoléon Jérôme Bonaparte (son of Jérôme) were elected to parliament – the latter, incidentally, from the leftist list.

The new government, formed immediately after the elections, was not Bonapartist either; it relied above all on the "men of order". In fact, it was a new-old government, as Odilon Barrot was still head of it, Passy remained finance minister and Falloux minister of education. Faucher was replaced by Jules Dufaure, and Tocqueville took over the foreign affairs portfolio.

The most important debate of the first weeks after the election concerned in fact a foreign question, the Rome issue. Rome had been a republic since the autumn of 1848, with Pope Pius IX taking refuge in Naples. In the spring of 1849, the French sent a small expeditionary corps to Italy under the command of General Charles

606 L. Faucher *Papiers inédits de Léon Faucher,* [in:] "La Révolution de 1848. Bulletin de la Société d'histoire de la Révolution de 1848", 1906, vol. 3, no. 14, pp. 92–93.

607 F. Furet *La Révolution Française II. Terminer la Révolution. De Louis XVIII à Jules Ferry (1814–1880),* Paris 1988, pp. 270–284. Typical in this respect, for example, was the speech delivered by Ledru-Rollin in the Legislature less than two weeks after the election, in which he spoke of an alleged conspiracy to reinstate the empire in France (A. Ledru-Rollin *Discours sur le projet attribué au gouvernement du rétablissement de l'empire (23 mai 1849,* [in:] A. Ledru-Rollin *Discours politiques et écrits divers*, vol. II, Paris 1879, pp. 316–321).

Oudinot, whose primary task at first was to protect the Eternal City from possible Austrian intervention. The matter was debated in the Assembly even before the election. On 7 May, a resolution was passed demanding that the French corps follow its original purpose, which was to shield the Roman republic. The Left was already concerned that the French soldiers in Italy could be used against the local republicans. Initially, in fact, President Bonaparte complied with the parliament's demands, sending Ferdinand de Lesseps (the later builder of the Suez Canal, a professional diplomat) on a diplomatic mission to the Eternal City. However, the Legislature elected in the same month was much less republican, more pro-papal. Bonaparte, who needed the support of the Church in France (the election of 1849 had shown how effective this support could be), immediately changed the course of his Italian policy. Lesseps was summoned to Paris, Oudinot was ordered to occupy Rome. 3 June 1849 marked the beginning of the siege of the city by the French, with the first clashes between the soldiers of the French and Roman republics[608]. As a result, another debate heated up in the Legislature on 11 June. That day, on behalf of the Mountaineers, Ledru-Rollin filed an indictment against the President and ministers guilty, in his view, of a clear violation of the Constitution, following a blatant disregard for a resolution of the Assembly[609]. In essence, however, the Mountaineers were primarily concerned with the fact of France's attack on its "sister" republic.

The House rejected their motion by an overwhelming majority (361 votes against 202). Louis Wolowski voted with the Conservatives on 7 May and 11 June. Patrice Markiewicz claims that he voted in favour of the Italian expedition "out of sympathy for the Italian cause". I do not agree with this interpretation: while Wolowski was indeed sympathetic to the Italians striving for unification, he was also keen to maintain the temporal power of the Pope. It was the second factor, along with probably a distrust of the revolutionary left, at the heart of his attitude towards the Roman cause in 1849.

Meanwhile, the Mountaineers decided not to lay down their arms and, faced with parliamentary defeat, intended to appeal to the street. On the morning of 13 June, the left-wing press titles published a call for revolt: "The president and ministers have violated the constitution. The part of the Assembly that supported them in yesterday's vote have contravened the constitution. The national guard is being formed. The workshops are closed. Let our brothers in the army remember that they are citizens, and their first duty is to protect the constitution. Let all people

---

608 R. de Félice *La journée du 13 juin 1849, à Paris. Ses origines. Son épilogue devant la Haute Cour,* [in:] "La Révolution de 1848. Bulletin de la Société d'histoire de la Révolution de 1848", 1909, vol. 6, nr 33, pp. 134–141.

609 A. Ledru-Rollin *Dépot sur le bureau de l'Assemblée Législative d'un acte d'accusation contre Louis Napoléon Bonaparte et ses ministres;* [in:] A. Ledru-Rollin *Discours politiques...*, pp. 334–339.

rise!". Next to it was an appeal, similar in tone, signed by a hundred deputies of the Mountain[610]. The latter was also on posters displayed in Paris. The intentions of the signatories of the appeal are unclear: whether it was to change power or just to put strong pressure on the House. However, it soon turned out that the people of Paris were not going to rise this time. At around midday, there were only a few thousand of them at the agreed starting point of the demonstration[611]. In a short time, the crowd partly dispersed, and was partly chased away by the army. Ledru-Rollin managed to escape. He was later to cross the Channel and settle as an immigrant in England[612].

Meanwhile, the members of the Legislature experienced several hours of fear and uncertainty when the House declared a state of siege in Paris and Lyon. Wolowski voted in favour. Apart from the nerve-wracking day of 13 June[613], like the vast

---

610 "La Réforme", "Démocratie Pacifique", "Le Peuple", "La Révolution démocratique et sociale", 13.06.1849.

611 Jean Dautry mentions 10,000 demonstrators, according to Agulhon and Vigier the number was negligible (J. Dautry *Histoire de la Révolution de 1848 en France*, Paris 1948, p. 283; M. Agulhon *1848 ou l'apprentissage de la République...*, p. 107; Ph. Vigier *La Seconde République...*, p. 69).

612 The reasons for the defeat of the left were probably manifold: the fatigue with the republic, the fact that Ledru-Rollin did not support the struggling workers in June 1848. Perhaps, however, as Sylvie Aprile writes, the decisive factor proved to be cholera. In May-June 1849, another wave of this nineteenth-century curse was sweeping through Paris, which probably stopped many potential demonstrators from mingling with the crowd. At the time, Count Rudolf Apponyi, attaché to the Austrian embassy, was strolling through the empty streets of Paris. He later noted in his diary: "We were saved this time by the fear of cholera: the suburbs of Saint-Antoine, Saint-Denis, Saint-Marceau [inhabited mainly by the poorer strata] have been so overrun that their population is entirely occupied with just that, and the 110th article of the constitution, allegedly violated by the president and his ministers, has seemed to their inhabitants a less important violation of the existence of a sovereign people than this terrible disease which kills in a few hours; I would never have imagined that cholera could be useful for anything, let alone that it would one day save us from anarchy." (R. Apponyi *25 ans à Paris (1826–1850): Journal du comte Rodolphe Apponyi, attaché de l'ambassade d'Autriche-Hongrie à Paris*, vol. IV, Paris 1926, pp. 283–284).

613 The mental state of the Assembly during this period is evidenced by a minor incident involving Wolowski. Deputy Antoine Mathé publicly stated that Prime Minister Barrot allegedly stated that the Minister of the Interior was in possession of the original of the Mountain's appeal openly calling for rebellion, together with the signatures. According to Mathé, Barrot said this in his office, to Wolowski and others. Wolowski immediately protested that Mathé was referring to "a backstage conversation between colleagues that was absolutely not intended for the

majority of the deputies, Wolowski probably believed that it was the protesters who violated the constitution and intended to carry out a coup d'état[614]. Therefore, in the days that followed, he was likely to vote "in favour" on a regular basis, whenever the authorities asked the House to authorise the arrest of a Left deputy or deputies (a total of 31 Mountaineers were affected). In this context, Markiewicz quotes a characteristic story by Joseph Benoit, another left-wing deputy:

> At the time of the events of 13 June (1849), the Government feared that a victorious Lyon could lead to a general uprising in the south and east of France... It expressed these fears by seeking out and notifying by telegraph Ledru-Rollin and Victor Considérant [both fugitive deputies]. It was presumed that they headed that direction. Knowing the importance that the Government attached to the arrest of the two citizens, it occurred to me to tell Wolowski, one of my colleagues in the [parliamentary] majority, who offered me his help in case I was also pursued, that they were indeed on their way to Lyon. The idea was to distract the justice system, which was looking for them in Paris, where they were located. Much to my surprise, half an hour later, Dufaure[615] announced to the congregation that he had ordered a search for them in this direction [Lyon][616].

Rome was captured by the French on 03 July 1849. The events of 13 June, however, had mainly internal repercussions. The parliamentary left was practically shattered. Five radical press titles were suspended (reinstated in September, all

---

Assembly". He explained that some deputies discussing the text had suggested that it might have been a government provocation. He also cited another rumour (making it clear that it was a rumour), that the law enforcement authorities had the original of the document in question, complete with signatures. („Moniteur Universel...", Paris 1849, pp. 2076–2077). Clearly, there were a lot of rumours, hearsay and distorted stories circulating in the corridors of parliament. The key question that parliamentarians were asking was simply which of them had signed the appeal in question.

614 Barrot's memoirs reflect the mindset of the parliamentary majority about the rebels: "Not only did they deny the rights of the parliamentary majority; they declared it illegitimate, then, defeated and seized with arms in their hands, they were surprised when they had to pay for their offences. [...] when the judiciary did what it was supposed to do; when prosecutors entered places where civil war was more or less openly being prepared, then these demagogues invoked parliamentary immunity with the insolence of almost old patricians." (O. Barrot *Mémoires posthumes*, vol. III, Paris 1876, p. 330).

615 Jules Dufaure (1798–1881) – Minister of the Interior between June and October 1849.

616 J. Benoit *Confessions d'un prolétaire,* Paris 1968, p. 186; quote as in P. Markiewicz *Louis Wolowski...*, p. 133. Markiewicz clearly misinterprets the story, citing it as an example of Wolowski's act of mitigating repression.

eventually disappeared in 1850), and on 19 June, the Assembly also suspended the law on freedom of association for a year. On 27 July, it introduced a new, more restrictive press law. On 9 August, in turn, it adopted new legal provisions on the state of siege.

Wolowski didn't participate in the latter votes. In fact, the archives of the Assembly preserve his request for leave from 15 July 1849, motivated by his wife's illness and the need to go to Ems for treatment[617]. He returned in early September at the latest. In 1849 he participated in two important debates: on workers' coalitions, and on the rights of foreigners in France. The latter involved a proposal whereby the Minister of the Interior would have the right at any time to revoke any foreigner's civil rights and expel them from France. This provision also applied to persons who had previously obtained a residence permit in France. Wolowski stressed in the Chamber that this would mean that people who had often been long-time residents of France, who had set up their own businesses there and had family ties, could be expelled at any time by administrative decision of the Minister, without any possibility of defence. Wolowski therefore demanded protection for immigrants from the whim or ill-will of a minister. He proposed that the administration should retain the right of expulsion, but after an appropriate decision by the Council of State. It is difficult not to get the impression that both Wolowski and most of the Assembly were concerned with the Poles. Wolowski must have remembered his friends – compatriots from the Hotel Lambert, as well as his family, Celina, and Mickiewicz. On the other hand, the conservative majority of the Assembly probably remembered 15 May 1848, Polish émigrés on the streets of Paris in February and March 1848, and the links some of them had with the revolutionary left[618]. Therefore, the fact that Wolowski's amendments were rejected and that the law of 03 December 1849 allowed the authorities to expel any foreigner from the Republic by purely administrative means comes as no surprise.

It was, however, a slightly different republic to that of August. For on 31 October 1849, Louis Napoleon thanked his previous ministers and formed a completely new government. The most important figure was General Alphonse Henri d'Hautpoul, Minister of War; Eugène Rouher was Minister of Justice, Ferdinand Barrot (Odilon's brother) became Minister of the Interior, Achille Fould, a well-known banker, was appointed Minister of Finance. Alphonse de Rayneval became Minister of Foreign Affairs, followed by Jean-Ernest Ducos on 17 November. Three elements were distinctive. Firstly, the new government lacked representatives of the party of order. Secondly, the president did not appoint a prime minister. Thirdly, there were no well-known names in the ruling team. The new ministers had been, at best, second-tier figures, lacking broader political support. And in fact, their

---

617 Archives Nationales, ref. C//976.

618 Sławomir Kalembka covers the activity of Poles in Paris during this time (*Wielka Emigracja 1831–1863...*, pp. 301–314).

only support was the president who completely took control of the government (personally run by him from then on), and finally broke with the conservatives. As Philippe Séguin – the most enthusiastic biographer of the future emperor – rightly writes: "The appointment of the new government [...] was a much more significant turn than it seemed. From then on, he [Louis Napoleon] played his own game with all the means at his disposal."[619].

Rémusat claimed spitefully that the sole purpose of the change was to rid the cabinet of any more prominent personalities, overshadowing the president himself[620]. He was wrong several times. Not all the new ministers were completely bland, "transparent" as he pictured them. Moreover, thanks to them, Bonaparte could become independent of the Conservatives and start to form his own political camp. And he was taking the helm of the executive, which, given his ambitions, proved crucial.

October 1849 ended the cooperation between the Prince President and the Conservatives and marked the beginning of a growing conflict. Like Faucher, Louis Wolowski clearly took the side of the party of order in this conflict. This is evidenced by his subsequent votes. The year 1850 brought two extremely significant ones. In both cases Wolowski sided with the majority. The first concerned a new education law. Its main author was Falloux, the former Minister of Education. Falloux had a well-deserved reputation for representing Catholicism in politics[621]. In turn, the school law he drafted mainly met the demands of the Church. Under the new provisions, almost anyone could open a school; all that was needed was a secondary school leaving certificate in the case of secondary school principals or a lower-level diploma in the case of primary schools. Moreover, these requirements applied only to lay people, not to the clergy. Falloux introduced representatives of the Church: bishops at central level, often replaced by priests at departmental level to the University, the institution responsible for supervising all education since Napoleonic times. When we consider that there was also a minister and senior civil servants, most often also with strong ties to Catholicism, Falloux was largely placing education in the hands of the Church. The effect was almost immediate: by 1853, 257 new secondary schools were established, mostly Catholic, including 13 Jesuit colleges[622].

---

619 Ph. Séguin *Louis Napoléon le Grand,* Paris 1990, p. 145

620 Ch. De Rémusat *Mémoires de ma vie,* vol. IV..., p. 420.

621 François Furet briefly describes Falloux as a "deputy of the Church" (F. Furet *La Révolution II...*, p. 288). Falloux's biography, published in 2010, is not coincidentally titled *Count de Falloux. Between Church and Monarchy* (G. Gobbi *Le Comte de Falloux (1811–1886). Entre Église et Monarchie*, Rennes 2010).

622 R. Dobek *Laicka czy katolicka? Szkoła jako kluczowy element francuskiej debaty politycznej w XIX wieku,* [in:] J. Dobosz, D. Konieczka-Śliwińska *"Powtórka przed...". XIII spotkania z historią dla uczniów szkół ponadgimnazjalnych i ponadpodstawowych, 24-25 września oraz 26-27 września 2019 r.*, Poznań 2019, p. 65.

Behind the new law was the parliamentary majority's belief in the necessary positive influence of the Church on society through education. The idea was again to stop anarchy and revolution, but this time at primary school level, through the values instilled by the Church. This was well expressed by Adolphe Thiers, as key politician of the party of order at the time, otherwise far from clericalism. He admitted, however, that "after the abyss in which we found ourselves some time ago, in view of what now is threatening us [...], in view of the dangers now weighing down on society, I have given my hand to those who fought me and whom I fought; my hand will remain, I hope, joined with theirs, for the common defence of society."[623] The Orléanist Thiers spoke of an alliance with the legitimists and the Church, an alliance directed against the left, an alliance of which the education law under way was a key element. Thiers' words reflected the conviction, typical of Orléanists at the time, that the "reds" could not be defeated without the help of the Church. The Orléanist liberals, traditionally rather sceptical of the bishops, were ready to temporarily hide their scepticism after the experiences of 1848 and 1849. This explains their vote on the Roman question and, in 1850, on the "Falloux Bill", as the new school law was henceforth called.

Louis Wolowski was probably no exception. He voted in favour of the Bill, most likely for the very reasons mentioned. He, too, had previously been associated with the Orléanist party. He, too, had kept a certain distance from the Church and religion, and he, too, had been horrified by the rise of socialist and revolutionary sentiment, the subsequent coup attempts and the vote of a section of the people in 1849. It is possible that, again, his roots played a role in the education debate, prompting him to remain silent on matters of religion. Although Wolowski took part in the discussion in March 1850, he did not challenge or criticise the key provisions of the Bill. He was only concerned with the wider recognition of vocational education; he therefore requested that the name be included in the text, where it did not appear initially. His comments, however, were indicative of his thinking about education in general. Wolowski stressed that in the French system, far too much attention was devoted to classical and literary education while it was lacking for vocational education: agricultural, industrial, and commercial. He quoted Heinrich Heine: "If the Romans had been obliged to learn Latin, they would never have found time to conquer the world."[624] The professor of the craftsmen's Conservatoire des Arts et Métiers was clearly thinking of changing the entire education system to a more practical one. In 1850, this was probably not possible, but 15 years later, a reform along these lines was carried out by Imperial Minister Victor Duruy. Only without Wolowski's involvement at any point[625].

---

623 A. de Falloux *Mémoires d'un royaliste*, vol. I, Paris 1888, p. 567.

624 "Moniteur Universel...", Paris 1850, p. 881.

625 Notably, Falloux belonged to Wolowski's circle of acquaintances, as evidenced by the former's surviving letter to the Pole (not dated, National Archives in Cracow, ref. AKPot 3204).

Another important law, with numerous political consequences (albeit not necessarily in accordance with the intentions of the originators), was the new electoral law; its draft was considered by the Assembly in May 1850, with the leaders of the party of order: Thiers, Faucher, Montalembert and Berryer, behind it.[626] Their meeting was later described by Emile Ollivier, back then associated with the moderate Republicans. The initiative to change the electoral law was attributed to Thiers. The former prime minister of Louis-Philippe suggested including in the electoral law the obligation to live in the place of voting for a minimum of three years. At the time, Thiers was to state explicitly that this would "eliminate several million of the most dangerous voters".[627] Thiers' concern stemmed both from the election of 1849 and the results of the Assembly by-elections held in March and April 1850, in which the Mountain was again successful. The aim of the amendment to the electoral law was simple: to disenfranchise some of the poorest voters, potential supporters of the Left. This is what happened: the law was passed on 30 May 1850 thanks to the votes of 433 legislators, including Louis Wolowski. He took no part in the discussion, but there is no doubt that the limitation of democracy did not bother him. Like most of the centre-right, Wolowski had a clear opinion on the principle of the popular vote between the autumn of 1848 and the spring of 1850. This may have partly stemmed from the presidential elections of 1848, but above all by the parliamentary elections of 1849, the result achieved by the Left, and then by the June events of the same year. In fact, Wolowski, like his parliamentary colleagues, was soon to learn that the attempt to restrict the voting rights of the French was a mistake.

He was taking a different approach to freedom of speech. When, in July of the same year, the Assembly dealt with the new press law, imposing high deposits and stamp duties on newspaper owners[628] and aimed explicitly against the democratic press, Wolowski voted against it. Apparently, his attachment to freedom of expression outweighed his dislike of the revolutionary left. However, he found himself in the minority in this case. The law came into force and had the effect expected by the conservatives. Within months, left-wing titles like "La Réforme", "Le Démocrate de l'Ouest", "Le Démocrate de Saone et Loire", "Le Travailleur", "Le Démocrate vosgien", and "Le Républicain du Rhin" disappeared.[629]

---

626 The process of the new electoral law was traced by Paul Raphaël in his text *La loi du 31 mai 1850* ("Revue d'histoire moderne et contemporaine", vol. 13, no. 3, 1909; vol. 14, no. 3, 1910).

627 E. Ollivier *L'Empire libéral: études, récits, souvenirs,* vol. II, Paris 1897, p. 281.

628 *Collection complète des lois, décrets, ordonnances, réglements, et avis du Conseil-d'État: publiée sur les éditions officielles du Louvre; de l'Imprimerie nationale, par Baudouin; et du Bulletin des lois, de 1788 à 1824 inclusivement, par ordre chronologique...,* Paris 1850, pp. 315–325.

629 C. Bellanger, J. Godechot, P. Guiral, F. Terrou (dir.) *Histoire générale de la presse française,* vol. II, *De 1815 à 1871,* Paris 1969, p. 237.

Louis Wolowski was undoubtedly attached to parliamentarism, a value central to Franciszek Wołowski and the entire Orléanist tradition. He continued to take his parliamentary duties extremely seriously. In 1849, he was a member of eight committees, including the important Budget Committee[630]. He continued to sit on the latter committee in 1850. He was rapporteur on the draft agreement with Bavaria on the Strasbourg – Spira railway line.[631]

He also took an active part in other, less high-profile discussions in parliament: he successfully defended the principle of remunerating workers in money – he stressed that the payment of wages in other, commodity-based forms was too often linked to abuse[632]. The protection of workers was the subject of a discussion of housing harmful to health. The idea was that workers' dwellings should be inspected by the city's sanitary committees; they would indicate to the city council the buildings in which changes were necessary. The council could in turn take care of such changes, in extreme circumstances closing the building. Wolowski not only explicitly advocated the substance of the new law but proposed extending it to include workshops. He also wanted towns to take on part of the burden of constructing new buildings with better sanitary conditions. In both cases, however, he lost[633]. The law was finally adopted, without Wolowski's amendments, on 13 April 1850. Historian Florence Bourillon describes it as innovative: for the first time, the French parliament addressed urban planning issues in general (not specific buildings). Bourillon also takes a very positive view of Wolowski's proposals; in her view, along with another discussant, the physician Théophile Roussel, they were "an epitome of the emerging scientific discourse."[634]

Let me focus for a moment on workers' housing. Perhaps Wolowski's interest stemmed from humanitarian and political motives alike. Between 1849 and 1851, the "Cité Napoléon", a complex of four buildings designed at the request of Louis Napoléon by Marie Gabriel Veugny for workers' housing, was constructed in Paris. Although ultimately the presidential work did not enjoy great recognition among the workers and was not continued, in 1850 it may have seemed that Bonaparte sought the support of the working classes[635]. Possibly, the attempt to discuss workers' housing was a response of a part of the Assembly to the presidential initiative.

---

630 "Moniteur Universel...", Paris 1849, pp. 2057, 2118, 2194, 2321, 2627, 3019, 3421, 3541

631 "Moniteur Universel... ", Paris 1849, pp. 2322–2323, 2328–2331.

632 "Moniteur Universel...", Paris 1850, pp. 339–340.

633 "Moniteur Universel...", Paris 1850, pp. 788 & 791.

634 F. Bourillon *La loi du 13 avril 1850 ou lorsque la Seconde République invente le logement insalubre*, "Revue d'histoire du XIXe siècle" no. 20/21, 2000,http://journals.openedition.org/rh19/212 (retrieved 25.03.2023)

635 C. Bruant *La Cité Napoléon: une expérience controversée de logements ouvriers à Paris*, Versailles 2011.

The debate of 20 December 1850 on the commercial status of Algeria was interesting for slightly different reasons, for this was the only moment when Wolowski made a clear statement about Algeria and – indirectly – colonisation in general. He asked if Algeria should be retained. He considered the question ultimately obsolete: given the earlier efforts and sacrifices, the honour, and interests of France, leaving the colony was no longer possible. In his opinion, Algeria should be linked to France by extraordinary economic ties, exempt from duties on agricultural or construction goods, among other things. He asked about the sense of the colony in general. And his reply was: "when the inhabitants of a country are too cramped, when there is not enough space, when life becomes too difficult, they move their intelligence, their labour, part of their capitals elsewhere. They seek more abundant work and an easier life. The question of colonisation considered this way becomes one aspect of the key question of cheap living, a question occupying nations and governments today." He presented colonisation in market terms, in which everyone had every right to seek the best possible living and working conditions in the country or its dominions. Wolowski referred to the American example, arguing that colonisation, when done well, defended itself and needed no additional commercial incentives from the state. With such obvious advantages as land available in abundance and no/ low taxation, the colonies attracted settlers. Wolowski argued against the proposed customs privileges for Algeria, pointing out that this would be unfair competition with French farmers and landlords, who pay rent and high taxes associated with the land[636]. Clearly, in this reasoning, Wolowski completely ignored the rights of the Algerians to their own land. He overlooked the religious, cultural, political, and moral problems associated with colonisation, reducing it to purely economic, free-market choices.

The fact that this was yet another parliamentary discussion in which Wolowski was told by visibly impatient deputies at the end of his speech that he should cut it short was quite characteristic. They shouted, "The end, the end".

Meanwhile, the conflict between the conservative Assembly and Bonaparte was growing. The focus of the dispute was the 45th article of the constitution, prohibiting the president from running for another term. Bonaparte sought to revise the said article. This was possible, as the revision of the constitution was provided for in Article 111, but it was a complicated process that required the approval of three quarters of the deputies at the outset, followed by a separate constitutional assembly. The President's chances were slim, given the number of republicans and conservatives in the Assembly who were unequivocally opposed to him, but this does not change the fact that the years 1850 and 1851 were largely spent in constitutional negotiations. The fact that the Prince President pursued his policy in two ways was also fraught with consequences. There were the traditional cabinet talks. In the same time, an active Bonapartist propaganda aimed at all sections

---

636 "Moniteur Universel...", Paris 1850, p. 3655.

of society. Above all, by the end of 1851, he had travelled almost all over France. He made 16 journeys, visiting nearly fifty departments. A typical programme for such a visit was quoted by Haussmann, then prefect of the Yonne department. The Prince President arrived by train, reviewed the local dragoon regiment, the National Guard, met with departmental authorities, municipal representatives. Most important, however, was the "warm welcome" and "cheers of enthusiasm" of the local population[637]. Most times, this enthusiasm was at least partly fuelled up by the local authorities, partly by the Bonapartists, but all in all, everything points to its authenticity. At the same time, Bonaparte skilfully distanced himself from the unpopular moves of the Assembly conservatives. This was notably the case with the electoral law. Although Louis Napoleon signed it, there were clear signals coming out of the presidential palace that he would not oppose the restoration of universal suffrage. William Nassau Sr cited his conversation with Hortense Cornu, a friend of Bonaparte. In it, Mrs Cornu described his attitude to the Bill: "I hear", I said to him, "but I do not believe it, that you support this Bill". "I do", he answered. "What," I said, "you, the child of universal suffrage, do you support a limited suffrage?". "You understand nothing about it," he replied, "je perds l'Assemblée [I lose the Assembly] ". "But", I said, "you will perish with the Assembly". "Not in the least," he answered. "When the Assembly goes over the precipice, je coupe la corde [I cut the rope]".[638] The propaganda of the presidential palace skilfully combined two themes in 1851: the restoration of the popular vote and constitutional revision.

The final cutting of the rope, however, was no simple matter. Bonaparte made sure he had the army's support. In January 1851, he got rid of General Changarnier, the reluctant commander of the army of Paris. Through a skilful policy of appointments, personal contacts, revues, and military parades, he could reach out to a sizable group of officers, otherwise reluctant for the most part to the republic[639]. At the same time, Bonaparte skilfully built up his own parliamentary group, consisting mainly of disillusioned conservatives and former monarchists. Alongside them, the party of order, however, strongly divided internally, and the Republicans still operated in the Assembly. The explicit opposition of the latter and some legitimists to the idea of constitutional revision meant that it was in practice impossible.

At the same time, according to Louis Girard, in the spring of 1851, "Everyone, even Thiers, agreed that Louis Napoleon would be re-elected, legally or otherwise."[640] Tocqueville wrote in January 1851 to Victor Lanjuinais: "I think that we

637 G.E. Haussmann *Mémoires du Baron Haussmann* vol. I..., pp. 437–440.

638 W. Nassau Sr *Conversations with M. Thiers, M. Guizot, and other distinguished persons, during the Second Empire*, vol. II, London 1878, p. 338.

639 The process of gaining supporters in the army was described in a memoir-like work by Albert du Casse (*Les Dessous du coup d'État, 1851*, Paris 1891, pp. 45–69).

640 L. Girard *Napoléon III...*, p. 134.

are fighting in vain; I also think that the nation is dragging us out of the zone of freedom."[641] The divided Assembly could not and did not stand up to the President's increasingly evident ambitions. For its part, the person concerned still hoped at the time for some form of peaceful solution[642]. Both sides were forced to cooperate, gripped by the fear of the Mountain. The result of this temporary agreement was a new government, formed in April 1851. A government which, again, included Léon Faucher, Wolowski's brother-in-law. This time, however, not only as Minister of the Interior, but also as de facto Prime Minister. In addition, the government consisted of Conservatives Prosper de Chasseloup-Lobat, Marie Jean de Crouseilhes and Louis Buffet, and the Bonapartists: Rouher, Fould, Pierre Jules Baroche, Jacques Randon and Pierre Magne. The government's primary task was to resolve the political crisis, and its programme was the result of a compromise between monarchists and Bonapartists. Indeed, Faucher wanted to bring about a constitutional revision without changing the electoral law. It was also very soon that de Broglie, an advocate of the revision, tabled a corresponding motion in the Assembly. On 19 July, the House voted: 446 deputies, including Wolowski, voted in favour of amending the constitution, 278 were against. The necessary majority, however, was 543 votes. It thus became clear that there would be no revision. Bonaparte now had a choice between total capitulation before the Assembly or a coup d'état. The answer was simple: it was at this point that the direct preparations for the coup began.

Notably, at this time exactly, on 7 October 1851, Wolowski received from the President the officer's cross of the Legion of Honour.[643] This was hardly a coincidence but rather, a symbolic, no-strings-attached nod from Louis Napoleon to the conservatives, Faucher in particular.

Now, however, the president's first move was to get rid of the government. Faucher and his ministers resigned in late October and were replaced by the president's men, generally from the second political tier. With one notable exception, however – the army was henceforth managed by General Armand Saint-Arnaud, a staunch Bonapartist.

The second move was a presidential proposal to revoke the May 1850 Electoral Bill. On 12 November 1851, the Assembly rejected this idea by a majority of seven

641 A. de Tocqueville *Oeuvres complètes d'Alexis de Tocqueville.* vol. VII, *Nouvelle correspondance entièrement inédite,* Paris 1866, p. 267.

642 The coup d'état, on the other hand, was contemplated by some of his closest associates, like Persigny. Persigny was to say, "I have made him, in spite of himself, deputy, in spite of himself, president of the Republic; I will not leave before I have made him, in spite of himself, emperor" (quote as in P. Clément *Persigny. L'homme qui a inventé Napoléon III,* Paris 2006, p. 122).

643 Dossier of the Legion of Honour of Louis Wolowski: Archives Nationales, ref. LH// 2762/26. He had the Knight's Cross from April 1845.

votes. Barrot described the mood among the deputies after the vote. Among them was the news conveyed by one of the police commissioners that Louis Napoleon had allegedly carried out a coup attempt on the same night. Forty of them spent the night in the Assembly building. The alarm, however, turned out to be false[644]. However, this indicates the state of tension among parliamentarians and a widespread expectation of a coup.

One part of the Assembly made another, utterly desperate attempt to defend itself. This was the so-called quaestors' proposal, according to which the President of the Assembly would have the right, in his defence, to appeal directly to the army, without the intermediary of a minister. While the proposal was legal, it was also dangerous and unrealistic. Dangerous, because it would have been, in practice, a declaration of war against the president. Unrealistic, since the army was completely outside the control of the parliamentarians, long disliked by the officers. Later, in a conversation with Nassau, Tocqueville assessed it unequivocally: "[M. Baze's] proposition was absurd only because it was impracticable. It was a precaution against imminent danger, but if it had been voted it could not have been executed. The army had already been so corrupted that it would have disregarded the orders of the Assembly. I have often talked over our situation with Lamoricière[645] and my other military friends. We saw what was coming as clearly as we now look back to it, but we had no means of preventing it."[646].

The Conservatives eventually split during the vote on the quaestors' proposal. Thiers voted in favour. Faucher and Wolowski against. The latter was probably not as perspicacious as Tocqueville; he was rather closer to the "Journal des Débats", which regarded the quaestors' proposal as provocative and unnecessary[647]. Perhaps the democrats' thesis, articulated by Michel de Bourges "Mandataries of the people, deliberate peacefully; the people, the invisible sentinel, watch over you," also spoke to him in some way[648].

In each case, he clearly miscalculated. 2 December 1851 marked the occurrence of what many believed had to come. On that morning, Louis Napoleon Bonaparte's decree was circulated in Paris, by which he dissolved the National Assembly and the Council of State, restored the popular vote, and introduced a state of siege. The decree was accompanied by the *Proclamation of the President of the Republic. An*

---

644 O. Barrot *Mémoires posthumes*, vol. IV, Paris 1876, p. 185.

645 Louis Juchault de Lamoricière (1806–1865) – a French general, made famous by his successes in Algeria, where he captured Abd-el-Kader in 1847. A staunch opponent of Louis Napoleon Bonaparte.

646 W. Nassau Sr *Journals kept in France and in Italy*, vol. II, London 1871, p. 229.

647 "Journal des Débats Politiques et Littéraires", 17 and 18.11.1851.

648 Quote as in J. Risacher *Michel Louis, Chrysostome, dit Michel de Bourges,* [in] *Le Maitron,. Dictionnaire biographique, mouvement ouvrier, mouvement social :* https://maitron.fr/spip.php?article35021 (retrieved 29.03.2023).

Appeal to the People, in which Bonaparte stated that the Assembly had become a "hotbed of conspiracies" preparing France for civil war. According to the President, the Constitution was written in such a way as to weaken his power in advance, despite the "6 million votes cast for him". He was therefore proposing a new Basic Law to France, strengthening the executive power decisively. The law was to guarantee the president a ten-year term of office and complete subordination to the ministers. Instead of the National Assembly, there was to be a legislature elected by universal suffrage, accompanied by an upper house, as yet unnamed, composed of the country's "most eminent figures" and guarding constitutional rights.[649] It is worth noting the explicit reference to the institutions introduced in France by Napoleon I. The proclamation, moreover, made direct reference to the Consulate; and everyone on the Seine remembered that it had been followed by the empire of the first of the Bonapartes. On 2 December, therefore, Louis Napoleon had already set France's path quite clearly.

That same morning, before Paris had time to wake up for good, 78 individuals potentially leading the opposition to the coup were arrested. Meanwhile, some 220 deputies gathered in the mayor's office of the 10th arrondissement of Paris. Here, they voted to put Louis Napoleon on trial; however, this was no longer of any consequence: the army immediately appeared on the scene, everyone was arrested.

The Mountaineers were counting on the "invisible sentinel" of the constitution, the people. Admittedly, Pierre-Joseph Proudhon, met on the street that day, warned Victor Hugo: "Bonaparte has an object in view. The Republic has made the People. He wishes to restore the Populace. He will succeed and you [opposition deputies – R.D.] will fail. He has on his side force, cannons, the mistake of the people, and the folly of the Assembly. The few of the Left to which you belong will not succeed in overthrowing the coup d'état. You are honest and he has this advantage over you – that he is a rogue. You have scruples, and he has this advantage over you – that he has none"[650]. The poet, however, did not believe him; it was the anarchist who was right. A few barricades had admittedly been erected, and on 3 December the Mountain deputy Alphonse Baudin, was killed on one of them. His death, incidentally, became one of the important elements of republican mythology. It was described by Victor Schoelcher, another deputy present at the scene: "Bitterness accompanied his death. *We don't want to sacrifice ourselves for 25 francs*,' one of the workers told him. [...] *You will see*,' replied Baudin, '*how you die for 25 francs*!' And he parted with his life at the feet of the Constitution, passing into eternity with that beautiful word." [651] This workers' refusal to die for 25 francs (a day's wages

---

649 "Journal des Débats Politiques et Littéraires", 03.12.1851

650 V. Hugo, *The History of a Crime*, English translation by Andrew Locker, Altenmünster 1977, p. 93.

651 V. Schoelcher *Histoire des crimes du 2 décembre*, vol. I, Bruxelles 1852, p. 204. Contrary to the repeated claims of French historiography, Baudin was not forgotten after his death. Instead, it is true that his death came back very strongly in

for a parliamentarian of the Second Republic) was symptomatic. The workers of the suburb of Saint-Antoine did not turn up at the barricade; more generally, the people of Paris did not join the revolt. In total, according to P. Milza, 1,000–1,500 people tried to resist, of whom 200–300 were killed[652]. The most tragic event, incidentally, occurred on 4 December, not at a barricade but on the boulevards of Montmartre and Poissonière, where the military opened fire uncontrollably on a crowd of gathered demonstrators and onlookers. There, at least 100 people were killed. In total, then, the coup d'état of Louis Napoleon Bonaparte resulted in the deaths of around 300–400 people in Paris. While this is a tragic number, given the revolutionary history of the city, relatively small[653].

Louis Wolowski participated in these events only to a small extent. Levasseur cites the following story: "On the morning of 2 December, aware of the coup attempt, he and a number of colleagues went to the Assembly to reflect on the possibilities of resistance. A cordon of troops surrounded the building, and it was impossible to get through. Wolowski threw his deputy card over a fence of bayonets: "The card will at least get in," he chuckled, and withdrew, powerless, determined no longer to take any part in the political life of the regime whose origins he condemned."[654] This discarded deputy's card is the only clear sign of Wolowski's opposition to Bonaparte's actions. He did not man any barricade, nor was his name among the deputies detained in the mayoralty of the 10th arrondissement[655]. Markiewicz also notes that he had found no trace of Wolowski's attempt at resistance on 2 December or the following days[656].

Republican propaganda and legend during the liberalisation of the Second Empire in the late 1860s (J-O. Boudon *Baudin et la barricade du 3 décembre 1851: histoire et représentation de l'Empire à la République*, [in :] A. Corbin, J.-M. Mayeur (dir.) *La Barricade*, Paris 1997, https://books.openedition.org/psorbonne/1182 (retrieved 29.03.2023).

652 P. Milza *Napoléon III...*, p. 260.

653 Serious opposition to the coup came also from outside Paris. Several dozens of smaller or larger revolts broke out in 27 departments of southern and central France. Significantly, these were mainly in villages and small towns – thus confirming the strength of republicanism in parts of the rural departments, evident in the elections of 1849.

654 E. Levasseur *La Vie et les travaux de Wolowski...*, pp. 17–18.

655 Their names are mentioned by Joseph Décembre and Edmond Alonier in *Le coup d'État du 2 décembre 1851: historique des événements qui ont précédé le coup d'État, physionomie de Paris, arrestations et barricades, types et portraits des principaux personnages, faits qui ont suivi la chute de la république, pièces et documents officiels* (Paris 1868, pp. 140–141).

656 P. Markiewicz *Louis Wolowski...*, p. 136.

Thus, Louis Wolowski's political career came to a temporary end. He was a fairly typical representative of the majority ruling the Second Republic since at least April 1848. Starting from its Orléanist roots: an important part of both Assemblies (the Constituent Assembly of 1848 and the Legislative Assembly of 1849) were precisely notables descended from the elites of the July Monarchy. He was one of the many republicans of tomorrow, supporters of a liberal constitutional monarchy, ready to accept a liberal republic provided the principles of parliamentarism and the rule of law were preserved. Instead, he was probably not a democrat at the time, and in any case the popular vote was not a necessary component of a state so conceived. Like the vast majority of moderate republicans, he was an opponent of the socialism that was emerging in the 1840s and increasingly evident during the Revolutions of 1848. In doing so, he did not distinguish between the various socialist schools, collectively treating them all as dangerous utopias. However, this does not mean, as I will show later, that he fully represented the social and economic views of the French bourgeoisie – especially on free trade, which was important to Wolowski, the differences were quite significant.

Even if after February 1848, like most republicans of tomorrow, Wolowski believed in establishing a harmonious republic that could be formed with the popular classes, the subsequent events of 15 May 1848, the June Uprising of 1848, the elections of 1849, and 13 June 1849, increasingly undermined this belief. Concerned (in May and June 1848 probably literally frightened), he voted increasingly conservative. In 1848 he favoured the arrest of Blanc and Caussidière, and unequivocally supported Cavaignac. In 1849, he supported action against the leaders of the left, and in 1850, he voted in favour of limiting the voting rights of the poorest French and in favour of a new school law, subordinating schooling to the Church. In fact, Wolowski was leaning more and more towards a conservative, parliamentary republic, but with little connection to the people. This vision was shared by other former Orléanists: Thiers, Barrot, Molé and Faucher, who was closest to Wolowski. The trouble was that a republic conceived like this lacked a key element: legitimacy, roots. It was not backed by tradition, or history, it had no support in religion, and it could not, finally and most significantly, appeal to the will of the people. The weakness of this concept, which Wolowski evidently failed to see, lay in its very foundations. It was clearly exposed by the conflict between the Assembly and Louis Napoleon Bonaparte, with its final dissolution on 2 December. It was a conflict in which conservative republicans like Wolowski were perhaps doomed. Through them, as Sylvie Mesure writes, "the republic was dissolving". Louis Wolowski participated in this process.

At the same time, he was not an idle tool of the parliamentary majority leaders. The votes on the death penalty in 1848 or the freedom of the press in 1850 clearly showed that he was able to behave independently in parliament. Nor was he devoid of social sensitivity, as evidenced, for example, by his approach to workers' coalitions or the harmful conditions in workers' housing. Characteristically, moreover, he found himself in the minority in all these cases.

Wolowski was certainly not a parliamentary leader. He was not one of the key figures in the party. Nor was he simply one of several hundred parliamentarians, not afraid to speak out, and in several cases his interventions had an impact on the outcome of the debate. He was distinguished by the academic style of his speeches, probably difficult for the rest of the congregation to tolerate. He referred profusely to the economic theory of the time, above all to statistical data, foreign examples, and partly to his own research.

All of this, however, does not change the fact that the final collapse of the Second Republic also placed a certain, limited burden on him.

Chapter V: The Crédit Foncier

1. The Second Empire

It also seems that Wolowski's passive attitude on 2 December 1851 and in the following days can be understood and explained. He had at least several reasons, the first being the fact that Wolowski was a Pole. Strongly associated with the Hotel Lambert, he was well aware that his possible opposition could further complicate what was already less than ideal relations between Czartoryski and Bonaparte[657], and affect negatively the perception of the entire Polish immigration by the new authorities[658]. Moreover, Wolowski probably remembered the unfavourable reaction of the Provisional Government, in particular Lamartine, to the revolutionary activities of the Polish democrats in February and March 1848. Secondly, his own views (shared with other former Orléanists) kept him naturally away from the barricades and any revolutionary actions. Thirdly, Wolowski may have rightly assumed the futility of any resistance. Fourthly and finally, he may also have had some personal interest in it.

The developments were taking place very quickly. As early as on 20 and 21 December 1851, the authorities held a plebiscite asking the people if they "wanted to maintain the power of Louis Napoleon Bonaparte and transfer to him the powers necessary to introduce a constitution based on his proclamation of 2 December 1851". Of the 8,165,000 voters, 7,481,000 answered "yes".

The new constitution, drafted by a small group of trusted collaborators[659], approved by Louis Napoleon, was ready as early as on 14 January 1852. While the

---

657 As Jerzy Skowronek and Jan Ziółek point out, Czartoryski was associated with the Orléans dynasty. Moreover, in 1848 he had set his sights on General Cavaignac, against Bonaparte. This resulted in his actual loss of influence and contacts in the executive in Paris after the presidential election, and 1851 only deepened this process (J. Skowronek *Adam Jerzy Czartoryski 1770–1861*, Warszawa 1994, pp. 471–472; J. Ziółek *Studia nad myślą polityczną Wielkiej Emigracji. Napoleon I i Napoleon III*, Lublin 1995, pp. 101–122).

658 That Wolowski used his influence and acquaintance in Polish affairs is evidenced by the 1849 letter of the "Polish people in Algier", in which the authors thank him for the fact that their complaint about the unbearable living conditions reached the highest French authorities and was favourably received. (*Ogół Polaków w Algierze do Ludwika Wołowskiego*, Biblioteka Polska w Paryżu, ref. BPP 2339, cc. 40-41).

659 They were Jean Gilbert Victor Fialin, Duke de Persigny, Charles de Flahaut, Jacques-André Mesnard, Raymond-Théodore Troplong and Eugène Rouher. Interestingly, there is a copy of Faucher's letter to Louis Napoleon, dated 03.12.1851, in the National Archives in Cracow, in which the former prime minister referred to the news (rumour) that he was to be part of this commission. He wrote: "I do not

Prince President (named explicitly in the constitution: Louis Napoleon Bonaparte) represented head of state, his powers were significantly expanded. He was henceforth in charge of foreign policy, deciding on matters of war and peace, alliances, and trade treaties. He appointed and dismissed all officials, including ministers, at his discretion. In practice, the entire executive apparatus was his tool.

The legislature, on the other hand, consisted of the Senate and the Legislative Body. The Senate was appointed entirely by the Prince President and acted as the guardian of the constitution and, possibly, the initiator of constitutional amendments. The Legislative Body was elected by universal suffrage. Deputies debated bills and voted on the state budget. However, they otherwise had no influence on the executive; the ministers could not be deputies and, according to the Constitution, should not appear in the Legislative Body at all. The body did not even elect its own president. The subordinate role of the legislature was explicitly enshrined in Article 3 of the Constitution: "The President of the Republic governs through ministers, the Council of State, the Senate and the Legislative Body."[660] The abolition of the parliamentary tribune was a symbolic act – the deputies were to speak from their own seats.

Top it with the restrictions on freedom of the press (more than 100 opposition newspapers disappeared in 1852), the system of official government nominations in elections, to get a picture of an authoritarian state. A state whose first victims were the 30,000 arrested and 10,000 deported after the coup d'état[661].

By 1852, everyone had been aware of the twilight of the republic and the fact that a new empire was probably imminent. This was indicated both by the policies of the Prince President and by the obvious historical antecedents. Prosper Barante, a veteran of the First Empire, wrote in January 1852: "a bastard empire is rising even faster than the accidental republic it freed us from"[662]. The institutions were virtually ready, all that remained was the formal abolition of the Second Republic and its transformation into the Second Empire. The preparation for this transformation was Louis Napoleon's long tour of central and south-western France.

---

recall allowing you to make such an insult." (National Archives in Cracow, ref. AKPot 3204).

660 http://www.conseil-constitutionnel.fr/conseil-constitutionnel/francais/la-constitution/les-constitutions-de-la-france/constitution-de-1852-second-empire.5107.html (website of the Conseil Constitutionnel, the French constitutional court, retrieved 20 August 2014).

661 A comprehensive bibliography of the coup d'état of Louis Napoleon Bonaparte and its aftermath: S. Aprile, R. Huard *Le coup d'État du 2 décembre 1851. Bibliographie,* [in:] "Revue d'histoire du XIXe siècle", no. 22, 2001, http://journals.openedition.org/rh19/252 (retrieved 31 March 2023).

662 P. de Barante, *Souvenirs du baron de Barante de l'Académie Française 1782–1866,* vol. VIII, Paris 1901, p. 23.

Persigny ensured that the President was regularly greeted not only with shouts of enthusiasm, but also with a repeated "long live the emperor!" (for which he rebuked him). The key moment came in Bordeaux on 09 October 1852, when Bonaparte uttered his famous words:

> Some people say 'Empire is war,' I say 'Empire is peace.' […] I admit, however, that, like the emperor [Napoleon I], I have other conquests to make. […] I want to conquer for religion, morality, prosperity such a large part of the population who […] today hardly enjoy their own bare necessities. We have vast uncultivated areas to develop, roads to build, ports to dig, rivers to regulate, canals to complete, and finally our railway network to complete. We have, opposite Marseille, a great kingdom to connect with France. We have our great western ports, which we should connect to America by fast means of transport, which we still lack. […] This is how I understand the Empire.[663]

Louis Napoleon thus clearly announced the return of the Empire and developed its programme. A programme, I should add, which he meant to implement.

On 7 November 1852, the Senate adopted, with one dissenting vote, the *senatus consultum*, calling on the people to respond to the question of whether "The people of France wish to restore the imperial dignity in the person of Louis Napoleon Bonaparte, with the right of succession by descendants, legitimate or adopted, and delegate to him the right to regulate the order of succession to the throne within the Bonaparte family, in accordance with the *senatus consultum* of this date."[664] The plebiscite took place two weeks later. 7,800,000 French people answered "yes", 253,000 answered "no". The Empire was officially proclaimed on the night of 1- 2 December 1852[665].

The new political system was not aligned with Louis Wolowski's views at all. He gave expression to this by withdrawing completely from political life. Moreover, many former Orléanists came to terms with the Empire over time, others joined the ranks of the parliamentary opposition in the 1860s, but Wolowski was not in any of these groups. In his *Dictionnaire Universel des Contemporains* of 1870, Gustave Vapereau wrote that in 1869, Wolowski's name was on one of the opposition electoral lists before the election, but the man himself is said to have withdrawn it.[666]

---

663 Napoléon III *Discours, messages et proclamations de S. M. Napoléon III, empereur des Français: 1849–1860*, Paris 1860, p. 247.

664 *Extrait du Moniteur Universel de 1852 contenant le texte du sénatus-consulte du 7 novembre 1852 sur le rétablissement de l'Empire et celui du décret du 2 décembre 1852 promulguant le sénatus-consulte*, Paris 1852.

665 Notably, unlike his predecessor, Napoleon III did not, either then or later, organise a ceremonial coronation.

666 G. Vapereau *Dictionnaire universel des contemporains: contenant toutes les personnes notables de la France et des pays étrangers*, Paris 18700, p. 1868.

Perhaps, at the beginning, the reason for Wolowski's attitude was the hope of Bonaparte's imminent demise. Nassau recalled a New Year's Eve breakfast with Wolowski in 1851. During it, the Conservatoire professor was said to have made it clear that "the general opinion is that this Government has some years to run". He went on to add philosophically: "I rather hope that such may be the case. We ought to be made to feel the value of liberty. We have enjoyed it as a man who has never been ill, enjoys health unreflectingly; three or four years of real tyranny would be a useful lesson."[667] If Wolowski indeed initially thought that Bonaparte would last three to four years, clearly, he underestimated him, yet again. On the other hand, he may have been partly right speaking of a necessary lesson in tyranny for the French.

The word "tyranny" used by Wolowski clearly defined his attitude to the rule of Louis Napoleon. Yet, the economic programme of the Second Empire formulated at Bordeaux suited Wolowski just fine. What is more, in one respect this tyranny proved far more effective than a constitutional monarchy or republic and brought about the change that the Pole had long expected and supported.

2. Wolowski's credit proposals

For here, on 28 February 1852, less than three months after the coup d'état, Louis Napoleon Bonaparte signed a *Decree on landed credit societies*. A month later, the president signed another one, referring to the first one and establishing the first landed bank. One of the founders and the first director of the Banque Foncière de Paris (the name of the new institution) was... Louis Wolowski[668].

This fact may shed more light on Wolowski's actions in December 1851. Indeed, we cannot rule out a possibility that some discussions concerning changes to the landed loan (discussions involving the presidential palace) had been underway in late 1851. Wolowski may have been involved in them.

To explain this state of affairs, however, it is necessary to go back in time. This is because Wolowski's interest in landed credits and the related legal issues dated back to his university time. The second part of his undergraduate dissertation was devoted to mortgage law in France. In his work, Wolowski was clear about the law's key weakness, subsequently influencing the deterioration of a landed credit: the opacity of the whole arrangement, due in part to the poor system of mortgage books, in part to the specific approach to women's rights[669].

---

667 W. Nassau Senior, *Journals kept in France and in Italy*, vol. I, London 1871, pp. 265–266.

668 J.B. Josseau *Traité du crédit Foncier suivi d'un traité du crédit agricole et du crédit Foncier colonial, contenant l'explication théorique et pratique de la législation spéciale*, Paris 1872, pp. 212–214.

669 A legal mortgage, not resulting from a contract but from the law itself, when it encumbered women, was not subject to the obligation of entry in the books.

Wolowski returned to the issue of mortgages and the related landed credit in the first issue of the "Revue de Législation et de Jurisprudence". Undoubtedly, this topic became a leading issue for him over the next few years. In his first text, the then young law graduate drew attention to the problem of secrecy of mortgages encumbering women and minors. This fact, he stressed, had an extremely negative impact on the real estate (primarily land) trade and the associated credit. He therefore advocated first and foremost a reform of the mortgage system and full disclosure of all mortgages, both to property buyers and lenders[670].

Wolowski addressed the issue again in the "Revue... " in 1839. This time, he emphasised the modernisation that the development of a landed credit system could provide. However, it was again about openness of mortgages, full information about the property and its encumbrances available to both the buyer and the financier of the purchase. Quite optimistically – as it was to turn out later – he thought that this would be enough to get landed credit off the ground"[671].

Happily, at the time, more people realised the weakness of the mortgage system in general and landed credit in particular, including representatives of the authorities. In 1841, the French Ministry of Justice asked several law faculties about a possible reform of the mortgage system. All those asked were in favour of a change[672]. Certainly, the reform also had opponents, mainly among landowners. They feared many things, among them an overly bureaucratic system in which the slightest encumbrance on a property was to be recorded in the books of so-called "mortgage offices". Landowners were also afraid of the competition that could come with cheaper credits and were reluctant to look at the obligation to fully disclose the encumbrances on their own estates.

Wolowski not only criticised the existing mortgage and credit system in France; he also tried to identify possible solutions. He was no longer concerned with mortgages themselves, the reform of which seemed to him straightforward, but above all with strengthening the credit system and credit for agriculture. To this end, he referred to the Polish and the German credit societies with which he was familiar. He assumed that French agriculture needed capital to a degree comparable to or even greater than industry. In 1844, he wrote in a separate pamphlet

---

According to Wolowski, this created a moral hazard, as the husband could easily convince his wife to be jointly liable with him for the repayment of the loan, but the mortgage on his wife's property was not disclosed. (L. Wolowski *Thèse pour la licence...*, pp. 29–32).

670 L. Wolowski *Régime hypothécaire,* [in:] "Revue de législation et de jurisprudence", vol. I, 1835, pp. 35–48 and 276–290.

671 L. Wolowski *De la mobilisation du crédit Foncier,* [in:] Revue de législation et de jurisprudence", vol. X, 1839, pp. 241–276.

672 P. Blajer *Z dziejów francuskiego modelu "la publicité foncière",* [in:] "Zeszyty prawnicze", vol. XVI, no. 1, 2016, p. 113.

on this very subject: "To put capital in front of needs, to provide it with sound and convenient investment opportunities, to activate its circulation, to strengthen all sources of production, to reduce the price of raw materials by providing the land with the instruments it lacks and by lowering interest rates – this is the complex problem whose solution lies, in our opinion, on the one hand in the establishment of agricultural banks and, on the other, in the organisation of extensive landed credit [...]."[673] Wolowski meant primarily a long-term credit linked to land. He cited the amount involved in France (around 12 billion francs in 1843) but stressed that only a small part of this sum went to agriculture. In his view this was due, in part, to the mortgage barriers already mentioned, in part to the excessive cost of the credit itself[674]. In France, it was simply that credit did not pay off for farmers.

Wolowski claimed that, in fact, French banks were reluctant to lend money for agricultural purposes. This was due to problems with securing the loan, but also to the length of the capital repayment period. From the lenders' point of view, the periods were simply too long in agriculture. Meanwhile, "for the landowner, the necessity of repaying all the capital in accordance with the creditor's wishes is not only a hassle but stands in flagrant contradiction to the very nature of land ownership"[675], Wolowski wrote. In other words, according to him, farmers could repay instalments and interest on the capital regularly over a long period of time, calculated in decades, but they could not repay the whole thing quickly.

To solve this problem, the son of Franciszek Wołowski referred to the Polish example of the Towarzystwo Kredytowe Ziemskie (Land Credit Society). Louis, as I have mentioned, had probably been in touch with it in his youth through his father. The purpose of the Society, as it is known, was to provide cheap credit to landed property. The value of the Society's loans could reach 3/5 of the value of the landed property itself. Loans were granted in the form of mortgage bonds with a 4% annual fee. These letters were, in turn, used to repay creditors. The system was reliable and secure insofar as the whole Society was responsible for the collection of debts. The state was an additional guarantor of the stability of the loan, the Society's largest shareholder and its largest borrower. Significantly, in the French context, the Society offered debtors up to 28 years to repay their debts[676]. Wolowski also referred to the experience of similar societies in Prussia, Bremen, Mecklenburg, Württemberg, and Bavaria. He proposed that smaller landowners should be allowed to join the credit (unlike in Poland), and – this is the most

673 L. Wolowski *Réforme hypothécaire: organisation du crédit Foncier*, Paris 1844, p. 4.

674 L. Wolowski *Réforme hypothécaire...*, pp. 10–17.

675 L. Wolowski *Réforme hypothécaire...*, p. 20.

676 B. Wachowicz *Towarzystwo Kredytowe Ziemskie w Królestwie Polskim w okresie powstania listopadowego*, "Annales Universitatis Mariae Curie-Skłodowska", vol. 37, 1983, pp. 62–63; T. Skałkowski *Towarzystwa kredytowe ziemskie w ziemiach polskich. Szkic historyczny*, Lwów 1892, pp. 23–25).

important change – that in France the role of the Society should be taken over by the state.

It is noteworthy, by the way, that while describing Polish or German examples, Wolowski disregarded the relevant experience of... France. In 1816, Olinde Rodrigues drafted the statutes of the Caisse Hypothécaire (Mortgage Fund), which was also to mediate between lenders and borrowers. The idea was to raise funds through bonds. The fund was launched four years later and wound down after another eight. The reason was lack of customers[677]. Wolowski may not have been familiar with the history of the Caisse Hypothécaire but, quite possibly, he disregarded it in his arguments because of its ultimate failure.

In the 1830s and 1840s, however, Louis Wolowski was only a contributor to his own journal and a professor at the Conservatoire des Arts et Métiers. Although his articles reached specialists, including perhaps one or two ministers, on the whole they had limited impact on the world of politics. This changed in April 1848. Now Wolowski could try to push his ideas through parliament.

As early as on 23 June 1848, he presented his bill on landed credit – a clear indication of the importance he attached to the issue. The text itself stemmed directly from his earlier thoughts and proposals. According to its first article, "Any property owner could apply to the Treasury for the issue of a certain number of mortgage bonds equivalent to the value of the property tax subject to 5% capitalisation", and the time of repaying the total loan was to be a maximum of 23 years[678].

Unfortunately, Wolowski chose a truly bad moment to discuss loans. For on 23 June, Paris of the workers, Paris of the national workshops, was just rising. In these circumstances, the majority of the people's representatives had absolutely no desire to discuss the timing of the repayment of the landed debt, its interest rate, etc. The debate was therefore postponed, and the Assembly did not reopen it until October 1848[679].

It seems, however, that the entire period was not suitable for in-depth legal or credit reforms, which, after all, was on Wolowski's agenda. For the incessant turmoil and the deep political conflicts were still accompanied by economic collapse. France had not yet recovered from the deep food and industrial crisis of 1846–1847. Moreover, this crisis was to develop into a stagnation that lasted until 1851[680]. As a result, in 1848 Wolowski's project eventually stalled in parliament, without even the voting.

The issue returned in 1849 in the Legislature. Wolowski even became a member of a parliamentary committee to consider various landed credit projects[681].

677 B. Gille *La Banque de France au XIX siècle. Recherches historiques*, Genève 1970, p. 110.

678 "Moniteur Universel...", Paris 1848, p. 1480.

679 "Moniteur Universel...", Paris 1848, p. 2781.

680 D. Barjot *Histoire économique de la France au XIX siècle*, Paris 1995, pp. 31–31.

681 "Moniteur Universel...", Paris 1849, p. 2118.

However, we do not know whether it was the committee that was so slow to act, or the Assembly had more pressing matters. In any case, the issue of mortgages and credit did not come up for discussion until 1850[682]. Wolowski became heavily involved in the polemic on the former. Traditionally, he had evident trouble breaking through the clatter of the Assembly. When he finally succeeded, he advocated first and foremost the abolition of legal mortgages. These, he reiterated, made it difficult if not impossible to make proper use of the landed loan. Moreover, according to Wolowski, farmers had to repay the loan too quickly, in instalments that were too large. The result, according to him, was that mortgages most often did not reach farmers at all[683]. The polemic with Wolowski was then taken up by Crémieux, former Minister of Justice of the Republic. He argued, among other things, that the form of credit and mortgage proposed by Wolowski would ruin land ownership. In his view, entering a mortgage at the request of the creditor, when the debtor would find himself in trouble for some reason, could only have served speculation and speculators. Such would be the side effects of the abolition of judicial mortgages. Wolowski countered these allegations by citing examples from other countries. A mortgage assigned to specific properties, could in no way harm the property or the landed loan. Moreover, in many German lands it was successful. In addition, the judicial mortgage, he stressed, was a sure alternative for creditors to another, much more dangerous tool, namely expropriation. He defended real estate mortgages ordered by court, registered by the court at the request of the creditor, which "played the same role with regard to personal credit as a prison for debt plays with regard to commercial debts", and were therefore, according to Wolowski, to be a guarantee for the repayment of a debt that was not secured by a mortgage under the contract[684].

The discussion ended in December 1850. In 1851, the Assembly did not manage to open it up again, and on 02 December 1851 the Assembly itself ceased to function.

Meanwhile, Wolowski also tried to convince other state bodies of his ideas. He was a member of the Council of Agriculture, Craft Production and Trade, operating under the Minister of Agriculture and Trade. Here, too, he took up the

---

682 "Moniteur Universel...", Paris 1850, p. 2151.

683 "Moniteur Universel...", Paris 1850, p. 2181. Wolowski makes an interesting observation, clearly like Tocqueville's, about the key elements of the Great Revolution: "Do you know why a country, seemingly greatly disturbed, need not fear deep revolutions concerning the core of its institutions? You owe it to the division of the land. In my opinion, France is today the safest country under the sun, and will be the safest, because this great revolution which handed over the land to a great number of landowners, this great revolution which elsewhere is only just beginning, in France has already taken place: this is the basis of our security today and in the future.".

684 "Moniteur Universel...", Paris 1850, pp. 3627–3628.

discussion on landed credit and succeeded in convincing the relevant committee. Its report to the Council and to the Minister contained Wolowski's propositions, only slightly modified. The Commission, proposing a solution like the Polish one, clearly reduced the role of the state and additionally introduced a guarantee fund in the company. Apart from this, however, its report repeated Wolowski's arguments almost word for word[685].

Thus, Wolowski personally experienced parliamentary impotence, the sluggishness of the people's representatives on what he considered a key issue. It was soon to transpire that authoritarianism worked much more quickly and efficiently, as Louis Napoleon signed the aforementioned decree *On landed credit societies* in late February. According to its first article, landed credit societies could have been established "after consultation with the Council of State, with the aim of providing landowners who wished to take out a mortgage with the opportunity to free themselves through long-term repayments."[686] The decree allowed the establishment of both lender and borrower societies (Article 2). A loan could only have been taken out in this way after all previous creditors had been paid off, so the property could not have been encumbered by any mortgage including an undisclosed mortgage (art. 6). The value of such a loan could have been up to half of the value of the property and was repayable in annual instalments (Article 10). The interest rate could not have exceeded 5%, amortisation 2% of the value of the loan (Article 11). Societies were given the right to issue bonds and mortgage bonds of a value not exceeding the value of the loan[687].

3. Bank director

The new law allowed to open the first landed bank just one month later. On 28 March 1852, Banque foncière de Paris (Landed Bank of Paris) was established by presidential decree. The new institution's share capital was to be 25 million francs, in 25,000 shares of five hundred francs each. The bank was to operate in an area of 7 departments, subject to the Paris Court of Appeal: Seine, Seine-et-Oise, Seine-et-Marne, Eure-et-Loire, Aube, Marne, and Yonne. Most significantly, Louis Wolowski was one of the venture's founders and its first director[688].

---

685 L. Wolowski L. *Rapport fait par M. Wolowski, Représentant du Peuple, membre du Conseil Général, au nom de la Commission chargée de la question relative au crédit Foncier*, Paris 1850.

686 J.B. Josseau *Traité du crédit Foncier...*, p. 187.

687 J.B. Josseau *Traité du crédit Foncier...*, pp. 188–189.

688 Initially, the still-forming bank was temporarily headed by Antoine Simon Hailig, former president of the Chamber of Notaries. The vice-presidents were Francois Bartholony, Ksawery Branicki and d'Eichthal. Wolowski became a director in August 1852 (a rough draft of a letter Wolowski probably addressed to the first

It also seems, as I have mentioned, that the preliminary discussions on the establishment of the new bank must have taken place much earlier, perhaps as early as on 2 December 1851. This is also indicated by the rough draft of a letter from Wolowski to the first shareholders of Banque Foncière de Paris, in which he indicated that in just three months, the matter of the banking decree had been managed by the competent administrative commission and the Council of State[689]. This would mean that preliminary work had begun by late December 1851 at the latest. It also seems more than likely that the decree on land credit societies was linked to the design of the new bank since the beginning. Wolowski must also have started convincing influential figures in Parisian finance about the new bank much earlier. In fact, the directory of the people behind the bank is impressive. It also illustrates well Wolowski's network of connections. The list contained in the decree of 28 March included:

> Mr Bartholony, banker; Mr. Drouyn de l'Huys, Vice-President of the Senate; Mr. Léon Faucher, former minister; Count Ksawery Branicki, landowner; Prince Sapieha, landowner; Mr Adolphe d'Eichthal, member of the Paris municipal commission; Mr Benoist d'Azy, former representative of the people; Count de Mouchy, deputy; Count Hervé de Kergorlay, deputy; Mr Emile Pereire, director of the Saint-Germain railway; Mr Thibaut, former notary; Baron Charles de Ladoucette, senator; Count de Gasparin, former par of France, former minister; Messrs. Paccard, Dufour and company, bankers; Mr de Waru; count de Plancy, deputy; Mr Achille Fould, senator; p. Hippolyte Passy, former minister; r Darblay senior, former MP; Mr Darblay the younger, MP; Léopold Javal, banker; Count de Chappedelaine, landowner; Mr Hély d'Oissel, former councillor of state; Mr Cotelle, former MP; Mr Léonce de Lavergne, professor at the agronomic institute at Versailles; count de Brosses, landowner; general, count Dunin-Wąsowicz; Mr Charles Rhoné, landowner; Mr de Renneville, former deputy; Mr Adolphe Dailly, head of the post office in Paris; Mr Wolowski, former representative of the people.[690]

The list brought together figures from a variety of seemingly very different backgrounds. So, it included the Bonapartists Edouard Drouyn de Lhuys, Philippe de Mouchy, Aymé-Stanislas Darblay, Kergorlay, Renneville; the Orléanists Passy, Faucher, Adrien-Etienne de Gasparin and Wolowski himself; the legitimist Denis Benoist d'Azy and a large group of figures well versed in both the politics of the July Monarchy and the Second Empire (like Achille Fould).

The names of the bankers were also very important in the context of the new institution's credibility. Most conspicuous was the presence of Emile Pereire, one

---

shareholders of the Banque Foncière de Paris, Archives Nationales du Monde du Travail, ref. PI39 2).

689 Archives Nationales du Monde du Travail, ref. PI39 2.

690 J.B. Josseau *Traité du crédit Foncier...*, pp. 211–212.

of the two famous brothers. François Bartholony was another important figure in the banking world. Although the most powerful (Rotschild) was missing, he was somewhat represented by the associated Paccard. At the same time, Pereire, Bartholony, Mouchy and Benoist d'Azy represented heavy industry. The Darblays, Kergorlays and Drouyn de Lhuys were all great landowners. A separate group of Poles: Ksawery Branicki, Eustachy Kajetan Sapieha, Stanisław Dunin-Wąsowicz, is worth noting.

This large, diverse, and extremely politically and financially influential group of people guaranteed stability of the enterprise. The names of the Bonapartists, on the other hand, testified to the crucial support of the authorities.

Wolowski was most likely the originator of the new bank as well as one of the keystones of the group. He had known the Orléanists for years. He may have been introduced to the Bonapartist milieu by Napoleon Joseph Ney, the Marshal's son, one of his acquaintances. In fact, Wolowski also knew Morny, Louis Napoleon's stepbrother, and an extremely influential figure in Bonapartist circles.

Through Ney, he may also have come into contact with the world of big finance earlier. For Napoleon Joseph's wife was Albine Étiennette, daughter of Jacques Laffitte, a key Parisian banker of the first half of the century (and minister, prime minister, and president of the Chamber of Deputies in 1830-31). In their salon, therefore, Wolowski could also have met other great financiers.

Importantly, in all these milieus, the Polish cause enjoyed some sympathy. Thus, Wolowski's origin was not a significant obstacle to his taking up a managerial post at the bank. In turn, it allowed him to attract the wealthiest Poles. Wolowski's reputation as an expert in landed credit, which he enjoyed thanks to his publications, was probably also of significance.

The bank quickly raised the required minimum capital and began operations in early October 1852[691]. However, before it was able to start its lending activities in earnest, it changed its area of operation and – for that matter – its name, as Wolowski came to an agreement with Persigny, the new Minister of the Interior. Significantly, this earliest of the Bonapartists, and most devoted to Louis Napoleon, was also a great supporter of the agricultural credit reform. In a circular to the prefects of 15 April 1852, he wrote, among other things: "For a long time now, agriculture has rightly complained about the high price of the money lent to it, the magnitude of the costs incurred in connection with loans, and the difficulty of having to repay capital quickly [...] This situation could not escape the attention of the President of the Republic. Convinced of the need for a swift and effective remedy, as requested by the official bodies representing the interests of agriculture, he stated that the time had come to take immediate action to provide landed

691 L. Wolowski *Circulaire de la direction du Crédit foncier de France, à MM. les notaires*, [in :] J.B. Josseau *Traité du crédit Foncier...*, pp. 304–306.

property with a credit tailored to its nature and needs."[692]. He therefore supported the efforts of Wolowski and the Banque Foncière de Paris to strengthen this credit for both financial and political reasons (the aim was to gain the support of the peasants, still the most numerous stratum in France). An important argument for Persigny was probably the fact that Wolowski's bank had virtually no significant competition[693]. Therefore, the Minister (no doubt with Louis Napoleon's knowledge) agreed to extend its activities throughout the country. This had to entail a change of name, as the institution was losing its strictly Parisian character. At the same time, the authorities did not want to irritate the only pan-French bank at the time, the Banque de France. Therefore, the word "bank" disappeared from the name of the company founded by Wolowski and was replaced by "Crédit" ("Credit"). The name of the bank was henceforth the "Crédit Foncier" ("Landed Credit") and the bank was to operate under this name for the next 157 years, until 2019, when, taken over by the BPCE group, it ceased operations.

Louis Napoleon's minister forced another clause on the bank: the Crédit Foncier undertook to lend a total of at least 200 million francs over the next four years for strictly agricultural purposes. In return, the state allowed the bank's share capital to be increased to 60 million francs and gave it a subsidy of 10 additional million. These arrangements were subsequently confirmed by an imperial decree of 10 December 1852[694].

This state support was due to the bank's troubles. Although Eliza Krasińska, sister of Ksawery Branicki, since the very beginning, a member of the new bank's board of directors, wrote in December 1852 that the Crédit Foncier (the name I shall use consistently from now on) was thriving, she was wrong. The bank was to finance itself by selling shares and bank bonds. Meanwhile, the sales were not going as planned. The institution artificially maintained the price of their shares on the Paris stock exchange, but eventually recorded a 3-million-franc loss in late 1853[695].

---

692 V. de Persigny *Circulaire de M. le ministre de l'intérieur sur l'application du décret relatif au (15 avril 1852)*, [in :] J.B. Josseau *Traité du crédit Foncier...*, p. 214.

693 Aline Raimbault and Henri Heugas-Darraspen write that between 1852 and 1853, a total of a dozen societies based their activities on the 28 February decree. However, quite a few of them did not take up their activities at all, while others were much weaker than Wolowski's bank and were taken over by it over time (H. Heugas-Darraspen, A. Raimbault *Crédit Foncier de France. Itinéraire d'une institution*, Paris 1994, p. 35)

694 *Convention passée entre M. le ministre de l'intérieur, de l'agriculture et du commmerce et la Banque foncière de Paris (société de crédit foncier)*, [in:] J.B. Josseau *Traité du crédit Foncier...*, pp. 231–234; *Décret du 10 décembre 1852*, pp. 230–231.

695 J.-P. Allinne *Banquiers et bâtisseurs : un siècle de Crédit Foncier, 1852–1940*, Paris 1984, p. 33.

The bank's problems do not seem to have been linked to Wolowski's management; rather, they resulted from external circumstances, initially perhaps disregarded by the founders of the Crédit Foncier. Firstly, the bank hardly marked its presence outside Paris. Although it had 29 branches in the province, this meant an average of one branch per three departments. This was still clearly not enough. In addition, the lending terms and conditions set out in the decree of 28 February proved too rigid for the bank. In other words, the Crédit Foncier's initial business was hardly profitable. While the agreement with Persigny improved its condition, it did not change the core of the problem. The key reform, moreover, was to come a short time later, in 1854. And it involved Wolowski losing his post.

4. On the board of the Crédit Foncier and the Crédit Agricole

To significantly improve the operations of the Crédit Foncier, it was imperative to change the law, so another state intervention was required. This finally took place on 06 July 1854 when Napoleon III signed a decree giving the bank a new statute. The emperor lifted previous restrictions on lending rates and allowed new short-term mortgages without amortisation. In return, however, the Second Empire assumed control of the bank's authorities. Henceforth, it was managed by a president ("gouverneur") together with two vice-presidents. The president chaired the board of directors, convened, and chaired the shareholders' general meetings, signed all documents[696].

The new regulations were modelled by the statutes of the Banque de France. This raised the prestige of the Crédit Foncier and presumably also allowed it to attract new clients and investors. In turn, the lifting of interest rate restrictions made credit more attractive, although not necessarily for agriculture. Characteristic was the fact that the word "agriculture" itself did not appear even once in the new statute. In contrast, enabling short-term mortgages, in principle made it possible to invest outside agriculture. It seems that the imperial authorities were thinking of redirecting money via the Crédit Foncier towards industry and cities. This was otherwise also in line with the wishes of the bank authorities[697]. All the more so as Haussmann had been appointed prefect of Paris a few months earlier. At the Emperor's request, the great reconstruction of the capital was beginning,

696 *6 juillet 1854. Décret relatif à la nouvelle organisation du Crédit foncier de France*, [in:] J.B. Josseau *Traité du crédit Foncier...*, pp. 256–258.

697 Among other things, a rough draft of a letter from Wolowski to the Minister of the Interior inquiring about the possibility of crediting municipalities, departments, and public institutions, has survived (Archives Nationales du Monde du Travail, ref. PI392).

requiring gigantic funds[698]. The Crédit Foncier, on the other hand, could have been a convenient vehicle for its financing.

Only that the bank's mission, so conceived, diverged completely from Wolowski's initial idea. Moreover, if, according to the new view, the Crédit Foncier was to be an important financial tool of the authorities, they had to assume full control over the bank. It is also possible that the gigantic sums of money that the bank handled brought it to the attention of influential figures in the Second Empire. As a representative of the Orléanists, in the Bonapartists' eyes Wolowski was always a somewhat uncertain figure.

On the other hand, Roulliet claims that the change in the position of president of the Crédit Foncier was due to personal rather than political reasons. However, he fails to cite them, hiding behind respect for Wolowski's privacy. The fact is that 1854 was a difficult year for the Wolowski clan. In December, Faucher died. The Mickiewicz family was also badly affected, above all Celina, who was soon to leave this world.[699] Whether Roulliet meant these as the personal reasons, or perhaps others were at play, remains unknown. Another thing is that Roulliet's explanation also seems uncertain; in the absence of further information in his text, although it is impossible to deny it, it is difficult to trust it completely.

In any case, in 1854 the president of the Crédit Foncier was Count Charles de Germiny: a loyal Bonapartist and short-lived finance minister in 1851. Markiewicz cites a story by an anonymous author of Wolowski's biography, according to which Germiny was said to have offered the Pole a large sum of money as a farewell gift.

---

698 A brief reminder that Haussmann completely remodelled Paris. He demolished almost all the buildings on the Ile de la Cité (evicting 15,000 people in the process), rebuilt the Les Halles quarter and the area around today's boulevards Saint-Germain, Voltaire, Malesherbes, Saint-Michel, and the Rivoli, Dumesnil, Gay-Lussac streets. His creation is the gigantic Étoile square, with its star-shaped avenues diverging from it, plus the squares of the Opera, the Republic, the Bastille, the Nation, Denfert-Rochereau, Italie and the buildings surrounding them (new or unveiled by the prefectural architects). He erected the new Gare du Nord and Gare de Lyon stations. He also built 560 km of sewers, new aqueducts to supply drinking water to the city, more than twenty new churches. He demolished a total of 27,500 houses, at the same time building more than 102,000 new ones (G.-N. Lameyre, *Haussmann,préfet de Paris,* Paris 1958, p. 144 ; R. Dobek *Paryż, 1871...*, pp. 18–22).

699 Władysław cites his mother's letter from late 1853. Celina wrote, among other things: "Since Kleinasia's departure I have been seriously ill, I have had cholera three times and am still not completely well. I also have constant worries about Marynia's health, who got such a persistent fever that, despite many remedies, she is still not healthy and needs great care and rest." Władyslaw went on to add: "My mother's health was declining more and more. The children did not suspect how dangerous her illness was." (W. Mickiewicz *Moja matka...*, p. 92).

Wolowski was said to have refused, stressing that "the Crédit Foncier organisation made it possible for me to repay my debt to my adopted homeland, and now I would just like to serve it with you, monsieur."[700] It seems, however, that Wolowski may have had entirely different reasons than simply a desire to "serve his adopted homeland". Because, like Branicki, he retained a position on the bank's board of directors. This meant not only a substantial salary but above all maintaining extremely important and influential contacts – in the world of politics and great finance alike. Contacts that could ultimately also contribute significantly to the fortune left by Wolowski in 1876.

Germiny did not hold his office for long: he left just three years later for the much more prominent and prestigious position of president of the Banque de France. He was then replaced by Louis Frémy, aged 52. Wolowski probably knew Frémy as he was the director of Faucher's ministerial cabinet and a friend of the latter's[701]. He was therefore probably part of Wolowski's extensive network of connections; this partly explains how Wolowski retained his position at the Crédit Foncier. A position so important that, in time, his brother Kazimierz was employed as head of one of the offices[702], later also Louis Passy, Wolowski's son-in-law. Juliusz Falkowski recalled that "Wolowski placed in the [bank] offices many immigrants"[703].

---

700 P. Markiewicz *Louis Wolowski...*, p. 336; No author provided, *Louis Wolowski (1810–1876)....*, p. 197.

701 A. Robert, E. Bourloton, E. Cougny *Dictionnaire des parlementaires français...*, vol. III, Paris 1891, p. 65.

702 *Crédit foncier de France. Conseil d'Administration. Registre des délibérations. Séance du 14.01.1853,* Archives Nationales du Monde du Travail, ref. 2001 26 1996, pp. 60–61.

703 J. Falkowski *Wspomnienia z roku 1848 i 1849,* part III, Warszawa 1908, p. 19; Julia Słupska mentions the names in this context: Bohdanowicz, Rymkiewicz, Kisielnicki, Grochowski, Mikulski, Łempicki, Zalewski and Józef Gałęzowski (J. Słupska Ksawery Branicki..., p. 47). Jerzy Skowronek adds to this list Karol Sienkiewicz's son, Władysław Artur, deputy office manager at the bank (J. Skowronek *Między Hotelem Lambert a karierami rodziny. Papiery rodziny Sienkiewiczów w Bibliotece Polskiej w Paryżu,* "Miscellanea Historico – Archivitica", vol. IV. 1994, p. 79). A passage from one of Lelewel's letters is also characteristic: "In those days, too, a Frenchman paid me a visit [...]. He was amazed by the great invasion of Polish people everywhere, namely in Paris. He confesses that Wolowski has done a very useful thing by founding the Banque Foncière, and in it he sees much of the Polish community in use" (Letter to Walenty Zwierkowski, Brussels, 17 March 1853, [in:] J. Lelewel *Listy emigracyjne Joachima Lelewela,* vol. IV *1849–1861 (no. 948–1261)*, Kraków 1954, p. 147).

Another important figure at the bank was its vice-president, Jean-Marie de Soubeyran. This young man (he was 31 when he took up the post in 1860) was, in turn, a protégé of Fould's, perhaps even the minister's illegitimate son.[704]

The Frémy – Soubeyran tandem was to run the Crédit Foncier from then on. Arguably, this was a personal failure for Louis Wolowski, the bank's originator and founder. However, it was a moderate failure and, for the reasons mentioned above, difficult to avoid. It was accompanied by the bank's complete reorientation. Wolowski intended his creation to primarily finance agriculture. Under the management of first Germiny, then Frémy, however, the bank invested elsewhere. The Crédit Foncier's money went mainly to the big cities (70 per cent to Paris) and fed the portfolios of builders and building owners[705].

The reasons for this were manifold. First and foremost, from the outset Wolowski overestimated the strength of French agriculture and its creditworthiness. The fees charged by the bank for credit were too high for French landowners, generally exceeding the income from the land. On the other hand, the developing towns could afford them. Loan repayment also presupposed many years of regularity, which was often lacking in the countryside for reasons that were quite natural. Added to this was the legal framework of the mortgage: the bank's client had to demonstrate undisputed ownership of the land. In 19th-century France, where land had often passed from father to son for decades or centuries, this was sometimes problematic. Finally, there was a mental factor, completely disregarded by the Polish economist: French peasants, often still illiterate, generally distrusted bankers coming from the city, and contracts they could not understand. Moreover, as I have already pointed out, the very route the interested party had to take to the bank branch was in many cases problematic.

However, mortgage ceased to be a problem. For here Wolowski succeeded; his writings, regularly quoted, contributed to a change in the law. In 1855, a new law abolished the secret mortgages so criticised by Wolowski and introduced full transparency of the records of encumbrances on real estate[706].

---

704 This is what Jean-Pierre Allinne suggests. The historian notes, among other things, Soubeyran's remarkably rapid promotions in the finance ministry, the ministry of state and at the bank during the periods when Fould was minister (J.-P. Allinne *Banquiers et bâtisseurs...*, p. 63).

705 H. Heugas-Darraspen, A. Raimbault Crédit *Foncier de France...*, p. 39. As André Gueslin writes, this trend was to continue until the end of the 19th century. By 1913, the bank had lent a total of 5.28 billion francs, of which only 1.37 billion went to agriculture (A. Gueslin *Les Origines du Crédit Agricole (1840–1914)*, Nancy 1978, p. 105).

706 R.T. Troplong R.T. *Privilèges et hypothèques, commentaire de la loi du 23 mars 1855 sur la transcription en matière hypothécaire*, Paris 1856, pp. 1–2.

As I have mentioned, the Crédit Foncier became one of the main lenders for the redevelopment of Paris, and (to a lesser extent) Marseille. For example, in the 1850s its credit was used by the Pereire brothers' company, Société Immobilière, responsible for the redevelopment of rue Rivoli, the Champs-Élysées and Malesherbes boulevards, as well as the Place de l'Opéra, the Place Vendôme and the square at La Madeleine[707]. However, in the following decade the bank in Paris played a much more important role. By 1 January 1868, the bank had lent 460 million francs to the city, 62 million of which had been repaid in the intervening period. More significantly, the procedure itself was legally highly questionable. Under it, entrepreneurs received vouchers from the city, which they then ceded to banks, the Crédit Foncier enjoying the predominant position. This procedure, in turn, allowed Haussmann to bypass the scrutiny of the Legislative Body and incur debts without the (theoretically necessary) approval of the mostly reluctant parliamentarians[708]. In addition, in 1860 the bank set up a kind of "subsidiary" – the Crédit Agricole. Formally speaking, this was an independent entity. In practice, the Crédit Agricole and the Crédit Foncier, apart from having a similar name (in both cases referring to agriculture), shared a similar statute and an identical composition of their governing bodies. This means that Louis Wolowski also sat on the board of the younger company.

In theory, in line with the company's name ("agricultural credit"), the idea was again to provide capital to agriculture. In fact, this was included in the statutes of the new bank[709]. However, since the beginning, this was a largely fictitious clause, and the reasons for this were like those of the Crédit Foncier. The Crédit Agricole fell, in effect, into the rut of its predecessor, again lending mainly to Paris. Moreover, from Haussmann's and the building constructors' point of view, the new bank was a much more convenient tool, as it could provide short-term mortgages. However, it soon became apparent that Frémy and Soubeyran lacked prudence and caution. The bank was lending too easily and too quickly for investments that, at best, could take many years to pay off. There were loans for ¾ of the value of the property, secured by 3rd or 4th degree mortgages[710]. The bank also invested outside France, including Egypt. As a result of all this combined, by the end of the 1860s, Crédit Agricole had already been under threat. Changing political conditions (liberalisation of the Empire, then its collapse) meant that the authorities could not

707 H. Heugas-Darraspen, A. Raimbault Crédit *Foncier de France...*, p. 63.

708 L. Girard, *Nouvelle histoire de Paris...*, p. 346 ; B. Marchand *Le financement des travaux d'Haussmann: un exemple pour les pays émergents?* 2011, https://halshs.archives-ouvertes.fr/halshs-00583457/document (retrieved 06.04.2023).

709 *Fondation de la Société du Crédit agricole*, [in:] J.B. Josseau *Traité du crédit Foncier...*, p. 96.

710 In France, the degree of a mortgage determines to this day the order in which creditors recover a claim after the sale of the property encumbered by it.

and would not help. Eventually, in 1876 the bank was again taken over by the Crédit Foncier[711].

Another thing is that Wolowski's work was also in serious trouble because the settlements between the bank and Paris, it had become the object of inquiry of the anti-imperial opposition, playing an increasingly important role in France in the 1860s. As a result, it could strike at Haussmann and, through him, at Napoleon III himself. In late 1867, Paris signed a settlement with the bank whereby the repayment of the city's debts was to be stretched over sixty years[712]. This agreement, however, gave rise to a parliamentary discussion in which the opposition launched a fierce attack on the Prefect of Paris. The key piece of this criticism was a pamphlet published in 1868 by Jules Ferry, a rising star of the Republican party, entitled *Les comptes fantastiques d'Haussmann*[713] . The debate took place in the press and in parliament; Wolowski decided to take part in it. Appearing before a committee of the Legislative Body, he defended one of the most significant works of his life. It does not come as a surprise that his argumentation was not entirely honest. For Wolowski insisted that the Crédit Foncier had acted entirely legally, simply buying up the city's liabilities from entrepreneurs. In doing so, however, he overlooked the obvious and well-known fact that Paris should not have entered such obligations without parliamentary approval[714]. In turn, he was most likely right to defend Haussmann against charges of mismanagement and the Crédit Foncier against charges of taking advantage of the city. He argued, perhaps somewhat exaggeratedly, that the bank's profits from the whole operation were minimal[715]. However, even the historian Jean – Pierre Allinne, highly critical of the Crédit Foncier's management at the time, admits that the terms offered to Paris by the bank were relatively favourable for France's capital city[716].

One other element is worth noting: from the point of view of the Crédit Foncier authorities, Wolowski was a valuable ally in 1868 and 1869. As a moderate republican, he was not politically associated with the Second Empire. On the other hand, he still had many acquaintances and colleagues from former years among

---

711 H. Heugas-Darraspen, A. Raimbault Crédit *Foncier de France...*, p. 58.

712 N. Chaudun *Haussmann Georges-Eugène, préfet – baron de la Seine*, Paris 2009, pp. 275–276.

713 J. Ferry *Les comptes fantastiques d'Haussmann*, Paris 1868. The title was a play on words. Read literally, it meant "Haussmann's fantastic accounts" but it sounded exactly like "Haussmann's fairy tales" and referred to "The Tales of Hoffmann" popular at that time.

714 L. Wolowski *Quelques observations présentées à la Commission du Corps législatif chargée de l'examen du traité entre la Ville de Paris et le Crédit Foncier*, Paris 1870, pp. 12–13.

715 L. Wolowski *Quelques observations...*, p. 30.

716 J.-P. Allinne *Banquiers et bâtisseurs...*, p. 82.

the opposition representatives. He was also a well-known economist, and his opinion was probably perceived more as that of an expert than that of a bank representative.

In the end, the parliamentary enquiry did not harm the bank. Although the parliamentarians demanded that the bank reduce its deposits, and that Frémy and Soubeyran withdraw from other financial entities, the latter demand was never fulfilled in practice. The Crédit Foncier even took advantage of the crisis to partially get rid of government supervision. In 1869, the bank introduced a new charter, raising its share capital significantly and increasing the freedom of its operations. Another thing is that this freedom also applied, according to Allinne, to the shareholders: on the receiving end of high dividends, they were not particularly inquisitive about the bank's operations[717].

In this context, Louis Wolowski's own responsibility for the actions of the Crédit Foncier and the Crédit Agricole becomes a nagging question. After all, Wolowski sat on the boards of directors of both banks. Unfortunately, I have not been able to access the minutes of their meetings, deposited in the Archives Natioles du Monde du Travail, but still subject to explicit access restrictions. Wolowski's personal position was undoubtedly too weak to significantly influence the directions of the two banks. On the other hand, he was probably aware of the most important operations of both companies. This is indirectly confirmed, in my view, by his resignation from the boards of both banks in 1873[718]. According to Markiewicz, this was a gesture of protest against the fact that the Crédit Agricole was not fulfilling its tasks towards agriculture[719]. Only that both banks did not meet them since the beginning: in the case of the older of the two, since 1852. It seems much more likely to me that Wolowski, familiar with the bank's operations, in 1873 already saw the Crédit Agricole's troubles on the horizon. And he did not want to take responsibility or be associated with a bankrupt company. Another reason for his resignation could also have been his health, clearly failing around that time.

Certainly, too, Wolowski, politically inclined against the Empire, did not help the opposition to use this bankruptcy against Napoleon III. This also seems fully understandable. Firstly, for legal reasons: he could not act to the detriment of the company on whose authorities he sat. Secondly, for obvious financial reasons.

---

717 J.-P. Allinne *Banquiers et bâtisseurs...*, pp. 88–89.

718 *Crédit Foncier de France. Compte-rendu présenté au nom de l'administration par M. L. Frémy. Assemblée générale ordinaire du 23 avril 1874*, "Journal Officiel de la République Française", no. 117, 29.04.1874, p. 3001; *Compte rendu au nom du Conseil administration du Crédit Agricole, par M. L. Frémy, gouverneur. Assemblée générale du 25 avril 1874*, "Journal Officiel de la République Française", no. 120, 02.05.1874, p. 3066. At the time, Wolowski was made an honorary member of the Crédit Foncier's Board of Directors.

719 P. Markiewicz *Louis Wolowski...*, p. 342.

Thirdly and finally, again because of his Polish activities. His presence on two boards of major banks, his regular contact with the most important politicians and entrepreneurs in France, gave him opportunities that the overwhelming majority of immigrants did not have. Let me recall again the words of Iwona Pugacewicz historian of the Polish School in Paris, "all the doors of the most important Parisian institutions were opened" to Wolowski.[720] The price for this influence was tacit approval of the semi-legal activities of the Crédit Foncier or the Crédit Agricole.

Louis Wolowski's banking activities should also be viewed from a somewhat broader perspective. For through the Crédit Foncier, the Pole took part in a banking revolution taking place in France, and in time throughout Europe. Indeed, Wolowski's ideas and concepts corresponded to the outlook on banking of real giants of the financial market, like the Pereire brothers, Paulin Talabot and Benoit Fould (Achille's brother). The Pereires were, moreover, related to Rodrigues, their cousin and friend, so they knew the history of the Caisse Hypothécaire. In 1852, arguably one of the most significant years in French banking history, they set up the Crédit Mobilier. Their idea was simple yet revolutionary. The bank was to finance largely public investment, above all the construction of the French railway network – something the emperor was particularly keen on. There was a new element, however: for the first time, the price of the bank's shares was low enough for medium and small holders to afford them. As a result, the Pereires appealed to a much broader financial base than the existing banks.[721] This was best expressed by the most important representative of "old banking", James de Rotschild: "The key difference between Rotschild and Pereire is that the former will always work primarily with his money, while the latter works primarily with the money of others."[722] Rotschild was wrong after all: the success of the Crédit Mobilier (with the admittedly imperial support) was so rapid and evident that as soon as in 1855, the most powerful of French bankers tried to set up his own company operating on similar principles. However, he did not get the approval of the government[723]. The Crédit Foncier was part of the change made by the Pereires. It is also no coincidence that the founders and first shareholders of the bank included the Pereires, as well as other former Saint-Simonists: d'Eichthal and Bartholony. Meanwhile, the Crédit Foncier became the largest deposit bank in France in the 1860s and 1870s, with 170 million francs in deposits. By 1875, the company had raised an additional 200 million through bonds. Over time, Wolowski's bank also participated directly or indirectly in the financing of railways, including Algeria. Within a few years,

720 I.H. Pugacewicz *Batignolles 1842–1874...*, p. 126.

721 H. M. *Davies Emile and Isaac Pereire. Bankers, Socialists and Sephardic Jews in the nineteenth-century France*, Manchester 2015, pp. 112–134.

722 Quote as in E. Anceau *Ils ont fait et défait le Second Empire*, Paris 2019, p. 193.

723 N. Stoskopf *Banquiers et financiers parisiens, Les patrons du Second Empire* series, part 7, Paris 2002, p. 316.

other banks were established, with – like Wolowski's work – a long future ahead of them. In 1859, the Crédit Industriel et Commercial (CIC) of Armand Donon and William Gladstone emerged. Louis Bischofsheim created the Banque de Crédit et de Dépots des Pays-Bas in 1863. Edouard Hentsch and Talabot were setting up Société Generale. Another member of the same group – Alphonse Pinard – established Crédit Colonial. The same people then set up Société Générale Algérienne (1866), the Banque Franco-Ègyptienne (1870), Paribas (1872), the Banque de l'Indochine (1875), the Société Francaise de reports et de dépots (1881). Over time, from this group the present-day BNP Paribas bank was to emerge. Finally, on 6 July 1863, Henri Germain founded the Crédit Lyonnais.

Wolowski thus operated among the great French and European bankers. It must be remembered, however, that in terms of wealth he was far from the most prominent. Suffice it to mention that Isaac Pereire, at the time of his death in 1880, left 33 million francs, his brother Emile Pereire, who died in 1875, 16 million (although at his peak in 1859 his fortune was estimated at 200 million)[724]. In 1894, Soubeyran's fortune was estimated by the press at 50–60 million francs[725]. Finally, the most powerful of them, James de Rotschild, bequeathed almost 100 million francs to his heirs[726]. Wolowski's political influence was also considerably less: in 1862, Napoleon III himself visited Rotschild at his estate in Ferrières for a few days, and the meeting was widely perceived as a significant political and financial event[727]. The Pereires had similar if not better (especially in the 1850s) access to the emperor. Fould was a minister and "a true friend of Louis Napoleon"[728]. Wolowski's opportunities for influence were much smaller. Thus, when writing about his banking achievements, the world of connections and informal influences in which he operated, it is important to remember that his role remained secondary.

724 N. Stoskopf *Banquiers et financiers parisiens...*, pp. 281 and 287

725 N. Stoskopf *Banquiers et financiers parisiens...*, p. 339.

726 N. Stoskopf *Banquiers et financiers parisiens...*, p. 318.

727 A. Muhlstein *James de Rothschild. 1792–1868*, Paris 1981, p. 236.

728 J. de Brabant *Achille Fould et son temps (1800–1867). L'homme clef du Second Empire*, Pau, 2001, p. 105.

Chapter VI: The Apogee

1. The demise of Mickiewicz

For Louis Wolowski, the 1850s and 1860s were a time of the highest activity and most important achievements, not only in banking. It was also a time of significant and uneasy family changes. As I have mentioned, Faucher died in 1854, and on 5 March of the following year, Celina Mickiewicz passed away. Maria Gorecka later recalled that, shortly before her death, her mother "still demanded that relatives whom she loved, Mrs [Tekla] Wołowska and Mrs Faucher, with whom she bid farewell, be brought to her, commending them to the care of some of the poor she had taken care of."[729] Unfortunately, this was not the end of the misfortunes. On 11 September 1855, Mickiewicz left Paris for Turkey: the Crimean War had been going on for two and a half years, with the French and English involved for 18 months. The poet's departure was agreed with the Hotel Lambert[730]. He was supposed to have persuaded Michał Czajkowski (Sadyk Pasha) to cooperate, and to have encouraged him to co-found Polish military formations with Władysław Zamoyski. Possibly, Louis Wolowski, associated with the Czartoryski camp, assisted the poet in his travel plans (although there is no clear evidence of this). Instead, the end of this journey was certainly tragic: Mickiewicz died suddenly in Istanbul on 26 November 1855. The cause of death was most likely violent Asian cholera. Mickiewicz had already suffered from cholerine (the precursory symptoms of cholera), which probably severely weakened his body, previously exhausted by the hardships of the journey[731].

---

729 K. Kostenicz *Ostatnie lata Mickiewicza...*, p. 375.

730 After a time of cool relations between 1848 and 1852, Prince Adam Jerzy Czartoryski established a somewhat closer relationship with Napoleon III. Czartoryski was primarily interested in extending the war into Polish territories, which would then bring independence to the Poles. Napoleon III, not entirely opposed to these ideas, nevertheless made implementation thereof dependent on Austria, so they ultimately came to nothing (M. Handelsman *Adam Czartoryski*, vol. III, part II, Warszawa 1950, pp. 391–393; M. Kukiel *Czartoryski a jedność Europy: 1770–1861*, Lublin 2008, pp. 277–279).

731 R. Koropeckyj *Adam Mickiewicz...*, pp. 562–563; Z. Sudolski *Mickiewicz. Opowieść biograficzna*, Warszawa 1995, p. 872. The poet's sudden death was immediately followed by rumours of its alleged unnatural causes. According to Sudolski, they resulted from the aura of mystery surrounding the his last moments. This, in turn, was linked to the fact that Mickiewicz's friends, wishing to transport his body to France, initially concealed the fact that he had died of cholera, rightly expecting the related transport problems.

The news of the poet's passing reached his children on 30 November. In all probability, the Wołowskis learned of it on the same or the following day. Meanwhile, on the Bosporus, a short-lived dispute arose over the poet's burial place. In Istanbul, the idea arose among local Poles that Mickiewicz, pending his return to Poland, should be buried in Turkish soil. One of the proponents of this solution was Władysław Zamoyski. In turn, the proponents of transporting the body to France were Lévy and Henryk Służalski, who stayed with Mickiewicz in Turkey. Wolowski, like the rest of the family, probably did not participate in this discussion, unless Czartoryski included him. For the prince had the final word. He made the decision to have Mickiewicz buried in France. The matter turned out to be complicated and lengthy as none of the naval companies wanted to risk quarantine in port. Wolowski even intervened with Ferdinand Alphonse Hamelin, Minister of the Navy, who promised to help.[732] It is not known if this was the minister's making but on 31 December, the coffin with Mickiewicz's body set off on its journey to France. On 9 January, it arrived in Paris and was transported from the Gare de Lyon, escorted by Wolowski and others, to La Madeleine. The Wolowskis also arranged for Celina's coffin, hitherto resting in the Père Lachaise cemetery, to be moved to Montmorency. Here, on 21 January 1856, the poet was buried beside his wife.

The issue of Mickiewicz's children remained open. At the time of her father's death, the eldest daughter, Maria, was 20, Władysław was 17, Helena was 15, Aleksander 13, Jan 10, and the youngest, Józef, was less than 5 years old. Under French law at the time, none of them were of legal age.[733] Their closest Parisian relatives were Zofia Szymanowska and the Wołowskis. The siblings had been in fact separated by their father before his departure. Maria wrote in a letter: "My brothers Oleś[little Aleksander] and Jaś [Jan] were given away by Papa to a Polish school. Helenka stayed at home with me. Fortunately, we have an aunt living with us, Mrs Zofia Szymanowska, our mother's sister, who came from Warsaw a few months before her [mother's] death and has stayed with us ever since. Władzio[Władysław] goes to school every day and only comes home in the evening. Papa gave our youngest brother Józio [Józef] to our friends, the Falkenhagen-Zaleski family."[734].

732 Letter from Louis Wolowski to an unknown addressee regarding the transport of Mickiewicz's corpse, 25.12.1855, Adam Mickiewicz Museum in Paris, ref. MAM 744

733 According to the Napoleonic Code, a woman came of age at the age of 21, while a man came of age at 25.

734 Quotation as in: J. W. Borejsza *Armand Lévy...*, p. 160. Maria Falkenhagen-Zaleska recalled the day Józio appeared in her family years later, emphasising the bond between Mickiewicz and Tekla Wołowska: "On the second day after your mother's funeral, towards evening, Mr Adam brought us a little boy with blue eyes, wrapped in a warm kerchief. He was accompanied by Mrs Wołowska, held by your father in high esteem." (K. Kostenicz *Ostatnie lata Mickiewicza...*, p. 379).

Wolowski later admitted that the Falkenhagen-Zaleskis became in fact a surrogate family for the youngest Mickiewicz[735].

Under French law, a board of guardians (so called *Conseil de famille*) looked after the children. Its members included Wolowski, Jules Michelet – the eminent historian and Mickiewicz's friend, Falkenhagen-Zaleski, Branicki, Lévy, Seweryn Gałęzowski, Aleksander Chodźko and Prince Napoléon-Jérôme Bonaparte. However, the composition of the council, the strong political and personal differences between its members meant that it was a non-functional body[736]. This made the function of the legal guardian of the children, performed formally by Louis Wolowski, all the more important.

His relationships with the children varied. It is also characteristic that while in the memoirs of Maria and Władysław, Tekla Wołowska, "grandmother" was regularly referred to in very warm words, just like Aleksandryna Faucher, a distance was evident in relation to Louis Wolowski. It is also reflected in his mother's letters quoted by Władysław, in which Aleksandryna was "Olesia", while Louis was invariably "Mr Louis" or "Wolowski".

The following extract from Celina's letter to Maria is quite telling: "Granny has been away for three months. She is angry with Papa's habit of not returning her visits, and at the same time, the great business of Mr Louis at the *Crédit Foncier* gives her *de l'importance* which we respect from afar."[737] The deaths of Celina and Adam did not significantly reduce this distance, at least in relation to the poet's sons.

As Jerzy Borejsza recalls, immediately after Mickiewicz's death a dispute arose over the custody of his eldest, Władysław. On one side of the dispute were Wolowski, Szymanowska and Służalski, and on the other Lévy. The Frenchman defended the will of Mickiewicz who, before his departure, had left Władysław full freedom to decide on his own life. It was known that the young Mickiewicz was closely associated with Lévy. Wolowski, on the other hand, advocated family care. This is how Borejsza commented on this dispute, which incidentally died down rather quickly: "It was simply that Szymanowska and the others were advised, as one might assume, to remove Lévy, a radical, a comrade of the Polish democrats and, most importantly, a man who was on a collision course with the "official Church", from the affairs of the Mickiewicz family."[738] Borejsza was probably quite

735 This is indicated by a letter from Wolowski to Falkenhagen-Zaleski which is in the National Library in Warsaw. (*Korespondencja Piotra i Marii z Korzeniowskich Falkenhagen-Zaleskich,* manuscript ref. IV 8954, c. 31).

736 Michelet was a republican, Lévy a radical republican. Their collaboration with Bonaparte was therefore extremely difficult. The prince's presence on the council, on the other hand, simply proved to be financially profitable. Indeed, the "Wiadomości Polskie" reported in 1857 that the Prince "took upon himself [fees for] the upbringing of the two sons of the late Adam Mickiewicz". (no. 18, 02.05.1857)

737 W. Mickiewicz *Moja matka...*, p. 89.

738 J. W. Borejsza *Armand Lévy...*, p. 169.

right, but I need to add a factor, perhaps the most important one: a very strong sense of community and family/clan affiliation among the Wołowskis and the descendants of former Frankists in general. In the case of Louis Wolowski, this seems to have been clearly more important than religious issues.

In the end, in fact, Louis Wolowski's influence on Władysław was relatively small. Although he was the formal legal guardian of all the children, de facto Lévy was much more important to the boys. This is well reflected in Władyslaw's *Memoirs*, in which Wolowski, unlike the Frenchman, appears rather sporadically. In a work on Polish emigration, Władyslaw also described Wolowski in an overly concise and cool manner: "he wrote and thought in French".[739] Borejsza and Władysław Mickiewicz's biographer, Andrzej Kłossowski, shared the impression[740]. The situation with the poet's two younger sons, Aleksander, and Jan was comparable. They eventually settled together with Lévy and Władysław. In 1862, despite Wolowski's resistance, they were joined by the youngest, Józef[741].

Wolowski's surviving letters to Mickiewicz's children raise doubts about the effectiveness of his educational methods. Around 1860, Louis wrote to the eighteen-year-old Alesander:

> I will always be happy to do anything that is useful or pleasant for you. You must know that when great disobedience forced me to punish you, I suffered greatly; for I only wish I could reward you for your work and conduct. You are no longer a child and should understand how important it is for your future to act righteously. Disobedience to the one who replaces your father (not only according to the law, but also because of the attachment he feels to you) is a sad precedent. I must say the same about your indifference to the sister who has taken your mother's place at your side, and when? When she herself became a mother and God gave you one more being to love in this world. Maria is deeply offended, as is Helena. As for your brother-in-law, a true gem of honour, he is deeply saddened. This must come to an end. As soon as your sister's health allows it, you must do what fraternal attachment should have prompted you long ago. [...] Farewell my dear Alesander, I embrace you with all my heart, as a devoted guardian should do.[742]

This letter which smack of somewhat stiff pedagogy, refers to the wedding of the eldest sibling, Maria. In 1857, she married Tadeusz Gorecki, a painter. However, the marriage was not accepted by her brothers, perhaps under the influence of Lévy, previously rejected by Maria[743]. Wolowski, in turn, supported her conduct. He was

---

739 W. Mickiewicz *Emigracya Polska 1860–1890,* Kraków 1908, p. 107.

740 W. Mickiewicz *Emigracya Polska...*, pp. 172–175; A. Kłossowski *Ambasador książki polskiej w Paryżu. Władysław Mickiewicz,* Wrocław 1971, pp. 18–22.

741 More on the fate of Mickiewicz's children: E.K. Kossak *Rodzina M.,*Warszawa 1991.

742 Adam Mickiewicz Museum in Paris, ref. MAM 925, pp. 91–94.

743 J. W. Borejsza *Armand Lévy...*, p. 161.

also inevitably involved in property disputes between the siblings. These mainly concerned the poet's memorabilia, and Wolowski seems to have tried to mediate between Maria and Władysław. In a letter to her brother, Maria Gorecka wrote in 1859: "Mr Wolowski proposed that the bust and the silver chalices be drawn by us after their value has been estimated. The one to whom the object falls at the division will repay others their value in money."[744] In time, however, these disputes fortunately died down. It seems that of the children of Adam and Celina, the Wołowskis were most attached to Maria, followed by Helena, as evidenced by later correspondence between members of the family[745]. When, in turn, Helena decided to marry a certain Edward Żeligowski in 1862, Wolowski, clearly concerned, asked Józef IgnacyKraszewski for his opinion on the candidate, allegedly a professionally and financially irresponsible man[746]. Ultimately, according to Ewa K. Kossak, the wedding did not take place after information received by the family from Brygida Zan, Tomasz's widow[747]. Helena soon married Ludwik Hryniewiecki – this time with the full consent of her guardian.

A separate problem was providing the Mickiewicz children with the means to survive after the death of their parents. As early as on 18 December 1855, the Committee for Contributions to the National Fund for Mickiewicz's Children was established in Falkenhagen-Zaleskis' flat in Paris. It was made up of Chodźko, August Cieszkowski, Gałęzowski, Seweryn Goszczyński, Eustachy Januszkiewicz, Józef Kaszyc, Stanisław Małachowski, Teodor Morawski, Roger Raczyński, Karol Sienkiewicz, Franciszek Szemioth, Piotr Falkenhagen-Zaleski, Amancyusz Żarczyński and Louis Wolowski. Ksawery Branicki was appointed President of the Committee, Gałęzowski and Raczyński Vice-Presidents, Falkenhagen – Zaleski was the Treasurer, Januszkiewicz – the Secretary. The Committee's task was to erect "a monument of our citizenship, a monument of Polish protection for the six under-age children of the great poet", i.e., to raise a fund for them through

744 J. W. Borejsza *Armand Lévy...*, p. 162.

745 The Goreckis met regularly with the Wołowskis, as attested by Louis's letters to Maria (ref. MAM 919, c. 227) and Zofia Lenartowiczowa, née Szymanowska (ref. MAM 986), preserved in the Adam Mickiewicz Museum in Paris. In turn, a letter from Aleksandryna Faucher to the same Zofia dated 04.02.1868, written after Gorecki's death, attests to the affectionate relations: "My address to you today is painful! Beloved, unlamented Tadeusz ended his suffering perhaps on Friday, 31 January, at 11 o'clock in the evening. It took him almost two days to die. When your letter arrived, we could barely read it, and it is difficult for us to understand its content. You will understand Marynia's terrible state. Let us ask God to give her the strength to endure this blow bravely and to be able to fulfil her maternal duties". (ref. MAM 986).

746 J. I. Kraszewski *Korespondencja Józefa Ignacego Kraszewskiego...*, c. 182.

747 E.K. Kossak *Rodzina M...*, p. 229.

contributions[748]. All the money donated by the Committee passed through Wolowski. The Wołowski family were also among the first and largest donors to the Committee. They contributed a total of 15,000 francs (of which 6,000 was donated by Tekla Wołowska, 5,000 by Aleksandryna, 4,000 by Louis and Kazimierz). By far the largest sum, 25,000 francs, was allocated for the children by Branicki[749].

The Committee held its last meeting on 26 November 1857. According to a report, the Committee noted that during its two years of activity, it managed to raise 103,680 francs, 6 Crédit Foncier shares and 36 metallurgical shares. From the money raised, the Committee purchased French government bonds for just under 55,000 francs, Prussian railway bonds for 46,000 francs, and two Crédit Foncier bonds. The committee donated the collected assets in full to "the legal guardian of Mickiewicz's children, Mr Louis Wolowski"[750]. He continued to pay out the funds in stages to the poet's six children. Maria Gorecka's surviving letters, by the way, indicate that these donations were meticulously accounted for[751].

2. The Academy

The 1850s brought another significant change to Wolowski, resulting in an unquestioned professional and prestigious advancement. For in 1855 he became a member of the Académie des Sciences Morales et Politiques (Academy of Moral and Political Sciences). The youngest of the academies of the Institut de France (Institute of France) was founded in 1832 by Guizot. The minister made no secret of the fact that the new Academy was intended to be a support to the government in combating intellectual and spiritual chaos in France. The academic corporation was thus to "exercise a salutary influence for the advantage of intellectual order, and may lend to power itself, if it knows how to maintain mutual relations."[752]. Significantly, however, Guizot was also absolutely convinced of the need to leave scholars almost complete freedom of research and discussion. Subsequent ministers adhered to this principle, so over time, academics necessarily moved well beyond the role of government experts. According to Corinne Delmas,

---

748 *Protokoły posiedzeń Komisji Funduszu Narodowego dla dzieci A. Mickiewicza, 1855–1857*, Adam Mickiewicz Museum in Paris, ref. MAM 914, pp. 1–7.

749 „Wiadomości Polskie", nr 8/9, 19.01.1856.

750 *Protokoły posiedzeń Komisji Funduszu Narodowego dla dzieci A. Mickiewicza...*, pp. 26–28.

751 In January 1858 Gorecka wrote to Wolowski: "We arrived in Dresden a few days ago after a successful journey, and I am taking advantage of the first free moment to arrange outstanding accounts and send you the notes you requested before our departure." (Biblioteka Polska w Paryżu, Biblioteka Polska w Paryżu, ref. BPP 2339.

752 F. Guizot *Memoirs to illustrate the history of my time*, vol. III, London 1860, p. 140.

> There was a tension in the work of the Academy arising from the body's various functions and positions. Indeed, moral sciences are accompanied by a diversity of human opinions. They function within the framework of the Academy, which can be perceived as a centre of an ideology akin to power, which it endows with the authority of science. In turn, such a role implies the presence of the academy in public life and a certain predominance of philosophy over other moral and political sciences. Hence the tension between theorists, philosophers and "exceptional figures" [politicians and entrepreneurs with intellectual inclinations gracing the academy – RD]. Hence the attempt to reconcile concerns for order and morality with sometimes less than obvious social diagnoses. Hence the ambivalent position of the liberal Academy sometimes demanding state intervention, while at the same time a conservative institution but shedding new light on social reality.[753]

The Academy of Moral and Political Sciences was (and still is) a part of the Institute of France, alongside the French Academy, the Academy of Inscription and Belles Lettres, the Academy of Sciences, and the Academy of Fine Arts[754]. It was divided into five sections: philosophy; morals; legislation, public law and jurisprudence; political economy and statistics; general and philosophical history. There were invariably thirty academics, which meant that this exceptionally honourable and prestigious title could only be conferred after the death of one of them[755]. In 1854, Blanqui, a friend of Wolowski's who had taught like him at the Conservatoire des Arts et Métiers, died, thus leaving the seat no 6 of the Academy's political economy section vacant. The election of a new member of the Academy took place on 19 May 1855. Wolowski had no counter-candidate. In the very first round, he received the votes of 22 academics out of a total of 32 cast. On 22 May 1855, Napoleon III approved this election[756].

The title of an academic was then and still is one of the most prestigious, if not the most prestigious title in the French academic and literary world. In fact, according to Roulliet, Wolowski was well aware of this: "He was among those who see a member of the Institute as most desirable, and who believe that such an award can either crown a lifetime of work or, anticipating the moment somewhat, provide an incentive for further hard work for a man who has already given evidence of it."[757]However, Roulliet failed to mention that Wolowski was probably

753 C. Delmas *Instituer des savoirs d'Etat. L'Académie des Sciences Morales et Politiques au XIX siècle*, Paris 2006, p. 75.

754 Therefore, from 1855 onwards, Wolowski appeared on all official documents, title pages of books, etc., as a "member of the Institute".

755 *Ordonnance du roi qui établit au sein de l'Institut royal de France l'ancienne classe des sciences morales et politiques,* [in:] *Collection complète des lois, décrets, ordonnances, réglemens, et avis du Conseil-d'État*, vol. 32, Paris 1832, p. 378.

756 *Élection à l'Académie des Sciences Morales et Politiques*, dossier Wolowski, Archives Nationales, ref. F/17/3589; A. Roulliet *Wolowski...*, p. 224.

757 A. Roulliet *Wolowski....*, p. 224.

well aware of the fact that the election was largely political, that social factors mattered, and that, finally, a regular election campaign had been conducted beforehand. We do not know what it looked like exactly in the case of Wolowski, but we can assume that either he or his supporters had visited almost all the academics beforehand. Wolowski certainly had many allies in the Academy in 1855. A look at its members suffices: at the time, they included the liberal Orléanists Cousin, Rémusat, moderate republicans close to Wolowski such as Jules Barthélemy-Saint-Hilaire, liberal economists like Louis Reybaud, Charles Dunoyer, Charles Dupin or Michel Chevalier, Passy, Troplong, Tocqueville and Beaumont, all of whom were still well known to him since the 1830s, as well as Michelet, a member of the Mickiewicz welfare board. In general, the Academy was clearly dominated by Orléanists, liberals and, economically, supporters of the free market. Wolowski connected with this profile perfectly.

Wolowski was one of the more active members of the Academy. He was a regular visitor to its meetings, as clearly show the reports contained in the periodical "Séances et travaux de l'Académie des Sciences Morales et Politiques" published by the Academy. He enjoyed the esteem of his colleagues, which is best demonstrated by the fact that, barely ten years after his election to the Academy, he became its President and served in this capacity for a year, coordinating the work of the academics.

3. Changes within the family

It seems that, despite the banking troubles, the late 1860s were a happy time for Wolowski. Above all, the family was growing. Wolowski consistently followed a strategy of expanding clan connections. As late as in 1859, Levasseur, his pupil, friend, and successor at the Conservatoire des Arts et Métiers, married Charlotte Nathalie Wołowska[758]. Levasseur's 1986 biography reads that she was the daughter of Jan Wołowski, a landowner, and Stéphanie Bosto, and "cousin of Louis Wolowski."[759] Unfortunately, if a few texts devoted to Levasseur repeat the information that Charlotte was a relative of Wolowski, none of them give a source for this claim. However, in the archives of the Institute of France (in the papers of Aleksandryna Faucher) I have found an obituary of Jan Wołowski. It clearly shows that Jan, who died in Barcelona in 1869, was indeed Nathalie's father and most likely Louis's cousin. Unfortunately, in the absence of any other information concerning Jan, it is impossible to determine the exact degree of this kinship. However, the correspondence preserved in the same ensemble, including that of Jan with

758 Archives de Paris, ref. V3E/M 1022.

759 *Levasseur Pierre Émile*, [in:] I. Havelange, F. Huguet, B. Lebedeff-Choppin *Les inspecteurs généraux de l'Instruction publique. Dictionnaire biographique 1802–1914*, Paris 1986, p. 468.

Aleksandryna, makes it possible to conclude that the family ties between them were indeed strong[760].

This probable affinity was, incidentally, the cause of the only attack on Wolowski in France on family grounds. In 1868, the then Minister of Education Duruy created a chair of political economy within the elitist École Normale Supérieure. It was then given to Levasseur. His rival was another economist, Jean-Gustave Courcelle-Seneuil. After awarding the chair to Levasseur, Courcelle-Seneuil complained in a letter published by the "Journal des Economistes" (the most important journal of French economists at the time) that Levasseur, whom he otherwise regarded as an able researcher and lecturer, had not told him explicitly that "Mr. Wolowski, his uncle, applied for this position for him". Courcelle-Seneuil thus accused Wolowski of nepotism[761]. On 05 February 1868, Wolowski responded at a meeting of the Society for Political Economy in a rather characteristic manner[762]. He denied any efforts to obtain a chair for Levasseur. He also stated that he was not Charlotte Nathalie's uncle. Arguably, he was mistaken in both cases. He was almost certainly a relative of Levasseur's wife. He also most likely strongly supported him

760 Bibliothèque de l'Institut de France, *Correspondances et papiers divers provenant de la succession d'Émile Levasseur*, sygn. MS 6029, dossier 3, Wolowski.

761 "Journal des Economistes....", series III, vol. V, January – March 1867, pp. 162–164.

762 The Society of Political Economy (Société d'Economie Politique) was founded in 1842 as the "Society of Economists". It was initially formed by Eugène Daire, Gilbert Urbain Guillaumin, Joseph Garnier, Adolphe Blaise and Pierre Hos. Almost in parallel, Rossi tried to set up his own society, which included Wolowski, Louis Leclerc, Pierre Clément, Hippolyte Dussard, Reybaud, Faucher, Horace Say, Théodore Fix, Dunoyer and Chevalier. However, it ceased to function after a few meetings, while its members joined the former one (*Société d'Economie Politique. Réunion du 5 février 1868,* "Journal des Economistes...", series V, vol. XX, October – December 1882, pp. 263–267). The Society had no governing body until 1845 when it was headed by Dunoyer. In the Society, offices were held for life; in the event of the death of any member his place was taken by the next in the hierarchy, entailing the promotion of others and the election of new ones to lower positions. Therefore, during Wolowski's lifetime, the Society had only two presidents: Dunoyer until 1862 and Passy in 1862–1882, with Garnier as secretary. In 1858, Wolowski became one of the Society's vice-presidents. The Society's members were economists, journalists, entrepreneurs, politicians, lawyers and, less frequently, landowners. The Society did not have its own journal, but it was closely personally linked to the *Journal des Economistes...*, and to a lesser extent to the *Annuaire de l'économie politique*, which published extensive reports of its meetings (Y. Breton *The Société d'Economie Politique of Paris (1842–1914),* [in:] M.M Augello, M.E.L. Guidi (dir.) *The Spread of Political Economy and the Professionalisation of Economists. Economic societies in Europe, America, and Japan in the nineteenth century,* London, New York 2001, pp. 53–62).

as a candidate. For in the resources of the Institute of France, his letters to a friend have been preserved which indicate this indirectly[763]. Courcelle-Seneuil eventually withdrew his charges[764].

In 1866, Wolowski's only and beloved daughter, Fanny, got married.[765]. Her chosen one was Louis Passy, son of the well-known geologist and botanist Antoine, a deputy under Louis-Philippe and undersecretary of state during the Second Republic, and nephew of Hippolyte, well known to Wolowski[766]. It was the latter, moreover, who introduced him to Wolowski. Passy turned out to be an excellent match: at the time of his marriage, he was a renowned historian and Doctor of Law, and later became a deputy (alongside his father-in-law) and undersecretary of state of the Third Republic[767]. The couple lived to have children quite late in

---

763 *Société d'Economie Politique. Réunion du 5 février 1868*, "Journal des Economistes...", series III, vol. V, pp. 315–316.

764 Bibliothèque de l'Institut de France, *Correspondances et papiers divers provenant de la succession d'Émile Levasseur*, ref. MS 6032. The correspondence reveals that Wolowski played an important role in Levasseur's election to the Academy of Moral and Political Sciences in the same year, 1868.

765 *Société d'Economie Politique. Réunion du 5 février 1868*, "Journal des Economistes...", series III, vol. V, Archives de Paris, ref. V4E 1025 no. 445.

766 His distant cousin was Frédéric Passy, the first historic winner of the Nobel Peace Prize.

767 The Goncourts described him somewhat mischievously under the character of Henri Mauperin in the novel *Renée Mauperin*:

> [...] when young, he was made much of, and it was rumoured that Henri Mauperin was a great favourite. He had a practical mind. He set up for being a believer in all that was useful., in mathematical truths, positive religions and the exact sciences. He had a certain compassion for art and maintained that furniture had never been made as well as at present. Political economy, that science which leads on to all things, had appealed to him when he went out into the world as a vocation and a career, consequently he had decided to be an economist. He had brought to this dry study a narrow-minded intelligence, but he had been patient and persevering, and now, once a fortnight, he published in important reviews a long article well-padded with figures which the women skipped and the men said they had read. (...) political economy had, of course, given to Henri Mauperin a colouring of Liberalism It was not that he belonged to a very decided Opposition: his opinions were merely a little ahead of Government principles. (...) He limited his war against the powers that were to the shooting of an arrow or to a veiled allusion, the key and meaning of which he would by means of his friends convey to the various salons. As a matter of fact, he was carrying on a flirtation, rather

life. In 1872, François Marie Antoine Casimir Passy was born. Unfortunately, the child died soon, in June 1875[768]. As Levasseur wrote, Wolowski was exceptionally happy with his grandson and felt strongly connected to him. The child's death was therefore a devastating blow from which he never recovered[769]. He did not live to see the birth of Fanny's other child in 1878. Marie Françoise Louise Adelaïde Passy happily survived childhood and died in 1966. In 1901 she married René Joseph de Varennes, Count de Bueil[770].The couple subsequently had three sons, whose descendants are still alive today. In this way, the process of social advancement and assimilation of the Wołowski family in France was completed.

Notably, the matrimonial strategy of Wolowski or, more broadly, the Wołowskis, was not an unusual phenomenon either among the French elite of the time or even among French economists. A typical example was the most influential among them (at least during the years of the Second Empire), Chevalier, who gave away three of his four daughters to Albert Le Play (son of the well-known thinker and politician Frederic Le Play), the economist Paul Leroy-Beaulieu and the Minister of Foreign Affairs of the Third Republic, Paul Flourens (son of the famous biologist), incidentally linking up with the Pereire clan[771].

---

than hostilities, with the Government in power. (E. and J. de Goncourt *Renée Mauperin*, Paris, 1864, pp. 72–73).

It is impossible not to notice that this description also partly fitted Wolowski.

768 Death certificate: Archives de Paris, ref. V4E 3526, no. 954.

769 E. Levasseur *La Vie et les travaux de Wolowski...*, p. 29.

770 Marriage certificate: Archives de Paris, ref. V4E 8877, no. 243.

771 L. Le Van-Lemesle *Le Juste ou le Riche...*, p. 251. Le Van-Lemesle emphasises, however, that both Chevalier and Wolowski owed their own careers primarily to themselves.

Chapter VII: The Twilight of Life

1. Franco-Prussian War and the Paris Commune of 1871.

However, the year 1870 brought events that, while changing the face of France as a whole, significantly affected the lives of Louis Wolowski and his entire family. On 19 July 1870, France declared war on Prussia. Tension between the superpowers had been growing since at least 1866 and the Prussian victory at Sadowa, widely perceived in Paris as a defeat not only for Austria, but also for French foreign policy. In 1867, Napoleon III demanded Luxembourg as a form of "compensation" to France for the Prussian acquisitions of the previous year. Thanks to Bismarck's skilful policy, Napoleon III did not obtain it, and, to add insult to injury, France was once again humiliated. The immediate cause of the war was the question of the throne of Madrid. The throne had been vacant since the abdication of Isabella II in 1868. In the first days of July 1870, the Spanish government officially offered the crown to Leopold Hohenzollern-Sigmaringen, outraging the French in the process. After a French diplomatic offensive, Wilhelm I of Prussia, head of the Hohenzollern dynasty, withdrew the candidacy, but this was not enough for the livid French. On 13 July, Ambassador Benedetti asked the king, staying in Ems, to confirm the Hohenzollerns' complete renunciation of their claim to the Spanish crown. Wilhelm politely declined and ended the conversation. However, Bismarck seized the opportunity and, in a note sent to the press, portrayed the meeting between the sovereign and the ambassador in a way that was insulting to France. The Chancellor wanted to provoke the French into a war, necessary in his view for the unification of Germany, and he succeeded[772].

It soon became apparent that, pitted against Prussia and its German allies (Bavaria, Baden, Württemberg, and Hesse), France was completely unprepared for war. As a result, divided into two armies, the French suffered defeat after defeat from the start. Marshal Patrice Mac Mahon's army was defeated on 04 August at Wissembourg, and on 06 August – at Froeschwiller-Woerth. On the same day, Marshal Achille Bazaine had to acknowledge the superiority of the Germans at Forbach-Spicheren, then on 14 August at Borny-Colombey. On 19 August, his army was completely blockaded at Metz. Meanwhile, Mac Mahon suffered one of the greatest defeats in French history: 100,000 French troops with Napoleon III and the Marshal at their head were first caught up, then encircled at Sedan. Powerless against German artillery, they capitulated on 02 September 1870. The disaster of the army was also the disaster of the Empire. With Napoleon III in captivity, no

---

772 L. Trzeciakowski, *Otto von Bismarck*, Wrocław 2009, p. 176.

one in Paris was going to defend the old government. Power was almost literally in the street, and the only grouping capable of raising it at this point were the Republicans. So, on 04 September, the Third Republic was proclaimed, again at the Hôtel de Ville. A new republican Government of National Defence was also formed, headed by Gen. Jules Trochu[773].

There is no indication that Wolowski participated in any way in these events. The war of 1870 clearly took him by surprise. It is not clear what he thought of it, or whether he expected – like most – a quick victory for the French. In any case, the start of the manoeuvres found him in England. However, aware of the impending siege of Paris, Wolowski returned to the capital city. Perhaps it should be attributed to his French patriotism, and his mother's deteriorating health was undoubtedly an important argument. Obviously, Wolowski – 60 years old at the time – could not actively take part in the fighting.

Wolowski returned to a city that just experienced another very serious twist in its turbulent history. Just two weeks after the proclamation of the republic, German troops stood outside the city and the siege began. The French capital had been preparing for it. Theoretically, the city had an armed force of more than half a million men, the vast majority of whom, however, were the national guards, or armed citizens. Only 130,000 defenders were in the army and had any military experience[774]. The city's strength, on the other hand, was its surrounding forts, well equipped with artillery.

For this reason, among others, the Prussians did not intend to conquer Paris, and were initially content with a complete blockade of the metropolis of almost two million people. It meant that the city was completely cut off from the rest of France in terms of communications and provisions. With it, the new republican government was cut off. Although a "government delegation" was set up in Tours on 9 September, and a month later it was headed by the Republic's most articulate and energetic politician, Interior Minister Léon Gambetta, the possibility of communication between him and the ministers remaining on the Seine was very limited[775]. This in turn made the coordination of military operations, for example, considerably more difficult. Moreover, the siege of Paris involved the cutting of almost all the vital railway lines radially coming out from the capital. At the same

---

773 More on the Franco-Prussian War: G. Wawro, *The Franco – Prussian War. The German Conquest of France 1870–1871,* Cambridge 2003; F. Roth *La guerre de 1870,* Paris 2011; N. Bourguignat, G. Vogt *La guerre franco-allemande de 1870. Une histoire globale,* Paris 2020. Pierre Cornut-Gentille writes about 4 September 1870 itself and the beginnings of the Third Republic in his book *Le 4 septembre 1870. L'invention de la République,* Paris 2020.

774 S. Rials, *Nouvellehistoire de Paris. De Trochu à Thiers 1870–1873,* Paris 1985, pp. 97–101.

775 J.P.T. Bury, *Gambetta Défenseur du territoire (1870–1871),* Paris 1937, p. 86.

time, it set the primary objective of France's further war effort – henceforth, the overriding task of all armies successively created by the Republic was to liberate the city.

The Parisians also tried to relieve themselves from the siege. The first clashes took place in the last decade of September. They did not bring about any significant change in the situation other than the loss of a few thousand men. The French were plagued with undoubtedly much lower fighting efficiency than those the German troops. Equally important was the attitude of the command, completely disbelieving in the possibility of victory. An additional disaster stroke when Bazaine's army surrendered at Metz on 28 October 1870. The blow was twofold: 170,000 of the then best French soldiers were taken prisoner, while an additional 200,000 Germans were now able to lay siege to the capital. "The faces are menacing. Some women are crying, others are spurring on their husbands, who need no spurring. They form groups in front of the doors, from which voices rise: 'Our men must move! No truce! We would rather blow Paris up than surrender!'. In all streets, the shops are closed. Concerned figures show in the windows; on the pavements people are loudly lamenting and despairing over the misfortunes of France"[776] – this is how the then writer Juliette Adam described the reaction of Parisians to the news of the fall of Metz.

Indeed, Paris was furious. And it is also true that the Parisians (if not all, a very significant part of them) did not intend to capitulate then or later. This, in turn, put those in power in an extremely difficult position, as they had to continue the war despite themselves. Under the influence of the street, Trochu, Jules Favre (Foreign Minister) did not believe in success, but they could not fly the white flag. Paris fell into a kind of war fever, with characteristic mood swings. Hope was mixed with disappointment. As was the case after 11 November, when troops of the so-called Army of the Loire (formed by Gambetta in the provinces) entered Orléans, previously occupied by the Germans. The news reached Paris and aroused enthusiasm. On 4 December, however, Orléans fell again, and the Army of the Loire ceased to exist[777]. Its defeat was coupled with a major defeat for the capital itself. On 29 November, the Army of Paris was to meet the Army of the Loire and strike south. The operation ended in another defeat; on 03 December the Parisians had to retreat into the city, having lost around 12,000 men[778]. Juliette Adam wrote at the time: "We are counting our dead, their list is endless."[779] An important factor contributing to this emotional swing of the residents of the City of Lights was the cut-off from the world. The streets of Paris, instead of real news, fed on fantastic

---

776 J. Adam, *Mes illusions et nos souffrances pendant le Siège de Paris,* Paris 1906, p. 161.

777 F. Roth *La guerre de 1870...*, pp. 276–295.

778 P. Milza„ *L'année terrible" La guerre franco-prussienne septembre 1870 – mars 1871,* Paris 2009, pp. 251–264.

779 J. Adam, *Mes illusions...*, p. 256

gossip and (often) illusions. Thus, as late as in early January 1871, Victor Hugo mentioned in his diary a supposed series of French victories in the provinces that would bring the final triumph. None of this information was true[780].

To make matters worse, the besieged city was slowly beginning to starve. Prices of food, especially meat and vegetables, were reaching sky-high levels[781]. In addition, the winter proved particularly unkind and difficult for the French. In December 1870 and January of the following year, temperatures reached -10℃, -15℃ [14°F, 5°F]. The town was slowly running out of wood. The administration helped the needy by issuing vouchers for meat, bread, and firewood. However, the city's supplies, hastily prepared in August and September, began to run out after three months. All these factors contributed to a marked increase in mortality in Paris, caused not so much by the fighting itself as by hunger and disease. In December and January, each week 2,500 to 4,000 people were buried (usually in mass graves)[782].

Paris was getting sick. This was not just a matter of ailments and mortality among the residents. The city was also gripped by a kind of political fever. There were discussions and arguments like rarely before. As it had been during the Great Revolution and the Revolution of 1848, the republican capital was once again home to dozens of political clubs, more or less radical. They slandered the rulers, discussed issues of national defence, put forward inventions to save France, denounced spies or "bad citizens", and sometimes proposed confiscating the wealth of the rich and distributing it to the poor. As Georges Bourgin, a historian, wrote, the clubs combined an irritated patriotism with a popular militarism and a simple-minded belief in the strangest rumours and claims[783]. In turn, their gradual radicalisation reflected the growing discontent across the city.

Old press titles ("Journal des Débats", "Le Temps", "Le Figaro", "L'Avenir National", "Le Rappel", "Le Réveil") were coming out, accompanied by new, usually ephemeral and revolutionary.

Under these conditions, the importance of the revolutionary left was inevitably growing in Paris. As early as on 31 October 1870, the Blanquists[784] and the

---

780 V. Hugo, *Choses vues...*, p. 1097.

781 É. Delalain, *Le Siége de Paris (Du 18 septembre 1870 au 28 janvier 1871). Journal historique et anecdotique*, Lille, Paris 1874, pp. 170–171.

782 S. Rials, *Nouvelle histoire de Paris...*, p. 201.

783 G. Bourgin, *La guerre de 1870–1871 et la Commune*, Paris 1971, p. 124,

784 It was about the followers of Louis Auguste Blanqui. At the time, he was in prison outside Paris. He advocated a very general organisation of the economy based on workers' associations, universal, free, and secular education. The most essential element of Blanquism, however, was its revolutionism. Blanqui was therefore an advocate of revolution, the germ of which was to be constituted, among others, by his disciples, a small, well-organised group of rebels. This revolution had to be ruthless and bloody to finally defeat the people's main enemy – the bourgeoisie.

neo-Jacobins[785] organised the first attempted coup. They were then stopped thanks to the attitude of some National Guard battalions loyal to the government. In response, on 03 November the government organised a plebiscite in Paris in which the population was asked to answer if they maintained full power for the Government of National Defence. More than 620,000 Parisians voted, of whom 550,000 answered "yes". Notably, this was the only form of legitimisation of the republican government at the time, while limited to Paris itself. Two days later, the citizens elected the mayors of the various districts – all Republicans, in two cases "red"[786]. However, from then on fatigue and discontent only grew along the Seine. And it exploded in March 1871.

Louis Wolowski returned to the city, where the temperature was constantly rising. Unfortunately, we do not know how much he got involved in the political events – probably not very much. Instead, he certainly took part in the meetings of the Academy of Moral and Political Sciences, still taking place. Levasseur, who often saw him at the time, wrote: "We begged him to rest, to leave, to take no more part in the work of the Institute, but we were asking too much! Work was his life, he didn't want to abandon it, he repeated that if he was going to die, he wanted to die standing straight. By force of will, and only by force of will, he overcame,

---

Blanqui therefore distrusted democracy: while he did not reject it altogether, he propounded the theory of the dictatorship of Paris for some time after the victorious revolution – to "prepare" the people for power. He was extremely critical of the bourgeois democrats, who, in his view, were in fact merely dressing up the oppression of the people in new clothes. The criticism of the bourgeoisie and capitalism was combined, in his case, with a very sharp anti-clericalism. For he saw the Church as a support of the old system, of darkness and enslavement of the poorer strata. More on the subject: M. Dommanget, *Blanqui*, Paris 1970; M. Agulhon et al., *Blanqui et les blanquistes*, Paris 1986; R. Dobek *Paryż, 1871...*, pp. 226–245.

785 The neo-Jacobins (e.g., Charles Delescluze, Félix Pyat) referred above all to the Jacobin tradition. They emphasised the principle of the sovereignty of the people, taken directly from Jean-Jacques Rousseau, and rejected the rule of the National Assembly in its name. Sovereignty could only be realised within a fully democratic republic. Like Blanqui, they emphasised compulsory education. Like him, they saw it as a means of liberating the people from the moral and intellectual tyranny of the Church. They were also advocates of a popular revolution, of which Paris was to be the vanguard. Only that, unlike the Blanquists, the neo-Jacobins did not mention any revolutionary dictatorship. One element, on the other hand, differed significantly from Robespierre, Saint-Just: their disciples of 1850–1871 accepted a certain decentralisation of the republic, a growing role for self-government. More on the subject: R. Dobek *Paryż, 1871...*, pp. 246–275; W. Serman, *La Commune de Paris (1871)*, Paris 1986, pp. 85–90.

786 "Journal des Débats Politiques et Littéraires", 08.11.1870.

seemingly, the sickness that consumed him from within."[787] Levasseur was doubly right: indeed, Wolowski did not slow down academically during this period. On 05 and 12 November 1870, he presented to the Academy excerpts from his work on the history of economic relations between France and England[788]. He continued to teach at the Conservatoire des Arts et Métiers[789]. And indeed, he was probably being consumed by the disease.

Two years earlier, Maria Walewska met him during a summer cure trip to a spa resort. She left what is probably the only literary portrait of him, which otherwise corresponds well with the surviving photographs. "He was in his fifties, his face unremarkable both for its ugliness and its original appearance. His eyes were bulging, too large, and had a long, misty gaze, full of kindness. The nose had a curve, slightly reminiscent of the Semitic race, but it was full of expression, completing what the eyes did not complete and giving the stamp of reflection, of concentration. The narrow mouth spoke of will, of precision and of a certain compression of self and others in the tight embrace of dutifulness. I remember people laughing at his protruding ears; [...] in an English frockcoat with a tall cylinder, clean-shaven, with small sideburns and a rose in a loop buttonhole, he looked like a jet-setting international gentleman with a refined superficial elegance."[790] Possibly, Wolowski was already taking treatment for his diabetes; this is what Kraszewski later wrote in "Dziennik Poznański".[791] If so, the siege, with its associated restrictions and sacrifices, more than likely had a fatal effect on his health. In late 1870, this "international gentleman of refined elegance" looked very different. André Lavertujon met him ailing in the street. "He frightened me, so gaunt and emaciated was he then. His eyes were shining from the fever; he almost didn't sleep anymore."[792] At the time, Wolowski still managed to beat the disease, although not for long.

Wolowski thus suffered along with all of Paris. He was also subject to similar mood swings. This is clearly shown in a text published in the *Journal des Economistes;* in December 1870, he wrote that France was "not only creating new armies when it was claimed that her great army had been destroyed; not only rebuilding her artillery when her artillery seemed to have been crushed; not only putting up a vigorous resistance which might turn into a fantastic offensive; France is doing even more: she is learning from her defeats for the future, she is purifying

787 E. Levasseur *La Vie et les travaux de Wolowski...*, pp. 385–386.

788 E. Levasseur *La Vie et les travaux de Wolowski...*, p. 386.

789 This is evidenced by the lecture announcements posted in the "Journal des Débats Politiques et Littéraires" of 07.11.1870 and 05.01.1871.

790 M. z Przezdzieckich Walewska *Polacy w Paryżu...*, p. 54.

791 J.I. Kraszewski *Ludwik Wołowski....*

792 A. Lavertujon *M. Wolowski....*

herself in her catastrophe, while her moral strength is growing to make amends in the future for the evils resulting from the collapse of her material strength."[793]

While France attempted to rebuild the artillery and created new armies, these did not stand much of a chance against the experienced and superbly commanded Prussian or Bavarian troops and were quickly defeated. Thus, this sobering "fantastic offensive" by the French never materialised. On 19 January 1871, the Parisians made a last, desperate attempt to break out of the encirclement. It no longer had a military justification: France was devoid of any prospect of victory. The reason for this action was purely political; it was a matter of convincing the inhabitants of the capital to capitulate. After one day of fighting, slight initial successes, the Battle of Buzenval effectively ended in another French defeat. 4,000 Frenchmen paid for it with their lives; the Germans lost 600 men[794]. On 26 January 1871, Foreign Minister Jules Favre signed an armistice at Versailles, which came into force two days later. In fact, it marked the capitulation of France. It was initially to last for three weeks, during which the French were to elect a parliament capable of subsequently signing peace. At the time, the Germans occupied 25 French departments, or just under a third of the country's territory.

How did Paris react? The eminent historian of the period, Jacques Rougerie, wrote of widespread agitation, rage, an impression of deceit, a desire for revenge.[795] The pages of the republican newspapers were full of proclamations, protests signed by battalions of national guards, citizens of various neighbourhoods, and so on. This was indeed the attitude of at least some Parisians. In many cases, however, it was accompanied by an entirely natural sense of relief. Supply difficulties were diminishing, food prices were falling, and life was slowly returning to normal. Robert Tombs, an equally excellent British historian, writes in this context of relief mixed with guilt for many of the population. Revolt, grief dominated the poorest strata. Wealthier or middle-income residents probably reconciled more easily with the inexorable reality. It is probably safe to assume, without much risk of error, that Louis Wolowski was among them.

Meanwhile, under the terms of the armistice, on 08 February 1871 France elected a new National Assembly. The election campaign mainly revolved around the question if the war should be continued. The results were quite telling as of the more than 600 deputies, about two thirds were various monarchists. In addition, about 150 declared republicans and 30 Bonapartists entered parliament.[796] Those

---

793 L. Wolowski *Comment un peuple se relève, Ouverture du cours d'histoire des doctrines et des faits économiques au Collège de France par M. Levasseur,* "Journal des Economistes...", series III, vol. XX, October – December 1870, p. 394.

794 F. Roth *La guerre de 1870...*, pp. 357–358.

795 J. Rougerie, *Paris libre 1871...*, p. 82.

796 F. Furet *La Révolution II...*, p. 412.

in favour of peace with Germany prevailed. On 8 February 1871, France came out clearly against the Second Empire and in favour of peace.

On the electoral map, however, Paris stood very clearly apart from the rest of the country. The capital sent 37 republicans to parliament (out of 43 elected deputies), many of them in favour of the continuation of the war effort. Characteristically, the largest number of votes went to Louis Blanc, Wolowski's opponent in 1848. Adolphe Thiers, arguably the closest to Wolowski among the candidates selected at the time, was only twentieth. What is more, there were several radicals among the elected individuals, such as Charles Delescluze, Benoit Malon, and Henri Rochefort[797].

The situation in the city was deteriorating. The newly elected Assembly met in Bordeaux on 12 February 1871. This was because Paris had not yet recovered from the siege, and a meeting in the capital was not possible for organisational reasons. On 17 February, Thiers, well known to Wolowski from 1848 to 1851, former Prime Minister of Louis-Philippe, became "head of the executive of the French Republic".[798] On 01 March 1871, the Assembly accepted the peace deal imposed by the Germans. France was to be truncated by losing Alsace and part of Lorraine and pay a gigantic war contribution of 5 billion francs in gold. Until it was repaid, some of the departments were to be occupied (the Germans would abandon them as further tranches were handed over).[799] On 01 March, under the terms of the truce agreed with Thiers, the Prussians entered the French capital, only to leave it two days later. Paris, thus humiliated, soon received another outrageous piece of news: on 10 March, the Assembly decided not to return to Paris for the time being, opting instead for nearby Versailles. From the point of view of most deputies, this decision was understandable: in Paris, they would have had to sit under constant pressure from an armed, largely revolutionary National Guard. Therefore, they had every right to fear a repeat of 1848. For the Parisians, however, it was another blow, and an incomprehensible one after months of siege. In addition, on the same day, the Assembly abolished the city's moratoria on trade debts and rent arrears. Both moves were blows, especially to the poorer and middle-income residents of the city, which had not yet managed to return to its usual industrial and commercial modes. Tension along the Seine thus continued to rise.

Unfortunately, we do not know how Louis Wolowski reacted to the authorities' subsequent moves, or how he perceived the mood in the city. What we do

---

797 "Journal des Débats Politiques et Littéraires", 15.02.1871.

798 G. Valance, *Thiers, bourgeois et révolutionnaire,* Paris 2007, pp. 316–317. The mostly monarchist deputies deliberately used the strange term "head of the executive" instead of "president". This was because the latter was associated with Louis Napoleon Bonaparte. Moreover, such a term emphasised the temporary nature of the republic, which was to be replaced in time by a monarchy.

799 "Journal des Débats Politiques et Littérraires", 04.03.1871.

know is that he was certainly there in mid-March 1871, as evidenced by further announcements about his courses, this time in "Le Constitutionnel" of 12 March 1871 and "Le Temps" of 14 March.

The revolution finally broke out four days later, on 18 March, when the government attempted to strip the National Guard of its artillery. This attempt failed, and the popular section of Paris once again revolted: the time of the Paris Commune had arrived. On Thiers' orders, on that day the army withdrew from the city towards Versailles. In the evening or night, almost all ministers and senior officials left Paris. The city was in the hands of the revolutionaries for just over two months.

I do not intend to describe the history of the Paris Commune in detail, especially as it remains unknown whether Louis Wolowski stayed in the city at all during this period, or for how long.[800] Suffice it to say that power was taken over by Blanquists, neo-Jacobins, Proudhon supporters and socialists of various sorts – people whom Wolowski equalled with dangerous utopians and bandits. He certainly referred to them with hostility. This is clear from J.S. Mill's letter to Gustave D'Eichthal of 21 May 1871. Mill recalled that he had recently seen Wolowski, who "is extremely vicious towards all those involved in the Paris movement."[801] Wolowski was therefore in England in May 1871, perhaps as early as in April. At this point, there was already an armed conflict in France. As early as on 18 March, two government generals, Claude Lecomte and Jacques Clément-Thomas, were killed in Paris. Both were assassinated by an enraged mob. On 02 April, the first skirmishes took place between the government army and the revolted Parisian National Guard. The following day, the Communards organised an armed expedition to Versailles, which eventually ended in total disaster on 04 April. Thus began the civil war. The government troops, better armed, better commanded, and much more disciplined, slowly approached the city walls and finally crossed them on 21 May 1871.

Wolowski's unusually harsh view of the Communards, mentioned by Mill, was linked to this very conflict. It worried the Englishman justifiably, as was soon to become clear. Wolowski's approach was not dissimilar to the views of most parliamentarians gathered at Versailles. As early as on 21 March, in a debate, Thiers spoke of a Parisian "party of robbery", "a hateful faction that no man of good faith could join", "the scoundrels who murdered Generals Lecomte and Thomas". Perhaps even more characteristic was the voice of Jules Favre, the Foreign Minister. Favre, unlike Thiers, had always been a republican. However, he

---

800 Kraszewski claimed that Wolowski was to give his last lectures during the Commune, which the revolutionaries eventually closed. According to the writer, Louis Wolowski left Paris on 18 May to join his son-in-law and daughter in Gisors (J.I. Kraszewski *Ludwik Wołowski...*). However, as is clear from Mill's letter (below), he must also have been in England in the meantime.

801 J.S. Mill *Correspondance inédite avec Gustave d'Eichthal: 1828–1842, 1864–1871*, Paris 1898, p. 233.

used a very similar vocabulary in relation to the rebellious city. Moreover, he accused the Communards of acting illegally, undermining the principle of the popular vote, and attempting to detach Paris from the rest of France. With the Germans occupying a third of the country, Favre saw the actions of the Communards virtually as treason. He also claimed unequivocally that they had already declared war on the rest of the country on 18 March. "Isn't this already a civil war, accompanied by cowardly murder and looting in the shadows?", he continued. "Do we not know that the requisitions have already begun, that private property will be raped and that we will see [...] how the whole of society, undermined from below, falls if those who should take up arms in its defence do not do so."[802] In fact, this ministerial speech from the early days of the Paris Commune contained all the elements characteristic of the Versailles vision of events. Most of the government and parliamentary representatives saw the Commune as a hotbed of criminals, traitors, thieves, false republicans, and false democrats. Favre's words, moreover, were received by the House with "lively approval and applause". A House that included many of Wolowski's acquaintances and political friends.

Let me quote Julian Klaczko, another person whom Wolowski knew well and with whom he cooperated. Klaczko strolled through the streets of Paris in late March 1871. He perceived the Communards almost as madmen: "Their method of reasoning now, their way of looking at the world and humanity, at social and political relations, at the past and the future, at the real and ideal conditions of existence – in a word, their thought and their speech and actions are so unusual, so eccentric, so far beyond the boundary posts of common sense, that one listens to them with the constant disbelief of some dreamy nightmare, that one looks into them as into the 'mirror up to nature' – according to Ophelia's sorrowful expression."[803] The Pole was already in Versailles in the first days of April. He described the fear of the Versailles people at the news of the Communards' expedition towards them[804]. He recalled the words of opponents of the Commune who fled the city: "Women stop passers-by, perfect strangers, and they tell them about the rapes committed by the Commune. *It's hell, sir, it's hell!* One poor old woman took my hand, sobbed and amidst her sobs she mentioned her two grandchildren who had died during the siege, her son killed by the Prussians, her husband who had been taken by les Communeux [the Communards – RD], and finally, with an expression of pain I'll never forget, she added: And yet it's Holy Week!..."[805]. Klaczko, like most residents of Paris and Versailles he met, did not usually distinguish between rumours, exaggerated gossip, and facts. He reported on alleged extortions carried

802 *Assemblée Nationale, Séance du mardi 21 mars 1871 à Versailles*, "Journal Officiel de la République Française", 22.03.1871.

803 J. Klaczko *Notatki z podróży,* Kraków 1871, p. 10.

804 J. Klaczko *Notatki z podróży...*, pp. 30–31.

805 J. Klaczko *Notatki z podróży...*, p. 39.

out in Paris against the wealthier residents, that "shooting already started". And he cursed Jarosław Dąbrowski and Walery Wróblewski "and so many others with a Polish name, but without Polish faith, without Polish conscience" who "stood in the ranks of the communists, among the main heroes of this despicable bunch".[806]

We can assume without much risk that Wolowski's opinion on the Paris revolution was very similar. This explains, moreover, the lack of any reaction on his part to the events of the last week of the Commune ("the bloody week") and the weeks immediately following it. His attitude to the Commune may also have been influenced by a personal tragedy. For his mother, Tekla Wołowska, died on 09 May 1871. She therefore passed away during the Commune, though undoubtedly of natural causes. The "Ateneum", already quoted, reads that Wolowski was in Versailles at the time. And that he arrived in Paris for the funeral, undisturbed by anyone[807]. While the latter statement seems plausible – indeed, even in May 1871, it was possible to move between Paris and Versailles, while Wolowski was not such a recognisable figure as to make the Communists particularly concerned about him – it is worth noting that Tekla Wołowska's death certificate was drawn up much later, not until 4 August 1871.[808] It is likely that the delay was related to the poor functioning of the administration (quite a number of officials had left the city with the government). It may also be that Wolowski, having arrived in the city quietly, nevertheless did not intend to throw himself in the face of the Communard authorities in May. One thing is certain, however, if the "Ateneum" is to be believed, at the time of his mother's death, he was not with her, most likely because of the Commune.

The situation had meanwhile escalated. Immediately after the defeat of the 04 April clash, the Commune adopted the so-called Hostage Decree, according to which the Communards could arrest people accused of collaborating with Versailles at any time. After the court verdict, they were to become hostages of Paris, whom the Communards could execute at any time in response to Versailles' actions[809]. In fact, the Commune had hostages somewhat earlier: after 18 March, the first gendarmes and policemen were arrested, together with several clergymen, and on 04 April the Archbishop of Paris, Georges Darboy, was imprisoned[810]. In turn, as the fighting and the subsequent minor successes of the Versaillesians continued, irritation grew among the Communards. Although it does not appear that Wolowski was personally threatened, in May 1871 he may have seen things differently. To understand Wolowski's attitude to the Commune, let me quote Michelet, another

806 J. Klaczko *Notatki z podróży* ..., p. 39.
807 "Ateneum: pismo naukowe i literackie", vol. 3 (3), part 9, Warszawa 1876, p. 636.
808 Death certificate of Tekla Wołowska: Archives de Paris, ref. V4E 3483 no. 6.
809 "Journal Officiel de la République Française sous la Commune", 06.04.1871.
810 More on the subject: A. Rastoul, *L'Église de Paris sousla Commune. Persécutions et martyrs*, Paris 1871.

of his acquaintances. An eminent historian of the Revolution, and a staunch republican, in the context of 1871 he wrote of the capital's barbarians paid by Bismarck, "the social monster we carry within us". He juxtaposed the Communards with the supporters of the restoration of the monarchy, treating one and the other as the perpetrators of the decay of society[811].

They were similarly treated by the government. Jules Favre proudly quoted a government proclamation of the period, addressed to Parisians: "[The Commune] is raping private property, arresting citizens to make them hostages, turning into deserts your streets and your public squares where the commerce of the whole world once flourished; suspending work in Paris and paralysing it all over France, stopping the prosperity that was already reviving, delaying the evacuation of the territory by the Germans and exposing you on their part to a new attack, which they claim they are ready to carry out if we do not stop the insurrection ourselves."[812]

In the same proclamation, Thiers and his ministers announced the imminent entry of the army into Paris. This indeed happened on 21 May 1871, the day that marked the beginning of the last, "bloody week" of the Commune. On 28 May the last barricade fell. By this day, some 3,000 Communards and just under a thousand soldiers had been killed in the fighting[813] which must be topped with around a hundred hostages murdered by Parisians (including Archbishop Darboy). Irrespective of the direct clashes, there was a real massacre of the Communards, after they had laid down their arms. It was the result of summary executions and the action of the so-called military prevotal courts, sentencing them to death in a flash. French historians estimate of the number of victims range from 10,000 to 35,000[814]. A gigantic war crime thus took place in Paris. The Commune was only marginally responsible for it – in proportion to the number of hostages murdered. Versailles was incomparably more to blame.

This crime was made possible by the tacit acquiescence of Versailles politicians, senior officers, and personalities such as Wolowski. The responsibility of the officers, with Marshal Mac Mahon in the lead, is brilliantly analysed by Robert Tombs in his book, demonstrating clearly that the rank-and-file soldiers were

---

811 J.-C. Caron *Jules Michelet, Correspondance générale, tome 12: 1871–1874 et suppléments, Textes réunis, classés et annotés par Louis Le Guillou*, Paris, 2001," Revue d'histoire du XIXe siècle" no. 22, 2001, pp. 226–229.

812 J. Favre *Gouvernement de la Défense nationale*, vol. III, *Du 29 janvier au 22 juillet 1871*, Paris 1875, p. 383.

813 Mac Mahon (Maréchal), *L'Armée de Versailles. Depuis sa formation jusqu'à la complète pacification de Paris,* Paris 1872, p. 44.

814 Robert Tombs writes about 10 000 (*La Guerre contre Paris 1871*, Paris 1997, p. 332), Rougerie mentions 34-35 000 (*Paris libre 1871..*, p. 257). The estimations of the others historians fall between these two numbers.

simply following orders or following the officers[815]. On 22 May 1871, Adolphe Thiers promised from the parliamentary tribune that the Communards who lay down their arms would be spared[816]. However, he later preferred to align himself with the majority of the National Assembly, which was clearly blood hungry.

2. Back to Politics

Wolowski, like Thiers, was silent on the issue. The problem of how to deal with the communards did not appear once in his texts. This absence was particularly striking in June 1871, during the next election campaign. For, in the wake of the events of the Commune and the earlier resignations of some of the Paris deputies, by-elections to Parliament were called on the Seine. Wolowski decided to stand as a candidate.

Unlike in 1848 and 1849, in 1871 he was part of a genuine electoral committee, the Union parisienne de la presse (the "Paris Press Union"), which brought together conservative and centrist press titles. He could count on the support of the Bonapartist "Le Constitutionnel", the Republican "La Presse", the Catholic "L'Univers", the legitimist "Gazette de France", the Orléanist "Journal des Débats Politiques et Littéraires", and "Le Figaro", "La France", "Le Gaulois", "Le Moniteur Universel", "La Patrie" and "Le Pays".[817] On the same list were representatives of all right and centre-right orientations: Maurice de Flavigny, a Bonapartist, Charles-Émile Freppel, the Bishop of Angers, Edmond de Pressensé, a conservative pastor, Joseph d'Haussonville, an Orléanist, Alexandre de Ploeuc, a legitimist, Edouard Laboulaye, a republican, and Wolowski. They shared a commitment to "order", property, and traditional values, and were divided by the attitude to the monarchy and republic. However, Wolowski did not mind; in one of his letters to Levasseur in 1871 (no date), he mentioned that he had sought such an agreement between moderate republicans and monarchists. Apparently, the shock and fear of a revolution that had just been put down was (temporarily) stronger than the differences that divided them.

Following the example of 1848 and 1849, Wołowski prepared a proclamation to the voters. It is worth quoting, bearing in mind that it was dated 19 June 1871:

> In the terrible situation in which we find ourselves because of the civil war and the external war, I have decided to accept the offer to stand for election on 02 July. No lengthy declarations are necessary here. You have known me for a long time, I was elected in 1848 with 134,000 votes to the Constituent Assembly; in 1849, in the

815 R. Tombs, *La guerre...*, pp. 315–317.

816 A. Thiers, *Discours parlementaires de M. Thiers,* t XIII, Paris 1882, p. 267.

817 More on the French press at the time and the political character of the various titles in C. Bellanger, J. Godechot, P. Guiral, F. Terrou (dir.) *Histoire générale de la presse française,* vol. III, *De 1871 à 1940,* Paris 1972, pp. 178–238.

> Legislative Assembly 120,000 votes renewed this mandate. My political career came to an end on 02 December 1851. I devoted myself to the study of economic issues and the defence of freedom of trade, both in the press and as chair of the Conservatoire des Arts et Métiers. If you place your trust in me, I will support the system of public order and tranquillity initiated in Bordeaux and recently reaffirmed at Versailles, based on the Republic, accepted by the enlightened decision of the entire country. We must all join forces to strengthen work, commerce, industry, agricultural production and recover from the disasters suffered and the crimes that have threatened public order.[818]

This text is by all means symptomatic as it was written in Paris, where the ruins of the Tuileries, the Hôtel de Ville, the Palace of the Legion of Honour and other buildings set on fire in an act of desperation by the Communards were still smoking. In a Paris where, until recently, rifles could be heard shooting rebels in prisons[819]. Wolowski despaired of the ruins[820] but failed to see the lawlessness and callousness of the repression of the defeated. He consistently sided with Thiers, the government and (once again) the party of order. In his declaration, however, another word is worth noting, namely "Republic". At the 08 February elections, France had not at all spoken clearly in favour of this form of government, but the results of the municipal elections held in April and May of the same year were much more promising for the Republicans. It was not a foregone conclusion which political shape would ultimately prevail. Louis Wolowski was therefore very clearly in favour of a republic from the outset in the discussion. In the end, he was also one of the deputies who brought about its consolidation.

---

818 L. Wolowski *Scrutin du 2 juillet 1871. Aux citoyens électeurs du département de la Seine,* Paris 1871. He briefly outlined more or less the same programme in a subsequent letter to Levasseur: "I intend only to defend the sacred principles of liberty and respect for the law, the foundation of any possible republic." (Bibliothèque de l'Institut de France, *Correspondances et papiers divers provenant de la succession d'Émile Levasseur*, ref. MS 6032).

819 Edmond de Goncourt wrote about them in his *Journal* (E. & J. de Goncourt *Journal des Goncourt. Mémoires de la vie littéraire,* vol. IV, *1870–1871,* Paris 1890, pp. 328–329). The poet Catulle Mendès, a fierce opponent of the Commune, described Paris of that time as follows: "The Commune is defeated, Paris is gloomy, immobile, naked. [...] Gloom has seized souls, just as loneliness has seized the streets. We are strangers to both anger and pity; we are broken, resigned, stupefied." (C. Mendès *Les 73 journées de la Commune (du 18 mars au 29 mai 1871,* Paris 1871, p. 326).

820 Wolowski was on a list published by the *Journal Officiel de la République Française* of 19.06.1871 (no. 170, p. 1460) of people financially supporting the rebuilding of the Palace of the Legion of Honour. At the time, he contributed 100 francs for this purpose.

On 02 July, Wolowski received 143,781 votes, the most of any Parisian candidate[821]. Markiewicz explains this success by his liberalism, appealing to the petite and middle bourgeoisie of Paris, the popularity of his lectures at the Conservatoire des Arts et Métiers, his Polish background, and his experience in 1848 and 1849[822]. "Ateneum", in turn, mentioned that some voters were said to have confused him with Walery Wróblewski, a Polish general of the Commune[823]. The latter argument seems questionable, as does the reference to Polish roots: in Paris, in July 1871, precisely because of the participation of Wróblewski, Dąbrowski and several hundred other Poles in the struggle of the Commune, it was not a good political recommendation. Arguably, Wolowski's liberalism and his moderate republicanism indeed suited many Parisians. Wolowski also mentioned his popularity among representatives of the workers – at least those who listened to his lectures at the Conservatoire[824]. However, another factor seems of utmost significance: of the twenty-one candidates promoted by the Union parisienne de la presse, as many as sixteen were selected. Thus, it was the list that most determined Wolowski's success.

The other thing is that, overall, Paris voted in favour of the republic and elected 16 republicans alongside only 5 monarchists. Nationwide, just over a hundred deputies were elected at the time, generally moderate republicans, declaring their support for Thiers, successful in these elections.[825].

In the French parliament, political camps did not yet emerge fully, their boundaries were fluid, with some deputies abstaining from any of them and others operating between several groups, but the centres of these parliamentary factions were quite visible. On the extreme right were some 80 legitimists, known as the "Chevau-légers", attached to Henri Count de Chambord ("Henry V"), the House of Bourbon pretender to the throne and, equally, to the conservative Catholicism of Pius IX. The key figures in this group included Edouard de Cazenoves de Pradines, Albert de Mun and Lucien Brun.

Alongside this group on the right were more moderate legitimists like Falloux, Charles de Lacombe, Camille de Meaux, who were close to the conservative Orléanists (Albert de Broglie and Gaston d'Audiffret-Pasquier). Together they advocated an agreement between the Bourbons and the Orléans in the name of

821 "Journal des Débats Politiques et Littéraires", 05.07.1871. 299,000 Parisians voted at the time, 458,000 were eligible (registered) to vote.

822 P. Markiewicz *Louis Wolowski...*, p. 143.

823 "Ateneum: pismo naukowe i literackie", vol. 3 (3), part 9, Warszawa 1876, p. 636.

824 Undated letter to Levasseur from 1871, Bibliothèque de l'Institut de France, *Correspondances et papiers divers provenant de la succession d'Émile Levasseur*, ref. MS 6032.

825 G. Hanotaux *Histoire de la France contemporaine (1871–1900)*, vol. I, *Le Gouvernement de M. Thiers*, Paris 1903, pp. 238–239.

dynastic restoration. While remaining Catholics, they were critical of the pontificate of Pius IX, in particular the dogma of papal infallibility and the *Syllabus of Errors*.

Louis Wolowski, on the other hand, associated himself with the Assembly's centre-left. A historian of French parliamentarism of this period described this group as follows: "Some of the Orléanists formed a centre-left group whose role was to prove crucial. It is difficult to clearly identify the elements that separated it from the centre-right, to the extent that some historians have deemed them only appearances. And yet the issue at stake is central to the entire history of the period. The same liberalism, the same belief in parliamentarism united one and the other. If even the centre-left, sceptical about the chances of the monarchy, eventually joined forces with the conservative Republic, it is difficult to see this as a clear criterion for classification – since Orléanism was not defined by attachment to a dynasty, but rather a peculiar state of mind, adapting well to various combinations. Ultimately, the divide was decided by the issue of religion. People of the centre-left, even if they were Catholics (and there were quite a few of them, like Dufaure) did not wish the Church to influence society too much or to retain the "privilege of respectability" (according to D. Halévy). Liberal Catholics, prominent on the centre-right like Archbishop Dupanloup or Falloux, even if accepted "modern freedoms", they nevertheless believed that the state should enforce respect for the Church. [...] This fracture was to slowly separate people seemingly so close to each other, forcing them into difficult coalitions – a union of the right and a union of the left."[826].

The axis of the centre-left's conception was thus liberal thought, combined with the popular vote and the republic. In 1863 Edouard Laboulaye, one of the most important representatives of this group, wrote in a text characteristic of the French liberals:

> The most important question today is the organisation of democracy; not by restriction, not by imprisonment in sterile forms, but by breaking its chains and accustoming it to live its own life. There are two types of democracy. One follows its master, flattering him, then subverts and insults him; this is the democracy of the Caesars, a revolutionary and ignorant democracy, the rule of the mob, of the instincts and the passions. The other is a Christian democracy, enlightened, industrious, in which everyone learns from a young age to manage their own lives, to respect the rights of others, the laws protecting those rights and the authority guarding them. [...] To provide every individual with full opportunity for development, to guarantee him total freedom to exercise his physical, intellectual, religious and moral faculties, to remove all obstacles, to promote universal progress by multiplying the means of education available to the least educated and poorest: this is the task of the State; I know of no more important or laudable one.[827]

---

826 J.-M. Mayeur *Les débuts de la Troisième République 1871–1898,* Paris 1973, pp. 17–18.
827 E. Laboulaye *Le Parti libéral: son programme et son avenir,* Paris 1863, p. 9.

Clearly, Wolowski's free-market and liberal ideas connected with this vision. If he mentioned a republic in his election declaration, it was precisely the kind of republic depicted by Laboulaye. In his text on the group, Jean Garrigues rightly noted that two events in 1871 were extremely important for them: the Commune and its suppression by Thiers' government, the other being the municipal elections. For the government's victory over the Commune showed that the republic did not need to be revolutionary but also that it had the strength to deal with the "reds". The electoral results, on the other hand, indicated that France was leaning towards a republic; Wolowski and like-minded deputies saw the parliamentary elections of 08 February as a specific case, resulting from an extraordinary historical context[828]. The key task for them was to combine the republic with liberal parliamentarism.

In total, the centre-left had around 170 deputies in the first half of the 1870s with Adolphe Thiers as the key figure. The faction revolved around support for his policies. His famous phrase "A republic is the form of government which divides us the least"[829], summarising the attitude of many Orléanists to the new system, represented almost its programme. More importantly, Orléanists like Thiers had learned from the events of 1850–1851 and did not intend to question the principle of the popular vote. This was also true of Wolowski. Among the group's most important politicians were also Auguste Casimir-Perier, well known to Wolowski, and Charles de Rémusat (a deputy since 1873). Above all, however, as Garrigues writes, there was an unusually large representation of the financial and economic world in the group. This included the banks: sitting on the benches alongside Wolowski were, among others, Germain of the Crédit Lyonnais, Eugène Gouin of the Banque de Paris et des Pays Bas and René Brice, the Pole's colleague from the Crédit foncier. Alongside them were board members of railways, steel companies and major French traders. Laboulaye was also an economist, regularly meeting Wolowski at the Society of Political Economy, as were Germain, Ernest Duvergier and Garnier.[830]

On the parliamentary left, in turn, was a group of around 150 deputies who were decidedly republican and anti-monarchist. They were led by the "four Jules": Jules Grévy, Jules Ferry, Jules Favre, and Jules Simon. Economically liberal, the Left had much in common with the group to which Wolowski belonged. They shared a clear dislike of any monarchy and a distrust of Thiers' policies.

Finally, on the extreme parliamentary left were Gambetta's supporters, the radical republicans. They were distinguished as much by their style of politics – much

828 J. Garrigues *Les élus du centre gauche en 1871*, „Parlement(s), Revue d'histoire politique", no. 2 (16), 2011, pp. 25–26.

829 Thiers uttered it on 13 February 1850 during a parliamentary debate ("Journal des Débats Politiques et Littéraires ", 14.02.1850)

830 J. Garrigues *Les élus du centre gauche en 1871...*, pp. 30–31.

more democratic than the others (Gambetta was not called the People's Tribune for nothing) – as by their anti-clericalism, which grew over time.

Thus, Wolowski found himself in a large and significant parliamentary group, well suited to his programme, consisting, for the most part, of familiar figures. He quickly got down to work. As always, he was primarily concerned with financial and economic issues. However, their weight and importance had changed somewhat in relation to the period of his first term in the Assembly: France, wishing to get rid of German occupation troops, had to repay its war contribution as quickly as possible. Almost all the proposals and financial problems discussed at the time were linked in one way or another to this very issue. So, in early August, Wolowski tabled a draft amendment to the tax on raw materials in the House. He proposed that instead of this, a two per cent tax should be introduced, charging all transactions except for food. Every invoice on a transaction was therefore to be given a seal of approval by the government.[831] In the end, the Assembly did not agree to his proposal.

In contrast, another discussion, also strongly related to finance, ended in success for Wolowski. Later that month, he proposed allowing postcards to be sold in France. His argument was based mainly on the revenue that France could generate from the related taxes. In doing so, Wolowski referred to examples from England and the United States, where the sale of postcards was expected to generate significant profits for the state. He also emphasised their impact on social bonds and cunningly added that the postcard had been introduced by Germany. And he went on to say, if France was thinking of revenge after losing the war, "there is the possibility of immediate revenge, which I support; it consists in seizing any tools of progress that may have contributed to France's defeat."[832]. The economist's idea was met with unexpected resistance. Some deputies were clearly concerned that the card would replace letters and thus lead to a drop in revenues from postage stamps. Perhaps more significant was the fact that the issue was simply ignored by the House. The Budget Committee, which should have dealt with the project, simply decided that it was not responsible for postal reform[833]. However, the Pole did not let up in this case, although sixteen months passed before he returned to the postcard. In December 1872, he made his proposal a second time, citing further countries where the postcard was in operation. Significantly, this time Wolowski was explicitly supported by Germain Rampont, Director General of the Post Office. Together they managed to convince the Assembly, which finally, on 19 December 1872, accepted the Pole's proposal[834]. In fact, Wolowski

831 "Journal Officiel de la République Française", 03.08.1871, pp. 2403–2404.

832 "Journal Officiel de la République Française", 24.08.1871, no. 235, pp. 2923–2924.

833 "Journal Officiel de la République Française", 25.08.1871, no. 236, p. 2943.

834 "Journal Officiel de la République Française", 20.12.1872, no. 350, pp. 7949–7954.

was so proud of this achievement that he still presented it at the Academy in 1873[835].

In December 1871, the liberal former director of the Crédit Foncier submitted yet another important bill to the Assembly, this time strictly financial. The idea was to allow the French central bank, the Banque de France, to issue an additional 100 million francs of money, in the form of 5- and 10-franc coins. In addition, the bill authorised a loan by the state to the Banque de France of 600 million francs. Justifying his project, Wolowski stressed that in post-war conditions, faced with the repayment of successive instalments of contributions, it seemed a necessity for the Banque de France to increase the issue of paper money. Wolowski, on the other hand, had long been its opponents. This time, too, he pointed out that the printing of money would lead to a fall in its value. Instead, he proposed a direct loan from the Banque de France to the state[836]. However, the project referred to a parliamentary committee, encountered stiff resistance from the government. Almost immediately, Wolowski was told by the Minister of Finance, Augustin Pouyer-Quertier, that France did not intend to take out new loans. This was, moreover, due to the general policy of the Thiers government, maintaining a balanced budget at all costs[837]. As a result, the Pole's idea was rejected.

Wolowski clashed with the government and Thiers in the same days on yet another financial issue, far more significant. For the banker and deputy Germain had come out with an initiative to introduce an income tax in France. Wolowski supported the idea of his factional colleague. In the parliamentary discussion, he referred above all to the example of England, where an income tax had been in operation since 1842 and – according to Wolowski – had worked well. According to him, this tax did not undercut the sources of the state's wealth. And at the right (relatively low) level, it could have brought huge revenues A key point of contention in this discussion, however, was not the amount of tax or the related state revenues, but the need to disclose revenues. Wolowski stressed that in England, the amount of individual incomes was known only to the relevant tax officials, and not fully at that. He also spoke of the egalitarian (in the positive sense of the word) nature of income tax, covering all types of income equally. He explicitly advocated the introduction of a tax allowance. Here, not for the first time, Wolowski departed from the principles of total laissez-faire. For "England has already introduced it [the tax allowance – RD] because England has understood that those who own more should also pay more; England has also understood that the tax should not burden those who own nothing at all." He also proposed that people earning little more than the minimum necessary for taxation could deduct 600 francs from their

835 L. Wolowski *La carte postale,* [in:] "Séances et travaux de l'Académie des Sciences Morales et Politiques", vol. XXIX (XCIX), Paris 1873, pp. 566–574.

836 "Journal Officiel de la République Française", 18.12.1871, no. 350, p. 5058.

837 G. Valance, *Thiers, bourgeois et révolutionnaire...*, pp. 359–360.

tax base. In fact, he was proposing a genuinely modern vision of an income tax which would in time, following the English model, replace other taxes. A vision indeed quite egalitarian in 1871, although it should be noted that his intention was primarily to supplement the revenues of the French budget rather than to distribute the tax burden more equitably. According to Wolowski, the time for this otherwise necessary discussion was to come only after the state's finances had been stabilised and contributions had been repaid.

Germain and Wolowski were answered on 26 December 1871 by Thiers himself. The answer was an unequivocal "no". Thiers argued that in many cases, an income tax would mean double taxation. He also accused it of arbitrariness; he asked the Assembly: "How do you gentlemen imagine the situation of a government forced to announce to the taxpayer: 'We know that you have 20,000, 30,000, 40,000 francs of annuities!' "Are you really going to delegate such a power to the government?". The head of government then outlined the structure of French taxation. He compared the English ones to arrive at the conclusion that in England the edifice of the budget was mainly borne by the lower classes, whereas in France the tax share of the upper classes was much more significant. Thiers concluded with a clear call to reject the income tax and a pledge not to allow it as long as he was in power. Judging by the reaction of the room, his speech made a big impression[838]. As his biographer writes, "Thiers had prepared a speech rich in figures, but – and this was his strength – he was able to present them in an interesting way. According to his words, the tax was going to hit income already taxed. Hatred, mutual grievances, and jealousies were to decide that one would pay more and the other less. So why introduce socialism into the country through the tax system?"[839]. Pierre Guiral is right: the head of government's stance seems to have been determined primarily by ideological, less by financial considerations.

Wolowski found himself in a difficult position. He had supported Thiers' government and usually supported his policies, as did the centre-left. As a result, he felt distinctly uncomfortable opposing him on such an important issue; he even pointed out that he had dared to debate one of the greatest figures of his time. Nor did he match Thiers oratorically. He sought to demonstrate that the latter was wrong in his tax calculations. However, he was on the losing end of the argument: the Assembly was clearly unwilling to listen to him, with shouts demanding from time to time that his speech be cut short. Moreover, after his speech, Pouyer-Quertier once again spoke out clearly against it. The House then rejected the income tax proposal[840].To the detriment, arguably, of France. Indeed, if Alain Plessis, a historian who juxtaposed the French and British tax systems of the period, is

---

838 "Journal Officiel de la République Française ", 27.12.1871, no. 358, pp. 5268–5274.

839 P. Guiral *Adolphe Thiers,* Paris 1986, p. 424.

840 "Journal Officiel de la République Française", 28.12.1871, no. 359, pp. 5288–5291 & 5297.

to be believed, the latter, which included also the income tax in the long run, performed much better. It was more flexible, better adapted to the needs of the modern state and, contrary to Thiers' assertions, placed a heavier burden on the richest than most European systems. France, on the other hand, only introduced income tax in 1907.

Louis Wolowski lost this battle but did not give up until the end. The following year, he published his parliamentary speech in defence of income tax in a separate pamphlet[841]. He also continued to be primarily preoccupied with tax issues in the Assembly. Thus, he protested against the government's capital gains tax proposal. The tax proposed by Pouyer-Quertier was to charge income from shares or other ownership in companies, bonds, redemption premiums, etc. Wolowski claimed that the reality was to protect land ownership and agriculture. Only that, according to him, the new tax would hit capital, which agriculture needed like no other. He was also concerned that the new tax would hit credit, which the whole economy would end up paying for.[842] Once again, he lost – in June the new tax was finally passed[843].

In January 1872, Wolowski made another tax proposal. This concerned a unique residence tax, levied only temporarily, of 15% of the rent. Interestingly, in this case Wolowski very quickly withdrew his proposal on grounds of illness and inability to defend it personally[844]. On 19 January 1872, his name was among others under the Financial Transaction Tax Bill. However, the bill was not passed.

During this period, Wolowski drew attention to his failing health on several occasions during speeches. In February 1872, he asked for three weeks' leave for this reason, and in March for ten more days. At that time, the Speaker of the Assembly informed the deputies that the Pole had had to stay at home following an accident[845]. In the end, however, he did not appear at Versailles until August 1872.

Some of the political issues that Wolowski spoke or voted on are worth mentioning. The burning issue was still the question of Paris and the return of

841 L. Wolowski *L'impôt sur le revenu. Discours de M.Wolowski, député de la Seine (Séances du 22 et 27 décembre 1871) avec des observations et des annexes sur l'impôt du revenu aux Etats-Unis et en Angleterre*, Paris 1872.

842 " Journal Officiel de la République Française", 09.01.1872, no. 8, p. 147.

843 Once again, Wolowski's lack of flair as a speaker was evident. The House again interrupted him, waiting for the end of his speech. Another thing is that, clearly out of form at the time, he complained about his health, which did not allow him to develop all his arguments fully ("Journal Officiel de la République Française", 09.01.1872, no. 8, p. 147).

844 "Journal Officiel de la République Française", 13.01.1872, no. 12, p. 246 & 16.01.1872, no. 15, p. 315.

845 "Journal Officiel de la République Française", 17.02.1872, no. 47, p. 1142, 17.03.1872, no. 73, p. 1894 & 13.03.1872, no. 72, p. 1776.

government institutions and parliament to the capital. Notably, the Assembly was still sitting at Versailles. From time to time, proposals to move to the Seine recurred. Wolowski voted clearly against, as did most of the House[846]. In another instance, however, he embraced Paris. This was because, in early August, he drew the attention of deputies to the fact that the department of the Seine (especially the environs of the capital) had been severely damaged during the siege and should therefore count on some help from the state. Unfortunately for Parisians, the Pole's speech had no follow-up.

In July 1871, the Assembly also considered the question of the so-called petitions of the bishops. Several petitions, clearly orchestrated by the French bishops, had arrived at Versailles, demanding French diplomatic intervention in the Roman question, namely in defence of the temporal power of the Pope. The Thiers government could not follow the wishes of the Church, for this would certainly have meant a marked deterioration in relations with Italy. At the same time, he wished to retain the favour of the French hierarchy. That is why the petition was eventually forwarded by the Assembly to the Minister of Foreign Affairs, which in practice meant that it was frozen. This is how Wolowski voted (as did the majority of the centre-left)[847].

Shortly afterwards, the Assembly held its first constitutional vote. To understand its significance, however, I must return to the general political situation in France. If the majority of the deputies elected on 08 February 1871 were in favour of the monarchy, there was certainly no agreement between the legitimists and the Orléanists on the vision of the future crown. There was also no agreement on the candidate for the throne. The legitimists stood by Henri de Chambord. The Orléanists, on the other hand, pinned their hopes on the sons of Louis-Philippe. The dynastic conflict could be resolved, for Chambord had no children. The legitimists were therefore able to agree to hand over the throne to the House of Orléans after his death. However, a more difficult question remained about the shape of the future monarchy. In turn, it was reflected in the question of the banner. Post-revolutionary France, the France of the constitutional monarchy, was associated with the tricolour banner. Pre-revolutionary France, the France of the Bourbons, the absolute monarchy, and the dominant role of the Church, was symbolised by the white royal banner. A condition of the Orléanists' consent to the coronation of the Count of Chambord was therefore the latter's acceptance of the tricolour, symbolising France of 1789. Chambord arrived in Paris in early July 1871 after forty years of living in exile. On 05 July, he published a manifesto in which he promised to introduce extensive decentralisation, local freedoms, the preservation of the popular vote ("fairly practised") and a bicameral parliament. At the same

846 "Journal Officiel de la République Française", 03.08.1871, no. 215, p. 2404 & 03.02.1872, no. 33, p. 792.

847 A. Robert, E. Bourloton, E. Cougny *Dictionnaire des parlementaires français...*, p. 565.

time, however, he insisted that monarchical law was the nation's historical legacy. Above all, he rejected the tricolour banner of France in favour of the old royal white. "I will not allow the banner of Henry IV, Francis I and Joan of Arc to be torn from my hands. It flew over my cradle, I want it to cover my tomb."[848] In reality, these words signified a rejection of post-revolutionary France together with the principles of constitutionalism and parliamentarism. They made any compromise with the centre-right impossible. Instead, they corresponded to the actual views of the grandson of Charles X. For as Georges Poisson, his biographer, writes: "In fact, Henry was, according to his own principles and traditions, in favour of a personal dictatorship in the Russian style. He admitted that it had to – here was a concession to the age – be limited by liberties (he preferred the plural to the singular) and certain constitutional rules, but these rules he intended to give himself after enthronement."[849] This vision, however, did not fit at all with the Orléanist parliamentarism embodied in the English maxim "the king reigns but does not rule". The reaction of the "Journal des Débats", moreover, was characteristic. John Lemoine, the newspaper's editor, wrote on 10 July: "the Count de Chambord gives the impression that he does not understand any times except those of his ancestors. [...] It is no accident that his vocabulary has been compared to the *Syllabus*. The monarchy is based on the same absolute declaration as the papacy; on both banners, or rather on the common banner, the same motto is inscribed: *Sit ut sunt, aut non sint*."[850]

When a monarchy was at least temporarily impossible, it became necessary to regulate the key constitutional issues and Thiers' power at least temporarily. Hence the so-called Rivet law, enacted on 31 August 1871. This kind of (mini) constitution of France consisted of three articles:

> Article 1. The Head of the Executive shall henceforth use the title of President of the French Republic and shall continue to exercise, under the supervision of the National Assembly until it has completed its work, the functions which were entrusted to him by the Decree of 17 February 1871. Article 2. The President of the Republic shall promulgate the laws as communicated to him by the National Assembly. He supervises the execution of the laws. His seat is the seat of the Assembly. He is heard by the Assembly whenever he deems it necessary, after informing the President of the Assembly. He appoints and dismisses ministers. The Council of Ministers and the ministers are accountable to the Assembly. Presidential acts must be countersigned by the relevant minister. Article 3. The President shall be accountable to the Assembly.

848 H. de Bourbon, c. Chambord *Manifeste de M. le comte de Chambord: 5 juillet 1871*, Montpellier 1871, pp. 6–7.

849 G. Poisson *Le Comte de Chambord. Henri V*, Paris 2009, p. 269.

850 "Journal des Débats Politiques et Littéraires", 10.07.1871.

The Assembly passed the new law by an overwhelming majority – 491 out of 585 voters.[851] Louis Wolowski was part of this majority. In fact, the text of the law was fully in line with his ideas: the word "republic" appeared, it was still headed by Thiers, but clearly subordinated to the parliament. While this was a temporary solution, both for Wolowski and all the other members of the House, including the legitimists, it was nevertheless moving in the direction he certainly desired.

Wolowski was one of the more active parliamentarians in 1871 and 1872, despite his visibly deteriorating health. He sat on several parliamentary and ministerial committees[852]. He was clearly most comfortable with financial and economic discussions; however, he was also the author of a resolution that all emigrants from Alsace and Lorraine were to be recognised as Frenchmen[853]. This was the only case in which the Chamber of Deputies unanimously adopted his proposal in a flash, even extending it to financial aid given to the neediest[854]. Another thing is that the problem of Alsatians and Lorrainians remaining in France and deprived of their livelihoods by annexation was clearly at the heart of this former émigré.

---

851 "Journal Officiel de la République Française", no. 243, 01.09.1871, pp. 3120–3125.

852 In 1871, these committees were as follows:
- on the draft law on bearer shares ("Journal Officiel de la République Française", no. 214 02.08.1871, p. 2385),
- on the cheque bill. Wolowski was its chairman ("Journal Officiel de la République Française", no. 238, 27.08.1871, p. 3012 and no. 240, 29.07.1871, p. 3125),
- considering a proposal to extend the term of office of the Assembly ("Journal Officiel de la République Française", no. 248, 06.09.1871, p. 3250),
- on a trade treaty with Germany ("Journal Officiel de la République Française", no. 259, 17.09.1871, p. 3538),
- considering his own project relating to the Banque de France ("Journal Officiel de la République Française", no. 347, 15.12.1871, p. 4986).
In 1872, Wolowski became a member of the following committees:
- ministerial for international exhibitions ("Journal Officiel de la République Française", no. 4, 05.01.1872, p. 57),
- budget ("Journal Officiel de la République Française", no. 123, 04.05.1872, p. 2992),
- examining his project concerning residents of Alsace and Lorraine ("Journal Officiel de la République Française", no. 321, 21.11.1872, p. 7167),
- on the cotton industry ("Journal Officiel de la République Française", no. 322, 22.11.1872, p. 7197),
- considering a draft postal agreement between France and Russia ("Journal Officiel de la République Française", no. 350, 20.12.1872, p. 7957),
- ministerial in charge of aid to residents of Alsace and Lorraine ("Journal Officiel de la République Française", no. 351, 21.12.1872, p. 7969).

853 "Journal Officiel de la République Française", no. 312, 12.11.1872, p. 6931.

854 "Journal Officiel de la République Française", no. 349, 19.12.1872, p. 7920.

The deputies set up a special commission to oversee the distribution of the aid. The Pole became a member of this commission, which was then usually referred to as the "Wolowski Commission". The commission provided aid and dealt with the relocation of Alsatian families – the "Journal Officiel" of 26.01.1875 (p. 686) reported 959 Alsatian-Lorraine families sent to Algeria by Wolowski's commission and another 160 in the process of being relocated. In late 1873, Wolowski still submitted a bill granting Alsatians and Lorrainians who had previously sold tobacco concessions in France.[855] Finally, the Pole donated 10,000 francs to the exiles of these two provinces.[856]

In 1873, Wolowski took part in a key parliamentary debate on child labour. According to the law in force in France since 1841, children as young as eight could work in factories or manufactories. Their work was limited in time: children under twelve could not work more than eight hours a day, between thirteen and sixteen years of age – 12 hours a day. Even these provisions were largely illusory, as the state had no control instruments. The impetus to change this law was, ironically, provided by the French war defeat – for its causes were also sought in the physical weakness of French recruits. This was also linked to French child labour. The new law was authored by Ambroise Joubert-Bonnaire, an industrialist who submitted it as early as in 1871. Joubert raised the age at which children were allowed to work in industry to twelve years. His draft also banned night work for boys under sixteen and girls under twenty-one in factories or manufactories. Most importantly, it established a state inspectorate responsible for compliance with the new provisions. The debate on the new law was held for a long time. The ideas contained in it corresponded to Wolowski's earlier beliefs.. While working on the 1841 law, he emphasised in his "Revue..." that children belonged first and foremost in the school, not in the factory. He pointed out that rapid development of education would have to be a necessary complement to the ban on younger children working in factories[857]. In 1868, Wolowski published a pamphlet on this issue where he wrote about the threat that the Industrial Revolution brought to poor children, the physical danger of working beyond their strength. Significantly, he was prepared to restrict the rights of parents in this case. Wolowski knew that parents most often sent minors to work. He even compared work beyond their strength to infanticide.[858] At the time, his proposal did not go as far as Joubert's later one: Wolowski wanted to ban child labour up to the age of ten, while between the ages of ten and thirteen it would be limited to six hours a day.[859] By the same

855 "Journal Officiel de la République Française", no. 351, 23.12.1873, p.

856 H. Baudrillart *M. L. Wolowski*, "Journal Officiel de la République Française", no. 322, 23.11.1876, p. 8607.

857 L. Wolowski *Bulletin législatif*, "Revue de législation et de jurisprudence", vol. 13, January – June 1841, p. 143.

858 L. Wolowski *Le Travail des enfants dans les manufactures*, Paris 1868, pp. 13–23.

859 L. Wolowski *Le Travail des enfants...*, p. 30.

age, night work was to be banned altogether. The latter provision was also to apply to women of all ages[860].

Joubert's draft thus went somewhat further than Wolowski's earlier idea. Unlike the latter, it also contained enforcement provisions. The difference was also related to the fact that Wolowski altogether prohibited night work for women. During the parliamentary debate, he supported the new provisions, but proposed that they be extended to include just such a prohibition. He invoked the rights of the family, of children, he also argued that this would be a reform that would effectively counter the development of socialist doctrines[861]. Typically, Wolowski referred to foreign examples, primarily the British one. He even postulated an international agreement on the issue: "For a long time now, nations have been making agreements that have led to the death of many people. I believe that the day has come when nations should agree to jointly introduce laws that protect human existence and prevent abuses that harm it".[862]

Wolowski's proposal was met with a clearly negative reaction. Questions were raised about freedom of competition, the distinction between a factory, manufactory and a small workshop and the lighter work that women could do at night. The speech by Pouyer-Quertier, who invoked the alleged immorality of British workers, who were more spoiled than French workers, was a real curiosity. According to the now former minister, in all countries where women's work was not restricted, workers were generally more moral. However, financial, not moral, considerations probably prevailed; Wolowski clearly lost the vote, and his amendment was defeated by 507 votes against 90[863].

The law "on the industrial labour of children and underage girls", was finally voted on 19 May 1874 (Wolowski, of course, supported it). Notably, as historian Karen Fiorentino points out, despite its obvious shortcomings and deficiencies, the law played an unambiguously positive role, significantly reducing child labour in industry and introducing genuine state control[864].

Another thing is that the debate on the bill showed once again all Wolowski's weaknesses in the Assembly. This was probably partly due to his frequent absences for health and professional reasons[865], partly due to his persistent "professorial"

---

860 L. Wolowski *Le Travail des enfants...*, pp. 32–34.

861 "Journal Officiel de la République Française", no. 35, 05.02.1873, p. 841.

862 "Journal Officiel de la République Française", no. 36, 06.02.1873, p. 870.

863 "Journal Officiel de la République Française", no. 36, 06.02.1873, p. 870.

864 K. Fiorentino *Protéger l'enfant ouvrier. La loi du 19 mai 1874, une „législation intermédiaire"?,* "Revue historique", no. 2 (682), 2017, pp. 327–358.

865 "Journal Officiel de la République Française" of 1873 recorded his numerous absences from votes (throughout January) or requests for leave. In issue 140 of 22.05.1873 (p. 3246), there was again an indication of absence due to illness. At the end of the month, his son-in-law, Louis Passy, wrote to the President of the Chamber about his father-in-law's prolonged indisposition (no. 144, 27.05.1873, p. 3559). As soon as his

manner. Characteristic in this respect was the tax debate of 1874, when Pouyer-Quertier clearly mocked the Pole, driving him to fury in the process. More importantly, however, he was portraying Wolowski as a detached intellectual, a theoretician rather than an economic practitioner. The laughter he provoked in the Chamber was clear proof that this criticism, otherwise unfair and unjust, was convincing to many deputies[866]. The economist, incidentally, was partly to blame. A month later, he found himself at the rostrum in connection with a debate on the salt tax. And he clearly confused a parliamentary speech with a university lecture: he began to present the entire history of the salt tax in France since the 17th century. The result was easy to predict: the Assembly soon began to show signs of weariness, interrupting the speaker with increasing frequency[867]. Shouts calling for him to shorten and conclude accompanied Wolowski's speeches in the 1870s on a regular basis. He clearly had trouble holding the attention of the Assembly. This was probably also reflected in the vote in late November 1873, when the Assembly was electing candidates for the Constitutional Committee. Wolowski received the second smallest number of votes[868].

In 1873, the Pole also took part in several important political and constitutional votes. On 13 March 1873, the Assembly adopted the so-called de Broglie Act, restricting the President's ability to address the Assembly. In essence, the aim was to reduce Thiers' influence on parliament – an influence that many deputies, including the centre-left, were finding now difficult to bear. Louis Wolowski, along with the centre as a whole, voted in favour of the proposal[869].

The real political turning point came in May 1873, in the absence of Wolowski. The Right had been intent on getting rid of Thiers for some time. The tamer of the Commune was becoming superfluous from its point of view: peace with Germany had long since been signed, the war contribution had almost been paid in full, the last occupation troops were to leave French territory in September of the same year. His strong personality clearly disturbed the monarchists. In May, the entire right – from the "Chevau-légers" to the Orléanists – joined forces to make him resign. As late as on 24 May, Thiers declared in the Assembly: "Here is the truth of which I have spoken, and which I repeat: yes, there is distrust and resistance

health allowed him to do so, Wolowski had to move to Vienna in the summer for the Universal Exhibition (letter from Wolowski to the President of the Assembly, "Journal Officiel de la République Française", no. 180, 03.07.1873, p. 4380).

866 "Journal Officiel de la République Française", no. 44, 14.02.1874, pp. 1253–1254. Another thing is that Wolowski did not always maintain parliamentary forms towards others. He loudly expressed his approval or disapproval and did not hesitate to interrupt speakers when their words evoked his clear resistance.

867 "Journal Officiel de la République Française", no. 72, 14.03.1874, pp. 1971–1973.

868 "Journal Officiel de la République Française", no. 326, 28.11.1873, p. 7256.

869 "Journal Officiel de la République Française", no. 72, 14.03.1873, p. 1766.

[to the Republic] in the upper classes, who care above all for order, and are right; but among the masses, you are under no illusion, the Republic has an enormous majority."[870] These words could only reinforce the monarchists' conviction that Thiers' resignation was imperative. Later the same day, the Assembly, by a slight majority, adopted a resolution clearly critical of the President[871]. He immediately resigned, which the right-wing majority of the Assembly accepted. The House instantly elected a new president: Marshal Mac Mahon, the infamous Sedan commander and commander-in-chief of the government troops fighting the Commune. Mac Mahon was aware that he would be a transitional president – until the return of the monarchy[872]. Wolowski was not present at Versailles that day, but his faction voted against Thiers' resignation and did not take part in the vote on Mac Mahon's candidacy. Such would probably have been his vote too – especially as Thiers' republican views certainly corresponded to his own.

The new president immediately appointed a new government headed by the most prominent representative of the monarchist majority, de Broglie. The majority thus once again hoped for the return of the king. And once again, its hopes were shattered by the stubbornness of Henri de Chambord. For in August, Louis-Philippe's eldest son recognised his right to the throne on behalf of the Orléanists. However, in late October, Chambord reiterated his unwavering commitment to the white banner. "I withdraw from nothing, I do not change my previous declarations in any way," – wrote the Bourbon in a letter published in the legitimist journal "L'Union"[873]. In this situation, the moderate monarchists decided to wait out the pretender to the throne. Hence the bill introduced by the government on 20 November 1873 to extend Mac Mahon's presidency to seven years (the centre-left, together with Wolowski, voted against it and lost)[874]. The objective was clear: to await the death of the childless Henry and hand over the crown to the Orléanists. The thing is, however, that time was not on the monarchy's side at all.

Among Wolowski's parliamentary activities in 1873, two bills are worth mentioning. The first, signed by him, completely abolished the death penalty in the French legal system. Wolowski thus returned to this issue after more than twenty years[875]. The effect was like the previous one: the Assembly rejected the project; the death penalty was only abolished in France in 1981.

870 "Journal Officiel de la République Française", no. 142, 25.05.1873, p. 3308
871 This was primarily to say that his recent ministerial appointments "did not give the Conservatives the satisfaction they had a right to expect" ("Journal Officiel de la République Française", no. 142, 25.05.1873, p. 3315).
872 Mac Mahon even said outright that "he would never stand in the way of the restoration of the Count de Chambord" (quote from G. de Broglie *Mac Mahon*, Paris 2000, p. 228).
873 "L'Union", no. 304, 30.10.1873.
874 "Journal Officiel de la République Française", no. 318, 20.11.1873, p. 7091
875 "Journal Officiel de la République Française", no. 351, 23.12.1873, p. 8046.

The second, completely different draft concerned the protection of brands and trademarks. Wolowski was the rapporteur for the committee dealing with this text. The idea was that brands and trademarks would be protected against counterfeiting by means of a state stamp, which would be paid for, and the law would also make it possible to prosecute foreign counterfeiters. The state stamp was also intended to provide customers with a guarantee of quality.[876] The bill received very clear support from Wolowski and was finally passed by the Assembly on 27 November 1873.

The Pole had also been a member of the presidential committee on trade, agriculture, and industry since 1873.[877] The Minister for Education appointed him a member of the council of excellence overseeing the Higher School of Commerce (Ecole Supérieure du Commerce)[878]. In the Assembly, he was also part of an important committee giving its opinion on the project to extend the presidency of Mac Mahon[879].

The year 1874 brought a long fiscal debate to which Wolowski actively contributed. After all, France had paid off the German war contribution, but as a result it found itself in a difficult financial situation and the government regularly sought new taxes that could support the budget.

Wolowski was primarily critical of any concept of additional taxation of capital. He acknowledged that income from capital could be taxed but capital itself could not. For Wolowski, capital was the basis of production and therefore the economy as such. Consequently, its taxation hit the entire economy. The Pole admitted that the new taxes were necessary, but they should have primarily covered the effects of production rather than its foundations[880]. In his opinion, the taxation of capital would be a blow to the owners as much as the wages of the workers. It is clear, moreover, that by capital he meant above all industry. Exceptionally, he allowed for an additional tax on landed property, as it was less productive than industrial capital.[881] Significantly, Wolowski regularly raised the argument throughout this

---

876 L. Wolowski *Assemblée Nationale. Année 1873. Annexe au procès-verbal de la séance du 27 février 1873 Rapport supplémentaire fait au nom de la commission du budget chargée d'examiner la proposition de loi de MM. Labelonye, Bozerian, Morin et plusieurs de leurs collègues pour l'établissement d'un timbre ou signe spécial destiné à être apposé sur les marques commerciales et de fabrique*, Paris 1873.

877 "Journal Officiel de la République Française", no. 153, 06.06.1873, p. 3578.

878 "Journal Officiel de la République Française", no. 197, 20.07.1873, p. 4882.

879 "Journal Officiel de la République Française", no. 307, 09.11.1873, p. 6801.

880 "Journal Officiel de la République Française", no. 34, 04.02.1874, pp. 984–985;

881 L. Wolowski *Assemblée Nationale. Séance du 24 décembre 1873. Discussion générale du budget. Discours de M. Wolowski, député de la Seine,* Paris 1874. In March 1874, Wolowski suggested slight changes to the way in which the value of landed property was assessed, so that the inheritance and gift tax should be raised as a result. However, his proposal was rejected by the Assembly ("Journal Officiel de la République Française", no. 76, 017.03.1874, pp. 2086–2087.

discussion that new taxes should primarily burden the wealthier, while the popular classes should be spared wherever possible.

There was, incidentally, a clear dispute between him and the rest of the Assembly over the salt tax; Wolowski called for it to be raised once. However, the tax on salt, as he was well aware, was associated with the wildly unpopular "gabelle" (a tax abolished in 1790). In the end, after assurances from the government that the budget was stable without changes to the tax on salt, the amendment under discussion was withdrawn by the proposers[882]. Not for long as the issue returned in July 1874 on the occasion of a budget discussion. This time Wolowski clashed directly with Pierre Magne, the then Minister of Finance, whom he accused of avoiding unpopular but necessary decisions, such as the introduction of a salt tax [883]. The Pole subsequently lost the vote, but the results show that he managed to convince the entire opposition, with a right-wing majority behind the government[884].

The tax on salt, however, was only a part of a wider tax battle that played out around the budget in July 1874. The government proposed raising some new taxes. The opposition protested, together with Wolowski, who represented the budget committee. The committee considered the government's proposals dangerous for the economy. In turn, instead of an increase in fiscal revenue, Wolowski proposed to postpone the repayment of part of the loan taken out by the state with the Banque de France. Of course, this was to be done with the Bank's consent: Wolowski argued that, for the Banque de France, the timing of the repayment of this 50 million (out of a total loan of 200 million) was of little importance, while such an extension could significantly relieve the state[885]. On behalf of the government, Magne firmly rejected Wolowski's proposal. In doing so, he cited contractual

882 In addition to Wolowski, the proposers were Léon Say and Pierre Tirard. Discussion of the amendment: "Journal Officiel de la République Française", no. 72, 14.03.1874, pp. 1971–1974; no. 73, 15.03.1874, pp. 1998–2002. Interestingly, the temperature of the rather harsh discussion was further raised considerably by Wolowski's proposal that the amendment vote should be secret. He was clearly concerned to avoid a situation where deputies would need to confess to their constituents for supporting an extremely unpopular tax. For the same reason, Wolowski's opponents in the debate demanded an open vote. Here are some of their voices: "Léopold Limayrac: The proposal to vote in secret undermines the dignity of the Assembly! L'Ebraly: The salt tax is an extremely unfair tax! We vote against it and want it to be known! Marquis de Castellane: We protest against a secret ballot whose sole purpose is to abandon the most sacred interests of our departments. Many members of the Assembly from the right: we demand an open vote." ("Journal Officiel de la République Française", no. 72, 14.03.1874, p. 1974).

883 "Journal Officiel de la République Française", no. 188, 11.07.1874, p. 4828.

884 "Journal Officiel de la République Française", no. 192, 15.07.1874, p. 4932.

885 "Journal Officiel de la République Française", no. 180, 03.07.1874, p. 4609.

certainty, the bank's freedom of action and lack of coercion by the state. The minister said: "I reject with all my might this proposal because it is inconsistent with the nature of things, because it is inconsistent with the Bank's statutes, because it harms the creditworthiness of the Bank and of you, and, finally, because it is the first blow to the prudent, wise, salutary credit system proposed by the previous government and adopted by the Assembly; also because, if the proposal of the Honourable Mr Wolowski were to be accepted, everything would be at risk, no one could guarantee that next year, instead of today's 50 million, there would not be an even more convenient proposal to default on 100 million; and thus the credibility of the bank, on which the power of money, crucial for all of us, is based, would be jeopardised."[886] Wolowski took up the gauntlet thrown down by the Minister and proved that the 50 million francs was of no great significance to the Banque de France, in no way undermining its credibility. He also made it clear that at stake was a voluntary adjustment of the contract between the State and the Bank. Magne replied that such an adjustment would necessarily contain an element of coercion, which the Pole clearly denied[887]. On 14 July 1874, the Assembly finally rejected the government's tax proposal. On 19 July 1874, by a majority of 5 votes, it accepted Wolowski's proposal[888]. Magne did not wait for the outcome of this vote: on 15 July he resigned. According to his biographers, the minister took the criticism of the House personally. In part, probably rightly so – during the debate he was reproached for his ministerial functions during the Second Empire, the conservative fiscal policy pursued at the time[889]. Wolowski did not use such personal arguments, but his interventions were crucial to the minister's downfall. Suffice it to say that Magne never returned to the government. The Banque de France agreed to revise the deal, but in the end, it proved unnecessary: budget receipts that year far exceeded expectations and the French state was able to repay the entire 200 million francs.

The year 1874 showed, however, that Wolowski's parliamentary activity was declining. He was regularly absent: partly due to travel (for example, he was briefly in England in April), but it seems that health was increasingly the reason for these absences. Moreover, the "Journal Officiel" mentioned only four parliamentary committees on which the Pole sat (although one of them was the key budget committee mentioned).[890]

---

886 "Journal Officiel de la République Française", no. 188, 11.07.1874, p. 4822.

887 "Journal Officiel de la République Française", no. 193, 16.07.1874, pp. 4848–4849.

888 "Journal Officiel de la République Française", no. 196, 19.07.1874, p. 5047.

889 G. Antonetti, F. Cardoni, M. Oliveira de. *Magne (Pierre)*, [in:] *Les ministres des Finances de la Révolution française au Second Empire*, vol. III, *Dictionnaire biographique 1848–1870*, Vincennes, 2007, http://books.openedition.org/igpde/1251 (retrieved 20.05.2023).

890 In addition to the budget commission ("Journal Officiel de la République Française", no. 37, 07.02.1874, p. 1075) there was a commission dealing with the cadastral tax

Wolowski's parliamentary victory over Magne was linked, more broadly, to the slow shift of political centre of gravity across France, including the Assembly, towards the republican left. Between 1873 and 1875, France elected 23 deputies in by-elections, 16 of whom belonged to the republican camp[891]. Significantly, the republicans triumphed despite the restrictions imposed by the government. A state of siege was still in force (since 1871) in many French cities. The government took advantage of this to close or restrict the distribution of more than two hundred republican newspapers, pamphlets and booklets were confiscated, and in some cases suspected republicans were taken into custody on various pretexts, sometimes before the court[892].

France still lacked a permanent constitution, and prolonging temporariness served no one. Meanwhile, the right-wing government coalition began to disintegrate in 1874. The "Chevau-légers" blamed the Orléanists for the failure of the royal restoration. On 16 May 1874, they voted jointly with the Republicans against the government. As a result, de Broglie and his government resigned[893]. President Mac Mahon then appointed another Orléanist – General Ernest Cissey. Magne was a minister in his government. The right-wing Orléanists, however, began to consider a change of ally and an agreement with the centre-left[894]. For the alternative was only a stalemate in the Assembly and likely a snap election. Judging by the results of the by-elections, this could only have resulted in losses for the Right.

The centre-left and centre-right finally came together in early 1875 with new constitutional laws. The key amendment to one of them, authored by the hitherto little-known deputy Henri Wallon, was voted through on 30 January 1875. At issue was a law on the organisation of public authorities, to which Wallon inserted one

("Journal Officiel de la République Française", no. 73, 15.03.1874, p. 2005), a committee working on a postal agreement between France and the US ("Journal Officiel de la République Française", no. 145, 29.05.1874, p. 3578) and the committee considering a draft 220 million franc loan to Paris ("Journal Officiel de la République Française", no. 343, 16.12.1874, p. 8333).

891 Although Charles Seignobos, followed by Alfred Lajusan, pointed out that these Republican victories were relative, partly related to the absenteeism of conservative voters, the general trend in favour of the Republicans was clear. Moreover, among the winning candidates of the left, several belonged to its radical wing (A. Lajusan *Les origines de la Troisième République. Quelques éclaircissements (1871–1876)*, [in:] "Revue d'histoire moderne", vol. 5, no. 30, 1930, pp. 419–438).

892 A.-D. Houte *Le triomphe de la République 1871–1914*, Paris 2014, p. 31.

893 "Journal Officiel de la République Française", no. 134, 17.05.1874, pp. 3299 & 3205–3206. Interestingly, Wolowski in this case voted for the government – unlike the vast majority of his own faction.

894 Wolowski made a small contribution to this process: indeed, the departure of Magne, a Bonapartist, contributed to the disintegration of the right-wing coalition.

sentence: "The President of the Republic is elected by the Senate and the Chamber of Deputies, combined into the National Assembly, by an absolute majority."[895] The key words were: "President of the Republic". Wallon's amendment passed by one vote (353 "for", 352 "against"). Wolowski supported it, but the key vote was by a section of the centre-right. Their attitude is best captured in a story by Paul Bosq, who described a meeting between the Duke d'Audiffret-Pasquier, one of the leaders of the Orléanist Right, and one of its deputies. D'Audiffret-Pasquier was said to have stated: "What are you doing, they tell me you are going to establish a republic!". However, he then added a little more quietly: "Unfortunately, this is the only possible way. Just be as solid as a rock."[896] After which he voted... against, and finally on 25 February supported the entire text of the law. In fact, the Wallon amendment simultaneously gave the green light to three constitutional laws. On 24 February 1875, the Assembly voted – this time by a clear majority – in favour of the Senate Bill. It established a 300-member Upper House of Parliament. Seventy-five senators were to be elected for life by the Chamber of Deputies, the rest (for a nine-year term) by electoral colleges made up of deputies and representatives of regional and municipal governments. The Senate had the legislative initiative and participated in the legislative process. If necessary, it could transform itself into a tribunal to try the president or ministers[897]. The following day, the law on the organisation of public authorities was adopted, this time by a crushing majority (467 in favour, 46 against). The law granted extensive powers to the president of the republic. Elected under the Wallon Amendment for seven years (with the right of re-election), he had the legislative initiative, appointed all civil and military officials, was responsible for the army, appointed the Council of State, and could dissolve the Chamber of Deputies at the request of the Senate. He was not accountable for his actions to anyone – except in situations of high treason[898]. The last of the three constitutional laws was adopted a little later, on 16 July 1875. It described the procedure for convening sessions of parliament, the relationship between ministers and the Houses (the former had the right of free entry and to be heard in the Houses on request). It delegated important foreign policy powers to the President, subject to ratification of treaties by the Houses. Finally, it guaranteed deputies and senators immunity in matters relating to their mandate[899].

France thus gained three constitutional laws that formed the foundation of its political system for the next 65 years. It was primarily the agreement of the centres: the centre-right and the centre-left that stood behind them. Louis

895 "Journal Officiel de la République Française", no. 30, 31.01.1875, p. 838.
896 P. Bosq *Souvenirs de l'Assemblée nationale, 1871–1875*, Paris 1908, pp. 302–303.
897 "Journal Officiel de la République Française", nr 55, 25.02.1875, p. 1447.
898 "Journal Officiel de la République Française", nr 56, 26.02.1875, p. 1485.
899 "Journal Officiel de la République Française", nr 194, 17.07.1875, p. 5452. This time, 520 deputies voted in favor of the law, 81 against.

Wolowski, of course, supported all three. He was part of a whole large group of former Orléans supporters who were building the new republic. This is reflected in its design. Indeed, the president, elected for seven years, resembled the Orléanist ideal – a monarch "reigning but not ruling"[900]. The key role was to be played by a bicameral parliament, with the Senate playing a moderating role vis-à-vis the democratic (popular) Chamber of Deputies. To a large extent, this vision flowed from the Orléanist conception of the state. It was about, as René Rémond wrote in his classic work, "a parliamentary regime, remaining at an equal distance from absolute power as from the dictatorship of the masses, being the guarantor of civil liberties."[901] This vision was otherwise perfectly suited to Wolowski. Characteristic in this respect was an episode from the March 1875 constitutional debate, when Gambetta demanded, in the name of the rights of the people, that the Assembly be dissolved, and new elections called. Wolowski then exclaimed to him that "only the Assembly has the right to determine the moment of its dissolution"[902] – emphasising the dominant position of parliament in the entire system.

It is also no coincidence that Rémond referred to the 1870s as the "golden age" of Orléanism. The Orléanists also prevailed in the new Buffet government formed in March 1875. In turn, Léon Say, Wolowski's colleague from the centre-left, from the Academy of Moral Sciences and the Society of Political Economy, became Minister of Finance. Thus, not only the new constitution, but also the new governmental dealings may have suited the Polish deputy.

This was clearly evidenced by the fact that the critic of the tax-raising policy of 1874 turned into its defender in 1875, for in June 1875 he acted as rapporteur for a parliamentary committee, defending a government bill on taxation that clearly raised taxes[903]. He defended other government projects as well – such as the text on the legal protection of the state monopoly of matches[904]. And when he happened to table a draft resolution in the House that did not correspond to the policies of the new government, "at the request of his friends", he quickly withdrew it[905].

He continued to be an active member of the budget committee, appearing on its behalf before the House on several occasions. He was a member of that committee for the year 1876 and was the rapporteur of its final report on the budget

---

900 Some Republicans even spoke of a "quasi-monarchical" constitution.(F. Démier *La France du XIXe siècle 1814–1914*, Paris 2000, p. 311).

901 R. Rémond *La Droite en France de la première Restauration à la Ve République*, Paris 1963, pp. 138–139.

902 "Journal Officiel de la République Française", no. 97, 19.03.1875, p. 2070.

903 "Journal Officiel de la République Française", no. 150, 03.06.1875, p. 3941.

904 "Journal Officiel de la République Française ", no. 206, 29.07.1875, p. 6021 & no. 226, 19.08.1875, pp. 6952–6953.

905 "Journal Officiel de la République Française", no. 76, 18.03.1875, pp. 2057 & 2059.

for that year[906]. He also participated, of course, in the work of less prominent committees[907].

Unfortunately, towards the end of the year, the health of the then 65-year-old Wolowski again deteriorated markedly. On 05 November 1875, he informed deputies that, for health reasons, he would not be appearing at the next few sittings of the House. Unfortunately, reality turned out to be more brutal: in early December 1875, he appeared again at Versailles, but only for a month. He did not yet know that this was the last month of his parliamentary activity.

He did, however, manage to take part in a vote of extreme importance to him. For, according to the new constitutional provisions, the House had to elect 75 senators for life. Wolowski was one of the candidates. The first vote took place on 09 December 1875. On that day, the Assembly elected just two Senators (d'Audiffret-Pasquier and deputy Louis Martel), with Wolowski receiving 322 votes, 22 votes short of the required majority. The following day, the vote was repeated, and this time Louis Wolowski received 349 votes, five votes more than the required minimum. On 10 December 1875, the Pole was thus elected senator of the French Republic for life[908]. This choice, undoubtedly the crowning achievement of the political career of the descendant of the Schors, was mainly due to the political set-up, but it also showed a certain recognition. Although in 1944 Daniel Halévy wrote, in the context of the choice of the first "immortals of the Senate", about "unknown mediocrities"[909], contemporary French historians have significantly changed that outlook. As Jean Marie Mayeur writes in the introduction to the collective study devoted to them, they were for the most part experienced and valuable people – even if they lacked among them the most important leaders of the factions[910]. Their age and selection (among the first twenty elected, only five

---

906 "Journal Officiel de la République Française", no. 136, 23.05.1875, p. 3636; no. 182, 05.07.1875, pp. 4980–4981; no. 185, 08.07.1875, pp. 5088–5091; no. 188, 11.07.1875, pp. 5204–5207.

907 These were the parliamentary committees responsible for:
- draft law on railway administration ("Journal Officiel de la République Française", no. 75, 17.03.1875, p. 2037),
- evaluation of the state contract with the Compagnies Maritimes ("Journal Officiel de la République Française", no. 135, 19.05.1875, p. 3525),
- preparation of the French section of the Universal Exhibition in Philadelphia ("Journal Officiel de la République Française", no. 170, 01.07.1875, p. 4810).

908 "Journal Officiel de la République Française", no. 338, 10.12.1875, p. 10180 and no. 339, 11.12.1871, p. 10215.

909 D. Halévy *La fin des notables. La République des ducs*, Paris 1944, p. 189.

910 J.M. Mayeur *Introduction,* [in:] A. Corbin, J.-M. Mayeur (dir.) *Les immortels du Sénat, 1875–1918: Les cent seize inamovibles de la Troisième République,* Paris: 1995. Online: http://books.openedition.org/psorbonne/67972 (retrieved 02.06.2023).

were under the age of sixty) meant that, in most cases, the senatorial seat was the culmination of a political career, sometimes a kind of retirement; however, this group also included future ministers and one prime minister.

The political composition of the nominees was also distinctive. The centre-left was clearly dominant. There were as many as twelve among the senators elected with Wolowski, two to the Republican left and only two to the centre-right[911]. Ironically, this was due to the eventual break-up of the right-wing coalition in the House. The "Chevau-légers" and legitimists preferred to support centre-left Republican candidates rather than their recent centre-right coalition partners. In the days that followed, the Assembly elected more life members. Out of a total of 75, 23 were associated with the republican left or the radical left, 32 came from the centre-left, 8 from the centre-right, 11 from the monarchist right, 1 was a Bonapartist[912].

Wolowski's last vote of deputies took place on 31 December 1875. On that day, the Assembly called new elections to the Chamber of Deputies and to the newly established Senate. The first round of deputy elections was held on 20 February, the second on 05 March 1876. Senators (except for those for life) were elected on 30 January 1876.

Louis Wolowski did not participate in any way in the election campaign. Firstly, because he had secured himself a senatorial seat, and secondly, his health no longer allowed him to do so. Moreover, the centre-left's chances of winning the senatorial elections were limited: the electors electing senators were often mayors of municipalities, appointed by the government. As a result, unlike with the life senators, the majority represented the centre-right: 93 elected, topped with 39 Bonapartists and 2 legitimists. The centre-left did not poorly with 51 senators, like the republican left, with a total of 40 senators. However, together with the life members, this gave a slight advantage to the right in the Senate (154 to 146)[913].

The situation in the lower house of parliament was completely different: the right wing, previously holding a clear advantage, lost decisively. Of the more than 500 deputies elected, 360 represented the centre-left or the left[914]. Viscount Camille de Meaux, the worried Minister of Agriculture and Commerce in several successive Conservative governments, later recalled:

> The predominance of the Conservative spirit in the rural communes, and of the rural communes in the departmental colleges, was such that the senators elected in the

911 The report of the proceedings of the House, moreover, refers to the outcry coming from the right after the announcement of the voting results. ("Journal Officiel de la République Française", no. 339, 11.12.1871, p. 10215).

912 O. Rudelle *Chap. II. Mars 1875, Janvier 1879: quelle république?* [in:] *La république absolue: 1870–1889*, Paris, 1982, online : http://books.openedition.org/psorbonne/71612 (retrieved 08.06.2023).

913 O. Rudelle *Chap. II. Mars 1875, Janvier 1879: quelle république?...*

914 O. Rudelle *Chap. II. Mars 1875, Janvier 1879: quelle république?....*

> departments restored the balance [in the Upper House] and even tilted it to our side. [...] On the contrary, the popular vote was moving away from us since France no longer felt threatened. The radicals and those who opened the way for them broke into the Chamber of Deputies as republicans. In this Chamber, Gambetta, whose very name still frightened people of order (and rightly so since he had not given up his radical doctrines and intended only to wait for the right time) was to rule undivided.[915]

De Meaux probably overestimated Gambetta's importance, but his further analysis of the balance of power was correct: "A conservative head of state, a radical House [of Deputies], a Senate hostile to radicalism but divided between those in favour of appeasement and those in favour of a policy of resistance, these were the powers that were to decide the fate of the country."[916] The election result thus already contained the seeds of further political conflicts.

Louis Wolowski, however, did not see them again. His health was clearly deteriorating. He did not appear at the first meeting of the Senate but sent a request for an excuse for absence at this and subsequent meetings[917]. The last trace of his Senate activity was another request for leave, sent in June 1876.[918]

By this time, Wolowski was staying at the estate of his son-in-law and daughter in Gisors. There he died at a quarter past midnight on 15 August 1876[919].

He passed away at a crucial moment for France (the years 1876–1879). In 1877, Mac Mahon dissolved the Chamber of Deputies, but the next election was clearly the Republicans' victory again, so the President had to accept a Republican centre-left government. In 1879, the Republicans first won a majority in the Senate, then Mac Mahon resigned, and Jules Grévy became president on 30 January 1879. The monarchists thus lost their last footholds in the governing bodies. The Third Republic was already ruling indivisibly. It lasted until 1940. After 90 years since the outbreak of the Great Revolution, France had finally achieved political stability as such.

Louis Wolowski was among those who contributed to this stability. They were leaving with him: the election of 1877 was a clear defeat for the centre-left, and within a few years it completely disappeared, in fact melting away among the

915 C. de Meaux *Souvenirs politiques: 1871–1877*, Paris 1905, pp. 271–272.

916 C. de Meaux *Souvenirs politiques...*, p. 272.

917 "Journal Officiel de la République Française", no. 73, 14.03.1876, p. 1780. Interestingly, the absent Wolowski was elected chairman of one of the Senate committees ("Journal Officiel de la République Française", no. 77, 18.03.1876, p. 1903).

918 "Journal Officiel de la République Française", no. 165, 17.06.1876, p. 4243.

919 Death certificate: Gisors, civil registration, death certificates 1876, no. 76, Wolowski Louis Michel Raymond. The exact cause of his death remains unknown. "Journal des Economistes" reported at the time that Wołowski had been struggling with illness for three years, as evidenced by his repeated absences from the Assembly ("Journal des Economistes...", series III, vol. XLIII, July – August 1876, p. 358).

Republicans. Moreover, at the same time as Wolowski, other important representatives of this political and ideological formation were dying. Above all, its most emblematic figure, Adolphe Thiers, died in 1877, Charles de Rémusat (1875) a little earlier, and Auguste Casimir-Perier (July 1876) almost at the same time as Wolowski. Thanks to their political flexibility, these moderate (conservative) liberals played a key role in the history of 19th century France. Their programme was outlined by Thiers in his famous speech "on the necessary liberties" in 1864, in which he demanded above all the full protection of the personal liberty of citizens, freedom of speech, free elections and the observance of the basic principles of parliamentarianism, including the parliamentary accountability of ministers.[920] For them, private property was an obvious value, naturally complementary to personal freedom but the Monarchy not necessarily so; after all, Thiers did not mention it in1864. This group, as I have stressed several times before, originated from the July Monarchy. It was therefore naturally linked to the Orléans dynasty, but unlike the House of Bourbon legitimists, this bond was not inseparable. In fact, Thiers, Rémusat, Léon Say, Jules Barthélemy-Saint-Hilaire and Wolowski were ultimately ready to accept any power that would guarantee these fundamental values. The historical process of working out this compromise lasted virtually all their active lives and was not without mistakes or twists and turns. The time of trials, experiences, including bad decisions, was largely the Second Republic for them. It was the first time when they had to confront the people of Paris who did not necessarily adhere to the rules of parliamentarism, and it was also then that they encountered the popular vote in practice. From their point of view, these first experiences were bad. 1848 and 1849 brought a fear of revolution and the related doctrines, also strongly evident in Wolowski, that these liberals were unable even to enter any discussion with them. This fear was also experienced in 1871, making it impossible for them to understand the Paris events and leading ultimately to the massacre of the last week of May 1871. The fear caused by the results of the 1849 election led them (including Wolowski) to vote to exclude some Frenchmen from the electorate a year later. In this case, however, they seem to have been able to draw the consequences of their mistake. After the collapse of the Second Empire, when the centre-left became the key political group, it sought a way to limit the negative (in the liberals' view) effects of the popular vote, but it had fully accepted the principle itself. This search in turn resulted in the constitutional laws of 1875, guaranteeing the strong position of the president and, above all, of the Senate, elected by the social elite. Thus, these moderate monarchists in their youth, then one of the mainstays of Louis-Philippe's monarchy, became the midwives of the Third Republic in their old age.

In many respects, Wolowski was a typical representative of this group. Personal freedom, freedom of speech, private property and the rule of law were key values

920 *Supplément,* "Journal des Débats Politiques et Littéraires", 12.01.1864.

back for Franciszek Wołowski. Louis largely inherited this thinking from his father. He was undoubtedly linked to the political and social elites of the July Monarchy. His relationship with the Orléans, however, was perhaps somewhat weaker than that of the other members of this formation. He seems to have come to terms with their departure as early as in 1848 and never particularly longed for the dynasty. This does not mean, however, that he enthusiastically embraced the republic; he always treated it as a means of achieving certain goals rather than as a value in itself.

It is important to remember that 19th century political groups did not resemble today's parties. They were much less disciplined, less organised, and often resembled a collection of strong personalities rather loosely connected by their views. Louis Wolowski was also such an independent personality, and so it often happened that he voted differently from his political friends. Wolowski was clearly at his best during economic and financial discussions in parliament. He was very well prepared for them each time, operating freely with statistical data and historical examples. Perhaps too freely and for too long – he often bored his listeners stiff. However, he was also able to stand up to the equal-minded Thiers on these issues. He contributed to the departure of Finance Minister Magne, and indirectly, to the collapse of the right-wing ruling coalition.

It seems that in some instances he was distinguished, not least in comparison to his own parliamentary group, by his greater social sensitivity. This is indicated by his votes and speeches in defence of the right of workers to form coalitions or to strike for wages, in favour of improving the standard of workers' housing in 1850, against imprisonment for debt in 1848, against the death penalty in 1848 and 1871 or in favour of restricting child labour two years later. On the other hand, this social sensitivity of Wolowski should not be overestimated. He lacked it decisively in June 1848, he lacked it when he voted against limiting the working day to 10 hours, he lacked it in May and June 1871.

To understand this shortage, it is necessary to go back to the events of 15 May 1848, to the workers' uprising of the same year, and to the associated terror of the people's representatives of the time, for a few hours or days uncertain of their fate. Wolowski, accustomed to academic debates and parliamentary forms, must have felt uncomfortable in the heated atmosphere of the clubs of 1848. There is much to suggest that the whole period between February and June 1848 left an indelible mark on the Pole. His later words about the heroic battles fought then, the volcano in which France found itself, etc., were a measure of the strength of the feelings that accompanied him. And the most important of these, it seems, was fear. A fear that returned in 1870 and 1871, when the economist could feel history recurring, in even more tragic circumstances.

Secondly, it is necessary to refer to Wolowski's liberal economic thought. This is because, to a large extent, it explains his view of the relationship between workers and employers, workers and the bourgeoisie, the state, and the free market.

Chapter VIII: The Economic Thought

1. The Method

The origins of Wolowski's economic thought were naturally linked to his legal education. In the "Revue... ", he regularly dealt with topics bordering on law and economics, including the mentioned credit issues and the mortgage system. The issue of joint-stock companies falls also into that category. In 1837, Wolowski devoted a text to them, in which he defended the freedom of their operation. In France, since Napoleon's times, these companies could only operate with the consent of the state. Wolowski called for the abolition of this restriction, seeing it as unnecessary, harmful to the economy and dangerous to individuals[921]. Wolowski's text was noted in the ruling circles but the restrictions on joint stock companies were only lifted by Napoleon III in 1863.

In his arguments, Wolowski often referred to the experiences of other European countries and the United States. This was, after all, the purpose of his academic journeys: to gather observations and other countries' legal and economic experiences. The Polish economist also enjoyed travelling back in time. In his deliberations, he regularly referred to examples and historical experiences from different eras. In doing so, he quoted from the German historical school (later referred to as the "older historical school"). Its main founder was Wilhelm Roscher, a friend of Wolowski's; they regularly met and corresponded[922]. In his writings, Roscher harshly criticised the classical school of economics for thinking too abstractly and mathematically. He did not completely reject the deductive method it proposed. However, according to him, it needed to be supplemented with a picture of the historical functioning of individual nations. At the same time, Roscher emphasised their complex nature, which consisted not only of law or politics, but also language, religion, art, and science. Another important founder of the school was Bruno Hildebrand. Hildebrand formulated the thesis of three degrees of social development: natural economy, monetary economy and credit economy, the latter being, in his view, only in its nascent stage. The third founder of the historical school was Karl Gustav Knies. He even rejected the statistical methods adopted by the first two (and Wolowski). He believed that political economy should focus

921 L. Wolowski *Des sociétés par actions*, [in:] "Revue de législation et de jurisprudence", vol. 7, October 1837–March 1838, pp. 180–195 & 258–304. Wołowski subsequently published the text as a separate booklet (L. Wolowski *Des Sociétés par actions*, Paris 1838)

922 Some of this correspondence is held in the Archiwum Państwowe w Krakowie (State Archives in Cracow, ref. AKPot 3206)

exclusively on the history of specific nations, on the basis of which, however, it could not formulate any general, abstract laws[923].

In 1857, Wolowski published his translation of Roscher's book with his own preface in the Guillaumin's publishing house. In it, the Pole attacked thinkers who, relying solely on abstract philosophy, intended to create social reality from scratch, with total disregard for the traditions and nature of individual nations. In their view, the world was becoming merely "a great laboratory in which to multiply the most dangerous experiences".[924] However, this remark was directed primarily at left-wing thinkers and reformers. On the other hand, Wolowski accused the conservative right of intending to put history on stop or take it back to the Middle Ages. Meanwhile, he stressed, the task of history was to point out the elements and characteristics inherent in each epoch. Thus, it necessarily had to be based on reality, rejecting abstraction. Wolowski referred to two directions: historical and rationalist, fighting each other in various areas of social life, including law and economics. He sided with the former. However, he added an important caveat: unlike Roscher, the Pole believed in the law of nature and saw man as an intelligent, free being, functioning among other similarly intelligent and free people[925]. In his opinion, the 19th century was to reconcile the historical method with the law of nature understood in this way. According to him, history confirmed his philosophical assumptions[926].

Wolowski invariably emphasised the importance of human intelligence. It was this, he wrote, that produced wealth through labour. The latter was not an end in itself, but merely a means of humanity's moral progress. The 19th century, in turn, brought with it incredibly rapid economic and technical changes. Humanity owed it to the French Revolution, which put into practice the very principles of natural law – equality and freedom. In turn, history and its teachings were intended to protect humans from straying from the path. It was therefore a necessary complement to political economy[927]. In this, Wolowski was distancing himself from Say, who in his view underestimated the importance of history, unlike, for example, Smith[928]. Instead, he invoked the German school of history, Knies and Hildebrand on top of Roscher. He wrote of them: "The historical point of view does not consist in a blind rendering of the past and a depreciation of the present, nor in seeing successive events as fluctuations without purpose and without bonding. Instead, it perfectly meets the real needs of progress: it shows the free and creative action

923 W. Stankiewicz *Historia myśli ekonomicznej*, Warszawa 2007, pp. 156–159.

924 L. Wolowski *Préface,* [in:] G. Roscher *Principes d'économie politique,* vol. I, Paris 1857, p. XVI.

925 L. Wolowski *Préface,* [in:] G. Roscher *Principes...*, p. XXI.

926 L. Wolowski *Préface,* [in:] G. Roscher *Principes...*, p. XXXII.

927 L. Wolowski *Préface,* [in:] G. Roscher *Principes...*, p. XXXVIII.

928 L. Wolowski *Préface,* [in:] G. Roscher *Principes...*, pp. XLI-XLII.

of humans, accompanying the growth of education, morality, and freedom."[929] Wolowski regarded this approach as diametrically opposed to the attitude of classical economists, relying on self-evident (in their view) principles and, based on those principles, determining, by deduction, the laws of economics. Wolowski thought of his "dear master" Rossi, accusing him of thinking in abstractions, reducing man to the role of a tool, "the sum of the services he can perform or the pleasures he can provide".[930] In doing so, he did not deny the principles of liberal political economy developed by Smith, Quesnay, or Rossi, and known to him since his student days through Skarbek and Kunatt. However, he demanded their analysis in the light of history. "The laws of economic development arise in the crucible of time. They emerge from it stronger and more flexible, devoid of the rigidity of mathematical calculations, resistant to the absolutism of purely speculative theories inclined to confuse the horizon of the epoch with eternity", he wrote four years later.[931]

In the same year, Wolowski repeated his theses before the Academy of Moral and Political Sciences. There he stated, among other things, that everyone was guided by self-interest, as Rossi, among others, had argued. And only a well-managed and expressed self-interest could contribute to the flourishing of the common interest. Misunderstood, uncontrolled, it turned into selfishness, in conflict with the common good. History has also provided a better understanding of how to manage individual interest.[932]

Wolowski assumed that history was not so much an auxiliary science of economics as its key and inalienable component. This entailed another assertion: political economy itself, seen as an "external manifestation of the spirit of peoples", was as old as humanity. Therefore, he opposed the classical school, which saw the

929 L. Wolowski *Préface,* [in:] G. Roscher *Principes...*, p. LII.

930 L. Wolowski *Préface,* [in:] G. Roscher *Principes...*, p. LVI. Wolowski put forward a similar thesis in the preface to another work – *Economie politique du Moyen Age* by the Italian author Louis Cibrario. There, in turn, writing about Adam Smith, he pointed out that he avoided simple "social arithmetic", the description of social life by simple "algebraic equations", and was able to reconcile his own doctrine with the teachings carried by history (L. Wolowski *Introduction de l'économie politique en Italie,* [in:] L. Cibrario *Economie politique du Moyen Age,* Paris, 1859, p. IV).

931 L. Wolowski *Introduction de l'économie politique en Italie...*, p. V.

932 L. Wolowski *Mémoire sur l'application de la méthode historique a l'étude de l'économie politique,* part I, "Séances et travaux de l'Académie des Sciences Morales et Politiques", vol. XXII (XLII), 1857, pp. 366–379; part II, "Séances et travaux de l'Académie des Sciences Morales et Politiques", vol. XXIII (XLIII), 1858, pp. 303–313, 450–465.

beginning of the history of political economy in the work of Smith. [933] Moreover, Wolowski himself reached much further back.

In his studies, he repeatedly referred to historical examples and to the thinking of medieval as well as modern authors. He pointed to economic elements in the works of Machiavelli[934] and Antonio Serra [935]. In 1843, he published a short text in the "Revue..." on the organisation of the economy and customs in France before Colbert. In it, he described medieval guilds and professional corporations as a tool in the hands of small merchants, craftsmen, guaranteeing them freedom and independence and protecting them from arbitrary power, with time transformed into an oppressive instrument. In effect, Wolowski saw a revolution between the 10th and 13th centuries that led to the rise of the Third State and opened the way to 1789[936].

In 1856, in turn, he published a short work on King Henry IV, in which the first Bourbon on the throne appeared as an extremely modern ruler. Wolowski described the "good King Henry" as an advocate of an active economic policy of the state: caring for infrastructure (digging canals), appreciating the importance of both agriculture and crafts, including luxury products. In fact, he adopted a policy that was in many respects to the active and innovative economic policy of Napoleon III[937] but Wolowski failed to mention it explicitly. He returned to the subject of Henry IV five years later. This time it was the foreign policy of the king whose death prevented him from realising the concept of a new European order. Again, it is hard not to get an impression that the Pole was essentially addressing the French emperor. In the conclusion, he wrote "Henry IV's great project can be measured by the momentum of his preparations: Voltaire argued that through alliances, through armies, through economics, the king intended to change the European set-up and become its arbiter; the world would then have avoided the devastating Thirty Years' War and would have seen more quickly an era of political equilibrium and religious tolerance."[938] "The arbiter of Europe" – this term must

---

933 Jean-Baptiste Say wrote that "if we read Smith as he should be read, we find that before him there was no political economy" (*Traité d'économie politique ou simple exposition de la manière dont se forment, se distribuent et se consomment les richesses*, vol. 1, Paris 1814, p. XLVIII). Ricardo, in turn, cited Turgot and Smith among the early fathers of political economy (D. Ricardo *Des principes de l'économie politique et de l'impôt*, Paris 1847, p. 1).

934 L. Wolowski *Introduction de l'économie politique en Italie...*, pp. XIII-XIV.

935 L. Wolowski *Introduction de l'économie politique en Italie...*, pp. XIX-XX.

936 L. Wolowski *De l'organisation industrielle et de la législation douanière de la France avant le ministère de Colbert*, "Revue de législation et de jurisprudence", vol. 17 (series 2, vol. 7), January–June 1843, pp. 273–274.

937 L. Wolowski *Henri IV économiste. Introduction de l'industrie de la soie en France*, Paris 1855.

938 L. Wolowski *Le Grand dessein de Henri IV*, Paris 1860, pp. 31–32.

have convinced Bonaparte. In turn, Wolowski was aware that such an arbitration would have significantly changed the position of the Poles. And this is probably what he was mainly concerned with, rather than a (dubious) historical analysis.

Three more works by Wolowski in which history played a key role are worth mentioning (in most of them, historical arguments were put forward). In all cases, it was linked to the most topical issues or discussions.

In 1862, Wolowski published two texts on the history of monetary theory. The first concerned Nicolas Oresme, a 14th-century French philosopher and mathematician, author of *Tractatus de origine, natura, iure et mutationibusmonetarum* (1355), a pioneering work on the theory of money. It was undoubtedly Wolowski's merit alone to evoke the memory of this interesting thinker. However, the most important thing for the Pole was that the Rouen canon's view of money corresponded largely to his own. Like Wolowski, Oresme did not confuse money with wealth, similarly advocated coinage based on silver and gold, and stressed that the ruler could not freely influence the value of money[939]. Interestingly, the book also included Oresme's quoted voice against tyranny: "a tyrant prince cannot long survive".[940] It is not clear if Wolowski had Napoleon III in mind, but that is how some readers perceived it[941]. The medieval thinker's ideas, however, primarily strengthened Wolowski's voice in the discussion among French economists in the 1860s about money, the role of banks in issue thereof, and mono- or bimetallism. Similar was also the thrust of Wolowski's text, two years later, on Nicolaus Copernicus' theory of money. Again, it was about stable coinage as a key tool of the economy. A coin based on silver and gold[942]. Finally, Wolowski referred to Copernicus in the context of a dispute over the meaning of paper money, of which he himself was a great opponent[943]. However, the brochure dedicated to Copernicus had another purpose, which the Pole did not try to conceal. Namely, it was a part of a dispute over the astronomer's nationality, which broke out in earnest in the

939 L. Wolowski *Un Grand économiste français du XIV siècle*, Paris 1862, pp. 15–23.

940 L. Wolowski *Un Grand économiste français...*, p. 26.

941 Montalembert wrote to Wolowski: "I do not think like Oresme that the slavery imposed on the French cannot last long. It seems to me that it lasts beautifully, and they are enjoying it more and more". (Montalembert to Wolowski, Biblioteka Polska w Paryżu, ref. BPP 2339, c. 37).

942 However, as Józef Zajda points out, there was an important difference between Copernicus and Wolowski in this respect. Wolowski was in favour of a rigid parity of silver and gold, while Copernicus left their relationship to the market (J. Zajda *Kopernikowska teoria pieniądza,* "Ruch Prawniczy, Ekonomiczny i Socjologiczny", no. 35, part 3, 1973, pp. 32–33).

943 L. Wolowski *La Monnaie. Entretien sur le traité de monnaie de Copernic*, Paris 1864, pp. 12–23.

19th century. In a text addressed to the French, Wolowski emphasised Copernicus' Polish origin and considered describing him as a German simply absurd[944].

In the same year, thanks to Wolowski, French translations of the works by Nicolas of Oresme and Copernicus were published[945]. Therefore, he contributed to restoring both thinkers to French and European economics and historiography.

In *Mazarin*, published in 1867, Wolowski praised the treaty between France and England concluded in 1655, particularly its economic aspects. As in other cases, it is difficult to deem it a historical work, as evidenced, for example, by the scant bibliography and lack of sources. Here, too, he was primarily looking for arguments in quite contemporary discussions. Cromwell's England was in his mind becoming the nucleus of a liberal, free-market rule of law[946]. Above all, however, *Mazarin* cannot be read in isolation from the discussion of the trade treaty with England signed by Napoleon III. While praising the Cardinal, Wolowski supported the treaty of 1860, criticised by many factions.

Wolowski very often supplemented his economic reflections supported by history with statistical elements. He was clearly fascinated by social statistics, booming in the first half of the 19th century. In 1874, he even became president of the Paris Statistical Society (Société de Statistique de Paris)[947]. Seven years earlier he said at the Society's meeting that "Political economy elaborates principles, drawn from the highest philosophical considerations, the laws of production and exchange. These laws, however, have meaning only insofar as they are confirmed by facts – carefully selected, tested, and collected long enough to avoid accidental perturbations. Constructions based on a pure ideal do not stand this test; only real and true concepts survive."[948] Wolowski made abundant use of statistical

944 L. Wolowski *La Monnaie. Entretien...*, p. 10.

945 N. Oresme i N. Copernic *Traictié de la première invention des monnoies de Nicole Oresme et Traité de la monnoie de Copernic*, Paris 1864.

946 Wolowski wrote: "The proper authorities assigned to the various interests, the protection of persons and property from the arbitrariness of power, the valuation of labour, open career opportunities for all, the careful control of public opinion introduced everywhere, the transformation into laws of the mature will of the people – this is what the English Revolution aimed at; it was the basis of true greatness, based on the free initiative and free activity of the citizens." (L. Wolowski *Mazarin. Fragment d'une histoire des relations commerciales entre la France et l'Angleterre. Lu dans la séance publique annuelle des cinq académies le 14 aout 1867*, Paris 1867, pp. 19–20).

947 "Journal Officiel de la République Française", no. 25, 26.01.1874, p. 766.

948 L. Wolowski *Allocution prononcée le 19 juillet 1867, à la première séance publique de la Société de Statistique de Paris*, Paris 1867. A similar description of the tasks of statistics and its relationship to political economy is also included in Wolowski's earlier work from twenty years before, *Études d'économie politique et de statistique* (pp. 397–417).

data – both in academic studies and in public speeches. Unfortunately, he lacked the tools to take a more critical approach to the content he presented. He also often failed to cite the sources. Interestingly, Thiers also used statistics regularly – their parliamentary disputes sometimes resembled a data duel, from which they drew completely contradictory conclusions.

Wolowski's "historical method" today also seems at least questionable. For it is evident that the Pole did not attempt to study the past to draw conclusions about contemporary problems based on this research. Moreover, he was not competent to do so, and the historical fragments of his works are largely a compilation of several French historians, above all Cousin. Incidentally, the peculiar philosophy of history contained therein, according to which the history of France and Europe was a time of gradual, uneven struggle for individual freedom (political, social, and economic) with a culmination and end point in 1789, is very reminiscent of Guizot's philosophy of history[949]. The key difference was that, for Guizot, history ended with the July Monarchy, which most perfectly embodied the principles of 1789 in combination with the required order. This is why Guizot, an Orléanist, never came to terms with democracy. Wolowski, also an Orléanist, looked at the achievements of 1789 in a similar way, but did not link them definitively and inextricably to the monarchy of Louis-Philippe. In turn, history in his works served primarily to confirm the theses already put forward[950]. If Wolowski looked to the

---

949 Guizot believed that up to the late 10th century, Europe was an arena of a clash between the Roman tradition of state and law and the tradition of freedom and independence of the barbarians. This was accompanied by a conflict between proponents of theocracy and concepts of the separation of state and Church. From these conflicts, feudalism emerged in the 10th and 11th centuries. In the Middle Ages, two processes prevailed: the creation of a modern state and centralised administration – through royal activity – and (here, in particular, the similarity with Wolowski), the gradual release of human energies on the basis of freedom and equality. In the latter, the bourgeoisie was to play a key role. The French Revolution was the moment of its ultimate triumph. In a way, for Guizot, history ended precisely in 1789, and the most perfect embodiment of the principles of liberty, equality, and order (on which that end was based) was to be the Orléans Monarchy. Guizot's most important works containing this vision of history include:
- *Histoire générale de la civilisation en Europe*, Paris 1828;
- *Histoire de la civilisation en France*, Paris 1830;
- *L'Histoire de France: depuis les temps les plus reculés jusqu'en 1789. Racontée à mes petits-enfants*, vol. I-V, Paris 1870–1875;
- *Mémoires pour servir à l'histoire de mon temps*, vol. I-VIII, Paris 1858–1867.

950 Wolowski formulated his views on money, its stability, and its role in the economy largely in the 1840s, so they clearly predated the publication of his study of Copernicus or Nicolas Oresme. The same was true of free trade, of which the Pole had been an advocate since the beginning of his economic career, or of the trade treaty

past, it was mainly to find support in it for contemporary discussions on liberalism, freedom of trade, the nature of money, the role played by banks (including a possible central bank). Inevitably, by appropriately selecting the periods, phenomena and events described – he found them. He therefore followed a model of behaviour known from his travels – there, too, theory preceded practice, while observations from his trips served mainly to confirm earlier ideas.

One more element clearly distinguished Louis Wolowski from the German historical school. If the latter assumed, as Wiktor Werner writes, that "human activities represent an inseparable unity and cannot be divided into economic, religious, artistic, etc.', they instead express "the specificity of a supra-individual Being: Spirit, Nation [...]"[951], in Wolowski's case, this unity is hardly visible, and the behaviour of individuals is in fact in all cases quite similar[952]. The descriptions of the German, British, Polish, or French states present different legal and political systems, but with individuals acting comparably.

It is noteworthy that, with such a view, the difference between Wolowski and the classical school, so clearly emphasised by him, ultimately became relatively minor. Like Ricardo, Say, Rossi or Bastiat, Wolowski took a completely free and rational individual as the basis of his reasoning. Like them, he assumed that the fundamental laws of economics – for example, the law formulated by Oresme and Copernicus of better money being displaced by worse money – apply regardless of time and system. The same assumption applied to supply and demand, the impact of freedom of trade on domestic industry, etc. His historical method only served to confirm these theses. As a result, Wolowski had to come to very similar if not the same conclusions as the classics – that is, a vision of an economy based on the free market and competition.

One more remark about Wolowski's method, or rather its invariability: he used a similar type of reasoning at the beginning of his economic career and at its end alike. Meanwhile, in the 1870s, it already seemed anachronistic. By then, Léon Walras had developed his mathematical theory of general equilibrium and, more broadly, was introducing mathematical methods into economics. However, Wolowski rejected his theory a priori, without even attempting to fully understand

---

with Great Britain, which he had defended since its conclusion in 1860, seven years before the publication of *Mazarin.*

951 W. Werner *Historyczność kultury. W poszukiwaniu myślowego fundamentu współczesnej historiografii,* Poznań 2009, p. 146.

952 Only Russia was an exception in Wolowski's concepts. The Pole emphasised the negative impact of history and the Orthodox Church. Even here, however, he was convinced that, once liberal reforms had been carried out, "freedom would lead through work to enlightenment and prosperity" (Discussion on the enfranchisement of peasants in Russia, *Société d'économie politique* [in:] "Journal des Economistes...", vol. XXXVIII, April – June 1863, p. 473).

it. At a meeting of the Academy of Moral and Political Sciences, he simply stated that "in attempting to transform political economy into an exact science, Mr L. Walras had failed to recognise its proper nature: political economy is a moral science, its starting point and goal is man."[953]

2. Capital, Labour, Free market

In most of the key economic and political discussions, Wolowski acted jointly with disciples of Say and Ricardo. They all took a similar view of competition and the free market in the economy and shared an opinion on the role of the entrepreneur. Like Ricardo, Wolowski accepted the labour theory of value: the goods produced by the economy were, according to Wolowski, always the result of a combination of property, capital, and labour[954]. He wrote of an interconnected system in which the labourer, the farmer who harvests the grain, the trader and middleman who stores and delivers that grain and other goods, the inventor who creates the tools and the entrepreneur who efficiently manages the business, all form a coherent whole[955]. All the elements of this whole had to be completely free and liberated. The greatest merit of the French Revolution, according to Wolowski, was that it brought freedom to employers and workers alike by abolishing state privileges and guild restrictions. In 1844, Wolowski spoke at the Conservatoire des Arts et Métiers: "Freedom is the strongest lever for the growth of production; the freedom of industry, supplemented by the freedom to operate the land, has led to a doubling of national income in less than half a century. It has enabled us to survive the conflict of the giants with the whole of Europe, it has made possible the sacrifices of the times of the Republic, the wars of the Empire, the repayment of war reparations for the Restoration – without depleting our resources. On the contrary, adding something year by year to the national wealth." He went on to add that attempting to restrict the freedom of an entrepreneur or employee would be akin to turning a river back with a stick. He also made it very clear that freedom could only function within an efficient rule of law. Therefore, it also required a limited but efficient repressive apparatus[956].

---

953 *Académie des Sciences Morales et Politiques. Séance du 16 aout 1873*, „Journal Officiel de la République Française ", nr 242, 04.09.1873, p. 5722.

954 L. Wolowski *Notions générales d'économie politique. Conférences populaires faites à l'Asile Impérial de Vincennes sous le patronage de S. M. L'Impératrice*, Paris 1868, p. 39; L. Wolowski *La Liquidation sociale*, "Journal des Economistes... ", ser. III, vol. XVIII, April– June 1870, pp. 116–117.

955 L. Wolowski *La Liquidation sociale...*, p. 117.

956 L. Wolowski *Cours de législation industrielle. Cinquième année 1843–1844. Première leçon (22 novembre 1843). Des fraudes commerciales*, Paris 1843, pp. 13–14.

Interestingly, Wolowski seemed at times to recognise the problem of the worker's freedom posed by socialists. On the sidelines of a discussion on credit, he wrote in 1848: "What kind of freedom will it be for the workers if they exchange guild bondage for the bondage of hunger?". In his opinion, the answer to the question was... austerity. "It is frugality that guarantees workers real freedom; it is frugality that allows them to discuss the terms of their contracts, allowing them to wait; it is frugality that allows them to obtain the tools of the trade and rise to the level of entrepreneurs."[957] Apparently Wolowski had little knowledge of the realities of life of Parisian workers[958].

He acknowledged that one of the key tasks of modern societies was to improve the lot of the working classes. He reiterated on several occasions that this had been largely achieved following the events of 1789. At the same time, he accepted that there was still much to be done. Poverty, he wrote in 1844, was to disappear in its entirety with the growth of education and knowledge in the working class[959]. That is why he emphasised then and later the importance of education and schooling of workers' children. In the 1840s, when the memory of the Luddites was still clear in France, Wolowski described the beneficial effects of machines. By guaranteeing an increase in production, in the long run they were to provide workers with an increase in wages and a reduced cost of living.

Part of the fight against poverty was also to give workers the right to form coalitions and defend their own wages.

Markiewicz is therefore right in emphasising that, unlike some of his economist friends, Wolowski did not believe in the natural class division of society or in the salutary economic effects of class differences[960]. In the end, however, this made

---

957 L. Wolowski *De l'organisation du Crédit Foncier. Troisième partie. Les caisses d'épargne et le crédit foncier*, "Revue de législation et de jurisprudence", vol. 3, IX-XII 1848, p. 247.

958 At the time, a worker earned on average 3.8 francs a day in Paris, a woman about 1.6 francs (A. Cochin, *Paris, sa population, son industrie. Mémoire lu à l'Académie des Sciences Morales et Politiques.Les 18 et 25 juin 1864*, Paris 1864, p. 46). If we add children, possible illnesses, periods without work, no long-term austerity was possible. Wolowski also received letters from workers describing the living conditions of the poorer classes – for example, a poignant complaint from a certain Antoine Auguste, preserved in the National Archives in Cracow, about working beyond his strength, and living conditions that were slowly destroying his body. (Archiwum Państwowe w Krakowie- ref. AKPot 3204).

959 L. Wolowski *Cours de législation industrielle. Sixième année...*, p. 6.

960 Louis Girard cites Dunoyer, who stressed the usefulness of the "social hell" and Rossi, for whom clear class divisions were a necessary part of progress, although at the same time they were to disappear with it (L. Girard *Les libéraux français...*, pp. 142–143).

little difference. After all, Wolowski shared the optimism of a whole liberal generation of economists, firmly believing that progress and the free market would bring salvation for all. Thus, as a panacea for the misery of the working classes, in 1840 he cited good legislation, morality, austerity, the ability to anticipate and cooperate with others and with machines[961]. He also believed in the natural solidarity between employers and workers. In 1868 he even said to the latter: "Love one another, for, owners and workers, you are all in solidarity as members of the great social family. This is not an illusion; it is a reality."[962] We can assume that his audience, the patients of the Asile Impérial de Vincennes – the imperial hospital for workers who had suffered accidents at work – did not entirely believe him...

Of course, according to the Polish economist, this harmony of interests was to be ensured by the free market. For throughout his political and economic career, Wolowski was a firm supporter of liberal economic freedom and full competition. In 1839, he wrote: "[Competition] is a uniquely fruitful battle, during which the industry, constantly pushed forward by mutual rivalry, tries to win the public's approval through good product quality and low price."[963] This involved a rejection of any form of statism. Wolowski also disagreed with any direct state aid to specific industries, not to mention specific entrepreneurs. As a rule, the free market was a sufficient panacea for emerging ills[964].

This did not mean, however, that Wolowski was an advocate of the state acting as a night watchman, the total withdrawal of government from the economy. French economists of the mid-19th century saw differently the role of the state in the economy. Gustave de Molinari wrote in 1849 that the principles of competition and the free market should also apply in the fields of justice and security[965]. Bastiat, in turn, argued that the activities of the state should include: "(a)

---

961 L. Wolowski *Cours de législation industrielle. Introduction...*, p. 23.

962 L. Wolowski *Notions générales d'économie politique...*, p. 68.

963 L. Wolowski *La concurrence et la coalition,* "Revue de législation et de jurisprudence", vol. X, IV-IX.1839, p. 369. In the same text, Wolowski pointed out that it was one thing to have fair competition, another to have unfair competition aimed solely at destroying other producers, not at benefiting the consumer. Although he did not use the word, he clearly meant dumping.

964 This was, for example, according to Wolowski, the case with the increase in prices for raw materials and unprocessed products in the 1870s (*Académie des Sciences Morales et Politiques, Séance du samedi 02 janvier 1875,* "Journal Officiel de la République Fraçaise", no. 6, 07.01.1875, p. 128).

965 G. de Molinari *Cours d'économie politique*, vol. II, Paris 1863], pp. 515–521. Murray Rothbard referred to Molinari in this connection as "the first anarcho-capitalist" (M. Rothbard Gustave de Molinari – the first anarcho-capitalist, https://mises.pl/storage/files/articles/2020/11/rothbard-gustave-de-molinari-pierwszy-anarchokapitalista.pdf, (retrieved 27.06.2023).

watching over public security, (b) managing common goods [rivers, forests, roads, etc.], (c) collecting contributions."[966] With the saint-simonist background, Chevalier saw the role of government much more broadly: he attributed to it a pivotal role in the construction of the credit system and road and rail infrastructure[967]. As Markiewicz notes, Wolowski positioned himself somewhere in the middle[968]. In his case, the state was of course responsible for the external and internal security of its citizens, including the administration of justice. However, it also had certain economic tasks. He described them briefly in 1848. These concerned the organisation of the credit system, the insurance system, the organisation of the great public works and, above all, education[969]. The importance of the state for the credit system was soon to become apparent to him when he became head of the Crédit Foncier. When writing about insurance, Wolowski had in mind the construction of the legal framework and supervision of the social insurance system. The state was not to own the insurance companies but was to create the appropriate legal conditions for their establishment and operation. Public works mainly involved transport and infrastructure: roads, canals, ports, railways. In the latter case, the state's task was not only to lay out the railway lines, but also to provide support, for example through appropriate guarantees, authorisations for banks, companies responsible for construction, and finally through a proper concession policy.

3. Free trade

All the mentioned economists were almost unanimous in one of the longest disputes shaking French public opinion and the French economy, that is, the dispute over free trade. Louis-Philippe's France pursued a protectionist trade policy, inherited from the House of Bourbon. The government tried to loosen this customs corset between 1832 and 1836. In the latter case, moreover, it succeeded in reducing some of the duties on certain cloths, haberdashery, parts of linen products and horses, among others. In 1841, there was a reduction in duties on steam engines and machine spare parts. However, all were clearly limited in nature, and all encountered significant parliamentary opposition with links to domestic manufacturers. The Guizot government later attempted to bring about a change in customs policy in the 1840s through a series of bilateral agreements with other countries, starting with a treaty with Belgium in 1842. However, the agreement was signed for only

---

966 F. Bastiat *Harmonie ekonomiczne,*[in:] *Dzieła* zebrane, vol. II, Warszawa 2009, p. 464.

967 M. Chevalier *Cours d'économie politique fait au Collège de France: Année 1841–42*, Paris 1842.

968 P. Markiewicz *Louis Wolowski...*, p. 264.

969 L. Wolowski *Études d'économie politique et de statistique...*, p. 327.

four years: opposition on both sides of the border virtually ruled out its extension and the idea of similar agreements in the future[970].

In response to pressure from the protectionist lobby, the Free Trade Association was established in 1846. Frédéric Bastiat was its main founder and driving force. The *Declaration of Principles of the Association*, which he wrote down, stated that trade (exchange) was a natural right just like property. Depriving individuals of freedom of trade was therefore theft and a violation of elementary justice. Free trade was also the result of God's will: for God endowed people with different climates, with resources, so that they could exchange the results of their labour. According to Bastiat, free trade was a condition for prosperity and development and an essential binder that united nations and thus prevented wars. The objective of the Free Trade Association, on the other hand, was the complete abolition of protectionism[971]. A circle of liberal economists quickly emerged around Bastiat, accompanied by producers of wine, industrial machinery, and silk products. Members of the Society included Dunoyer, Blanqui, Rossi, Garnier, Faucher and Wolowski. However, as Olivier Todd writes, this group, further united under the Society for Political Economy, had very little influence on public opinion. They could count on the support of the "Journal des Débats" but compared to the supporters of protectionism, their political clout was small[972].

The Association therefore organised a series of open meetings at which its members defended trade freedom. One of these was led by Wolowski, who described economic protectionism as industrial chauvinism. He called for the liberation of all European peoples[973]. In contrast, in a text from 1847, he emphasised the importance of the community created by international trade and its peaceful impact. For "Freedom of trade is based on a principle, the healthy observance which makes it possible to eliminate the causes of quarrels and conflicts between nations. [...] political economy has shown [...] that peoples are in solidarity both in successes and in failures."[974] He referred again to Henry IV, Turgot, and the Anglo-Portuguese Methuen treaties. Finally, he emphasised that free trade promoted more efficient,

---

970 J. Bordas *Chapt. III Du gouvernement de Juillet au début du Second Empire, 1830–1860,* [in:] *Les directeurs généraux des douanes, l'administration et la politique douanière, 1801–1939,* Vincennes, 2004, http://books.openedition.org/igpde/13947 (retrieved 14.06.2023).

971 F. Bastiat, duc d'Harcourt, *Déclaration de principes (1846),* "Le Libre-échange: journal du travail agricole, industriel et commercial ", no. 22, 25.04.1847, p. 169.

972 O. Todd *L'Identité économique de la France. Libre-échange et protectionnisme (1814–1851),* Paris 2008, pp. 333–344.

973 O. Todd *L'Identité économique de la France...,* p. 346.

974 L. Wolowski *De la liberté commerciale,* [in:] L. Wolowski *Études d'économie politique et de statistique,* Paris 1848, p. 240.

better matched, and more competitive production and labour. This meant that it protected the interests of workers much better than a protectionist system[975].

Wolowski also referred to another extremely important argument during this period. He stressed that in the face of a possible bad harvest, free trade in cereals was the country's surest protection against famine, which also made it possible to avoid the danger of speculation.[976] He therefore referred to the concepts of customs protection of the domestic agricultural market as "inverted servitude", in which the interests of consumers, i.e. the vast majority of French people, were subordinated to those of a small group of agricultural producers[977].

The opponents of trade liberalisation were quite busy during this period, too. They came together in the Association pour la Défense du Travail National (Association for the Protection of National Labour), which brought together many French entrepreneurs and industrialists. The association founded by Bastiat was much smaller, poorer, and less influential than the protectionists. It was also beset by internal conflicts, with Wolowski being a party in one of them. In April 1847, he and Faucher left the board of the Association. They gave their reasons for this decision in a letter published by "Le Libre Echange", a journal of free trade advocates. In it, they wrote that it was one thing to have a duty as a tool to defend a section of producers, and another to have a duty understood as part of fiscal policy and revenue to the treasury. Meanwhile, when advocating the abolition of tariffs altogether, the Association gave an impression that it was simultaneously launching a campaign against taxes in general. According to Wolowski and Faucher, there was no need to abolish duties on exotic products that were not manufactured in France at all. They were also concerned that the tax burden on products made in France should be more or less like that on foreign products.[978] However, Wolowski did not abandon the Association and did not give up defending free trade.

975 L. Wolowski *De la liberté commerciale...*, pp. 285–315.

976 L. Wolowski *Lettres à M. De Lamartine sur le commerce des grains. Deuxième lettre, Paris le 4 octobre 1846,* [in:] L. Wolowski *La Liberté commerciale et les résultats du traité de commerce de 1860,* Paris 1869, pp. 132–137.

977 *Société centrale de l'Agriculture*, „Journal des Economistes..." series III, vol. I, January–March 1866, p. 494.

978 "Le Libre-Echange. Journal du Travail Agricole, Industriel et Commercial", no. 23, 02.05.1847. The split among the supporters of free trade was immediately noticed by their opponents. Their organ, "Moniteur Industriel. Journal de la défense du travail national" described with evident satisfaction "the schism among the opponents." The language was also distinctive in this case – Bastiat, Chevalier, Say and Wolowski were treated like religious fanatics, detached from reality (no. 1131, 25.04.1847). Wolowski's response – "Moniteur Industriel. Journal de la défense du travail national", no. 1132, 29.04.1847.

Markiewicz argues that in the early days of the Second Republic, the Pole held out hope for the democratic triumph of free trade. Unfortunately, this thesis remains unproven. If this was the case, it would demonstrate a certain naivety on the part of Wolowski: the chances of a radical reduction of customs duties amid a massive economic crisis were rather slim. Other issues soon began to occupy the French political and economic elite. Wolowski, as already mentioned, gradually shifted towards the conservatives, many of them being supporters of protectionism. Meanwhile, the Free Trade Association was dying out. In 1848, the last issue of "Le Libre Echange" was published; the organisation itself had virtually ceased to function. In 1850, its central force, Bastiat, passed away. Thiers, a key player in the Assembly, unequivocally sided with the protectionists. This ultimately doomed the already slender chances of change.

Change came, however, only ten years later; it was not brought by the democratic Second Republic, but by the autocratic Second Empire.

Louis Napoleon Bonaparte probably encountered the Manchester School and Richard Cobden during his stay in Britain between 1846 and 1848. Later, between 1853 and 1856, his imperial decrees gradually reduced the duties on coal, iron, steel, industrial machinery, and raw wool. However, his attempt at a major reform of the customs system in the Legislative Body in 1856 sparked such violent protest that the project was abandoned[979]. Napoleon III was still contemplating reforms of the customs policy. The opportunity came when, in 1859, Cobden arrived in Paris with a proposal for a trade agreement[980]. Once the Emperor had given the green light, the negotiations moved very quickly. It was no coincidence that France was represented by a strong advocate of free trade, a close associate and adviser of Napoleon III, Chevalier, also an acquaintance of Wolowski. The agreement was signed on 22 January 1860. "The economic coup d'état", as the Chevalier-Cobden treaty was later referred to, was written for ten years. It completely abolished tariffs on food and raw materials on the French side, tariffs on industrial products not exceeding 30%. Similar treaties were subsequently signed by France with Belgium (1861), the German Customs Union (1862), Italy (1863), Switzerland (1864), followed by Sweden and Norway, Bremen, Hamburg and Lübeck, Mecklenburg, the Netherlands (1865), Portugal and Austria (1866) and the Papal States (1867).[981]

---

979 G. Unger *Histoire du Second Empire,* Paris 2018, pp. 167–168.

980 Alfred A. Iliasu points out that the key factor influencing France's attitude was not Napoleon III's liking or dislike of the idea of free trade, but the international situation, above all the desire to reach an agreement with Great Britain in the context of Italian affairs (A.A. Iliasu *The Cobden-Chevalier Commercial Treaty of 1860,* "The Historical Journal", vol. 14, no. 1, 1971).

981 W. Bruyère-Ostells *Napoléon III et le second Empire,* Paris 2004, pp. 137–138, J. Walch *Michel Chevalier. Economiste, Saint-Simonien 1806–1879,* Paris 1975, pp. 73–75.

Wolowski had no influence on the treaty and was probably also unaware of the negotiations until the very end. He accepted it with obvious satisfaction. He subsequently defended its provisions on a number of occasions. Indeed, the treaty was regularly attacked by protectionist circles and Britain's numerous opponents in France. As early as in 1860, in a series of lectures at the Academy of Moral and Political Sciences, he sought to demonstrate that historically all attempts to open France's trade had paid off[982]. When, in 1868 and 1869, the opposition, led by Thiers, attacked the treaty in the Legislative Body[983], Wolowski responded in 1869 with a publication on the issue of the treaty and free trade. In it, he stressed first and foremost that the workers in the industries genuinely interested in special customs protection were a distinct minority in France – while most French people were content to keep customs duties as low as possible. He therefore completely rejected the worker protection argument used by Thiers. This was also because, he pointed out, the work truly in the interests of the nation was that which made the best use of workers' abilities. The protectionists, on the other hand, demanded the protection of the weakest branches of French industry, where the labour input was disproportionate to the results achieved. Wolowski also returned to the thesis of freedom of exchange as one of the key human freedoms, and to the argument of its peaceful internationalism[984].

Wolowski's voice meant much less than Thiers's, but the key factor was the attitude of Napoleon III, who did not intend to abandon the treaty. Another thing is that, with a conflict with Prussia slowly approaching, this would probably have been unwise.

Inevitably, however, the issue returned after the collapse of the Second Empire, in early 1872. Not only because of the change of power in France, but also because the treaty had to (or not) be extended. This time, Wolowski took part in the debate as a deputy. Again, using figures, he stressed that everyone, above all farmers, would lose from an increase in tariffs, while only a few would gain. He also contradicted Thiers, stating explicitly that throughout the treaty period the French trade balance with Britain had been positive. In general, he regarded the

---

982 L. Wolowski *Les Droits de douanes et les anciens traits de commerce entre la France et l'Angleterre*, "Séances et travaux de l'Académie des Sciences Morales et Politiques", vol. II–IV (LII–LIV), Paris 1860 & vol. VIII (LVIII), Paris 1861.

983 Thiers gave a long parliamentary speech on 13 May 1868 in which he tried to prove that since 1860 French imports had grown much faster than exports, agriculture was being ruined, together with the textile and heavy industries. "I ask only two things: free us from trade treaties, give us back our freedom so that we can decide for ourselves the fate of the country by approving tariffs." ("Journal des Débats Politiques et Littéraires", 14.05.1868).

984 L. Wolowski *La Liberté commerciale et les résultats du traité de commerce de 1860...*, pp. 1–60.

thought of leaving the treaties as an unserious attempt to achieve a kind of platonic satisfaction that could only worsen relations with Britain.

In this case, Wolowski was up against the Thiers government, keen to raise some of the tariff barriers, primarily on raw materials. The head of government, however, encountered considerable opposition, with the Duke of Decazes in the lead. Eventually, threatening to resign, he pushed through his project. Only that he was still facing new negotiations with Britain. Negotiations which, according to Jean Bordas, ultimately yielded little: the new agreements signed with Britain in November 1872 and early 1873 changed little, and in some provisions were even less favourable to France[985]. A fundamental change in trade relations between France and Britain did not occur until 1882.

A question must be asked: who was right? Was it the supporters of free trade and defenders of the 1860 Treaty, including Wolowski, or the protectionists and opponents of the Treaty led by Thiers? Historians do not have a clear-cut answer, although contemporary historiography seems to prove that the pros of the treaty rather outweighed the cons. In a text devoted solely to the consequences of the treaty, Gabrielle Cadier assesses that, on balance, the treaty proved more profitable for Paris than for London: exports from France to England grew markedly faster than imports during the period of the treaty. In her view, in the 1860s the treaty also contributed to a reduction in prices for basic goods on the Seine with fixed or higher wages.[986] The unequivocal right of Napoleon III (and therefore of free trade) is conceded by Walter Bruyère-Ostells[987]. Pierre Milza mentions an "act of political courage" to improve the lot of the working classes and modernise the French economy[988]. Eric Anceau, assesses the economic turnaround of 1860 as "undoubtedly profitable in a long term", although difficult for contemporaries to assess clearly[989]. Frédéric Barbier and Gérard Unger are more circumspect, pointing in turn to the relatively poor economic growth of the 1860s and the persistent underdevelopment against English industry[990]. Dominique Barjot, on the other hand, mentions in general terms the failure of the economic policy initiated in 1860 – but not due to the treaty itself, but to the global conjuncture (the US Civil War) and the conservative budgetary policies of the successive governments[991].

---

985 J. Bordas, Chapt. *V. La Troisième République, 1871–1914,*[in:] *Les directeurs généraux des douanes…*, http://books.openedition.org/igpde/13957 (retrieved 15.06.2023)

986 G. Cadier *Les Conséquences du traité de 1860 sur les échanges franco-britanniques*, [in:] F. Crouzet (dir.) *Le négoce international, XIII – XX siècle*, Paris 1989, pp. 205–212.

987 W. Bruyère-Ostells *Napoléon III…*, p. 138.

988 P. Milza *Napoléon III…*, p. 456.

989 E. Anceau *Napoléon III*, Paris 2012, pp. 380–381.

990 F. Barbier *Libre-échange* [in:] J. Tulard (dir.) *Dictionnaire du Second Empire*, Paris 1995, pp. 733–738 ; G. Unger *Histoire du Second Empire…*, pp. 169–170.

991 D. Barjot *Histoire économique de la France…*, p. 173.

4. Banque de France's monopoly on issuance

Louis Wolowski also participated in two important economic discussions in France, which significantly divided the community of economists. The first concerned the French banking system and the position of the Banque de France. The other one – the issue of silver-gold parity[992].

A reminder: the Banque de France had existed since 1800. The bank was private, at the same time closely linked to Napoleonic power since the very beginning. In 1803, it obtained a monopoly on the issue of banknotes in Paris. In 1806, the emperor changed the bank's statutes; from then on, its administrators were appointed by the sovereign[993]. The bank gradually opened branches in more French cities with a local monopoly of issue. In 1848, faced with a financial panic, the government ordered the merger of all branches with the head office. In practice, this meant that the Banque de France's issuing monopoly was extended to the whole of France. In 1857, the bank's privilege was prolonged for forty more years[994].

In the same year, as the Banque de France's issuing monopoly was extended, a heated debate broke out among French economists between opponents of the monopoly, supporters of the banks' freedom and defenders of the privileged position of the Banque de France. Among the former, Michel Chevalier undoubtedly played a key role. He was among Napoleon III's circle of important (and listened to) advisers. Moreover, and significantly, Chevalier was linked to the Pereires. The brothers and their banking group, built around the Crédit Mobilier, competed fiercely with the "old banking", including the Banque de France. Meanwhile, Chevalier belonged to the governing bodies of the Crédit Mobilier and several of its subsidiaries[995]. However, let me make it clear that Chevalier's views had taken

---

992 More about Wolowski's voice in these two debates in Alain Raybaut's *Money and banking in the French Liberal School: Wolowski and the debates on banking regulation in the 1860s.*(https://shs.hal.science/halshs-03504232/document, (retrieved 26.06.2023).

993 The first shareholders of the Banque de France included the First Consul Napoleon Bonaparte, his brothers Joseph and Jérôme and Hortense de Beauharnais. The bank's founders Frédéric Perregaux and Jean-Barthélemy Le Couteulx were among the earliest supporters of the 1799 coup d'état, and it is possible that they were funding Bonaparte at the time. Notably, the bank's authorities were formally independent of the state, and Bonaparte himself strongly emphasised their autonomy (A. Plessis *La Banque de France, une des grandes institutions napoléoniennes*, "Revue du Souvenir Napoléonien", no. 430, 2000, pp. 35–43).

994 J.P. Domin *La question du monopole d'émission de la monnaie: Le débat banque centrale contre banque libre chez les économistes français (1860–1875*), "Revue européenne des sciences sociales", vol. XLV, no. 137, 2007, pp. 186–187.

995 A. Plessis *La politique de la Banque de France de 1851 à1870*, Genève 1985, p. 54.

shape in part beforehand and were supported by a vast majority of economists not connected with banking in any way.

Chevalier treated banking, including the issuing of banknotes, as a regular economic activity, and therefore equally subject to the rules of competition and the free market. Banks and bankers were to act exactly like all other entrepreneurs. This was linked to another fundamental statement: Chevalier saw money as a commodity, a substitute for other commodities as well as operating in the market according to its basic principles. From the saint-simonist tradition still came his belief in credit and its salutary importance for the economy, a belief shared with the Pereire brothers, other former saint-simonists. That is why, during the Senate debate on the Banque de France in 1864, Chevalier explicitly demanded that the bank makes credit more accessible by lowering the interest rates. He criticised the bank's issuing monopoly on historical grounds (Napoleon I did not want it). He completely rejected the claim that the issue of banknotes was a prerogative of the state (Chevalier clearly distinguished between banknotes, treated as bank securities, and paper money), leaving it entirely to the banks. According to him, competition between banks was to lead to cheaper and more easily accessible credit. On the other hand, Chevalier was clearly concerned about the dependence of a bank with a monopoly on banknote issuance on the state. In his view, it could be forced into various "courtesies" towards the state, like large loans on preferential terms, precisely because of the privileges it held[996]. Similarly, Courcelle-Seneuil wrote a little earlier: "If, by its mere issue, a banknote could hold more or less value than the sum of the metal money it expresses, thus leading to a breach of contract, the motives that grant the government the supervision and even the monopoly of money manufacture would have it also grant it the supervision or monopoly of banknote issue. Otherwise – no." "And how could a banknote," the economist further asked rhetorically, "when exchanged for money by the bearer, be worth more or less than the sum of money it expresses?"[997]. Alongside him, Gustave de Puynode argued that "Full freedom of banknote issue strengthens banking activity most, allows it to reach the industrial workshop; gives banks the most capital and [...] reduces the use of coins to the greatest extent".[998] Garnier, Passy, Dunoyer,

---

996 M. Chevalier *Rapport de M. Michel Chevalier sur l'ouvrage de M. Horn, intitulé:" La liberté des banques"*, "Journal des Economistes...", series III, vol. III, July – September 1866, pp. 350–359.

997 J.-G. Courcelle-Seneuil *Introduction,* [in:] Ch. Coquelin *Le crédit et les banques,* Paris 1859, p. 8. Seneuil wrote critically about the position of the Banque de France back in 1840 in his *Le Crédit et la banque.*

998 G. Du Puynode *De l'indépendance des banques et de la loi qui régit l'émission de leurs billets,* "Journal des Economistes...", series II, vol. XXXVI, October – December 1862, p. 169.

Edouard Horn and Henri Baudrillart were also supporters of the freedom of the banks[999].

In this dispute, Louis Wolowski found himself on the other side of the barricade. He was initially alone among economists, only supported by Léon Say in 1867. He did, however, have the support of some bankers, politicians (e.g., Rouher) and lawyers. He also seems to have been supported by most members (at least those who spoke on the issue) of the Academy of Moral and Political Sciences[1000]. Above all, he could count on the active support of the Banque de France, encouraging journalists, for example, to repeat his arguments[1001].

Wolowski laid them out clearly in his 1864 work *La question des banques* (*The question of banks*). Unlike Chevalier, he did not regard money as a commodity like any other. Indeed, he emphasised that money was at once a tool of exchange and an evaluation of other goods. This in turn, was enough not to treat it as an element of economic activity subject to the ordinary rules of the free market[1002]. For Wolowski, money, including banknotes, was a key, ordering element of the entire state economy. A consequence of this, in turn, was the statement that "The state cannot remain indifferent to the issue of banknotes, functioning like money; for it is not a matter of mere economic activity, but an element of order."[1003] In a letter to Jules Duval, editor-in-chief of the "*Economiste français*" magazine, he wrote that the state had to supervise the circulation of money if it wanted to avoid "Proudhon anarchy"[1004]. The first director of the Crédit Foncier also tried to defend himself against being labelled an opponent of banking freedom by Chevalier and others. He stressed that the freedom of the banks, of which he was a great advocate, did not mean complete freedom to issue banknotes. Banks retained, for example, rightly full freedom of their credit policy. Only, he insisted, the banknote was not a form of credit[1005]. Moreover, Wolowski warned against a situation of inter-bank competition in banknote issuance. This would lead to a mutual undermining of confidence in the paper issued by the competition, to an unhealthy fight for customers, resulting, for example, in too large an issue of successive batches of banknotes. This in turn could have a disastrous effect on the entire economy.[1006].

---

999 A. Plessis *La politique de la Banque de France...*, p. 54.

1000 So says Yves Leclercq in his book *La banque supérieure. La banque de France de 1800 à1914* (Paris 2010, p. 182).

1001 A. Plessis *La politique de la Banque de France...*, p. 56.

1002 L. Wolowski *La question des banques*, Paris 1864, p. 6.

1003 L. Wolowski *La question des banques...*, p. 12.

1004 L. Wolowski *Lettres à M. Jules Duval, directeur de l'Economiste français*, [in:] L. Wolowski *La Banque d'Angleterre et les banques d'Ecosse*, Paris 1867, p. 361

1005 L. Wolowski *La question des banques...*, p. 30.

1006 L. Wolowski *La question des banques...*, p. 132.

The polemic between Wolowski and Chevalier also found its way into the press, while taking on a relatively strident tone. In a letter to Wolowski, subsequently published by the latter in the collection *La Banque d'Angleterre et les banques d' Ecosse*, the Frenchman was clearly ironic about the alleged recognition of the Pole's views in England. Above all, however, he stressed once again that a bank note, a bank security, was not money but a form of credit, "a promise made by a bank of greater or lesser repute and trust that it will pay the person holding [the note], or, as it is said, the bearer, the proper sum in gold or silver."[1007] In another text, published on 22 June 1864 in the "Journal des Débats Politiques et Littéraires", Chevalier placed Wolowski in one line with the enemies of liberty. He also accused him of misrepresenting other people's views. In response, Wolowski accused Chevalier of confusing a banknote with a bill of exchange. He stressed once again that the banknote was not a substitute for the coin but had a very similar role in practice. It was therefore extremely important to the financial system as a whole and therefore the state, in this case through the Banque de France, had to control its issue[1008]. When, in turn, he attempted to respond to the text of the emperor's adviser in the "Journal des Débats", his opponent was said to have disagreed. The text, containing Wolowski's now-familiar claims about the banknote and money and defending himself against accusations of distorting the views of other economists and politicians, was eventually published in "Le Constitutionnel"[1009].

Finally, in 1864, there was a vote in the Senate, won by those in favour of preserving the monopoly of the Banque de France. Chevalier then suggested that a special commission be set up to study the issue. Napoleon III agreed to this idea, but also asked Rouher to head the commission. It was made up of members of the Council for Commerce, Agriculture, and Industry (Conseil Supérieur du Commerce, de l'Agriculture et de l'Industrie), the government's advisory body. The Council heard from dozens of people, almost all European economists, including Louis Wolowski. At the end of the hearings, the Council had to answer the question posed by Rouher: "Should the issuance of fiat money [i.e., banknotes – RD] be entrusted to a single, privileged bank?". The overwhelming majority then answered: yes. This was a key moment: as Jean-Paul Domin writes, although the theoretical debate was still ongoing, it was gradually weakening. Ultimately,

1007 M. Chevalier *Lettre de M. Michel Chevalier, membre de l'Institut, à M. Wolowski, membre de l'Institut, sur la question des banques,* [in:] L. Wolowski *La Banque d'Angleterre et les banques d'Ecosse...*, p. 196.

1008 L. Wolowski *Réponse à la lettre de M. Michel Chevalier, sénateur, membre de l'Institut, sur la question des banques,* [in:] L. Wolowski *La Banque d'Angleterre et les banques d'Ecosse...*, pp. 250–292.

1009 L. Wolowski *Lettre de M. Wolowski au „Journal des Débats" (23 juin 1864),* [in:] L. Wolowski *La Banque d'Angleterre et les banques d'Ecosse...*, pp. 293–300.

however, the issuing monopoly of the Banque de France remained intact until the end of the 20th century. Largely, I should add, thanks to Louis Wolowski.

5. Money, gold and silver

The debate on the monopoly of issue was somewhat surprisingly connected with another extremely important economic discussion on mono- and bimetallism. At issue was the question of whether the French franc should be based on silver and gold (as before), or on gold alone. At first glance, the two issues were not related. Nevertheless, as Claire Silvant observes, "It is characteristic that the economists in favour of banks' freedom of issue (above all Courcelle-Seneuil, Chevalier, Coquelin, J. Garnier, Puynode and Parieu) were also proponents of gold parity."[1010] And the linking element between the two problems was the Banque de France.

However, let me start with a brief reminder of the French monetary system in the 19th century. It was based on the so-called "germinal franc". Under the law of the 17th germinal of the year XI (07 April 1803), the franc became the official currency of France, based on gold and silver[1011]. The system proved to be quite stable. Plessis mentions relatively minor troubles that the "germinal franc" faced: for a time, in the early 19th century, older coins, including pre-revolutionary ones, were still used by inertia by the French. In addition, "gold francs" (coins with gold) were hardly put into circulation. After all, gold was so rare that the ratio of its market price to that of silver was only slightly greater than the official parity of 1:15.5. It therefore paid to keep gold francs at home, using silver francs on a daily basis. In the middle of the century, with the influx of Californian and Australian gold, the situation began to change abruptly, and gold became cheaper. This led to a wave of speculation; it became profitable to exchange gold coins for silver coins, which were then shipped out of France to be sold more expensively. Another change came in the 1870s, with massive silver mining in the Rocky Mountains, among other places, and the German monetary reform, introducing the gold-based mark[1012].

1010 C. Silvant *L'école libérale française et la question du bimétallisme (1860–1885). Enjeux économiques et politiques de la controverse,* "Oeconomia. Hitory, methodology, philosphy", no. 2–3, 2012, online: https://journals.openedition.org/oeconomia/1314 (retrieved 23.06.2023).

1011 The one-franc coins thus contained 4.5 g of pure silver, while the quarter, half, two and five-franc coins also had a proportional admixture of silver. Twenty- and 40-franc coins, on the other hand, contained an admixture of gold (5.2 g and 10.4 g, respectively). The parity of silver and gold was therefore 1 to 15.5 (A. Redish *The Persistence of Bimetallism in Nineteenth-Century France,* "The Economic History Review", vol. 48, no. 4,1995, p. 724).

1012 A. Plessis *Le franc au XIXe siècle,* [in:] *D'or et d'argent: La monnaie en France du Moyen Age à nos jours,* Vincennes, 2005, http://books.openedition.org/igpde/10568 (retrieved 23.06.2023).

Importantly, the central bank (Banque de France) was obliged to issue a parity-compliant quantity of bullion in exchange for money if requested. However, bimetallism allowed the bank to choose gold or silver. Thus, when gold rates were high, the bank was willing to sell off silver – and vice versa. The bank's management also argued that bimetallism allowed it to react more efficiently in the face of fluctuations in gold or silver prices[1013].

The same arguments that caused the Banque de France to advocate bimetallism determined Chevalier and Courcelle-Seneuil to speak out strongly against it. The former wrote in 1866 that "a system of sub-divisible parity leads, as logic inevitably indicates, to consequences that are manifestly incompatible with unshakeable equality and with the security of contracts."[1014] His point was that a person making any obligation through a contract would be inclined to repay it in a coin containing relatively less valuable bullion, at a loss to the other party. The same objection, by the way, applied to the Banque de France: indeed, the bank could repay its own notes with any denomination it chose. With fluctuating gold or silver prices, this meant, according to Chevalier and other mono-metallists, an incalculable loss for customers. The Frenchman further invoked John Locke's opinion that "Two metals such as gold and silver cannot at the same time serve in the same country as a measure of exchange, for the reason that the measure must always be the same, in the same proportion to value." In practice, Locke's theory was to be proved by the monetary system of the United States and France, from which gold-doped coins disappeared at one time and silver-doped coins at another. Chevalier added that, in fact, when two metals make up a monetary system, one of them is the main element according to which parity is arranged.[1015]

Du Puynode took a similar view of the matter. He added that in bimetallic systems, sooner or later, money based on the cheaper bullion simply pushes coins containing the more expensive one[1016]. Puynode, like Chevalier, in the end advocated exclusive gold parity[1017].

The opponents of bimetallism included Molinari, Frédéric Passy, Clément Juglar and Levasseur. Their objections revolved mainly around the rigid gold-silver exchange rate (1:15.5) imposed in 1803. They saw this regulation as an unauthorised state intervention in the market, practically ineffective. They also pointed to the British example.

This time, Wolowski, an advocate of double parity, was no longer as alone among economists as he was in the case of the Banque de France monopoly. Garnier, Paul Cauwès and Henri Cernuschi were among defenders of bimetallism.

1013 C. Silvant *L'école libérale française et la question du bimétallisme....*

1014 M. Chevalier *Cours d'économie politique,* vol. III, *La Monnaie,* Paris 1866, p. 151.

1015 M. Chevalier *Cours d'économie politique...,* pp. 140–146.

1016 G. du Puynode De *la monnaie, du crédit et de l'impôt,* vol. I, Paris 1863, pp. 17–18.

1017 G. du Puynode De *la monnaie...,* pp. 25–26.

The Pole agreed with his opponents to the extent that he also acknowledged that fluctuations in silver and gold prices affected the circulation of different types of coin. Indeed, he wrote, an increase in gold prices resulted in an increased circulation of silver money. Only that this resulted in a compensatory mechanism: the increased circulation of silver coinage increased the demand for silver, so silver prices had to go up.[1018] According to him, of equal importance was the security buffer that bimetallism offered to economies. In 1868 (some twenty years after the discovery of the Californian and Australian gold deposits), he wrote: "What would have happened if gold itself had acted as a universal monetary instrument since the beginning of the century? A tripling of its quantity on the market in twenty years would have led to a profound revolution in prices and in all long-term commitments. The coexistence of silver and gold in the world market has protected it from a massive shock."[1019] Wolowski repeatedly stressed then and later that the interchangeable use of silver and gold simply guaranteed greater stability of the entire monetary system[1020].

He therefore warned against any sudden attempt to move universally to gold parity. In October 1868, addressing a special meeting of the combined academies of the Institut de France, Wolowski spoke of the potential consequences of such a move: a drastic increase in the price of gold, resulting in a deteriorated situation of all those paying any monetary obligations. He calculated that France's public debt would then rise almost overnight by 3 billion francs[1021]. Did double parity favour debtors? This is what its opponents claimed, and Wolowski rejected the thesis. If only because the lender could reserve the coin in which he would be repaid[1022]. In turn, analysing the history of the franc germinal, he stated that it too did not support this allegation[1023].

He also rejected the claim that in the case of bimetallism, the export of the more expensive metal always caused a loss for the state. Nobody in their right mind, said Wolowski, would export the more expensive metal at a loss to themselves if they could use the cheaper one. In addition, in this case the whole state would gain.

1018 L. Wolowski *Quelques notes sur la question monétaire*, Paris 1868, p. 12.

1019 L. Wolowski *Quelques notes...*, p. 34.

1020 *La question monétaire à la société d'économie politique de Paris. Réunion du 1 juin 1867*, [in:] L. Wolowski *La Question monétaire*, Paris 1869, p. XVII.

1021 L. Wolowski *L'Or et l'argent. Mémoire lu le 7 octobre 1868 à la séance des cinq académies de l'Institut impérial de France*, [in:] L. Wolowski *La Question monétaire...*, p. 36; L. Wolowski *L'Or et l'argent. Question monétaire*, "Séances et travaux de l'Académie des Sciences Morales et Politiques", vol. XIX (LXXXIX), Paris 1869, p. 361.

1022 L. Wolowski *L'Or et l'argent. Mémoire...*, pp. 210–211.

1023 L. Wolowski *Les origines de la loi de Germinal*, "Séances et travaux de l'Académie des Sciences Morales et Politiques", vol. XXII (XCII), Paris 1869, p. 424.

Indeed, bi-metallism has proved useful in maintaining trade relations with countries using only one metal or the other. In the event of fluctuations in the exchange rate of one of the metals, it was even possible to make some profits[1024].

As was the case of the Banque de France, the discussion between Chevalier and Wolowski was sometimes very heated. Years later, Jules Simon recalled meetings of the Academy of Moral and Political Sciences from this time: "The Academy still remembers the arguments between Wolowski and Chevalier around the issue of banks. Wolowski preached the doctrine of a single national bank, Chevalier advocated not so much freedom as a plurality of banks of issue. As for the monetary question, Wolowski defended double parity and a fixed relationship between silver and gold while Michel Chevalier recognised only one parity. [...] While Chevalier no longer had his youthful verve or lightness, Wolowski, full of learning and good intentions, was never light or brilliant. At times the office had to intervene between the warring parties to bring peace again."[1025]

The dispute over the role of silver and gold, like the discussion around the monopoly of the Banque de France, also went far beyond the economic milieu. In 1870, the matter came before the Council of Commerce, Agriculture, and Industry. Wolowski appeared before the Council as an expert, repeating already deployed arguments. He also predicted at the time that Germany, in the process of unification, would adopt silver and gold parity, while Great Britain would remain the only European country with exclusive gold parity[1026]. This time, however, he clearly lost. The majority of the Council supported Chevalier and the mono-metallists[1027].

In 1868, Wolowski wrote: "One need not be a prophet to foresee that gold and silver will always be money".[1028] He proved to be a very bad prophet. In part, this was due to the new wave of silver from America flooding into Europe. In part, it was linked to the gigantic war contribution that the French had to pay back in gold. And partly it was because the German Reich, freshly reunified, had adopted – contrary to Wolowski's predictions – gold parity, which threatened France with an influx of demonetised silver. Even at the time, Wolowski claimed that France

---

1024 L. Wolowski *L'Or et l'argent. Mémoire ...*, p. 213.

1025 J. Simon *Notice historique sur la vie et les travaux de M. Michel Chevalier*, 1889, https://www.academie-francaise.fr/notice-historique-sur-la-vie-et-les-travaux-de-m-michel-chevalier (retrieved 26.06.2023). A partial transcript of one of these discussions was included in "Séances et travaux de l'Académie des Sciences Morales et Politiques", vol. VIII (LXXVIII), 1866, pp. 120–137.

1026 Conseil Général du Commerce *Enquête sur la question monétaire. Déposition de M. Wolowski*, Paris 1870.

1027 Conseil Supérieur du Commerce, de l'Agriculture et de l'Industrie *Enquête sur la question monétaire: Dépositions: procès-verbaux des délibérations du Conseil Supérieur; résumé de l'enquête; documents; tables*, Paris 1872, p. 414.

1028 L. Wolowski *L'Or et l'argent. Mémoire ...*, p. 229.

should not be afraid of this flood of silver, adding that a more dangerous threat to France would be a rise in the price of gold, bought up *en masse*[1029]. His voice, rather isolated in the Assembly, could no longer influence the authorities' decision. In 1873, France stopped minting silver coins. The money hitherto in circulation continued to do so but was gradually withdrawn. France thus switched to gold parity. By the end of the 1870s, all European countries had done so. The time of gold had come. However, Wolowski did not see it.

In one respect, throughout the monetary discussion, Wolowski was in full agreement with Chevalier and with all the other French economists. None of them accepted the vision of fully paper money, or even of paper money representing a significant part of the sum in circulation. To all without exception, this concept was associated with the state assignats of the Great Revolution period. Wolowski said of the assignats that they were a reflection of non-existent national assets and led to a complete collapse of credit. They were also a glaring example of state intervention incompatible with free market principles, which was bound to end badly[1030]. The mechanism for the use of paper money, according to Wolowski, was in fact always and everywhere the same. For the temptation to print money was strong. Further, Wolowski wrote, "nothing could limit the natural development of things any longer; as banknotes multiplied, paper displaced coin, bullion exports increased, exchange fell, while the nominal prices of commodities rose."[1031] Inflation, familiar to the French from the revolution, followed suit. He referred those who, through the printing of money, wanted to increase the sum of social wealth, as "modern alchemists who want to magically turn lead into gold again".[1032] This, moreover, was linked to another argument he strongly emphasised. Wolowski

---

1029 "Journal Officiel de la République Française" no. 352, 24. Dec.1873, pp. 8072–8073. On the occasion of a parliamentary discussion on bimetallism, a minor incident involving Wolowski occurred. Speaking afterwards, deputy Alexandre Clapier, who, like Wolowski, belonged to the centre-left, stated that all supporters of bimetallism were speculators and people who personally made money from it. The offended Pole immediately reacted by demanding an explanation. Clapier eventually stated that he had used words that could have been misinterpreted and retracted any accusations against Wolowski ("Journal Officiel de la République Française" no. 352, 24. Dec.1873, p.8074)

1030 *Discussion sur Les Finances de la France sous la Révolution*, "Séances de l'Académie des Sciences Morales et Politiques", vol. I (LI), Paris 1860, p. 77.

1031 L. Wolowski *Les finances de la Russie*, Paris 1864, p. 40; L. Wolowski *L'Influence du change sur le marche monetaire. Extrait de la Revue des Deux Mondes, Livraison du 15 septembre 1868*, Paris 1868, pp. 28–29.

1032 *Enquête sur les principes et les faits généraux qui régissent la circulation monétaire et fiduciaire. Déposition de M. Wolowski, membre de l'Institut. Séances des 21, 28 et 30 novembre 1865*, Paris 1866, p. 19.

repeatedly reminded that money is not yet wealth, it is only a tool for creating wealth.

At the same time, the Pole did not completely reject the concept of paper money: as I have mentioned, he allowed it to be issued by the Banque de France. Wolowski saw the advantages of paper, which facilitated exchange, especially of larger sums. And it functioned exactly like bullion-based coinage. However, he stressed its functioning based on the possibility of exchanging it at any time for coinage.[1033] The bank therefore had to hold adequate collateral in coin, silver, or gold in its safes. Consequently, the issue of paper money had to be strictly controlled and limited. Wolowski used the issuing policy of Great Britain during the Napoleonic Wars as an example. In describing it, however, he ultimately stressed again: "Excessive issuance of paper money always provokes a rise in prices, an appreciation of gold and a depreciation of the exchange rate of the currency."[1034]

While not completely rejecting paper, Louis Wolowski remained clearly distrustful of it. Chevalier similarly stressed that "Whenever the issuance of paper money is excessive, crises arise, which disrupt the interests of business and bring unrest to the states. Governments, on the other hand, first show a complete lack of restraint in the printing of money, then, amazed at the lack of success, attribute the blame to various factors: human meanness, party interests, the evil inherent in the very nature of things."[1035] This was in fact a view shared by all French economists and most politicians. It is clear, moreover, that the French thinking about money was extremely influenced by the negative example of the assignats, and to a somewhat lesser extent by the history of John Law's system. In almost every longer speech about paper as a means of payment, sooner or later the assignats appeared as a negative reference point. Wolowski was no exception[1036].

What kind of economist, then, was Louis Wolowski? In my opinion, methodologically he combined the classical school with the historical school imported from Germany. However, the classical element prevailed in his work. For he did not expect history to explain economic phenomena, but rather to confirm the laws of the free market and free exchange. Michel Lutfalla wrote that Wolowski's political

---

1033 L. Wolowski *Le Change et la circulation*, Paris 1869, p. 243.

1034 L. Wolowski *Un chapitre de l'histoire financière de l'Angleterre. La suspension des payements de la Banque et le bullion-report*, Paris 1865.

1035 M. Chevalier *Cours d'économie politique...*, p. 676.

1036 It is worth recalling at this point that France abandoned gold parity altogether (something that neither Wolowski nor Chevalier could even imagine) in 1936. Although gold returned to France as a yardstick after WWII under the Bretton-Woods system, it was only in international exchange. The gold era thus came to an end with the collapse of Bretton-Woods in the 1970s. (Van Hoang Thi Hong *La thésaurisation de l'or en France depuis 1914: d'une thésaurisation monétaire à une thésaurisation refuge*, "Revue numismatique ", vol. 168, 2012 p. 121).

economy had a clearly moral purpose, which was to solve social problems, above all the question of poverty[1037]. We can partially agree with him: indeed Wolowski, an economist and politician, was not insensitive to the plight of the popular classes, above all the working classes. This is evidenced by his statements on child labour, the restriction of working hours and workers' housing. The trouble was, however, that he hardly knew this workers' world and reality. Moreover, in many respects he remained a classical liberal. He firmly believed that the best tools for improving their lives were the free market, competition, the individual entrepreneur. Like all liberal economists, he combined this belief with a conviction of the fundamental commonality of interests between workers and employers, workers, and the bourgeoisie. Indeed, on many occasions during his lectures, he convinced the workers present of a policy of agreement and cooperation with entrepreneurs. In his view, both the worker and the owner of a factory or capital had a place in the process of production, and thus also in the progress of society as a whole, that was unique to him.

This community of interests also involved entire nations. In this case, its most effective tool was to be free trade. Wolowski was convinced that the liberalisation of exchange between European states would lead to an increase in turnover, increase the efficiency of the exchange (if only through the division of labour), a fall in the price of food and basic raw materials, and thus a fall in prices in general combined with an increase in production. In his view, this was to help above all the poorest and neediest members of society. Wolowski was also no stranger to a kind of free-trade pacifism: the conviction that by tightening relations not only between states, but also between their citizens, trade could lead, if not to the complete disappearance, then at least to a reduction in the number and intensity of inter-state conflicts. This is why he spoke unequivocally in favour of the liberalisation of France's international trade in the 1840s, and why he defended the provisions of the Chevalier-Cobden Treaty of 1860 until his death. At the same time, Wolowski exercised restraint in his demands; he was aware of the fact that the complete abolition of customs barriers was impossible for budgetary reasons and undesirable for economic reasons. This differentiated him from the more radical free market advocates like Bastiat and Molinari.

He differed from them in another extremely important respect: Wolowski was far from postulating a complete withdrawal of the state from the economy, a "night-watchman state" according to Ferdinand Lasalle's famous phrase. Firstly, he assumed that the state should take care of the legal cadres of the free market economy. This, however, was not enough. The professor of the Conservatoire des Arts et Métiers also emphasised the role of the state in the organisation of education, above all vocational education. The state also had to play a decisive role in

1037 M. Lutfalla *Louis Wolowski ou le libéralisme positif*, "Revue d'histoire économique et sociale", no. 54 (2), 1976, p. 175.

the formation of a proper banking and credit system. Unlike Chevalier, he did not believe that credit created capital. Instead, he acknowledged that it facilitated its circulation, linking capital to the sectors of the economy that needed it most and spent it most efficiently. He was, incidentally, one of the few French economists who also kept agriculture in mind. The state, in Wolowski's view, was also responsible for the framework within which workers' savings, self-help and pension funds could function. The state, in cooperation with entrepreneurs, was able to develop programmes to build roads, railways, ports and canals. In fact, Wolowski saw this not only as creating infrastructure for the economy, but also as an important impetus given by the authorities for its development. This is also why Wolowski found his way so well into the Second Empire: he did not share the authoritarian political views of Napoleon III; his economic views largely did.

According to Wolowski's economic thinking, the state had another key task. It had to ensure the stability of the monetary system. According to him, the foundation of a healthy economy was a stable, confidence-inspiring currency. Therefore, the authorities were to indirectly control the issue of money in any form – a billon or a paper banknote. Indirectly, because Wolowski did not intend to place the ability to print money entirely in their hands. His bimetallism was also related to this. According to him, it offered greater possibilities for the Banque de France to operate, and thus provided a greater guarantee of stability for the entire system.

All these considerations led Wolowski throughout his life to criticise the emerging theories of the early socialists – above all Blanc, but also Fourier, Cabet and Leroux. He regarded their ideas as dangerous, incompatible with the most important laws of economics, inconsistent with logic and counter-productive in the long run, leading to economic collapse, thus fuelling social conflict, and threatening civil war. The events of 1848–1849 and 1871 only strengthened his conviction.

Thus, Louis Wolowski was an important figure in France's economic life and the French economic thought of the 1840s, 1850s and 1860s. In the key debates concerning the Banque de France's monopoly of issue and French bimetallism, his voice was undoubtedly among the most important theoretical opinions. However, it must be clearly noted that his economic (and more broadly, economic and political) thought was not particularly original.

This remark applies not only to Wolowski, but to the entire French liberal school of the period. The Pole was undoubtedly one of its most important representatives. However, it lacked figures of the likes of Say, their contemporary J. S. Mill, or the somewhat later Walras. The economic thought of Chevalier, Garnier, Molinari or du Puynode, shaped back in the 1830s and 1840s, brought little new to the theses of Smith, Say, Ricardo or Malthus. As a result, as François Etner and Claire Silvant write, it became less and less able to cope with changing realities over time. France and Germany became industrial states, and with big industry came syndicalism and a new socialism. In France, on the other hand, economic stagnation set in for a long time in the early 1870s. Economists born under Napoleon I and still repeating the theses of Adam Smith could no longer handle these problems.

Chapter IX: The Polish Cause

1. Polish Literary Society

Louis Wolowski's economic, political, and business activity was linked to his Polish activity almost until the end of his life. However, its intensity varied. In 1832, Louis's signature appeared alongside that of his father among the founders of the Polish Literary Society. Unlike his father, however, the then Sorbonne student and young lawyer did not join any émigré committees, nor did he participate in the émigré political disputes of the 1830s. He would not publish any polemical texts in émigré periodicals. Initially, however, he was quite active in the PLS. In 1832, he regularly took the minutes of the Society's meetings. As Lubomir Gadon wrote, the Society's members usually met on Thursdays to discuss articles sent to French or English newspapers, letters and news from home, emigration issues, and to read dissertations. Because of the occasional presence of foreigners, the meetings were held in French, and news of the meetings was printed by the "Kronika Emigracji Polskiej" (Chronicle of Polish Emigration)[1038]. In May, Wolowski presented a text on post-insurrection repression in Poland, in the form of a letter from across the country's border. The long list of Russian crimes and abuses ended with the assurance that Europe would not be fooled by Russian autocracy, a combination of "late Empire Greek cunning and Moscow barbarism".[1039] In 1833, he prepared, probably also for the Society, a text outlining the activities of a Parisian society assisting those accused in court and acquitted who had since lost their jobs[1040]. In the same year he became second deputy editor of the PLS publications. However, as early as in February 1834, in a letter to Plater, he resigned from his post on account of his professional duties. He also assured that he would continue to take an active part in the Society's meetings. However, this was not the case. Wolowski appeared less and less frequently at the PLS during this period. In time, he stopped turning up altogether. Most likely, he did not have the time: between 1834 and 1835, he was working in Dalloz's chancellery, had just created the "Revue Wolowski", and later wrote for "Le Siècle". Plus, he had a family. His formal withdrawal from the Society with his father in December 1843 was therefore only a confirmation of the situation. However, Wolowski returned to the Society after almost twenty-five years: in 1868 he became a "distinguished member of the Society's Council",

1038 L. Gadon *Z życia Polaków we Francyi...*, pp. 12–13.

1039 Biblioteka Polska w Paryżu, ref. BPP 1378, c. 37-40.

1040 Biblioteka Polska w Paryżu, ref. BPP 1360. The library description: "On the Society for the relief of prisoners and the freed, but without life resources" is probably incorrect, as it is rather about the "Society for the relief of acquitted persons who have lost their jobs".

replacing Zamoyski who died that year[1041]. It does not come as a surprise that this honour was bestowed on the professor of the Conservatoire des Arts et Métiers not because of his previous activities for the Society, but because of his emigration merits (to be discussed later) in general. The function was purely honorary, nor did it require much commitment from Wolowski.

Wolowski's position in exile changed as his professional and political career developed. If in the 1830s he essentially played a secondary and auxiliary role in the Literary Society, by the 1840s, as a recognised professor at the Conservatoire des Arts et Métiers, he meant more. Thus, in 1847, during the celebration of the seventeenth anniversary of the outbreak of the November Uprising, he acted as one of the speakers; this would probably have been unlikely ten years earlier. Undoubtedly, his election to deputy in 1848 and 1849 and his close ties with Faucher further strengthened his position. Indeed, from then on, he became an important force in the politics of the Hotel Lambert. Finally, when he lost his political position on the Seine, he gained a financial one. Suffice it to say that when, in 1853, the Poles purchased the building that was henceforth to house the Polish Library, almost half of the required sum was raised in the form of a loan from the Crédit Foncier[1042]. As Janusz Pezda notes, further loans connected with changes in the ownership of the building (which at one time belonged partly to Zamoyski) were taken in 1859 and 1872 again from the Crédit Foncier[1043]. It seems doubtful that the choice of the bank with Wolowski and Branicki on board was accidental in this context.

2. The Polish School of Batignolles

In the 1850s, Wolowski was wholeheartedly involved in yet another Polish project. In 1853, he became a member of the Council of the Polish School in Paris[1044]. The

1041 *Sprawozdanie Towarzystwa Literacko-Historycznego w Paryżu*, vol. VII, *Sprawozdanie z czynności Towarzystwa Historyczno-Literackiego od 1 kwietnia 1867 do 1 kwietnia 1868*, Paris 1868, pp. 4–5.

1042 The building, still standing at number 6 on the Quai d'Orléans, Île Saint-Louis, cost 80,000 francs. Of this, 40,000 was borrowed from Wolowski's bank (Bibliothèque Polska in Paris, ref. BPP 1574, pp. 53–54). This debt was formally incurred by Władysław Zamoyski under the mortgage of his own house.

1043 J. Pezda *Historia Biblioteki Polskiej w Paryżu w latach 1838 – 1893*, Kraków 2013, pp. 110, 120–121.

1044 The Council was then headed by Alojzy Biernacki, and its members were Gałęzowski, Mickiewicz, Antoni Hłuszniewicz, Eustachy Januszkiewicz, Józef and Władysław Ordęga, Feliks Wrotnowski and Józef Bohdan Zaleski (A[gaton] G[iller] *Dr Seweryn Gałęzowski. Wspomnienie*, [in:] "Ruch Literacki. Tygodnik poświęcony Literaturze, Sztukom pięknym, Nauce i Rzeczom społecznym", vol. I, 1878, p. 266). After Biernacki's death in 1854, the Council was headed by Gałęzowski, Mickiewicz

school was founded in 1842. Its first premises were in Châtillon-sous-Bagneux, then it moved to Paris, at number13 in rue Fossés-Saint-Jacques, finally settling in 1846 for the next thirty years on Boulevard des Batignolles. This address gave the school its most common name – the "Batignolles School". At the time of Wolowski's arrival, the school had nine classes for children between the ages of 6 and 14. The older pupils of the school simultaneously attended the French Collège (Lycée) Bonaparte[1045], giving them later an opportunity to pursue higher education. The School Council was an extremely important body, electing the school's principal, appointed teachers and officials, admitted students, approved regulations, plans, and the budget[1046]. The school was intended for the children of emigrants, in many cases from mixed marriages. Its primary purpose, therefore, was to protect them from denationalisation. However, the school was not only concerned with the language or historical awareness of its pupils. Children were to be educated as good citizens of the future Poland, ready to fight for it and then work for it. On the other hand, since the beginning, the school's aim was also "academic education" at the highest level, enabling it also to function efficiently on French soil[1047]. As Iwona H. Pugacewicz notes in her excellent monograph on the school, a certain tension soon emerged between these two educational goals. Hipolit Klimaszewski, the school's headmaster from 1847 to 1853, emphasised above all the Polish nature, traditional Polish values, and the Catholic religion. In turn, he saw the school's pupils as future Poles, assuming that sooner or later they would all return to Poland. A completely different vision was presented by Gałęzowski, a key figure in the Council. According to Pugacewicz, "While trying to create a strong academic potential in the school, to build an establishment that would compete boldly for the palms of precedence with the best French establishments, he pushed its future service function towards the subjugated homeland into the background."[1048] In this dispute, Louis Wolowski was an entirely natural ally of Gałęzowski. Like Gałęzowski, he saw education as an instrument of technical and moral progress for the whole of humanity. Like Gałęzowski, he emphasised practical elements in education. Unlike Klimaszewski, on the other hand, he did not assume an imminent

---

became its vice-president, while Karol Sienkiewicz and Teofil Januszewicz joined the Council. In 1860, Julian Klaczko became its member, almost ten years later – Edmund Chojecki, in 1872 – Ludwik Nabielak. (I.H. Pugacewicz *Batignolles 1842–1874...*, pp. 165–173).

1045 This was the same prestigious school where the young Wolowski spent his first year of schooling in Paris (fn. 271). In 1848, it changed its name from Collège Bourbon to Lycée Bonaparte.

1046 N. Gris *Szkoła polska w Paryżu,* Warszawa 1962, p. 116; I.H. Pugacewicz *Batignolles 1842–1874...*, p. 134.

1047 N. Gris *Szkoła polska w Paryżu...*, pp. 90–95.

1048 N. Gris *Szkoła polska w Paryżu...*, p. 127.

return of emigrants to Poland. As a result, with the support of Wolowski and others (Biernacki, Mickiewicz and Zaleski), Gałęzowski removed Klimaszewski from the school in 1853[1049]. The changes included more than just the post of headmaster. By 1854, the council hired 17 new teachers[1050]. It opened the school up to external cooperation and won the school extremely important support, namely Prince Napoléon Jérôme Bonaparte. This probably happened through Branicki[1051]. Equally vital was the direct assistance of the Count himself, who, every year since Gałęzowski took the helm of the Council, supported the school financially[1052]. His attitude was undoubtedly influenced by Wolowski, his acquaintance with both the President and the Vice-President of the Council.

1049 That Wolowski was involved in the removal of Klimaszewski is evidenced by the minutes of the Council's vote of 23.10.1853 (Biblioteka Polska w Paryżu, ref. BPP 2361). Also, by a letter from Gałęzowski to Zaleski of 11 November 1853:

> Dear Bohdan, Thank God I am finally coming to terms with Klimaszewski. The day before yesterday he no longer considers himself to be the principal, having communicated to him the approval of the Minister of the Enlightenment of the appointment of Malinowski as headmaster of the school in his place, as it was written in the Rescript of the Rector of the Academy. We communicated this to him in both the Professors and Caretakers of the school and he could not but humble himself before the decision of the Government, to which he appealed. He has not yet got over all this, rushing from Ministry to Ministry for days on end with complaints. However, we expect him to remedy that too soon. Today we have a meeting at Biernacki's, to discuss how we should proceed in certain details; Mickiewicz, Ordęga, Hłuszniewicz and I will be there. We regret that Wolowski has left for Montmorency." (S. Gałęzowski *Listy Seweryna Gałęzowskiego do Bohdana Zaleskiego*, "Acta Medicorum Polonorum" no. 2, 2012, p. 127).

Klimaszewski himself, in turn, complained that he had been removed because he had "crawled under the Board's skin". His biographer writes that it was about the political views of the members of the School Board, Klaczko and Ordęga. However, she omits Klimaszewski's clear anti-Semitism, who did not accept Klaczko because of his Jewish origin, which he did not hide. This could also have influenced Wolowski's attitude towards the dismissed director. (E.Z. Wichrowska *Hipolit Klimaszewski – nieznana karta z dziejów Wielkiej Emigracji*, Warszawa 2012, pp. 30–31).

1050 I.H. Pugacewicz *Batignolles 1842–1874...*, p. 128.

1051 I.H. Pugacewicz *Batignolles 1842–1874...*, p. 171.

1052 I.H. Pugacewicz *Batignolles 1842–1874...*, pp. 171–172.

Indeed, the professor of the Conservatoire des Arts et Métiers became Vice-President in 1855, replacing the late Mickiewicz[1053]. Thus, according to Pugacewicz, he became Gałęzowski's right-hand man. The historian's opinion on the functioning of the Council under the administration of Gałęzowski and Wolowski is worth quoting:

> Gałęzowski's Council was undoubtedly more open to diversity and more tolerant, as best demonstrated by the private beliefs and spiritual choices of its members – led by the school's first patron, accused of religious Unitarianism and anti-Catholicism and whose voice in defence of the Jews was known throughout the exile. In this context, mention should also be made of the conversion from Judaism to Catholicism of the highly respected Julian Klaczko, still bearing in mind the activity of the staunch enthusiasts of Towiański, Mickiewicz's friends – Goszczyński and especially Nabielak – on behalf of the school. This body also boasted a peculiar internal and mutual solidarity, a truly fraternal assistance provided to each other in times of need, relations different from those under General Dwernicki, and more friendly. [...] [and the conviction] that working for the school was their mission in life, high personal dignity, and respect for each other.[1054]

Let me add that the men met many times in various configurations in other bodies: the Historical and Literary Society, the Hotel Lambert, the Committee for Contributions to the National Fund for Mickiewicz's children, the guardianship council of the young Mickiewiczes, and so on.

Most important, however, was the effect of their joint efforts. According to Pugacewicz, 300 students were educated at the school every year during Gałęzowski's presidency. They achieved excellent results: by the early 1870s its students had won more than 300 prizes at the Lycée Bonaparte and at the Sorbonne, where they were, after all, competing with their French peers. Almost 25% of Batignolles graduates continued education at universities in France[1055].

Wolowski made a tangible contribution to this success, topped with Gałęzowski purchasing the school building after 1852. In 1858/59, having bought new land, he expanded it. As the emigrants' contributions proved insufficient, he had to resort to a commercial loan. He took it out to the tune of 175,000 francs, obviously from the Crédit Foncier. Four years later, Wolowski's bank lent the school another 50,000 francs, "when, after the fall of the last uprising, all aid from the country suddenly ceased, and the influx of new refugees to France made it even more necessary to maintain the school."[1056]

1053 Minutes of the meeting of the School Council of 03.12.1855, Biblioteka Polska w Paryżu, ref. BPP 2361.

1054 I.H. Pugacewicz *Batignolles 1842–1874...*, p. 174.

1055 I.H. Pugacewicz *Batignolles 1842–1874...*, p. 131.

1056 *Sprawozdanie Szkoły Polskiej na Batignolles: od 1 października 1869 do 30 września 1872 roku*, Paris 1873, p. 6.

Wolowski's Batignolles activities came to an end with his last, unfortunately unsuccessful, mission. In 1865, the school was granted the title of a public institution, facilitating financing thereof[1057]. It seemed that the school had gained a sustainable financial foundation. Unfortunately, the years 1870 and 1871 were a gamechanger: the siege of Paris and the Paris Commune prevented Batignolles from functioning normally until June 1871. To make matters worse, the Thiers government withdrew the subsidy previously provided annually by the French administration to the school. This decision was partly due to strictly political reasons: after the fall of the Commune, a "bad time" had come for Poles on the Seine. The significant participation of emigrants like Jarosław Dąbrowski, Walery Wróblewski, August Okołowicz and several hundred other Poles resulted in the subsequent repression of the victorious Versailles government on emigration[1058], while Polish institutions were reluctantly tolerated. More important, however, was probably the collapse of the French budget due to the war, the Commune and the war reparations paid to Germany until 1873. In this situation, the French looked everywhere for savings, with the Batignolles school falling victim to this policy at the outset. By virtue of his political position, Louis Wolowski became heavily involved in its defence. Unfortunately, his intervention yielded little. In August 1871, the undersecretary of state at the Ministry of the Interior told Wolowski in reply that the sum of 32,000 francs allocated for the next school year would be the government's last subsidy[1059]. In this situation, maintaining the building at Batignolles was no longer possible. There were also no young men to maintain it for – the number of pupils had fallen to 25% of what it had been a decade before[1060]. The final decision to sell it was taken in December 1873. It was purchased by the

---

1057 J. Żebrowski *Szkoła polska na Batignolles w Paryżu w służbie polskości i wychowania narodowego (geneza, rozwój, struktura)*, "Studia Gdańskie. Wizje i rzeczywistość", no. 10, 2013, p. 340; I.H. Pugacewicz *Batignolles 1842–1874...*, p. 15.

1058 Krystyna Wyczańska mentions five to six hundred Polish communards (K. Wyczańska *Polacy w Komunie Paryskiej 1871 r.*, Warszawa 1957, pp. 163–200). This number seems exaggerated, but it is no longer possible today to determine the exact proportion of Poles in the Commune (R. Dobek Paris, 1871..., pp. 204 and 306). Even the Lvov Society, founded in 1870, intervened in the case of persecuted Poles (Letter of Walerian Podlewski, president of the Society, to Wolowski of 1871., Biblioteka Polska w Paryżu, ref. 2339, c. 63-64).

1059 Letter from M.A. Calmon to Wolowski, Versailles 19.08.1871, Biblioteka Polska w Paryżu, ref. BPP 2351, p. 264. Previously, the government subsidy had been more than 100,000 francs (Minutes of the School Council meeting of 22 Dec. 1873, Archives Nationales, ref. F/17/9084).

1060 Minutes of the School Council meeting of 22 Dec. 1873, Archives Nationales, ref. F/17/9084.

Department of the Seine, for 700,000 francs; the school was represented there by Wolowski[1061]. In 1874 it moved to 15 Lamandé Street.

It is noteworthy that during this difficult time, the Polish professor tried to care not only for the students of Batignolles, but also for the graduates. Indeed, Władysław Mickiewicz recalled: "In these difficult circumstances, an 'Association of educated Polish youth in higher scientific establishments in France' was formed; it set itself the goal of supporting the efforts of young people wishing to further their education in Paris. [...] Thanks to the intercession of Prince Władysław Czartoryski, the government provided students at technical colleges with permanent aid of 600 francs per person per year. As a result of Louis Wolowski's efforts, many students of medicine received monthly aid from the government, albeit by half as much."[1062]

Wolowski remained vice-president of the School Board until the end, alongside Gałęzowski. However, the stage of its history associated with Lamandé Street was no longer his. This does not change the fact that he gave back to the pupils of Batignolles, to good effect, a good part of the last twenty-three years of his life.

A loan from the Crédit Foncier thus allowed the purchase of the Polish Library building in Paris, a loan from the Crédit Foncier enabled the expansion of the Batignolles school. The Institution of Worship and Bread[1063] deposited its assets in an account with the Crédit Foncier. The Crédit Foncier employed Poles. The wealthy invested in the bank's shares. Apart from the mentioned Sapieha, Branicki and Dunin-Wąsowicz, this included Prince Adam Jerzy Czartoryski himself[1064]. Wolowski's bank was therefore undoubtedly an important financial anchor for the emigration.

1061 *Extrait du registre des procès-verbaux des séances du Conseil Général du département de la Seine. Séance du 22 novembre 1873,* Archives Nationales, ref. F/17/9084)

1062 W. Mickiewicz *Emigracya Polska...*, p. 132.

1063 It was founded as the Tax Association in 1862. Two years later it changed its name to the Worship and Bread Institution. Its purpose was to provide support to deserving compatriots, mainly former insurgents in need. Until 1884, its president was Bohdan Zaleski, and the institution had up to 1,200 members paying regular contributions of varying amounts. 75% of the proceeds went to pensions, aid for widows, etc., with the rest forming an inviolable endowment fund (K. Adamczyk *Władysław Zamoyski i Instytut Czci i Chleba,* [in:] B. Kosmanowa (ed.) *Rola książki w integracji ziem polskich w XIX w.*, Bydgoszcz 2000, pp. 125–133). Louis Wolowski was not a member of the institution, but his brother Kazimierz played a role in it. Zaleski even wrote in 1871 that it was "under the closer control of Kazimierz Wołowski and me, and the further control of the Supervisory Board". (D. Zaleski (ed.) *Korespondencya Józefa Bohdana Zaleskiego,* vol. V, Lviv 1903, p. 244).

1064 J. Pezda *Ludzie i pieniądze: finanse w działalności Adama Jerzego Czartoryskiego i jego obozu na emigracji w latach 1831–1848*, Kraków 2003, p. 155.

Louis Wolowski's importance in exile, however, went far beyond school or financial matters. Its apogee was undoubtedly during the January Uprising.

3. The January Uprising

The situation in Poland was gradually deteriorating; in the late 1850s, the first secret student circles were formed in Warsaw. In 1859, a clandestine committee was set up with Narcyz Jankowski at its head. The young people associated with it organised the first large public demonstration during the funeral of the widow of General Sowiński's (a heroic defender of Wola from 1831). The atmosphere in Poland was also heated by echoes of Italian events, Garibaldi's "red shirts" fighting in Sicily. The 30th anniversary of the November Uprising was celebrated in a solemn tone. On 25 February 1861, radical students organised another demonstration – on the anniversary of the 1831 Battle of Grochów. It was dispersed by Russian gendarmes but followed by an even bigger demonstration two days later. This time, soldiers fired on the demonstrators, killing five of them. The funeral of the five in early March turned into another demonstration. The tsarist authorities responded with concessions. The Council of State and the Government Commission for Religion and Education, headed by Aleksander Wielopolski, were reactivated. For several days, standing at the head of the Government Commission of Justice, Jan Kanty Wołowski cooperated with him. Wielopolski immediately dissolved two Polish organisations: the radical City Delegation and the conservative Committee of the Agricultural Society. Warsaw residents responded with further demonstrations – this time bloodily suppressed. On 8 April, more than a hundred people were killed by Russian bullets. The shock caused by these events did not, however, break the Poles. Masses for the Fatherland continued to be organised, more historical anniversaries were celebrated, and ladies wore patriotic outfits. As a result, in October 1861 the authorities imposed martial law. The Poles thus went underground. Its radical, "red" part set up the Municipal Committee, in which Jarosław Dąbrowski, the later general of the Paris Commune, played an increasingly important role. The Reds intended to regain independence through a victorious uprising. They planned to draw the popular masses into it through social reforms, above all the enfranchisement of the peasants. The more moderate "Whites", comprising mainly the landed gentry and bourgeoisie, formed the so-called Rural Directorate. Leopold Kronenberg, known to Louis Wolowski, was a member, as was Edward Jürgens and Karol Majewski.

Meanwhile, the Tsar's brother, Grand Duke Konstantin Nikolaevich, had become Governor of Congress Poland. In June 1862, Wielopolski was appointed head of the civil government. Despite his efforts, the situation continued to escalate. In June 1862, the Reds carried out the first terrorist attack on Alexander Lüders, Governor in 1861–1862. On 3 July, in turn, shots were fired in the direction of Grand Duke Konstantin. There were also two attempts to assassinate Wielopolski, neither of them successful, arousing resistance from a large part of Polish society in the process. Organised around a new entity, the Central National Committee, the Reds abandoned these tactics, and instead made intense preparations for an uprising. Wielopolski, not fully aware of the strength and scope of the conspiracy, was aware of the general state of turmoil in the country. His response was the *branka* or forced conscription of young people into the army. This posed a potential threat of splitting the independence movement. The Reds' response therefore became the slogan for an uprising. It finally broke out on 22 January 1863.[1065]

Louis Wolowski followed these events closely. This was not only because he was linked to them through Jan Kanty. More important was the fact that, from 1861, Wolowski was one of Prince Władysław Czartoryski's closest associates. In 1858, a so-called Council was set up on Île Saint-Louis by his father, Prince Adam. It was transformed in 1860 into the Bureau for Polish Affairs (Bureau des affaires polonaises), later abbreviated as the "Bureau". Apart from the Prince, it consisted of his two sons, Witold and Władysław, as well as Jan Działyński (spouse of Izabella, daughter of Prince Adam), Władysław Zamoyski, Stanisław Barzykowski, Andrzej Koźmian and Teodor Morawski.[1066] Contrary to what Sławomir Kalembka wrote (following Marceli Handelsman), Wolowski probably did not join the Bureau in 1860, but only in the autumn of 1861, after the death of Prince Adam[1067]. The economist certainly shared Władysław Czartoryski's political programme in exile, as presented, for example, in his speech on the 31st anniversary of the outbreak of the November Uprising. In it, the prince emphasised the principle of national unity in the face of the partitioners, the idea of voluntary renunciation of serfdom by the nobility, cooperation between Poles and Jews, revolutionary youth and moderate representatives of the Agricultural Society, and loyalty to the Church. Perhaps even more importantly, he explicitly stressed the merely auxiliary role of emigration, leaving the key political decisions to "domestic men familiar with the local circumstances". In turn, emigrants were to "enlighten Western governments and opinion", so that the Polish cause remained part of "European interests" and a "European future".[1068].

1065 More on the run-up to the uprising and preparations for it: S. Kieniewicz *Powstanie Styczniowe,* "Dzieje narodu i państwa polskiego" series, Warszawa 1987, pp. 1–40; S. Kieniewicz *Powstanie styczniowe,* Warszawa 1983, pp. 9–358.

1066 S. Kalembka *Cz. II Polskie zabiegi dyplomatyczne między powstaniem listopadowym a styczniowym (koniec 1831 – 1860 r.),* [in:] L. Bazylow (ed.) *Historia dyplomacji polskiej,* vol. III, *1795–1918,* Warszawa 1982, pp. 422–423.

1067 This is confirmed by the minutes of the Bureau's meeting of 11 Nov. 1861: "The President declares that Mr Wolowski, having received the unanimity of votes required by the statutes, becomes a member of the Bureau." ([in:] W. Czartoryski *Pamiętnik 1860–1864. Protokoły posiedzeń Biura Hotelu Lambert cz. I i II. Entrevues politiques,* Warszawa 1960, p. 205).

1068 W. Czartoryski *Mowa xięcia Władysława Czartoryskiego miana na posiedzeniu Towarzystwa Literacko-Historycznego w Paryżu dnia 29 listopada 1861 roku,* Paryż 1861, pp. 6–9.

To a large extent, Władysław Czartoryski's Bureau continued the earlier policy of the Hotel Lambert, making attempts to coordinate Polish efforts abroad, involved in intensive propaganda activity, and finally maintaining contacts with the country. It had a permanent network of correspondents, and benefited from the family, private and professional ties of its members and supporters. Quite importantly, Czartoryski eschewed conspiratorial methods, strongly recommending that his national correspondents act legally but in consultation with the Bureau[1069]. In practice, this meant that in Congress Poland, the Bureau was in contact mainly with the Whites. The Bureau met regularly on Tuesdays. Initially, its meetings were chaired by Prince Adam, but over time the baton was passed to his younger son, Prince Władysław.

Wolowski played an important role in it due to his financial and political contacts. He also contributed to the funding of the Bureau[1070]. He represented it at peculiar informal political conventions, such as the summer stays in Wiesbaden in 1861 and 1862. This was a place of meetings with landowners and wealthier bourgeoisie from the Polish territories[1071] and agreeing on positions[1072]. Since the very beginning, his French connections were very important. When, in 1861, the Bureau was considering a possible petition to the French Senate, it was Wolowski who pointed out the senators to count on[1073]. He also contacted Prince Napoléon on the same issue[1074]. When the Bureau sought contact with Louis de la Guéronnière, a Bonapartist close to the emperor and owner of the newspaper "La France Politique", Wolowski was a natural choice[1075]. The same thing happened when, in November 1862, the Bureau tried to contact another important title, "Le

1069 M. Handelsman *Adam Czartoryski*, vol. III, part II..., p. 640.

1070 E.g., the minutes of 25 Nov. 1861 reported his donation of 1,000 francs to the Bureau (W. Czartoryski *Pamiętnik...*, p. 209).

1071 A.Koźmian, staying in Wiesbaden together with Wolowski in August 1861, described it as follows: "So we have our circle and we are good together. We drink and stroll together, we dine together, we spend evenings together. The circle is made up of Louis Wolowski, Józef Mycielski from Kobylepole, Aleksander Przeździecki and Adolf Kurtz. There's also Siemieński, Matiasz Rosen from Warsaw, a Rotschild of Polish Jews, some Czetwertyński, Trębicki, a former adjutant to the grand duke, now a senator." (A. Koźmian *Listy Andrzeja Edwarda Koźmiana*, vol. IV..., p. 336).

1072 Henryk Wereszycki even wrote about an "unofficial convention of a dozen landed politicians in Wiesbaden" in 1861. (H. Wereszycki *Hotel Lambert i obóz Białych przed wybuchem powstania styczniowego*, "Przegląd Historyczny" no. 50 (3), 1959, p. 524.

1073 W. Czartoryski *Pamiętnik...*, p. 210.

1074 W. Czartoryski *Pamiętnik...*, p. 211.

1075 Minutes of the Bureau of 28 July 1862, [in:] W. Czartoryski *Pamiętnik...*, p. 283.

Temps"[1076]. Of significance were also his former journalistic acquaintances from "Le Siècle" and "Journal des Débats".

Louis Wolowski's Polish contacts were also important. In addition to the landowners, he corresponded with Józef Ignacy Kraszewski and August Cieszkowski. In 1862, it was Cieszkowski who approached Wolowski with the initiative to condemn the attacks on Wielopolski[1077]. The Bureau did not do so in the end, but Wolowski, strongly moved and outraged by the events, wrote on his behalf to Primate Leon Przyłuski with a proposal to organise official prayers "for an end to the secret killing". The Primate, however, declined it because of the "great uncertainty in the very origins of these sad incidents"[1078]. Wolowski's contacts from Galicia, Poland, also mattered. Preserved in the Polish Library in Paris are, among other things, two letters addressed to him by Kazimierz Grocholski, then a member of the Polish Circle within the Austrian Council of State, both dated 1863. In them, Grocholski inquired, among other things, about the position of Poles in Berlin on the issue of Schleswig and Holstein. He stressed the need to coordinate Polish policy on this issue, clearly assuming in an understated way that the coordinating body would be the Bureau in Paris[1079].

In the same year, Wolowski joined the finance committee of the Bureau[1080]. As a result, he was later responsible for its accounts and controlled all major expenditure.

Importantly, Wolowski clearly communicated well with Czartoryski. Thus, when the Prince was away, it was Wolowski who was asked to preside over meetings in his place. And when, in May 1863, they joined together the Polish Committee in Paris set up by the National Government, Czartoryski wrote: "I and Wolowski represented [in the committee] the right wing, and I dare not say that we represented the reasonable party".[1081] When an acrimonious dispute arose in the Bureau in 1862 between Wolowski and Walerian Kalinka (then an employee of the Bureau), the other members supported the economist. Facing Czartoryski's silence, Kalinka resigned[1082]. Finally, it was Wolowski who brought

1076 Minutes of the Bureau of 29 Dec. 1862, [in:] W. Czartoryski *Pamiętnik*... p. 318.

1077 Minutes of the Bureau of 11 Aug. 1862, [in:] W. Czartoryski *Pamiętnik*... p. 287.

1078 Letter from Primate Przyłuski to Louis Wolowski, Biblioteka Polska w Paryżu, ref. BPP 2339, c. 46-47.

1079 Letters of Kazimierz Grocholski to Louis Wolowski, Biblioteka Polska w Paryżu, ref. BPP 2339, c. 11-12.

1080 Minutes of the Bureau of 02 Dec. 1861, [in:] W. Czartoryski *Pamiętnik*..., p. 211.

1081 W. Czartoryski *Pamiętnik*..., p. 139.

1082 Minutes of the Bureau of 03 Nov. 1862, [in:] W. Czartoryski *Pamiętnik*..., pp. 303–304. Wolowski accused Kalinka of having arbitrarily sent Mr Lasserre on a mission to Rome without first informing the Bureau. At a subsequent meeting, Wolowski offered his "regrets" for Kalinka's resignation. The latter, by the way, continued work for the Bureau in the Foreign Agencies Department.

August Trzetrzewiński, a Warsaw barrister associated with the White Directorate in 1862–1863, to a meeting of the Bureau. Trzetrzewiński subsequently became the Bureau's official correspondent at the Directorate[1083].

Like the whole of the Hotel Lambert, Wolowski took a cautious and distrustful approach to the Uprising in the early days. The turning point was the Alvensleben Convention, signed between Russia and Prussia on 08 February 1863. The agreement between the two partitioning powers in fact internationalised the Polish cause and opened the way for Western diplomacy to intervene. Czartoryski must have soon received some signals from the French, for as early as on 16 February, he sent a message to Cracow quite clearly urging them to persist. This was also the green light for the Whites to join the rebellion[1084]. Although the authorities on the Seine did not promise anything specific to the prince beyond general assurances of diplomatic action, he was convinced that the situation was heading towards a European war. "War is inevitable and desired by Napoleon," he wrote to Warsaw on 14 May 1863[1085]. Wolowski was probably thinking along similar lines. He may also have been somewhat influenced by the attitude of Jan Kanty. For the latter wrote to Levasseur in March 1863: "You probably know that in our situation, only one thing occupies all minds, and please believe that only one feeling and one wish can be found in all Polish hearts. All states, all opinions have united; when it comes to national existence Poles do not retreat from any sacrifice, and (a unique thing in history) they march to death without fear, with a sense of duty, while with a feeling of happiness, they sacrifice part of their fortunes."[1086]

Like Prince Władysław, Louis was also critical of the English activities of Władysław Zamoyski: for, contrary to the Bureau's recommendations, Zamoyski convinced the English that it was only a matter of the government in London denying Russia any rights to Poland and recognising the Poles as a belligerent party. This, however, meant that the British, even those most supportive of the Polish cause, had absolutely no thoughts of war, which the Poles in turn wanted. Wolowski, together with Czartoryski and Klaczko, subjected Zamoyski's actions in this connection in April 1863 to clear criticism, which, however, was not accepted by the General[1087].

1083 Minutes of the Bureau of 20 Oct., 15 Dec. 1862, and 19 Jan. 1863, [in:] W. Czartoryski *Pamiętnik...*, pp. 299–300, 315 & 321.

1084 T. Szarota *Dyktatura Langiewicza a przystąpienie Białych do powstania,* "Przegląd Historyczny", vol. 54, Warszawa 1963, p. 271 and the next.

1085 A. Lewak (ed.) *Polska działalność dyplomatyczna w 1863–1864 r. Zbiór dokumentów.* vol. I, Warszawa 1937, p. 262.

1086 Letter from J.K. Wołowski to E. Levasseur, 25 March 1863, Bibliothèque de l'Institut de France, *Correspondances et papiers divers provenant de la succession d'Émile Levasseur,* ref. MS 6032. Let me recall that Jan Kanty Wołowski attested to these words with his own life.

1087 Minutes of the Bureau of 13 April 1863, [in:] W. Czartoryski *Pamiętnik...*, p. 327.

In the meantime, he continued to be an active intermediary between the Bureau, later the Polish Committee in Paris, and the French. He had several conversations with Prince Napoléon Jérôme, with Adolphe Billault (minister without portfolio), with Morny and other familiar journalists and politicians. On 30 March 1863, he was one of two Poles (along with Leonard Chodźko) to become a member of the French-Polish Central Committee. It was headed by Prince Eugène d'Harcourt. In 1846, d'Harcourt chaired the Free Trade Association, so Wolowski knew him well. He also came across other acquaintances on the Committee: Barrot, Montalembert, Beaumont, a large group of former representatives of the people from 1848 to 1849. The editors-in-chief of major press titles also sat on the Committee: Adolphe Guéroult of "L'Opinion Nationale", Auguste Nefftzer of "Le Temps", Pierre Scudo of "Revue des Deux Mondes", Léonor Havin of "Le Siècle", Delamarre of "La Patrie". The Committee's declared aim was to provide material support for the fighting Poles by organising collections, fund-raisers, etc. and to coordinate similar activities on a national scale. Equally important, however, was the establishment of a platform for the exchange of information and the coordination of political and propaganda efforts. The Committee undoubtedly supported the political and diplomatic activities of Czartoryski[1088]. Again, Wolowski's informal role was crucial.

The well-known economist was also a member of the Polish Committee in Paris established by the insurgent National Government in May 1863. Did he believe, like Czartoryski, in a great European war? It would seem so. Among other things, Wolowski was behind the Committee's manifesto published on 26 June 1863. In it, the Committee called upon "the nations of the West" to take up the struggle against Eastern despotism, and concluded by saying that God and justice would give Poland victory[1089]. At the same time, Wolowski was aware that the uprising's success would only be possible with military support from the West. This belief in victory was also echoed in the speech he gave at the closing ceremony of the school year in Batignolles on 12 August 1863.[1090] Earlier, in July, he

1088 This is evidenced, for example, by the Committee's proclamation of 30 October 1863 to the French senators. The idea was to put pressure on the government to formally recognise the Poles as a war party (*Comité Central Franco-Polonais: aux Amis de la Pologne: aux Amis de la Justice et de l'Humanité*, Paris 1863).

1089 A. Lewak (ed.) *Polska działalność dyplomatyczna...*, p. 139. Perhaps this was also due to some general optimism on the part of Wolowski. Krasiński wrote, for example, of Wolowski's "rosy hopes" in the context of the Crimean War in 1854 (Letter from Zygmunt Krasiński to August Cieszkowski, 24 July 1854, [in:] Z. Krasński *Listy do Augusta Cieszkowskiego...*, p. 687). Similarly, Eliza Krasińska described him as "rosy [optimistic] Wolowski". (E. z Branickich Krasińska *Świadek epoki. Listy Elizy z Branickich Krasińskiej z lat 1835–1876*, vol. III..., p. 244).

1090 *Ecole nationale Polonaise. Distribution solennelle des prix. Année scolaire 1862–1863*, Paris 1863. Echoes of Wolowski's speech also reached the Russians through Julian Bałaszewicz. The spy and provocateur reported that Wolowski's speech "was full

wrote to Czartoryski that he was "full of hope: the Russians have had plunged up to their necks, only England was behaving terribly".[1091] As late as on 10 December, he and the other members of the French-Polish Committee signed a proclamation to the members of the Legislative Body stressing that "Only France, France united without distinction between parties in her sympathy for Poland, can, by the force of her vote or her arm, stop a work of destruction hitherto unknown in the history of civilised nations."[1092]

It seems that Wolowski succumbed to the same illusion as Czartoryski for similar reasons. The French acquaintances of the Pole – mainly representatives of the Parisian elite – were probably behind him. Parisian public opinion was decidedly pro-Polish. As Pierre Milza wrote: "In 1863-64, everyone was an enthusiast of Poland and Poles in the same way that thirty or forty years earlier everyone had become an enthusiast of everything Greek".[1093] This Parisian and elite section of society also accepted a potential war with Russia. The thing is, however, that rural France, departmental and provincial France, numerically clearly dominant over Paris, if it even sympathised with the Poles, it did not want war. This was clearly indicated by the reports of prefects or attorneys-general[1094]. This part of France was relatively poorly known to Wolowski (or Czartoryski). Nor did the Polish Committee or the Franco-Polish Central Committee once mention possible

---

of puffed-up praise for the revolution, slanders against Russia and exhortations to the students to follow in the footsteps of their fathers who had fallen in the defence of independence." (A. Potocki (J. Bałaszewicz) *Pamiętnik szpiega*, vol. I, Warszawa 1973, p. 386). Bałaszewicz was lying – while appreciating the sacrifice of the insurgents, Wolowski was not calling on children to die for the Fatherland, but to study for it. In this context, it is also worth quoting a fragment of the funeral speech delivered by Wolowski a year earlier over Lelewel's coffin. It was a kind of programme for young generations: "Lelewel knew only two passions to which he remained faithful to the end: love of the homeland and love of science (...) Chronology, genealogy, geography, politics, history, legislation, yearbooks, manuscripts, monuments, memoirs, coats of arms, customs, costumes, he took everything into account, he understood everything." (Copy of Wolowski's funeral speech, Biblioteka Polska w Paryżu, ref. BPP 2357/10, c. 17-30).

1091 Letter from Louis Wolowski to Władysław Czartoryski, Biblioteka Książąt Czartoryskich, ref. 7243 IV.

1092 *Comité Central Franco-Polonais a Messieurs les membres du Corps Législatif, Paris 10.12.1863,* [in:] L. Chodźko *Papiery dotyczące komitetów francusko-polskich i innnych działających za granicą na rzecz powstania 1863 r. i emigracji postycznioweј,* Biblioteka Narodowa, ref. Rps 10022 II.

1093 P. Milza *Napoléon III...*, p. 621.

1094 S. Bóbr-Tylingo *Napoléon III, l'Europe et la Pologne en 1863-4*, "Antemurale" no. VII–VIII, Romae 1963, pp. 276–277.

French losses during the war, which Napoleon III, after all, had to reckon with. As a result, on 05 August 1863, during a meeting of ministers at Saint-Cloud, it was decided that France would not enter the war. In practice, in view of the clear reluctance of England and Austria to any wartime adventure, this put an end to the Polish cause. Meanwhile, Czartoryski continued to believe in war – it was only in April 1864 that he broke the news to Warsaw that "The situation, unfortunately, is most dismal and does not give us any hope either of safer external aid or even of greater European complication."[1095]

This was also the end of Wolowski's activities related to the Uprising. When, on 8 June 1864, the Bureau renewed its activities, his name was no longer on the list[1096].

However, this did not mean that he ceased his émigré activities altogether, or even that he gave up his political collaboration with Czartoryski. When the Czechs František Palacký and František Rieger appeared in Paris in 1867, a meeting with them on behalf of the Hotel Lambert was attended by, among others, Wolowski[1097]. That same year, on the inauguration of a monument to Adam Mickiewicz in the Montmorency cemetery, the latter again stressed: "Poland lives and will live."[1098] Above all, however, he continued to support the Batignolles School and the Historical and Literary Society. He also belonged to the Council of the Institute of Polish Maidens.[1099] He was associated with the Institution of Worship and Bread through his brother, with another extremely important émigré work – St. Casimir's Institution – this time through his sister. Mrs Faucher was in fact the cashier of this useful enterprise from 1868 onwards.[1100] Father Syski, an Interwar historian of the Institution, described her role after 1871 as follows: "A great help in obtaining government subsidies for St Casimir's Institution and in dealing with all matters

---

1095 A telegram from W. Czartoryski to the National Government, Paris 17 April 1864, [in:] A. Lewak (ed.) *Polska działalność dyplomatyczna...*, p. 458.

1096 J. Zdrada *Zmierzch Czartoryskich*, Warszawa 1969, p. 24.

1097 J. Zdrada *Zmierzch Czartoryskich...*, p. 184.

1098 L. Wolowski *Inauguration du monument d'Adam Mickiewicz à Montmorency (21 mai 1867). Allocution de M. Louis Wolowski*, Librairie du Luxembourg, Paris 1867, p. 3.

1099 "Rocznik Towarzystwa Historyczno-Literackiego w Paryżu", Paris 1869, p. IX. Information about Wolowski's presence on the Institute's Council appeared in subsequent copies of the Yearbook until his death. The Institute itself was an educational institution where daughters of Polish refugees were educated since 1845 (more on the subject: no author provided *L'Institut polonais: souvenirs et fragments*, 1845 à 1895, Paris 1895).

1100 St Casimir's Institution (House) was established in 1846. It served as a shelter for Polish orphans and elderly people no longer able to work, mainly veterans of the uprising (more on the subject: A. Syski *Zakład Św. Kazimierza w Paryżu. Szkic historyczny*, Łuck 1936).

with the government, was wife to Leon Faucher, née Wołowska. Her husband was a minister for a long time, and she had a close relative, Mr Louis Passy, a very influential deputy for many years, through whom she did a great deal."[1101] It is not difficult to guess that if Aleksandryna benefited from her brother's son-in-law, all the more reason why she must have benefited from the influence of Louis himself.

4. Applicants, acquaintances, friends, family

A coverage of Wolowski's Polish activities should include his social standing. It was largely linked to his professional opportunities. Letters that have survived in the Polish Library in Paris, the Czartoryski Library or in the State Archive in Cracow, often contain requests for patronage, assistance in finding a job or outright employment at the Crédit Foncier. There are also acknowledgements for his support albeit less frequent. What is more, compatriots whose financial situation was good or very good also benefited from Wolowski's assistance. For example, he was an attorney for Jerzy Henryk Lubomirski and his wife, Cecylia née Zamoyska, in a succession case after the latter's mother, Róża Zamoyska, who died in 1862[1102]. When, in turn, Aleksander Wołodkowicz was on a deathbed in Paris, he asked Wolowski to take care of his last property dispositions[1103]. Zygmunt Krasiński, writing in 1851 about a French visa for Stanisław Małachowski, recommended that the latter apply specifically to Wolowski[1104].

Louis Wolowski's compatriots in the country benefited from his assistance; a case in point is the Cracow Scientific Society (the predecessor of the Akademia Umiejętności – "Academy of Learning"). In a special letter of 1857, its president, Franciszek Wężyk, thanked the banker for his financial assistance to the Society.[1105] As it happens, Wolowski had been a member of the Society since 1849[1106], a foreign member of the Academy of Learning since 1874[1107], and an honorary member of

1101 A. Syski *Zakład Św. Kazimierza...*, pp. 110–111.

1102 Letters from Jerzy Henryk Lubomirski to Louis Wolowski (1866), Biblioteka Polska w Paryżu, ref. BPP 2339, c. 26-31.

1103 A. Koźmian *Listy Andrzeja Edwarda Koźmiana*, vol. IV..., p. 402.

1104 "I always think that the easiest and most skilful way is through Wolowski, let him whisper a word to Faucher and he to Szweycer', he wrote (Letter from Z. Krasiński to S. Małachowski, 01.05.1851, [in:] Z. Krasiński *Listy Zygmunta Krasińskiego do Stanisława Małachowskiego*, Kraków 1885, p. 251.

1105 Biblioteka Polska w Paryżu, ref. BPP 2339, c. 65-66. Louis Wolowski was a member of the Cracow Scientific Society since 1849.

1106 J. Zdrada *Między Wschodem a Zachodem*, [in:] *Towarzystwo Naukowe Krakowskie w 200-lecie założenia (1815–2015)*, Kraków 2016, p. 69.

1107 Approval of the election of Wolowski as a member of the AL: Archives of the Polish Academy of Sciences and the Polish Academy of Arts and Sciences in Cracow, ref. PAU KSG 70/1874.

the Poznań Society for the Advancement of Arts and Sciences. [1108] After his death, Józef Ignacy Kraszewski recalled Wolowski's help during his stays in Paris[1109]. He also forwarded him some letters of recommendation before the writer's trip to Italy [1110].

Importantly, the favours that Wolowski rendered to others were not only the result of his kind heart but of a policy he pursued. Symptomatic in this respect was his letter to Princess Anna Czartoryska (unfortunately, without a date). In it, on behalf of Mr Bixio, Wolowski asked for a place at the Institute of Polish Ladies for a young Polish woman, his protégé. In doing so, he made it clear that Bixio was among "our most ardent and influential friends"[1111]. In this way, Wolowski also built up the network of acquaintances and contacts mentioned many times, which he then used to his personal and national benefits.

These activities were specifically complemented by Wolowski's active and extensive social life. It was related at least in part to the conduct described above, and probably in part to the traits of his character. As for the Polish milieu, his closest friends and acquaintances could be described as undoubtedly elitist. They included the oft-mentioned Andrzej Edward Koźmian, who regularly attended dinners at the Wolowskis' with Roger Raczyński; Wołodkowicz frequented the circle as well. Ksawery Branicki was a close friend of the Wolowskis. Louis regularly visited

1108 *Sprawozdania z czynności Towarzystwa Przyjaciół Nauk Poznańskiego: od stycznia 1860 do grudnia 1862*, "Roczniki Towarzystwa Przyjaciół Nauk Poznańskiego", vol. 2, Poznań 1863, p. 91. The Pole also belonged to academies and scientific societies in Brussels, Madrid, Milan, Turin, Florence, Naples, Kazan, Toulouse, and Geneva. (P. Larousse *Grand dictionnaire universel du XIXe siècle: français, historique, géographique, mythologique, bibliographique*, vol. 15 *Testam – Z*, Paris 1876, p. 1370).

1109 J.I. Kraszewski *Ludwik Wołowski....* There is a distinctive text associated with Kraszewski's stay in Paris, given to him by his compatriots. At the time, Kraszewski received a ring with the inscription "Fides invicta fidis manibus" and an address, also signed by Wolowski and containing, among other things, the following, somewhat surprising words: "Our guest, from your hometowns long farewelled, you have lived a few days among us fraternally. Your name is widely known in the country. You wrote and printed a lot. Your books we do not all know, or we do not all know them: but your tireless activity and exemplary civic vigilance we have long admired and unanimously adored." (Dyonizy Zaleski (ed.) *Korespondencya Józefa Bohdana Zaleskiego,* vol. III, Lvov 1902, p. 22).

1110 J. I. Kraszewski *Korespondencja Józefa Ignacego Kraszewskiego...*, c. 188, 190, 192.

1111 Biblioteka Książąt Czartoryskich, ref. 7032 IV vol. 7. It is about Jacques Alexandre Bixio, head of the cabinet of the Provisional Government in 1848, a conservative republican, a short-lived Minister of Agriculture in December 1848, and a host of the famous "Bixio dinners" attended by Eugène Delacroix, Alexandre Dumas (father), Prosper Mérimée and François Ponsard, among others.

Branicki's castle in Montrésor in the summer[1112]. In his autobiographical novel, Ksawery's son, Augustyn, portrayed Wolowski as follows:

> In his youth, during his holidays, Jean Griff [the novel counterpart of Augustyn Branicki] hurt his arm and his only amusement became strolling in the park of the Château de Monpavan [Montrésor]; his companion was Mr Rapowski [Wolowski], a member of the Institute. He hated hunting with a passion, so that while the other guests were on the hunt, he spent his days working until the hour of his daily walk. He was a professor of political economy at the Collège de France [Conservatoire des Arts et Métiers], one of the founders of this science, and he liked to lecture even outside the official course, in front of any audience. Thus, taking advantage of the presence of a sole listener, he introduced Jean, as the Peripatetic philosophers once did, to the arcana of the laws that govern society and interests.[1113].

Wolowski also met Aleksander This before his death in Paris, and even published his obituary in the "Revue..."[1114]. He and his wife regularly visited the Czartoryski family; however, it was probably not friendship but rather social and political meetings. For family reasons, Wolowski's closest circle included the Mickiewicz family – until the deaths of Celina and Adam, and later their daughters, Maria and Helena, together with their husbands. This circle included, of course, the Fauchers, the Passys and the Levasseurs.

By all accounts, Wolowski's Polish political environment was primarily associated with the Hotel Lambert, as was he himself. Although representatives of all émigré camps wrote to him, he probably had no friends among the member of the Polish Democratic Society, democrats, not to mention revolutionaries like Dąbrowski and Wróblewski.

His death coincided with the twilight of Polish emigration on the Seine in general. Above all, the generation of the November Uprising was passing away. Of Wolowski's colleagues from the Bureau for Polish Affairs, Koźmian had been dead since 1864, Zamoyski died in 1868, Chodźko passed away in 1871, Barzykowski in 1872, Morawski in 1879, Działyński in 1880, and Kalinka, who survived longest, died in 1886. Among the deceased was Roger Raczyński (1864), Ksawery Branicki and Seweryn Gałęzowski (both (1879). Kazimierz, Louis's brother, passed away a year after him, Feliks lived until 1893.[1115] Władysław Czartoryski, considerably

1112 J. Słupska *Ksawery Branicki...*, p. 39.

1113 A. Branicki *ANATKH. Roman radiographique*, Paris, no date provided, pp. 421–422. According to this work, Branicki was to ask Wolowski one day about his son's abilities. The answer was supposed to be: "he is a dummy." (p. 21).

1114 "Revue de législation et de jurisprudence" 1846, vol. 1 (25), pp. 490–492.

1115 Interestingly, in the family of Louis, Kazimierz, and Feliks Wołowskis, women proved to be noticeably more long-lived than men. Their mother was 84 years old at the time of her death in 1871, Aleksandryna died in Paris in 1905 at the age of 93 (death certificate: Archives de Paris, ref. 9D101, no. 584), Laure, Louis'

younger than Louis, died in 1894, but had moved from Paris to Cracow twenty years earlier. In practice, this meant the end of the Hotel Lambert.

A second factor in the decline of emigration in Paris was the political changes taking place after 1871. France, slowly rebuilding its international position after its war defeat, sought an agreement with Russia[1116]. The ruling Republicans tended to silence the Polish cause, while the remaining Polish immigrants were followed by the police. It was characteristic, moreover, that the funerals of famous Poles, including Wolowski, were also held under police surveillance[1117].

Wolowski's death, in turn, undoubtedly exacerbated this process of decline in the importance of Poles in Paris. It marked disappearance of a man extremely active, and associated with many Polish undertakings, not only political ones. Wolowski was an important figure for the Polish school, the Institute of Polish Ladies, and indirectly St Casimir's Institution, the Institution of Worship and Bread and the Polish Library. Above all, he was among the most influential, and in the 1870s arguably *the* most influential Pole in French public life, an indispensable link between the Polish and French political worlds. When he died, there was no one who came even close to his position on the Seine.

---

wife, passed away in 1899, aged 85 (inscription on her tomb in the Père-Lachaise cemetery, author's information). She outlived her daughter by four years. Fanny was the only one to die relatively young, on 16 March 1895, at the age of 50 (obituary: Bibliothèque de l'Institut de France, Correspondances et papiers divers provenant de la succession d'Émile Levasseur, ref. MS 6029, dossier 3, Wolowski).

1116 Jerzy Borejsza is right, however, pointing out that this process had begun in the second half of the 1860s, when Napoleon III was seeking a rapprochement with St Petersburg (J. W. Borejsza *Emigracja polska po powstaniu styczniowym*, Warszawa 1966, pp. 279–285).

1117 J. W. Borejsza *Emigracja polska po powstaniu styczniowym...*, p. 402.

Conclusion

Louis Wolowski was a remarkable figure, yet at the same time difficult to grasp for a historian. The Frankist roots and habits of the Wołowskis were quite unusual. Wolowski undoubtedly belonged to a generation for which Frank's teachings were almost irrelevant. However, certain elements associated with Frankism survived and were reflected in his biography: his marriage to Laure Guérin, who came from another Frankist family, or, above all, the very strong emphasis on family ties, evident in his relationships with Jan Kanty Wołowski, with the Mickiewiczes, with Passy and Levasseur. It also involved a deliberate strategy of establishing new connections through marriages, from the marriage of his sister to Faucher, his cousin's marriage to Levasseur, to his daughter's union with Passy.

The Frankist origins, however, were a clear burden in Congress Poland at the time. Despite the full assimilation of the Wołowskis, their Polish neighbours and associates in Congress Poland remembered their Jewish roots very well, reproaching them, for example, to Franciszek Wołowski in 1831. From the point of view of Orthodox Jews, the Frankists were apostates, deviates, dead to the community of believers.

Therefore, in my view, the family past may have had a significant influence on Louis Wolowski's decision to remain in France in 1831 and quickly acquire French citizenship. For in Paris, the Frankist history of the Wołowskis was unknown and was no barrier to a possible career. Wolowski never returned to it either.

The family itself was unusual. Even a cursory glance at Louis Wolowski's ancestors, closer and more distant cousins, or relatives, reveals at least a dozen heroes of the *Polish Biographical Dictionary*, which, it should be recalled, has not yet covered the letter W. Significantly, four of these PBD heroes were women. Thus, among the Wołowskis and their relatives the Szymanowskis, Leszczyńskis, Brzezińskis and Lanckorońskis, there were unusually many (by the 19th century standards) people who were well educated and extremely talented. Education, including tertiary education, was evidently also a key tool for them to first advance, and then to maintain their social position.

This remark also applies to Louis Wolowski's immediate family, above all to his father Franciszek. His mother, Tekla Wołowska, also had intellectual ambition and a certain historical and literary culture, as best evidenced by her work *Historya Polska*. However, Franciszek Wołowski undoubtedly remained the family's central figure and the point of reference for the sons until his death in 1844. The renowned Warsaw lawyer, educated in Halle, took care of his son's education. It seems likely that Louis's choice of law studies was also significantly influenced by Franciszek. However, the father's importance in his son's life went beyond just the choice of schools. The political activity of the younger of the Wołowskis was also strongly linked to his father, and this had been the case since 1831. Characteristically, Wolowski co-founded the Literary Society in Paris with his father and left it together with his father. The dominant figure was undoubtedly Franciszek Wołowski. It also seems that Louis inherited some of his views from him: a commitment to the rule of law, to personal freedoms, including a strong emphasis on freedom of speech. The lawyer father therefore left a significant mark on the economist son.

Louis Wolowski's career in France was also extraordinary, incomparable to the career of any other Pole[1118]. It was a career based on three intertwined elements: economic thought, banking activity, and political activism. In all these areas, Wolowski achieved notable success, first as an economist. Wolowski was undoubtedly one of the most important economic theorists in France in the 1840s, 1850s and 1860s. As I have mentioned, this was no longer a generation as significant for the development of economic thought as the previous ones and Louis Wolowski, Michel Chevalier or Joseph Garnier do not occupy a place in economics textbooks like Smith, Ricardo or Say. However, this does not change the fact that Wolowski took part in several very important economic debates and his voice was among the most prominent. These are above all the discussions on the monopoly of issue of the Banque de France, mono- or bimetallism, paper money, and free trade. In all these cases, Wolowski's views were shared by other economists, as well as politicians, businessmen and, via the newspapers, the French public. The ideas he defended did not always triumph; suffice to mention his prediction of the European triumph of money based on silver and gold, which rapidly became outdated. On the other hand, Wolowski can be in part attributed to maintaining the monopoly of the Banque de France. All these discussions were translated into practice – the stability and strength of the French franc, the condition of French agriculture and industry in competition (and cooperation) with that of Britain. Theoreticians like Wolowski provided arguments for decision-making ministers or deputies. In one other instance, the son of the owner of Kaski can claim important credit – his early writings contributed to the reform of the French mortgage system. And while it is probably impossible to decide unequivocally who was right in the disputes over free trade, bi-metallism or the Banque de France, in the case of mortgages, the change proposed by Wolowski and introduced by Napoleon III was undoubtedly to France's benefit.

The issues of mortgages were linked to the second (until 1852) pillar of Wolowski's professional activity in France, namely banking. The Pole combined economic theory with practice. He was not alone; Chevalier also sat on the boards of several companies. Importantly, however, the Créditt Foncier was his idea and his creation. The very longevity of the bank, its strength, and its importance in the

1118 I have disregarded Alexandre Colonna-Walewski, Minister of Foreign Affairs, Minister of State and President of the Legislative Body during the Second Empire. However, Walewski, unlike Wolowski, no longer saw himself as Polish after the November Uprising and his entry into the French diplomacy.

1860s and 1870s are altogether testament to the success of this work. Objections can, of course, be multiplied: Wolowski had only been at the head of the bank for two years, the Crédit Foncier ultimately lent only marginally to agriculture, but took a fundamental part, under the management of Frémy and Soubeyran, in the illegal financing of the redevelopment of Paris and in more or less speculative investments abroad. The Pole was most likely aware of this. However, this does not change the fact that, through the Crédit Foncier, Wolowski played a (small) part in the fundamental change in the French banking and credit system that gradually took place since the mid-19th century. A change that subsequently contributed to similar developments in other European countries.

Finally, towards the end of his life, Wolowski could also boast a successful political career. It ran clearly at two speeds: the first stage took place during the Revolutions of 1848, the other one after 1871. Throughout this time, Wolowski was above all a classical liberal: emphasising, following Constant, Mill and his father, the importance of personal liberty, free courts, freedom of speech, parliamentarism, but also private property, the free market, entrepreneurial freedom and so on. He also placed significant emphasis on the family, while his view of the role of women in society was conservative, in keeping with the times. What distinguished him from the most ardent supporters of laissez-faire was that he saw in economic life an area of action for the state. The state was to stabilise money and the economy as a whole, on the one hand, and indirectly propel it, on the other, through skilful action in the spheres of banking and infrastructure. At the same time, for the liberal Wolowski, the issue who governed was far less important than how to protect the most important individual freedoms. For this reason, the liberal monarchy of Louis-Philippe certainly suited the Pole, but he was also able to quickly come to terms with a possible democratic republic, provided liberal freedoms were preserved. However, the first approach proved unsuccessful: the events of 1848 and 1849 terrified Wolowski and pushed him towards the conservative right. It was, however, a temporary and rather artificial alliance. For the rest of his life, Wolowski had friends among French monarchists and conservative Catholics, but he was never quite one of them. The differences were clearly visible in the 1870s. Indeed, the Second Empire interrupted his political career, but he returned to the National Assembly in 1871. Interestingly, he was back again in alliance with the Right, this time prompted by the events of the Paris Commune of 1871, which to Wolowski must have seemed like a deepened repetition of the history of 1848. However, when it became clear that the republican authorities had dealt with the revolution, when a democratic and conservative republic, based on what he saw as a balance of order and freedom, was possible, Wolowski immediately accepted it. And he contributed both through his political votes and his financial powers – to its eventual consolidation. He thus belongs to the co-creators of republican France.

Ironically, Louis Wolowski was probably much more interested in contributing to the restoration of an independent Poland. He took a direct part in the November Uprising, while during the January Uprising, he participated in the diplomatic and propaganda efforts of the Hotel Lambert, in both cases with equally negative results. It is therefore possible that he died with a sense of defeat, probably ill-grounded: through his activity at the Polish school, and his financial assistance to Polish institutions, Louis Wolowski certainly did his first homeland a significant service.

An open question remains why deputy and senator Wolowski never become a minister. Why, even when France was governed by his friends, was he not even mentioned among the candidates for ministerial posts? More broadly, why did he remain rather a man of the second rank until the end of his life? Politically, Thiers, Faucher, Barrot, Rémusat and other leaders always stood before him. Among the Poles, he was one of a whole series of figures associated over the years with the Hotel Lambert, not necessarily the most important. He gave up his function as director of the Crédit Foncier after only two years, thereafter, functioning clearly in the shadow of Frémy and Soubeyran.

This touches on the other side of Louis Wolowski, his peculiar elusiveness. The simplest answer is that Wolowski was not a born leader. This is probably part of the truth. Indeed, neither during the Revolution of 1848 nor after 1871, was he one of the most important personalities in French politics. He probably lacked charisma and, unusually in 19th century politics, was not the best speaker. All parliamentary leaders of the time were good orators. Wolowski clearly was not. He was always well-prepared for his speeches, introducing an academic element to them, but in effect tiring rather than enthralling his listeners. It is also possible that his Polish origin may have been a barrier for the French, a barrier of which he was fully aware. Nor can I completely rule out the possibility that Wolowski may simply not have had such far-reaching ambitions. All the more so because he fulfilled himself somewhat differently. Wolowski was a person who forms a backbone of society. Through his diverse activities and extremely wide-ranging acquaintances and connections, he brought together people from different political and national groups, with sometimes very different horizons of thought. This is well reflected in his activities during the January Uprising, when the professor of the Conservatoire des Arts et Métiers was an important intermediary between Czartoryski or the Polish Committee and the French, as well as some national circles and personalities. Wolowski, moreover, harmoniously combined Poland and France in his own soul, which was indeed fully Polish and French at the same time. There is nothing to deny his patriotism, be it Polish or French, and his genuine attachment to his two homelands. At the Academy of Moral and Political Sciences, Wolowski necessarily worked with people drawn from both the republican left and the monarchist right. He managed to attract both supporters of the emerging Second Empire and its staunch opponents, liberals, and supporters of authoritarianism to the Banque Foncière de Paris project. He was one of the bridges between economists and politicians. The only group that remained clearly outside the perimeter of his contacts (and interests) were the radicals, revolutionaries, and early socialists of the time. The year 1848 seems to have dug a chasm between them and Wolowski that he was no longer able to cross.

This, it seems, was largely the strength and importance of Wolowski. He created bridges between different groups and individuals. In many cases, these links must have been based on mutual small favours, of which traces are often hard to find today. To a considerable extent, he undoubtedly benefited from them himself. At the same time, he was one of those public figures without whom no society can function. By remaining in the second tier, he assisted if not enabled the politicians of the first tier to operate. He was an important part of the glue that keeps societies from crumbling into wall-separated rival groups or coteries. He quietly wove an intricate web of social and political connections. He certainly did not play a role like Thiers, Broglie (father and son) Passy, Faucher, Czartoryski or Zamoyski. However, without the support of Wolowski and people like him, the former could not have functioned.

Selected Bibliography:

Articles and books by Louis Wolowski:

Gaszyński Konstanty, transl. Wołowski Ludwik *Wiersz do Henrjetty Sontag*, Warszawa 1830

Wolowski Louis *Aux électeurs du département de la Seine*, Paris 1849.

Wolowski Louis *Communication verbale sur l'exposition de 1862. Extrait du compte-rendu de l'Académie des Sciences Morales et Politiques rédigé par M. Charles Verge. Sous la direction de M. le Secrétaire perpétuel de l'Académie*, Imprimerie E. Colas, Orléans 1862.

Wolowski Louis *Assemblée Nationale. Année 1873. Annexe au procès-verbal de la séance du 27 février 1873. Rapport supplémentaire fait au nom de la commission du budget chargée d'examiner la proposition de loi de MM. Labelonye, Bozerian, Morin et plusieurs de leurs collègues pour l'établissement d'un timbre ou signe spécial destiné à être apposé sur les marques commerciales et de fabrique*, Assemblée Nationale, Paris 1873.

Wolowski Louis *La Banque d'Angleterre et les banques d'Ecosse*, Guillaumin, Paris 1867.

Wolowski Louis *La Monnaie. Entretien sur le traité de monnaie de Copernic*, Didier et Cie, Paris 1864.

Wolowski Louis *Allocution prononcée le 19 juillet 1867, à la première séance publique de la Société de Statistique de Paris, par M. Wolowski, membre de l'Institut, Président*, Paris 1867.

Wolowski Louis *Assemblée Nationale. Séance du 24 décembre 1873. Discussion générale du budget. Discours de M. Wolowski, député de la Seine*, Assemblée Nationale, Paris 1874.

Wolowski Louis *Aux citoyens électeurs du département de la Seine*, Paris 1848.

Wolowski Louis *Communication verbale sur l'exposition de 1862. Extrait du compte-rendu de l'Académie des Sciences Morales et Politiques rédigé par M. Charles Verge. Sous la direction de M. le Secrétaire perpétuel de l'Académie*, Imprimerie E. Colas, Paris 1862.

Wolowski Louis *Conseil Général du Commerce. Enquête sur la question monétaire. Déposition de M. Wolowski*, Paris 1870.

Wolowski Louis *Cours de législation industrielle. Cinquième année 1843–1844. Première leçon (22 novembre 1843). Des fraudes commerciales*, Paris 1843.

Wolowski Louis *Cours de législation industrielle. Introduction. Discours prononcé à l'ouverture du cours, le 9 janvier 1840, par M. L. Wolowski, Avocat à la Cour Royale de Paris, Professeur de législation industrielle au Conservatoire des Arts et Métiers,* Paris 1840

Wolowski Louis *Cours de législation industrielle. Sixième année. Première leçon (27 novembre 1844). De l'organisation du travail,* Paris 1844.

Wolowski Louis *De l'organisation du travail,* „Le Siècle ", 09.04.1848.

Wolowski Louis *De la division du sol. Extrait de la « Revue des Deux Mondes », livraison du 1 aout 1857,* Imprimerie J. Claye, Paris 1857.

Wolowski Louis *De la Monnaie,* Hachette, Paris 1868.

Wolowski Louis *Des Sociétés par actions,* Paris 1838.

Wolowski Louis *Discours prononcé à la séance publique annuelle de la société centrale d'agriculture de France tenue le dimanche 27 juin 1875 par M. Wolowski, député de la Seine, président de la société,* Paris 1875.

Wolowski Louis *Discours prononcé au 17 anniversaire de la Révolution polonaise (29 novembre 1847),* Paris 1848.

Wolowski Louis *Eloge de Quételet. Discours prononcé par M. Wolowski de l'Institut devant la Société de Statistique de Paris,* Imprimerie Berger Levrault et Cie, Nancy 1874.

Wolowski *Louis Enquête sur les principes et les faits généraux qui régissent la circulation monétaire et fiduciaire. Déposition de M. Wolowski, membre de l'Institut. Séances des 21, 28 et 30 novembre 1865,* Imprimerie Impériale, Paris 1866.

Wolowski Louis *Études d'économie politique et de statistique. Le Paupérisme des Flandres. Exposition agricole et industrielle de Bruxelles. Le commerce des grains. L'Union douanière. Da la liberté commerciale. De la stastistique,* Guillaumin, Paris 1848.

Wolowski Louis *Henri IV économiste. Introduction de l'industrie de la soie en France,* Firmin Didot frères, Paris 1855.

Wolowski Louis *Inauguration du monument d'Adam Mickiewicz à Montmorency (21 mai 1867). Allocution de M. Louis Wolowski,* Librairie du Luxembourg, Paris 1867.

Wolowski Louis *Introduction,* [in:] Cibrario Louis *Economie politique du Moyen Age,* Guillaumin, Paris 1859.

Wolowski Louis *Introduction,* [in:] L. Faucher *Mélanges d'économie politique et de finances. Histoire financière* , Paris 1856, pp. I–XIX.

Wolowski Louis *L'impôt sur le revenu. Discours de M. Wolowski, député de la Seine (Séances du 22 et 27 décembre 1871) avec des observations et des annexes sur l'impôt du revenu aux Etats-Unis et en Angleterre,* Assemblée Nationale, Paris 1872.

Wolowski Louis *L'Influence du change sur le marché monétaire. Extrait de la Revue des Deux Mondes, Livraison du 15 septembre 1868,* J. Claye, Paris 1868.

Wolowski Louis *La Banque d'Angleterre et les banques d'Ecosse,* Guillaumin, Paris 1867.

Wolowski Louis *La Crise financière de l'Angleterre. Extrait de la „Revue des Deux Mondes". Livraison du 15 aout 1866*, Paris, 1866.

Wolowski Louis *La Liberté commerciale et les résultats du traité de commerce de 1860*, Guillaumin, Paris 1869.

Wolowski Louis *La question des banques*, Guillaumin, Paris 1864.

Wolowski Louis *La Question monétaire*, Guillaumin, Paris 1869.

Wolowski Louis *Le Change et la circulation*, Guillaumin, Paris 1869.

Wolowski Louis *Le Grand dessein de Henri IV*, Firmin Didot frères, Paris 1860.

Wolowski Louis *Le Travail des enfants dans les manufactures*, Guillaumin, Paris 1868.

Wolowski Louis *Les finances de la Russie*, Guillaumin, Paris 1864.

Wolowski Louis *Les résultats du traité de commerce de 1860. Conférence faite sous les auspices de l'Association polytechnique le 10 mai 1868*, Chaix et Cie, Paris 1868.

Wolowski Louis *Mazarin. Fragment d'une histoire des relations commerciales entre la France et l'Angleterre. Lu dans la séance publique annuelle des cinq académies le 14 aout 1867*, Firmin Didot frères, Paris 1867.

Wolowski Louis *Mémoire sur le cours de politique constitutionnelle de Benjamin Constant, lu à l'Académie des Sciences Morales et Politiques*, Guillaumin, Paris 1862.

Wolowski Louis *Notions générales d'économie politique. Conférences populaires faites à l'Asile Impérial de Vincennes sous le patronage de S. M. L'Impératrice*, Hachette, Paris 1868.

Wolowski Louis *Préface,* [in:] G. Roscher *Principes d'économie politique,* t.I, Guillaumin, Paris 1857.

Wolowski Louis *Quelques notes sur la question monétaire*, Hennuyer et fils, Paris 1868.

Wolowski Louis *Quelques observations présentées à la Commission du Corps législatif chargée de l'examen du traité entre la Ville de Paris et le Crédit Foncier*, Paris 1870.

Wolowski Louis *Rapport sur le concours relatif à l'administration de Colbert. Fait au nom de la section d'économie politique et de statistique. Lu à l'Académie des Sciences Morales et Politiques, dans les séances du 5 avril, 24 mai et 18 octobre 1856*, Firmin Didot frères, Paris 1860.

Wolowski Louis *Rapport verbal sur l'exposition universelle de Vienne*, Guillaumin, Paris 1874.

Wolowski Louis *Rapport, Représentant du Peuple, membre du Conseil Général, au nom de la Commission chargée de la question relative au crédit Foncier*, Paris 1850.

Wolowski Louis *Réforme hypothécaire: organisation du crédit Foncier*, Guillaumin, Paris 1844.

Wolowski Louis *Réforme hypothécaire: organisation du crédit foncier*, Guillaumin, Paris 1844.

Wolowski Louis *Résultats économiques du paiement de la contribution de guerre en Allemagne et en France*, Paris 1874.

Wolowski Louis *Scrutin du 2 juillet 1871. Aux citoyens électeurs du département de la Seine*, Paris 1871.

Wolowski Louis *Thèse pour la licence*, Paris 1832.

Wolowski Louis *Un chapitre de l'histoire financière de l'Angleterre. La suspension des payements de la Banque et le bullion-report*, Paris 1865

Wolowski Louis *Un Grand économiste français du XIV siècle*, Firmin Didot frères, Paris 1862.

Wolowski Louis *XXVI Jury. Papiers de teinture, meubles etc.*, [in:] *Exposition universelle de 1851. Travaux de la Commission française sur l'industrie des nations: publiés par ordre de l'Empereur*, t. VII, Paris 1855, pp. 1–45.

Wołowski Ludwik *Jedność, zapomnienie*, „Orzeł Biały. Dziennik polityczny", no. 4, 14.12.1830, pp. 25–32.

French National Assembly :

- *Annexe au procès-verbal de la séance du 27 février 1873. Rapport supplémentaire fait au nom de la commission du budget chargée d'examiner la proposition d loi de MM. Labelonye, Bozerian, Morin et plusieurs de leurs collègues pour l'établissement d'un timbre ou signe spécial destiné à être apposé sur les marques commerciales et de fabrique. Par M. Wolowski, membre de l'Assemblée nationale*, Paris 1873.
- *Proposition relative à l'Organisation du Crédit territorial, présentée le 24 juin 1848 par le citoyen Wolowski*, Paris 1848.
- *Rapport au nom de la Commission chargée d'examiner la proposition de MM. Wolowski, Scheurer –Kestner, le vicomte d'Haussonville, Lefebure, Martin (Henri), De Pressensé, Passy, Dietz-Monnin, Laboulaye, Georges Claude, Varroy, comte d'Harcourt, Leblond, Berlet, Claude, Bamberger, Keller, Scherer et Schoelcher, membres de l'Assemblée nationale, en faveur des Alsaciens et Lorrains qui conservent la qualité de Français, par M. Wolowski, membre de l'Assemblée nationale*, [in:] „Assemblée nationale. Impressions. Projets de lois, propositions, rapports, etc. Tome XXX, numéros 1417 à 1517", Versailles 1873.
- *Rapport fait au nom de la Commission du budget de 1850, sur le projet de loi tendant à accorder au Ministre de l'agriculture et du commerce, sur l'exercice de 1850, un crédit extraordinaire de 70 680 fr. 16 c. pour l'installation de l'Institut agronomique et à annuler pareille somme sur les exercices de 1848 et 1849. Par M. Wolowski, Représentant du peuple*. Séance du 1 juillet 1850, Paris 1850.
- *Séance du 1 février 1872. Discussion du projet relatif à la dénonciation du traité de commerce de 1860 avec l'Angleterre. Discours de M. Wolowski, député de la Seine*, Paris 1872.
- *Séance du 10 juillet 1874. Discussion du budget. Proposition relative au remboursement de la Banque de France. Discours de M. Wolowski*, Paris 1874.

- *Séance du 13 février 1874. Discussion sur l'impôt des chèques. Discours de M. Wolowski*, Paris 1874.
- *Séance du 24 décembre 1873. Discussion générale du budget. Discours de M. Wolowski, député de la Seine*. Paris 1873.
- *Session de 1871. Annexe au procès-verbal de la séance du 2 aout 1871. Proposition de loi ayant pour objet un impôt de 2 p. cent sur la fabrication et la vente de toutes marchandises autres que celles destinées a l'alimentation, au moyen d 'un timbre proportionné sur les factures. Par M. Wolowski, membre de l'Assemblée Nationale*, Paris 1871.

„Revue de Législation et de Jurisprudence" – selected articles[1119]:

- *Bulletin législatif*, vol. 13, 1841, pp. 143–151.
- *Congrès pénitentiaire de Bruxelles*, vol. 3 (30), 1847, pp. 184–223.
- *De l'enseignement du droit et de l'institution des concours*, vol. 9, 1838–1839, pp. 241–253.
- *De l'organisation du Crédit Foncier*, vol. 3 (33), 1848, pp. 193–304.
- *De l'organisation industrielle et de la législation douanière de la France avant le ministère de Colbert*, vol. 17, 1843, pp. 265–299.
- *De la mobilisation du crédit foncier*, vol. 10, 1839, pp. 241–276.
- *De la peine de mort*, vol. 3 (33), 1848, pp. 111–121.
- *De la société conjugale*, vol. 1(25), 1846, pp. 164–192 ; vol. 1(43), 1852, pp. 5–21, 62–94.
- *Des droits du travail et de l'action de l'état*, vol. 1 (31), 1848, pp. 143–160.
- *Des sociétés par actions*, vol. 7, 1837–1838, pp. 180–195, 258–304.
- *La concurrence et la coalition*, vol. 10, 1839, pp. 367–371.
- *La législation anglaise sur les coalitions*, vol. 2(41), 1851, pp. 97–132.
- *Le Crédit foncier en Belgique*, vol. 3 (39), 1850, pp. 193–221.
- *Législation industrielle en Allemagne. Des brevets d'invention*, vol. 15, 1842, pp. 405–438.
- *Notice biographique sur Alexandre This*, vol. 1(25), 1846, pp. 490–492.
- *Observations sur les réformes à apporter à notre régime hypothécaire*, vol. 16, 1842, pp. 442–478.
- *Quelques observations sur le principe fondamental de la législation en matière de procédure civile et sur les conditions essentielles qui en dérivent*, vol. 3, 1835–1836, pp. 30–39.
- *Rapport fait au Conseil Général de l'Agriculture, du Commerce et des Manufactures par M. Wolowski, Représentant du peuple, membre du Conseil général, Au nom de*

1119 Full bibliography of Louis Wolowski's texts from „Revue de Législation et de Jurisprudence": *Tables analytiques de la "Revue de législation"...*, pp. 80–81.

la Commission chargée de la question relative au crédit foncier, vol. 2(38), 1850, pp. 97–128.
- *Réforme administrative. Des conditions d'admission et d'avancement dans les fonctions publiques. Création de Facultés des sciences administratives*, vol. 22, 1845, pp. 203–219.
- *Réforme hypothécaire*, vol. 2 (35), 1849, pp. 78–116 ; vol. 3 (39), 1850, pp. 244–315.
- *Régime hypothécaire*, vol. 1, 1834 – 1835, pp. 35–48, 276–290.
- *Représentants du peuple. Contrainte par corps*, vol. 1(40), 1851, pp. 110–128.
- *Statistique de la justice civile et commerciale pour 1842*, vol. 19, 1844, pp. 557–568.
- *Statistique de la justice criminelle pour 1842*, vol. 20, 1844, pp. 225–231.

„Journal des Economistes" – selected articles[1120]

- *Le travail national. – De l'union douanière entre la France et la Belgique. – Deuxième Mémoire de la Chambre de commerce de Bordeaux. – Défense du travail national. – Compte-rendu par le comité central à ses commettants*, vol. 6, 1843, pp. 377–396.
- *Comment un peuple se relève, Ouverture du cours d'histoire des doctrines et des faits économiques au Collège de France par M. Levasseur*, vol. 20, 1870, pp. 393–397.
- *De la réforme hypothécaire*, vol. 27, 1850, pp. 305–324.
- *La Liquidation sociale* , vol. 18 (ser. III), 1870, pp. 112–126.
- *Question des banques*, vol. 128 (ser. II), 1864, pp. 282–290.
- *Revue des recueils étrangers consacrés à l'étude de l'économie politique. – Essai sur la politique et la statistique des systèmes de culture (d'après M. ROSCHER, professeur à l'Université de Gœttingue)*, vol. 6 (ser. II), 1855, pp. 65–83, 228–264.

„Séances et travaux de l'Académie des Sciences Morales et Politiques" – selected articles[1121].

- *Communication sur le commerce extérieur de la France en 1855*, vol. XXXVIII, 1856, pp. 277–285.
- *De l'affranchissement des serfs en Russie*, vol. XLVI, Paris 1858, pp. 189–221, 343–365.

1120 Full bibliography of „Journal des Economistes" : *Table complète du Journal des Economistes* https://www.institutcoppet.org/table-complete-journal-economistes/ , (retrieved 03.08.2023).

1121 Full bibliography of Louis Wolowski's texts from „Séances et travaux de l'Académie des Sciences Morales et Politiques" : *Séances et travaux de l'Académie des Sciences Morales et Politiques. Table alphabétique et bibliographique des matières et des auteurs figurant dans les 130 premiers volumes*, Alphonse Picard, Paris 1889, pp. 302–305.

- *De la société conjugale,* vol. IX, Paris 1846, pp. 990–104, 267–280.
- *Des coalitions en Angleterre,* vol. XIX, 1851, pp. 473–487.
- *Etudes sur l'industrie suisse,* vol. XII, 1847, pp. 167–182.
- *L'Economie politique en Italie, vol.* XLVII, Paris 1859, pp. 197–248.
- *L'Exposition universelle de Vienne,* vol. CI, 1874, pp. 77–96, 195–205.
- *L'Or et l'argent, vol. Question monétaire,* vol. LXXXIX, Paris 1869, pp. 337–364.
- *La carte postale,* vol. XCIX, Paris 1873, pp. 565–576.
- *La dernière exposition de l'industrie à Zurich,* vol. XI, Paris 1847, pp. 388–403.
- *La propriété littéraire et le droit de copie,* vol. XLVIII, Paris 1859, pp. 115–148.
- *La suspension des paiements de la Banque d'Angleterre,* vol. LXXV, Paris 1866, pp. 47–85, 267–320.
- *Le Change. Rapport sur la théorie des changes étrangers par M. George Goschen,,* vol. LXXIX, Paris 1867, pp. 5–56 ; vol. LXXX, Paris 1867, pp. 25–64.
- *Le Renchérissement des moyens d'existence,* vol. CIII, 1875, pp. 481–499.
- *Les Droits de douanes et les anciens traités de commerce entre la France et l'Angleterre,,* vol. LII, Paris 1860, pp. 425–447 ; vol. LIII, Paris 1860, pp. 433–458 ; vol. LIV, Paris 1860, pp. 187–243 ; vol. LVIII, Paris 1861, pp. 218–379.
- *Les métaux précieux et la circulation fiduciaire,* vol. LXXVI, Paris 1866, pp. 249–270 ; vol. VIII (LXXVIII), Paris 1866, pp. 353–384.
- *Les origines de la loi de Germinal,* vol. XC, Paris 1869, pp. 386–416 ; vol. XXI (XCI) Paris 1869, pp. 419–442 ; vol. XCIII, Paris 1870, pp. 233–249, 429–455.
- *Mémoire sur l'application de la méthode historique a l'étude de l'économie politique,* vol. XLII, Paris 1857, pp. 361–381 ; vol. XLIII, Paris 1858, pp. 301–315, 449–474.
- *Mémoire sur la division du sol,* vol. XLII, 1857, pp. 95–112, 257–296.
- *Mémoire sur l'administration de Henri IV, ancienne législation sur le commerce des grains,* vol. XXXIV, 1855, pp. 321–348.
- *Mémoire sur l'Administration économique de Henri IV et sur l'introduction de l'Industrie de la soie en France,* vol. XXXIV, 1855, pp. 33–54.
- *Rapport sur un ouvrage de M. Frédéric Passy intitulé: Les Machines, leur influence sur le développement de l'humanité et sur le cours d'économie industrielle de l'Association Polytechnique,* vol. LXXVIII, Paris 1866, pp. 463–476.
- *Rapport verbal à propos d'un ouvrage de M. R. Greg intitulé « Political problems for our age and country ». Le nouveau régime,* vol. XCIX, Paris 1873, pp. 85–95.
- *Rapport verbal sur divers ouvrages de M. Cibrario,* vol. XXXV, 1856, pp. 401–404.
- *Rapport verbal sur la correspondance et la vie parlementaire de Léon Faucher,* vol. LXXXIV, Paris 1868, pp. 159–160.
- *Rapport verbal sur le Congrès International de Statistique tenu à Florence en septembre 1867,* vol. LXXXII, Paris 1867, pp. 469–475.
- *Rapport verbal sur le dernier compte-rendu de l'administration des postes en Angleterre,* vol. XCIX, Paris 1873, pp. 160–168.
- *Rapport verbal sur trois ouvrages de M. Levasseur intitulés: 1. Notions fondamentales de l'économie politique 2. La Prévoyance et l'épargne 3. Les Assurances,* vol. LXXXIII, Paris 1868, pp. 203–205.

- *Rapport verbal sur un ouvrage de M. Blüntschli intitulé: Dictionnaire politique,* vol. XLIV, Paris 1858, pp. 461–462 ; vol. LI, Paris 1860, pp. 295–300.
- *Rapport verbal sur un ouvrage de M. Engel intitulé: Preussiche Statistik,* vol. LXXV, 1866, p. 173.
- *Rapport verbal sur un ouvrage de M. le comte Cieszkowski, intitulé: Des salles d'asile envisagées comme instituts d'éducation populaire,* vol. XXXVII, 1856, pp. 163–171.
- *Rapport verbal sur un volume de la statistique de la France relatif au mouvement de la population en 1851, 1852 et 1853,,* vol. XLI, 1857, pp. 285–292.

Entries in a dictionary:
Coquelin Charles, Guillaumin Gilbert (dir.) *Dictionnaire de l'économie politique: contenant l'exposition des principes de la science, l'opinion des écrivains qui ont le plus contribué à sa fondation et à ses progrès, la bibliographie générale de l'économie politique par noms d'auteurs et par ordre des matières avec des notices biographiques et une appréciation raisonnée des principaux ouvrages,* vol. I, A – I, Guillaumin, Paris 1852 :

- *Conservatoire des Arts et Métiers,* pp. 461–463.
- *Crédit Foncier,* pp. 497–508.
- *Dessins de fabrique,* pp. 552–553.
- *Hypothèques, pp.* 886–897.

Archives:

Archives de l'Assemblée Nationale, Paris.

Archives de Paris, Paris.

Archives Nationales du Monde du Travail, Roubaix.

Archives Nationales, Paris.

Archiwum Archidiecezjalne Warszawskie, Warsaw.

Archiwum Główne Akt Dawnych, Warsaw.

Archiwum Państwowe, Cracow.

Archiwum Państwowe, Warsaw.

Archiwum Polskiej Akademii Nauk i Polskiej Akademii Umiejętności, Cracow.

Biblioteka Jagiellońska, Cracow.

Biblioteka Książąt Czartoryskich, Cracow.

Biblioteka Narodowa, Warsaw.

Biblioteka Polska w Paryżu, Paris.

Mairie de Gisors, actes de l'état civil, Gisors.

Musée Carnavalet, Paris.

Muzeum Adama Mickiewicza w Paryżu, Paris.

Contemporary publications, memoirs, diaries, letters:

Adam Juliette *Mes illusions et nos souffrances pendant le Siège de Paris*, Alphonse Lemerre, Paris 1906.

Almanach des 25,000 adresses des principaux habitans de Paris, Henri Dulac Editeur, Paris 1835–1848.

Almanach Impérial, Veuve Berger-Levrault et fils, Paris 1853–1868.

Apponyi Rodolphe *25 ans à Paris (1826-1850): Journal du comte Rodolphe Apponyi, attaché de l'ambassade d'Autriche-Hongrie à Paris*, vol. IV, Plon-Nourrit, Paris 1926.

Barante Prosper de *Souvenirs du baron de Barante de l'Académie Française 1782–1866*, vol. VIII, Calmann Lévy, Paris 1901.

Barrot Odilon *Mémoires posthumes*, vol. II–IV, Charpentier, Paris 1875–1876.

Bartkowski Jan *Wspomnienia z 1830/31 roku (fragment)*, Drukarnia Władysława Łozińskiego, Lwów 1898.

Bastiat Frédéric *Dzieła* zebrane, vol. II, Wydawnictwo Prohibita, Warszawa 2009.

Benoit Joseph *Confessions d'un prolétaire*, Éditions sociales, Paris 1968.

Berg Nikolai *Zapiski o polskich spiskach i powstaniach*, vol. II, Druk. A.VOL. Jezierskiego, Warszawa 1906.

Blanc Louis *Histoire de la Révolution de 1848*, vol. I, C. Marpon et E. Flammarion, Paris 1880.

Bosq Paul *Souvenirs de l'Assemblée nationale, 1871–1875*, Plon, Paris 1908.

Branicki Augustyn *ANATKH. Roman radiographique*, V. Villerelle, Paris.

Caussidière Marc *Mémoires de Caussidière, ex-préfet de police et représentant du peuple*, vol. II, Michel Lévy Frères, Paris 1849.

Chambord, Henri de Bourbon *Manifeste de M. le comte de Chambord: 5 juillet 1871*, Pierre Grollier, Montpellier 1871.

Chateaubriand François René de *De la Monarchie selon la charte*, Impr. Lenormant, Paris 1816.

Chateaubriand François René de *Génie du christianisme*, Migneret, Paris 1802.

Chateaubriand François René de *Voyages en Amérique et en Italie*, Ladvocat, Paris 1827.

Chevalier Michel *Cours d'économie politique*, vol. III, *La Monnaie*, Capelle, Paris 1866.

Chevalier Michel *Cours d'économie politique fait au Collège de France: Année 1841-42*, Capelle, Paris 1842.

Cochin Augustin *Paris, sa population, son industrie. Mémoire lu à l'Académie des Sciences Morales et Politiques. Les 18 et 25 juin 1864*, Durand, Duniol, Paris 1864.

The Code Napoleon. The Lawbrook Exchange, London 2015.

Coin-Delisle Jean-Baptiste-César, Million Charles *Tables analytiques de la "Revue de législation" et de la "Revue critique de législation et de jurisprudence": précédées des tables de la "Thémis" et de la "Revue de droit français et étranger"*, Cotillon Editeur, Paris 1860.

Collection complète des lois, décrets, ordonnances, réglemens, et avis du Conseil-d'États. vol. 32–34, 50 A. Guyot et Scribe, Paris 1832–1834, 1850.

Comité Central Franco-Polonais: aux Amis de la Pologne: aux Amis de la Justice et de l'Humanité, Paris 1863.

Conseil Général du Commerce. *Enquête sur la question monétaire. Déposition de M. Wolowski*, Guillaumin, Paris 1870.

Conseil Supérieur du Commerce, de l'Agriculture et de l'Industrie *Enquête sur la question monétaire: Dépositions: procès-verbaux des délibérations du Conseil Supérieur; résumé de l'enquête; documents; tables*, Imprimerie Nationale, Paris 1872.

Constant Benjamin *Cours de politique constitutionnelle*, P. Plancher, Paris 1818–1820.

Constant Benjamin *De la liberté des Anciens comparée à celle des Modernes*, Plancher, Paris 1819.

Constant Benjamin *De la religion considérée dans sa source, ses formes et ses développements*, Bossange, Paris 1824–1831.

Constant Benjamin *O Monarchii konstytucyjnej i rękojmiach publicznych*, Wolters Kluwer, Warszawa 2016.

Copernic Nicolas, Oresme Nicolas *Traictié de la première invention des monnoies de Nicole Oresme et Traité de la monnoie de Copernic*, Guillaumin, Paris 1864.

Courcelle-Seneuil Jean Gustave *Introduction*, [in:] Ch. Coquelin *Le crédit et les banques*, Guillaumin, Paris 1859.

Courcelle-Seneuil Jean Gustave *Le Crédit et la banque*, Pagnerre, Paris 1840.

Czartoryski Władysław *Mowa xięcia Władysława Czartoryskiego miana na posiedzeniu Towarzystwa Literacko-Historycznego w Paryżu dnia 29 listopada 1861 roku*, Biblioteka Polska, Paryż 1861.

Czartoryski Władysław *Pamiętnik 1860–1864. Protokoły posiedzeń Biura Hotelu Lambert part I, II. Entrevues politiques*, PWN, Warszawa 1960.

Darasz Wojciech *Pamiętnik Emigranta*, Ossolineum, Wrocław 1953.

Daumier Honoré *Album comique*, vol. II, *Les représentants représentés*, Aubert, Paris 1849.

Décembre Joseph, Alonnier Edmond *Le coup d'État du 2 décembre 1851: historique des événements qui ont précédé le coup d'État, physionomie de Paris, arrestations et barricades, types et portraits des principaux personnages, faits qui ont suivi la chute de la république, pièces et documents officiels*, Décembre-Alonnier, Paris 1868.

Delalain Edouard, *Le Siége de Paris (Du 18 septembre 1870 au 28 janvier 1871). Journal historique et anecdotique*, J. Lefort Imprimeur Editeur, Lille, Paris 1874.

Dembowski Leon *Moje wspomnienia*, vol. II, Księgarnia K. Grendyszyńskiego, Petersburg 1898.

Dernałowicz Maria *Kronika życia i twórczości Mickiewicza. Paryż, Lozanna. Czerwiec 1834 – październik 1840*, Instytut Badań Literackich PAN, Warszawa 1996.

Doktór Jan (oprac.) *Księga Słów Panskich. Ezoteryczne wykłady Jakuba Franka*, vol. I, Wyd. Semper, Warszawa 1997.

Domeyko Ignacy *Listy do Władysława Laskowicza*, Instytut Wydawniczy PAX, Warszawa 1976

du Casse Albert *Les Dessous du coup d'État, 1851*, Albert Savine Editeur, Paris 1891.

du Puynode Gustave *De la monnaie, du crédit et de l'impôt*, vol. I, Guillaumin, Paris 1863.

Durand Hippolyte *Commentaire de la loi du 13 décembre 1848 sur la contrainte par corps et du tarif du 24 mars 1849*, Videcoq fils aîné, Paris 1850.

Dyaryusz Sejmu z r. 1830–1831, vol. I–VI, Wyd. Roztworowski Michał, Kraków 1907–1912.

Ecole nationale Polonaise. Distribution solennelle des prix. Année scolaire 1862–1863, Paris 1863.

Eisenbach Artur, Michalski Jerzy, Rostworowski Emanuel, Woliński Janusz (red.) *Materiały do dziejów Sejmu Czteroletniego*, vol. VI, Zakład Narodowy Imienia Ossolińskich, Wydawnictwo Polskiej Akademii Nauk, Wrocław-Warszawa-Kraków 1969.

Enquête sur les principes et les faits généraux qui régissent la circulation monétaire et fiduciaire. Déposition de M. Wolowski, membre de l'Institut. Séances des 21, 28 et 30 novembre 1865, Imprimerie impériale, Paris 1866.

Extrait du Moniteur Universel de 1852 contenant le texte du sénatus-consulte du 7 novembre 1852 sur le rétablissement de l'Empire et celui du décret du 2 décembre 1852 promulguant le sénatus-consulte, Paris 1852.

Falkowski Juliusz *Wspomnienia z roku 1848 i 1849*, part III, Wyd. K. Gadomska, Warszawa 1908.

Falloux Alfred de *Mémoires d'un royaliste*, vol. I, Perrin, Paris 1888.

Faucher Léon *Papiers inédits de Léon Faucher*, „La Révolution de 1848. Bulletin de la Société d'histoire de la Révolution de 1848 ", 1906, vol. 3, no. 14, pp. 91–111.

Faucher Léon *Correspondance*, vol. I, Amyot, Paris 1867.

Faucher Léon *Léon Faucher. Biographie et correspondance*, Librairie Auguste Thomas, Paris 1888.

Ferry Jules *Les comptes fantastiques d'Haussmann*, Guy Durier Editeur, Paris 1868.

Fourier Charles *Le Nouveau monde industriel et sociétaire*, Bossange père, Paris 1829.

Fourier Charles *Théorie de l'unité universelle*, vol. 1–4, Bossange père, Paris, 1822–1823.

Gałęzowski Seweryn *Listy Seweryna Gałęzowskiego do Bohdana Zaleskiego*, „Acta Medicorum Polonorum" no. 2, 2012, pp. 122–138.

Garnier-Pagès Louis – Antoine *Histoire de la Révolution de 1848*, vol. V, 3, Pagnerre, Paris 1866.

Giller Agaton *Dr Seweryn Gałęzowski. Wspomnienie*, „Ruch Literacki. Tygodnik poświęcony Literaturze, Sztukom pięknym, Nauce i Rzeczom społecznym", vol. I, 1878, pp. 265–266.

Gomulicki Wiktor *Warszawa wczorajsza*, Czytelnik, Warszawa 1961.

Goncourt Edmond and Jules de *Journal des Goncourt. Mémoires de la vie littéraire*, vol. IV, *1870–1871*, G. Charpentier et E. Fasquelle, Paris 1890.

Gorecka Maria *Wspomnienia o Adamie Mickiewiczu*, Spółka Wydawnicza Polska, Kraków 1897.

Guizot François *Des moyens de gouvernement et d'opposition dans l'état actuel de la France*, Ladvocat, Paris 1821.

Guizot François *Histoire de la civilisation en France depuis la chute de l'Empire romain*, Pichon et Didier, Paris 1830.

Guizot François *Histoire générale de la civilisation en Europe*, Pichon et Didier Editeurs, Paris 1828.

Guizot François *Histoire générale de la civilisation en Europe*, Pichon et Didier, Paris 1828.

Guizot François *L'Histoire de France: depuis les temps les plus reculés jusqu'en 1789. Racontée à mes petits-enfants*, vol. I–V, Hachette, Paris 1870–1875.

Guizot François *Memoirs to illustrate the history of my time*, vol. III, Richard Bentley Publisher, London 1860.

Haussmann Georges Eugène *Mémoires du Baron Haussmann* vol. I *Avant l'Hotel de Ville*, Victor-Havard Editeur, Paris 1890.

Helman Zofia, Skowron Zbigniew, Wróblewska – Straus Hanna (ed.) *Korespondencja Fryderyka Chopina*, vol. I–II, Wydawnictwa Uniwersytetu Warszawskiego, Warszawa 2009–2017.

Hube Romuald *Pisma*, vol. I, nakł. M. Arcta, Warszawa 1905.

Hugo Victor *Choses vues. Souvenirs, journaux, cahiers*, Gallimard, Paris 2002.

Hugo Victor *The History of a Crime*, English translation by Andrew Locker, Jazzybee Verlag, Altenmünster 1977.

Janowski Jan Nepomucen *Notatki autobiograficzne*, Zakład Narodowy im. Ossolińskich, Wrocław 1950.

Janowski Józef Kajetan *Pamiętniki o powstaniu styczniowem*, vol. II, Druk. Jan Cotty, Warszawa 1925.

Januszkiewicz Eustachy *Notatki i wspomnienia z życia Adama Mickiewicza*, „Czas", no. 120, 25.05.1859

Jełowicki Aleksander *Moje wspomnienia*, E. Wende i Spółka, Poznań 1877.

Jenerał Zamoyski 1803–1868, vol. III, *1832–1837*, Biblioteka Kórnicka, Poznań 1914.

Josseau Jean-Baptiste *Traité du crédit Foncier suivi d'un traité du crédit agricole et du crédit Foncier colonial, contenant l'explication théorique et pratique de la législation spéciale*, Cosse, Marchal et Billard Editeurs, Paris 1872.

Kicka Natalia *Pamiętniki*, Instytut Wydawniczy PAX, Warszawa 1972.

Klaczko Julian *Notatki z podróży*, Uniwersytet Jagielloński, Kraków 1871.

Kostenicz Ksenia *Kronika życia i twórczości Mickiewicza. Ostatnie lata Mickiewicza, styczeń 1850 – 26 listopada 1855*, Instytut Badań Literackich PAN, Warszawa 1978.

Koźmian Andrzej Edward *Listy Andrzeja Edwarda Koźmiana*, vol. III-IV, Gubrynowicz i Schmidt, Lwów 1894 – 1896.

Koźmian Kajetan *Pamiętniki*, vol. III, Zakład Narodowy im. Ossolińskich, Wrocław – Warszawa – Kraków – Gdańsk 1972.

Krasińska z Branickich Eliza *Świadek epoki. Listy Elizy z Branickich Krasińskiej z lat 1835–1876*, vol. II-III, Wyd. Ancher, Warszawa 1996.

Krasiński Zygmunt *Listy do Augusta Cieszkowskiego, Edwarda Jaroszyńskiego, Bronisława Trentowskiego*, vol. I, Państwowy Instytut Wydawniczy, Warszawa 1988.

Krasiński Zygmunt *Listy do różnych adresatów*, vol. I-II, Państwowy Instytut Wydawniczy, Warszawa 1991.

Krasiński Zygmunt *Listy Zygmunta Krasińskiego do Stanisława Małachowskiego*, Drukarnia "Czasu" Fr. Kluczyckiego i sp., Kraków 1885.

La Mennais Félicité de *De la religion considérée dans ses rapports avec l'ordre politique et civil*, Paris 1825.

La Mennais Félicité de *Des progrès de la révolution et de la guerre contre l'Église*, Belin-Mandar et Devaux, Paris 1829.

Laboulaye Edouard *Le Parti libéral: son programme et son avenir*, Charpentier, Paris 1863.

Lamartine Alphonse de *Mémoires politiques*, Paris 1863.

Le droit au travail au Luxembourg et à l'Assemblée Nationale, Michel Lévy Frères, Paris 1849.

Ledru-Rollin Alexandre *Discours politiques et écrits divers*, vol. II, G. Baillière, Paris 1879.

Lelewel Joachim *Listy emigracyjne Joachima Lelewela*, vol. III, 1842–1848, Polska Akademia Umiejętności, Kraków 1952.

Lelewel Joachim *Listy emigracyjne Joachima Lelewela*, vol. III, IV, V, Ossolineum, Polska Akademia Umiejętności, Kraków-Wrocław 1952–1956.

Lewak Adam (red.) *Polska działalność dyplomatyczna w 1863–1864 r. Zbiór dokumentów*. vol. I, Wydawnictwo Ministerstwa Spraw Zagranicznych, Warszawa 1937.

Lewandowski Kazimierz *Pamiętnik wychodźca polskiego*, Instytut Wydawniczy PAX, Warszawa 1977.

Lipiński Tymoteusz *Zapiski z lat 1825–1831*, K. Bartoszewicz, Kraków 1883.

Loi électorale en date des 8 et 28 février et 15 mars 1849, „ Bulletin officiel du Ministère de l'intérieur ", n.3, Paris 1849, pp. 73–91.

Lucas Alphonse *Les clubs et les clubistes: histoire complète critique et anecdotique des clubs et des comités électoraux fondés à Paris depuis la révolution de 1848*, E. Dentu, Paris 1851.

Mac Mahon Edme Patrice Maurice de (Maréchal), *L'Armée de Versailles. Depuis sa formation jusqu'à la complète pacification de Paris*, A. Ghio, Paris 1872.

Makowiecka Zofia *Kronika życia i twórczości Mickiewicza. Mickiewicz w Collège de France. Październik 1840-maj 1844*, Państwowe Wydawnictwo Naukowe, Warszawa 1968.

Manifeste du Comité Central Franco-Polonais de France et adresses des Comités Polonais de Suède, de Suisse et de Belgique: suivies des Réponses du Comité central Franco-Polonais, Paris 1863.

Meaux Camille de *Souvenirs politiques: 1871–1877*, Plon – Nourrit, Paris 1905.

Mendès Catulle *Les 73 journées de la Commune (du 18 mars au 29 mai 1871*, Lachaud, Paris 1871.

Mickiewicz Adam *Listy*, part II, *1830–1841*, (*Dzieła*, vol. XV), Spółdzielnia Wydawnicza Czytelnik, Warszawa 2003.

Mickiewicz Władysław *Moja matka*, Krakowska Spółdzielnia Wydawnicza, Kraków 1926.

Mickiewicz Władysław *Emigracya Polska 1860–1890*, Spółka Wydawnicza Polska, Kraków 1908.

Mickiewicz Władysław *Pamiętniki*, Wyd. Iskry, Warszawa 2012.

Mill John Stuart *Correspondance inédite avec Gustave d'Eichthal: 1828–1842, 1864–1871*, F. Alcan, Paris 1898.

Mill John Stuart *The Subjection of Women*, Nine Books, New Delhi 2015.

Mill John Stuart *On Liberty*, Longmans, Green and Co., London 1864.

Młocki Alfred *Księga wspomnień Alfreda Młockiego,* Wyd. A. Giller, P. Zbrożek, Paryż 1884.

Mochnacki Maurycy *Pisma krytyczne i polityczne,* vol. I, Instytut Badań Literackich Polskiej Akademii Nauk, Kraków 1996.

Mochnacki Maurycy *Powstanie narodu polskiego w roku 1830 i 1831.,* vol. II, Księgarnia J.K. Żupańskiego, Poznań 1863.

Molinari Gustave de *Cours d'économie politique,* vol. II, Guillaumin, Paris 1863.

Napoléon III *Discours, messages et proclamations de S. M. Napoléon III, empereur des Français: 1849–1860,* Mirecourt, Paris 1860.

Nassau (Senior) William *Conversations with M. Thiers, M. Guizot and other distinguished persons, during the Second Empire,* vol. II, Hurst and Blackett, London 1878.

Nassau (Senior) William *Journals kept in France and in Italy,* vol. I, Henry S. King and Co., London 1871.

Niemcewicz Julian Ursyn *Pamiętniki Juliana Ursyna Niemcewicza: dziennik pobytu za granicą od dnia 21 lipca 1831 r. do 20 maja 1841 r.: według autografu w Bibliotece Towarzystwa Historyczno-Literackiego w Paryżu,* vol. 2, Księgarnia Jana Konstantego Żupańskiego, Poznań 1877.

Ollivier Emile *L'Empire libéral: études, récits, souvenirs,* vol. II, Garnier frères, Paris 1897.

Ordonnance du 26 septembre 1839 relative au Conservatoire Royal des Arts et Métiers ; [in:] Valserres Jacques de *Manuel de droit rural et d'économie Agricole,* G. Thorel, Paris 1847, pp. 875–876.

Ostrowski Antoni *Pamiętnik z czasów powstania listopadowego,* Zakład Narodowy im. Ossolińskich, Wrocław – Warszawa – Kraków 1961.

Pecqueur Constantin *Théorie nouvelle d'Économie sociale et politique ou Études sur l'organisation des sociétés,* Capelle, Paris 1842.

Périer Casimir *Opinions et discours de M. Casimir Périer,* vol. III, Paulin, Paris 1838.

Pikulski Gaudencyusz *Złość żydowska Przeciwko Bogu y bliźniemu Prawdzie y Sumnieniu. Na objaśnienie Talmudystów. Na dowód ich zaślepienia y Religii dalekiey od prawa Boskiego przez Moyżesza danego,* Drukarnia Jana Filipowicza, Lwów 1760.

Poklękowski, Eugeni Aleksander *Akt oskarżenia w sprawie przeciwko osobom oddanym pod Najwyższy Sąd Kryminalny w Królestwie Polskiem w zarzucie spełnienia zbrodni, wyłączonych od ogólnego przebaczenia,* Warszawa 1834.

Polak Bogusław (oprac.) *Virtuti Militari 1815–1831. Wybór źródeł,* vol. II, Wydaw. Uczelniane PK, Koszalin 2001.

Potocki Albert (Bałaszewicz Julian) *Pamiętnik szpiega,* vol. I, Państwowy Instytut Wydawniczy, Warszawa 1973.

Potrykowski Józef Alfons *Tułactwo Polaków we Francji. Dziennik emigranta*, vol. II, Wydawnictwo Literackie, Kraków 1974.

Proudhon Pierre – Joseph *Carnets*, Les Presses du Réel, Dijon 2004.

Rastoul Alfred *L'Église de Paris sous la Commune. Persécutions et martyrs*, C. Dillet, Paris 1871.

Réglement de la Société Littéraire Polonaise, Paris 1832.

Rémusat Charles de *Mémoires de ma vie*, vol. IV, *Les dernières années de la monarchie. La Révolution de 1848. La Seconde République (1841–1851)*, Plon, Paris 1958.

Ricardo David *Des principes de l'économie politique et de l'impôt*, Guillaumin, Paris 1847.

Ricardo Dawid *O zasadach ekonomii polityczne i o podatku*, Druk. Księży Pijarów, Warszawa 1826 – 1827.

Roscher Guillaume *Principes d'économie politique*, vol. I, Guillaumin, Paris 1857.

Saint-Edme Benoit, Sarrut Germain *Biographies polonaises extraites de la Biographies des hommes du jour par G. Sarrut et B. Saint-Edme*, Impr. Poussielgue, Paris 1836.

Saint-Simon Claude Henri de *Catéchisme des industriels*, impr. de Sétier, Paris 1823–1824.

Saint-Simon Claude Henri de *Du système industriel*, Antoine-Augustin Renoir, Paris 1822.

Saint-Simon Claude Henri de *Nouveau christianisme*, Bossange père, Paris 1825.

Say Jean-Baptiste *Traité d'économie politique ou simple exposition de la manière dont se forment, se distribuent et se consomment les richesses*, vol. 1, Antoine, Augustin Renouard, Paris 1814.

Schoelcher Victor *Histoire des crimes du 2 décembre*, vol. I, Bruxelles 1852.

Skarbek Fryderyk *Dzieje Księstwa Warszawskiego*, vol. 2, Drukarnia Artystyczna Saturnina Sikorskiego, Warszawa 1897.

Skarbek Fryderyk *O ubóstwie i ubogich*, Drukarnia Gałęzowskiego, Warszawa 1827.

Skarbek Fryderyk *Ogólne zasady nauki gospodarstwa narodowego, czyli czysta teorya ekonomii politycznej*, Księgarnia Samuela Orgelbranda, Warszawa 1859.

Sprawozdanie Szkoły Polskiej na Batignolles: od 1 października 1869 do 30 września 1872 roku, Drukarnia Karola Rouge'a, Paryż 1873.

Sprawozdanie Towarzystwa Literacko-Historycznego w Paryżu, vol. VII, *Sprawozdanie z czynności Towarzystwa Historyczno-Literackiego od 1 kwietnia 1867 do 1 kwietnia 1868*, Biblioteka Polska, Paryż 1868.

Stern Daniel (d'Agoult Marie), *Histoire de la révolution de 1848*, A. Le Chevalier Libraire-Éditeur, Paris 1869.

Sydow Bronisław Edward (oprac.) *Korespondencja Fryderyka Chopina*, vol. II, Państwowy Instytut Wydawniczy, Warszawa 1955.

Szokalski Wiktor Feliks *Wspomnienia z przeszłości*. vol. I. *1811–1837*, Stowarzyszenie Nauczycielstwa Polskiego, Wilno 1921.

Szymanowska-Malewska Helena *Dziennik*, Ancher, Warszawa 1999.

Tabella miast, wsi, osad, Królestwa Polskiego, z wyrażeniem ich położenia i ludności, alfabetycznie ułożona w Biórze Kommissyi Rządowćy Spraw Wewnętrznych i Policyi. vol. II, *M-Z*, Warszawa 1827.

Table générale des Archives des Missions Scientifiques et Littéraires comprenant les trois séries jusqu'au tome XV inclus, E. Leroux, Paris 1890.

Thiers Adolphe, *Discours parlementaires de M. Thiers*, t XIII, C. Lévy, Paris 1882.

Tocqueville Alexis de *Listy*, Znak/Fundacja im. S. Batorego, Kraków, Warszawa 1999.

Tocqueville Alexis de *Democracy in America*, translated by Arthur Goldhammer, Library of America, New York 2004.

Tocqueville Alexis de *Oeuvres complètes d'Alexis de Tocqueville*. vol. VII, *Nouvelle correspondance entièrement inédite*, Michel Lévy frères, Paris 1866.

Tocqueville Alexis de *The Recollections of Alexis de Tocqueville*, MacMillan Co., New York 1896.

Troplong Raymond Théodore *Privilèges et hypothèques, commentaire de la loi du 23 mars 1855 sur la transcription en matière hypothécaire*, C. Hingray, Paris 1856.

Tyszka Andrzej Tadeusz (oprac.) *Nekrologi „Kuriera Warszawskiego"*, vol. I, *1821–1845*, Biblioteka Publiczna m. st. Warszawy, Warszawa 2001.

Walewska z Przeździeckich Maria *Polacy w Paryżu, Florencji i Dreźnie. Sylwetki i wspomnienia*, Księgarnia F. Hoesicka, Warszawa 1930.

Walras Léon *Mélanges d'économie politque et sociale*, Económica, Paris 1987.

Wężyk Władysław *Kronika rodzinna*, Państwowy Instytut Wydawniczy, Warszawa 1987.

Wołowska Tekla *Historya Polska*, vol. I, Druk. L. Martinet, Paryż 1860.

Wolowski Casimir *Méditations religieuses*, Charles Douniol Libraire-Editeur, Paris 1863.

Wołowski Franciszek *L'Empereur Nicolas et la constitution polonaise de 1815*, Paris 1832.

Wołowski Franciszek *Podróż do Szwajcaryi i Włoch rozpoczęta w 1825 roku*, Druk. Maulde i Renou, Paryż 1845.

Wysocki Piotr *Pamiętnik Piotra Wysockiego o powstaniu 29 listopada 1830 roku*, vol. II, Księgarnia Luxemburska, Paryż 1867.

Xięga pamiątkowa w 50-letnią rocznicę powstania roku 1830 zawierająca spis imienny dowódców i sztabs-oficerów tudzież oficerów, podoficerów i żołnierzy Armii Polskiej w tymże roku krzyżem wojskowy „Virtuti Militari" ozdobionych, Drukarnia Ludowa, Lwów 1881.

Zaleski Dyonizy (oprac.) *Korespondencya Józefa Bohdana Zaleskiego*, vol. III, V, Lwów 1902–1903.

Zamoyska Jadwiga *Jadwiga Zamoyska między Londynem a Stambułem. Wspomnień część II*, Fundacja Zakłady Kórnickie, Kórnik 2014.

Życie ś.p. Franciszka Wołowskiego deputowanego na Sejm Królestwa Polskiego: czytane na posiedzeniu Towarzystwa Literackiego Polskiego w Paryżu dnia 16 maja 1844 roku, Druk. Maulde ie Rengu, Paryż 1844.

Magazines, newspapers:

„Allgemeine Zeitung des Judenthums", no. 2, 04.01.1838.

„Annales de l'Assemblée nationale: compte rendus in extenso des séances, annexes" 1871–1876.

„Ateneum: pismo naukowe i literackie", vol. 3 (3), n. 9, Warszawa 1876.

„Das Judische Literaturblatt", no. 27, 05.07.1882.

„Dziennik Narodowy" 1844.

„Dziennik Poznański" 1876.

„Dziennik Praw Królestwa Polskiego", vol. IX, no. 37, Warszawa 1824.

„Feuilletons", Assemblée Nationale Constituante, 1848–1849.

„Journal des Débats Politiques et Littéraires" 1841–1876.

„Journal des Economistes. Revue mensuelle de l'économie politique, des questions agricoles, manufacturières et commerciales " 1843–1876.

„Journal du Palais. Lois, décrets, règlements et instructions d'intérêt général suivis d'annotations", Paris 1848.

„Journal Officiel de la République Française" 1871–1876.

„Kronika Emigracji Polskiej" 1834–1838.

„L'Union", no. 304, 30.10.1873.

„La Presse" 1841 – 1876.

„Le Charivari ", 08.10.1836.

„Le Constitutionnel" 1848 – 1876.

„Le Correspondant" 1875.

„Le Libre-échange: journal du travail agricole, industriel et commercial" 1846–1848.

„Le National" 05.III.1848.

„Le Siècle" 1837–1876.

„Le Temps" 1861–1876.

„Moniteur Industriel. Journal de la défense du travail national", 1847.

„Moniteur Universel. Journal Officiel de la République Française" 1848 – 1851.

„Pielgrzym Polski" 1832 – 1833.
„Polak Sumienny" 1831.
„Revue critique de législation et de jurisprudence" 1854 – 1876.
„Revue de législation et de jurisprudence" 1834 – 1853.
„Rocznik Towarzystwa Historyczno-Literackiego w Paryżu" 1867–1879.
„Roczniki Gospodarstwa Krajowego" vol. XLIII, poszyt 1, Warszawa 1861.
„Trzeci Maj" 1844–1848.
„Tygodnik Petersburski. Gazeta urzędowa Królestwa Polskiego" 1834.
„Wiadomości Polskie" 1856–1861.

Entries is encyclopedias and dictionaries:

Barbier Frédéric *Libre-échange* [in:] Tulard Jean (dir.) *Dictionnaire du Second Empire*, Fayard, Paris 1995, pp. 733–738.

Borzymińska Zofia, Żebrowski Rafał (red.) *Polski słownik judaistyczny.* vol. I, *Dzieje, kultura, religia, ludzie*, Prószyński i S-ka, Warszawa 2003.

Bourloton Edgar, Cougny Gaston, Robert Adolphe *Dictionnaire des parlementaires français...: depuis le 1er mai 1789 jusqu'au 1er mai 1889...*, vol. III, V, Bourloton Editeur, Paris 1891.

Burakowski Tadeusz *Wołowski Franciszek,* [in:] *Słownik biograficzny adwokatów polskich S-Ż,* vol. I, Wydawnictwo Prawnicze, Warszawa 1982, p. 476.

Cała Alina, Węgrzynek Hanna, Zalewska Gabriela *Historia i kultura Żydów polskich. Słownik,* Wydawnictwa Szkolne i Pedagogiczne, Warszawa 2000.

Dreżepolska Ewa *Brzeziński Kazimierz,* [in:] *Słownik biograficzny adwokatów polskich A-F,* vol. I, Warszawa 1980, pp. 43–44.

Fontanon Claudine, Grelon André (dir.) *Les professeurs du Conservatoire national des arts et métiers. Dictionnaire biographique 1794–1955,* vol. I, *A-K,* Institut national de recherche pédagogique, Paris 1994.

Gerber Rafał *Studenci Uniwersytetu Warszawskiego (1808–1831). Słownik biograficzny,* Zakład Narodowy im. Ossolińskich, Wrocław – Warszawa – Kraków – Gdańsk 1977.

Havelange Isabelle, Huguet Françoise, Lebedeff-Choppin Bernadette *Les inspecteurs généraux de l'Instruction publique. Dictionnaire biographique 1802–1914,* Institut national de recherche pédagogique, Paris 1986.

Kamela Małgorzata *Szymanowski Wacław,* [in:] *Polski Słownik Biograficzny,* vol. L, Polska Akademia Nauk, Polska Akademia Umiejętności, Warszawa – Kraków 2014, pp. 102–106

Kaski, [in:] Chlebowski Bronisław, Sulimierski Filip, Walewski Władysław (red.) *Słownik geograficzny Królestwa Polskiego i innych krajów słowiańskich,* vol. III, Warszawa 1882

Kiepurska Halina, Konarski Stanisław *Leszczyński Stanisław Andrzej Wiktor,* [in:] *Polski Słownik Biograficzny,* vol. XVII, Zakład Narodowy im. Ossolińskich, Wydawnictwo Polskiej Akademii Nauk, Wrocław-Warszawa-Kraków-Gdańsk 1972, pp. 144–146.

Konarski Stanisław *Leszczyński Jan Nepomucen,* [in:] *Polski Słownik Biograficzny,* vol. XVII, Zakład Narodowy im. Ossolińskich, Wydawnictwo Polskiej Akademii Nauk, Wrocław-Warszawa-Kraków-Gdańsk 1972, pp. 119–120.

Larousse Pierre *Grand dictionnaire universel du XIXe siècle: français, historique, géographique, mythologique, bibliographique,* vol. 15 *Testam – Z,* Paris 1876.

Lewicka-Depta Zofia *Szymanowska (Szymanowska-Lenartowicz) Zofia,* [in:] *Polski Słownik Biograficzny,* vol. L, Polska Akademia Nauk, Polska Akademia Umiejętności, Warszawa – Kraków 2014, pp. 47–49.

Łapinowa Irena *Guérin Laura (1817–1883),* [in:] *Polski Słownik Biograficzny,* vol. IX, Zakład Narodowy im. Ossolińskich, Wydawnictwo Polskiej Akademii Nauk, Wrocław-Warszawa-Kraków-Gdańsk 1960 – 1961, p. 138.

Łyczywek Roman *Leszczyński Stanisław,* [in:] *Słownik biograficzny adwokatów polskich* G-Ł, vol. I, Wydawnictwo Prawnicze, Warszawa 1981, pp. 213–215.

Łyczywek Roman *Wołowski Ludwik Franciszek Michał Rajmund,* [in:] *Słownik biograficzny adwokatów polskich S-Ż,* vol. I, Wydawnictwo Prawnicze, Warszawa 1982, pp. 482–485.

Nowakowski Jan *Lenartowicz Teofil Aleksander,* [in:] *Polski Słownik Biograficzny,* vol. XVII, Zakład Narodowy im. Ossolińskich, Wydawnictwo Polskiej Akademii Nauk, Wrocław-Warszawa-Kraków-Gdańsk, 1972, pp. 39–43.

Ochlewski Tadeusz *Brzezińska Filipina,* [in:] *Polski Słownik Biograficzny,* vol. III, Polska Akademia Umiejętności, Kraków 1937, p. 36.

Ostrowska Teresa *Henryk Podowski,* [in:] *Polski Słownik Biograficzny* vol. XXVII, Zakład Narodowy im. Ossolińskich, Wydawnictwo Polskiej Akademii Nauk, Wrocław – Warszawa – Kraków-Gdańsk – Łódź, 1982–1983., pp. 187–188.

Osuchów, [in:] Chlebowski Bronisław, Sulimierski Filip, Walewski Władysław (red.) *Słownik geograficzny Królestwa Polskiego i innych krajów słowiańskich,* vol. VII, Warszawa 1886, p. 741.

Pędowski Karol *Wołowski Jan Tadeusz,*[in:] *Słownik biograficzny adwokatów polskich S-Ż,* vol. I, Warszawa 1983, pp. 480–481.

Risacher J. *Michel Louis, Chrysostome, dit Michel de Bourges,* [in:] *Le Maitron,. Dictionnaire biographique, mouvement ouvrier, mouvement social:* https://maitron.fr/spip.php?article35021 (retrieved 29.03.2023).

Różycki Jan *Brzeziński Kazimierz,* [in:] *Polski Słownik Biograficzny,* t. III, Polska Akademia Umiejętności, Kraków 1937, p. 40.

Vapereau Gustave *Dictionnaire universel des contemporains: contenant toutes les personnes notables de la France et des pays étrangers,* Hachette, Paris 1870.

Books, articles, essays:

Adamczyk Kazimierz *Władysław Zamoyski i Instytut Czci i Chleba*, [in:] Kosmanowa Bogumiła (red.) *Rola książki w integracji ziem polskich w XIX w.*, Bydgoszcz 2000, pp. 125–133.

Agulhon Maurice and others *Blanqui et les blanquistes*, SEDES-CDU, Paris 1986.

Agulhon Maurice *1848 ou l'apprentissage de la République, 1848–1852*, Ed. du Seuil, Paris 1992.

Allinne Jean-Pierre *Banquiers et bâtisseurs: un siècle de Crédit Foncier, 1852–1940*, Editions du CNRS, Paris 1984.

Anceau Eric *Ils ont fait et défait le Second Empire*, Editions Tallandier, Paris 2019.

Anceau Eric *Napoléon III*, Editions Tallandier, Paris 2012.

Antonetti *La Faculté de droit de Paris à l'époque où Boissonade y faisait ses études*, „Revue internationale de droit comparé", no. 43 (2), 1991, pp. 333–356.

Aprile Sylvie *1815–1870. La Révolution inachevée*, Folio, Paris 2020.

Bałtruszajtys Grażyna (red.) *Zarys dziejów Wydziału Prawa i Administracji Uniwersytetu Warszawskiego*, Wolters Kluwer, Warszawa 2016.

Barańska Anna *Wymarsz korpusu wielkiego księcia Konstantego z Królestwa Polskiego w świetle wspomnień Nadieżdy Iwanowny Golicyny*, „Teka Komisji Historycznej Oddział PAN w Lublinie", 8 (2011), pp. 16–30.

Barjot Dominique *Histoire économique de la France au XIX siècle*, Nathan Université, Paris 1995.

Bazylow Ludwik, Kalembka Sławomiir, Wereszycki Henryk, Zahorski Andrzej, Zdrada Jerzy *Historia dyplomacji polskiej*, vol. III, *1795–1918*, Państwowe Wydawnictwo Naukowe, Warszawa 1982.

Bellanger Claude, Godechot Jacques, Guiral Pierre, Terrou Fernand (dir.) *Histoire générale de la presse française*, vol. II – III, Presses Universitaires de France, Paris 1969–1972.

Bielecki Robert *Belwederczycy i podchorążowie*, Krajowa Agencja Wydawnicza, Warszawa 1989.

Bieliński Józef *Królewski Uniwersytet Warszawski (1816–1831)*, vol. II-III, Księgarnia E. Weende i S-ka, Warszawa 1911–1912.

Bienaymé Gustave *Le coût de la vie à Paris à diverses époques*, „Journal de la société statistique de Paris", vol. 37, 1896, pp. 375–390.

Biernat Andrzej, Kłosowicz-Krzywicka Barbara, Zaworonko-Olejniczak Hanna *Na obcej ziemi – groby polskie na cmentarzach paryskich i Montmorency. En terre d'exil: tombeaux polonais dans les cimetières de Paris et de Montmorency*, Regards Multiples, Fundacja TRES, Paris 2011.

Blajer Paweł *Z dziejów francuskiego modelu "la publicité foncière"*, [in:] „Zeszyty prawnicze", vol. XVI, no. 1, 2016, pp. 89–133.

Bóbr-Tylingo Stanisław *Napoléon III, l'Europe et la Pologne en 1863-4*, „ Antemurale " no VII–VIII, Romae 1963, pp. 1–294.

Borejsza Jerzy W. *Emigracja polska po powstaniu styczniowym*, PWN, Warszawa 1966.

Borejsza Jerzy W. *Sekretarz Adama Mickiewicza. Armand Lévy i jego czasy 1827–1891*, Wyd. Słowo/obraz terytoria, Gdańsk 2005.

Bortnowski Władysław *Łuna nad Solcem 1830. Blaski i cienie nocy listopadowej*, Wydawnictwo Ministerstwa Obrony Narodowej, Warszawa 1982.

Bourgin Georges, *La guerre de 1870–1871 et la Commune*, Flammarion, Paris 1971.

Bourguignat Nicolas, Vogt Gilles *La guerre franco-allemande de 1870. Une histoire globale*, Flammarion, Paris 2020.

Brabant Jacques de *Achille Fould et son temps (1800–1867). L'homme clef du Second Empire*, Editions Cairn, Pau 2001.

Breton Yves *Les économistes français et les écoles historiques allemandes: rencontre entre l'économie politique et l'histoire? 1800–1914*, „Histoire, Économie et Société", vol. 7, no. 3, 1988, pp. 399–417.

Breton Yves *The Société d'Economie Politique of Paris (1842–1914)*, [in:] Augello Massimo M., Guidi Marco E.L. (dir.) *The Spread of Political Economy and the Professionalisation of Economists. Economic societies in Europe, America and Japan in the nineteenth century*, London, New York 2001, pp. 53–62.

Broglie Gabriel de *Guizot*, Perrin, Paris 1990.

Broglie Gabriel de *La monarchie de Juillet*, Fayard, Paris 2011.

Broglie Gabriel de *Mac Mahon*, Perrin, Paris 2000.

Bruant Catherine *La Cité Napoléon: une expérience controversée de logements ouvriers à Paris*, LéaV, Versailles 2011.

Bruyère-Ostells Walter *Napoléon III et le second Empire*, Vuibert, Paris 2004.

Burnell Joel *Revivals in Eighteenth-Century Poland. Jonathan Edwards and the Conversion of Polish Jews*, [in:] Bezzant Rhypp. S. (ed.) *The Global Edwards. Papers from the Jonathan Edwards Congress held in Melbourne, August 2015*, Wipf & Stock, Oregon 2017, pp. 103–117.

Bury John Patrick Tuer *Gambetta Défenseur du territoire (1870–1871)*, Editions de la Nouvelle Revue Critique, Paris 1937.

Cabanis Jose *Karol X. Król – ultras*, Państwowy Instytut Wydawniczy, Warszawa 1981.

Cadier Gabrielle *Les Conséquences du traité de 1860 sur les échanges franco-britanniques*, [in:] Crouzet François (dir.) *Le négoce international, XIII – XX siècle*, Economica, Paris 1989.

Caron Jean-Claude *Jules Michelet, Correspondance générale, tome 12: 1871–1874 et suppléments, Textes réunis, classés et annotés par Louis Le Guillou*, Paris, 2001, "Revue d'histoire du XIXe siècle" no. 22, 2001, pp. 226–229.

Castelot André *Louis-Philippe le méconnu,* Perrin, Paris 1994.

Charléty Sébastien *Histoire de la monarchie de Juillet 1830–1848,* Perrin, Paris 2018.

Chaudun Nicolas *Haussmann Georges-Eugène, préfet – baron de la Seine,* Actes Sud, Paris 2009.

Chevalier Louis *Classes laborieuses et classes dangereuses à Paris pendant la première moitié du XIX siècle,* Tempus Perrin, Paris 2007.

Clément Pascal *Persigny. L'homme qui a inventé Napoléon III,* Perrin, Paris 2006.

Cornut-Gentille Pierre *Le 4 septembre 1870. L'invention de la République,* Tempus Perrin, Paris 2020.

Cybulska Kamila *Laura Guérin (1817–1883) – zapomniane tradycje oświaty dla kobiet,* „Piotrkowskie Zeszyty Historyczne", vol. 22, part 3, 2021, pp. 43–62.

d'Avenel George *Le Prix et le Loyer des maisons en France depuis le moyen âge jusqu'à nos jours,* „Revue des Deux Mondes", no. 123, 1894, pp. 811–829.

Dautry Jean *Histoire de la Révolution de 1848 en France,* Editions Hier et aujourd'hui, Paris 1948.

Davies Helen M. *Emile and Isaac Pereire. Bankers, Socialiists and Sephardic Jews in the nineteenth-century France,* Manchester University Press, Manchester 2015.

Delmas Corinne *Instituer des savoirs d'Etat. L'Académie des Sciences Morales et Politiques au XIX siècle,* L'Harmattan, Paris 2006.

Démier Francis (dir.) *Louis Blanc. Un socialiste en république,* Créaphis, Paris 2005.

Démier Francis *La France du XIXe siècle 1814–1914,* Seuil, Paris 2000.

Dernałowicz Maria *Avant que Mickiewicz n'entre au Collège de France...,* „ Actes de la Société Historique et Littéraire Polonaise ", vol. IV, Paris 1998, pp. 43–52.

Dobek Rafał *Ludwik Wołowski (1810–1876): potomek Eliszy Szora, polski powstaniec, francuski senator,* [in:] J. Kita, M. Korybut-Marciniak (red.) *Życie prywatne Polaków w XIX wieku,* vol. IX, *Kariera w optyce prywatności,* Wyd. Uniwersytetu Łódzkiego, Łódź-Olsztyn 2020, pp. 29–44.

Dobek Rafał *Ludwik Wołowski and His Contribution to the French Credit Revolution of the 19th Century,* "Studia Historiae Oeconomicae", vol. 39, 2021, pp. 3–32.

Dobek Rafał *Paris and Poznań in 1848,* [in:] P. Matusik (ed.) *A Polish, european city: studies in the history of Poznań,* Wydawnictwo Miejskie Posnania, Poznań 2022

Dobek Rafał *Paryż, 1871,* Wydawnictwo Poznańskie, Poznań 2013.

Dobek Rafał *Sojusz tronu z ołtarzem we Francji w okresie Burbonów (1815–1830) i II cesarstwa (1852–1870),* [in:] P. Zając OMI (red.) *Od Rewolucji Francuskiej do Nowej Ewangelizacji. Wokół osoby I charyzmtu św. Eugeniusza de Mazenoda (1782–1861) w 150 rocznicę śmierci,* Poznań 2012, pp. 65–83.

Doktór Jan *Jakub Frank i jego nauka,* Instytut Filozofii i Socjologii Polskiej Akademii Nauk, Warszawa 1991.

Doktór Jan *Śladami Mesjasza-Apostaty. Żydowskie ruchy mesjańskie w XVII i XVIII wieku a problem konwersji*, Fundacja na rzecz Nauki Polskiej, Wrocław 1998.

Doktór Jan *Warszawscy frankiści*, „Kwartalnik Historii Żydów" 2001, no. 2 (198), pp. 194–209.

Domin Jean-Paul *La question du monopole d'émission de la monnaie : Le débat banque centrale contre banque libre chez les économistes français (1860–1875)*, „ Revue européenne des sciences sociales ", vol. XLV, no. 137, 2007, pp. 185–202.

Dommanget Maurice *Blanqui*, Études et documentation internationales, Paris 1970.

Duker Abraham *Polish Frankism's Duration: From Cabbalistic Judaism to Roman Catholicism and from Jewishness to Polishness*, "Jewish Social Studies", no. 25 (4), 1963, pp. 287–333.

Dzieszyński Ryszard *Sedan 1870*, Belona, Warszawa 2009.

Etner François, Silvant Claire *Histoire de la pensée économique en France. Depuis 1789*, Economica, Paris 2017.

Fastyn Arkadiusz *Problem powstania i charakteru prawa małżeńskiego z 1836 roku*, „Czasopismo prawno-historyczne", vol. XLIV, 2012, part 2, pp. 193–207.

Félice Raoul de *La journée du 13 juin 1849, à Paris. Ses origines. Son épilogue devant la Haute Cour*, „ La Révolution de 1848. Bulletin de la Société d'histoire de la Révolution de 1848 ", 1909, t 6, no. 33, pp. 133–157.

Fiorentino Karen *Protéger l'enfant ouvrier. La loi du 19 mai 1874, une „législation intermédiaire" ?*, „Revue historique", no. 2 (682), 2017, pp. 327–358.

Furet François *La Révolution Française II. Terminer la Révolution. De Louis XVIII à Jules Ferry (1814–1880)*, Pluriel, Paris 1988.

Gadon Lubomir *Wielka Emigracja w pierwszych latach po powstaniu listopadowym*, Księgarnia Polska w Paryżu, Paryż 1960.

Gadon Lubomir *Z życia Polaków we Francyi. Rzut oka na 50-letnie koleje Towarzystwa Historyczno-Literackiego w Paryżu, 1832–1882*, Biblioteka Polska w Paryżu, Paryż 1883.

Gałkowski Adam *Polski patriota, obywatel Francji i Europy, czyli krótka opowieść o Ludwiku Wołowskim*, [in:] A. i Z Judyccy (red.) *Polacy we Francji: historia i współczesność: materiały VIII Międzynarodowego Sympozjum Biografistyki Polonijnej: Stella-Palge, Vaudricourt, 2–3 października 2004*, Wyd. CCAN, Warszawa 2004, pp. 37–44.

Garrigues Jean *Les élus du centre gauche en 1871*, „Parlement(s). Revue d'histoire politique", no. 2 (16), 2011, pp. 23–32.

Gille Bertrand *La Banque de France au XIX siècle. Recherches historiques*, Librairie Droz, Genève 1970.

Girard Louis *Les libéraux français 1814–1875*, Aubier, Paris 1985.

Girard Louis *Napoléon III*, Hachette, Paris 1986.

Girard Louis *Nouvelle histoire de Paris. La Deuxième République et le Second Empire 1848–1870,* Association pour la publication d'une histoire de Paris, Paris 1981.

Gobbi Gérald *Le Comte de Falloux (1811–1886). Entre Église et Monarchie,* PUR, Rennes 2010.

Gołba Zdzisław *Rozwój władz Królestwa Polskiego w okresie powstania listopadowego,* Zakład Narodowy im. Ossolińskich, Wrocław, Warszawa, Kraków, Gdańsk 1971.

Gribaudi Maurzio, Riot-Sarcey Michèle *1848, la révolution oubliée,* La Découverte, Paris 2009.

Gris Noah *Szkoła polska w Paryżu,* Państwowe Zakłady Wydawnictw Szkolnych, Warszawa 1962.

Gueslin André *Les Origines du Crédit Agricole (1840–1914),* Université de Nancy II, Nancy 1978.

Guiral Pierre *Adolphe Thiers,* Fayard, Paris 1986.

Hahn Hans Henning *Dyplomacja bez listów uwierzytelniających. Polityka zagraniczna Adama Jerzego Czartoryskiego 1830–1840,* Państwowe Wydawnictwo Naukowe, Warszawa 1987.

Halévy Daniel *La fin des notables. La République des ducs,* Grasset, Paris 1944.

Handelsman Marceli *Adam Czartoryski,* vol. III, part II, Towarzystwo Naukowe Warszawskie, Warszawa 1950.

Handelsman Marceli *Konwencya bajońska 1808,* [in:] Tegoż *Pod znakiem Napoleona, Studya historyczne ser. II,* Zakł. Graf. Tow. Akc. S. Orgelbranda S-ów, Warszawa 1913, pp. 1–72.

Hanotaux Gabriel *Histoire de la France contemporaine (1871–1900),* vol. I, *Le Gouvernement de M. Thiers,* Combet, Paris 1903.

Harbut Juliusz Stanisław *Noc listopadowa w świetle i cieniach procesu przed Najwyższym Sądem Kryminalnym: (jeden z największych procesów politycznych w dziejach narodów),* Książnica-Atlas, Warszawa 1926.

Hayat Samuel *Quand la République était révolutionnaire. Citoyenneté et représentationn en 1848,* Seuil, Paris 2014.

Heugas-Darraspen Henri, Raimbault Aline *Crédit Foncier de France. Itinéraire d'une institution,* Éditions du Regard, Paris 1994.

Houte Arnaud – Dominique *Le triomphe de la République 1871–1914,* Editions du Seuil, Paris 2014.

Iliasu Alfred A. *The Cobden-Chevalier Commercial Treaty of 1860,* „The Historical Journal", vol. 14, no. 1, 1971, pp. 67–98.

Jeske – Choiński Teodor *Neofici Polscy. Materyały historyczne,* P. Laskauer i S-ka, Warszawa 1904.

Kalembka Sławomir *Wielka Emigracja 1831–1863,* Wydawnictwo Adam Marszałek, Toruń 2003.

Kallenbach Józef *Zygmunt Krasiński. Życie i twórczość z lat młodych (1812–1838)*, vol. I, Księgarnia Polska B. Połonieckiego, Lwów 1904.

Karbownik Krzysztof *Polskie formacje zbrojne w armii tureckiej w wojnie krymskiej 1853–1856*, [in:] „Przegląd Historyczno-Wojskowy" no. 64/4 (242), 2012, pp. 215–233.

Karpińska Małgorzata *„Nie ma Mikołaja! " Starania o kształt sejmu w powstaniu listopadowym 1830–1831*, Wydawnictwo Neriton, Warszawa 2007.

Karpińska Małgorzata *Senatorowie, posłowie i deputowani Księstwa Warszawskiego i Królestwa Polskiego*, Wyd. Sejmowe, Warszawa 2002.

Kaźmierczyk Adam *Rodziłem się Żydem... konwersje Żydów w Rzeczpospolitej XVII-XVIII wieku*, Księgarnia Akademicka, Kraków 2015.

Kędzierski Tomasz *Proces „dyktatora Nocy Listopadowej" – Piotra Wysockiego*, „Palestra", no. 21/11 (239), 1977, pp. 45–51.

Kieniewicz Stefan (red.) *Dzieje Uniwersytetu Warszawskiego 1807–1915*, Państwowe Wydawnictwo Naukowe, Warszawa 1981.

Kieniewicz Stefan *Powstanie Styczniowe*, Krajowa Agencja Wydawnicza, Warszawa 1987.

Kieniewicz Stefan *Powstanie styczniowe*, PWN, Warszawa 1983.

Kieniewicz Stefan *Społeczeństwo polskie w powstaniu poznańskim 1848 roku*, Towarzystwo Naukowe Warszawskie, Warszawa 1960.

Kizwalter Tomasz (red.) *Dzieje Uniwersytetu Warszawskiego 1816–1915*, Wydawnictwa Uniwersytetu Warszawskiego, Warszawa 2016.

Kłossowski Andrzej *Ambasador książki polskiej w Paryżu. Władysław Mickiewicz*, Zakład Narodowy im. Ossolińskich, Wrocław 1971.

Koropeckyj Roman *Adam Mickiewicz. Życie romantyka*, Wydawnictwo W.A.B., Warszawa 2013.

Kossak Ewa K. *Rodzina M.*, Czytelnik, Warszawa 1991.

Kowalski Jacek, Loba Anna i Mirosław, Prokop Jan *Dzieje kultury francuskiej*, Wydawnictwo Naukowe PWN, Warszawa 2007.

Kraushar Alexander *Frank i frankiści polscy. 1726–1816. Monografia historyczna osnuta na źródłach archiwalnych i rękopiśmiennych* vol. I–II, Gebethner i Spółka, Kraków 1895.

Królikowski Lech *Szkolnictwo dawnej Warszawy. Rzecz o korelacji pomiędzy rozwojem miasta a szkolnictwem (Od połowy XVII wieku do wybuchu drugiej wojny światowej)*, Muzeum Historyczne m. st. Warszawy, Warszawa 2008.

Kukiel Marian *Czartoryski a jedność Europy: 1770–1861*, Instytut Europy Środkowo-Wschodniej, Lublin 2008.

Labrousse Ernest (red.) *Aspects de la crise et de la dépression de l'économie française au milieu du XIX siècle 1846–1851*, La Roche sur Yon, 1956.

Lajusan Alfred *Les origines de la Troisième République. Quelques éclaircissements (1871–1876)*, „Revue d'histoire moderne", vol. 5, no. 30, 1930, pp. 419–438.

Lameyre Gerard-Noël *Haussmann, préfet de Paris*, Flammarion, Paris 1958.

Le Van-Lemesle Lucette *Le Juste ou le Riche. L'enseignement de l'économie politique 1815–1950*, Comité pour l'Histoire Économique et Financière de la France, Paris 2004.

Leclercq Yves *La banque supérieure. La banque de France de 1800 à 1914*, Éditions Classique Garnier, Paris 2010.

Levasseur Emile *L'enseignement de l'économie politique au Conservatoire des Arts et Métiers*, „Revue internationale de l'enseignement", no. 41, 1901, pp. 211–228.

Levasseur Emile *La vie et les travaux de Wolowski*, Imprimerie Viéville et Capionot, Paris 1877.

L'Institut polonais: souvenirs et fragments, 1845 à 1895, Imprimerie Adolphe Reiff, Paris 1895.

Lustman François *De l'émancipation à l'antisémitisme: Histoire de la communauté juive de Paris 1789–1880*, Honoré Champion, Paris 2006.

Lutfalla Michel *Louis Wolowski ou le libéralisme positif*, „Revue d'histoire économique et sociale ", no. 54 (2), 1976, pp. 169–184.

Maciejko Paweł *Wieloplemienny tłum. Jakub Frank i ruch frankistowski, 1755–1816*, Wyd. w Podwórku, Gdańsk 2014.

Makuch Michał *Organizacja sądownictwa cywilnego w Królestwie Polskim okresu konstytucyjnego (1815–1831*), „Zeszyty Naukowe Instytutu Administracji AJD w Częstochowie", part 1 (13), Częstochowa 2016, pp. 67–78.

Markiewicz Patrice *Louis Wolowski. Un intellectuel et un représentant du libéralisme en France au milieu du XIXe siècle*, doctorate Paris X – Nanterre, 1994.

Martin-Fugier Anne *Louis-Philippe et sa famille 1830–1848*, Tempus Perrin, Paris 2012.

Maurer Jadwiga *„Z matki obcej..." Szkice o powiązaniach Mickiewicza ze światem Żydów*, Polska Fundacja Kulturalna, Londyn 1990.

Maurer Jadwiga *Celina Szymanowska as a frankist*, „The Polish Review", vol. XXXIV, no. 4, 1989, pp. 335–347.

Mayaud Jean-Luc (dir.) *1848: actes du colloque international du cent cinquantenaire, tenu à l'Assemblée nationale à Paris, les 23–25 février 1998*, Société d'histoire de la révolution de 1848 et des révolutions du XIXe siècle, Paris 2002.

Mayeur Jean-Marie *Les débuts de la Troisième République 1871–1898*, Editions du Seuil, Paris 1973.

McKay Donald Cope *The National Workshops. A study in the French Revolution of 1848*, Harvard University Press, Cambridge Massachusetts 1933.

Mencel Tadeusz *Sumy bajońskie,* „Roczniki historyczne", rocznik XIX, Poznań 1952, pp. 133–164.

Mercier Alain *Un Conservatoire pour les Arts et Métiers,* Gallimard, Paris 1994.

Milza Pierre *„L'année terrible" La guerre franco-prussienne septembre 1870 – mars 1871,* Perrin, Paris 2009.

Milza Pierre *Napoléon III,* Perrin, Paris 2006.

Mondonico-Torri Cécile *Les réfugiés en France sous la monarchie de juillet: l'impossible statut,* „Revue d'histoire moderne et contemporaine" no. 47 (4), 2000, pp. 731–745.

Muhlstein Anka *James de Rothschild. 1792–1868,* Gallimard, Paris 1981.

Niecks Frederick *Fryderyk Chopin jako człowiek i muzyk,* Narodowy Instytut Fryderyka Chopina, Warszawa 2011.

Novak Charles *Jacob Frank, le faux Messie. Déviance de la kabbale ou théorie du complot,* Ed. L'Harmattan, Paris 2012.

Pezda Janusz *Historia Biblioteki Polskiej w Paryżu w latach 1838 – 1893,* Towarzystwo Wydawnicze „Historia Iagellonica", Kraków 2013.

Pezda Janusz *Ludzie i pieniądze: finanse w działalności Adama Jerzego Czartoryskiego i jego obozu na emigracji w latach 1831–1848,* Universitas, Kraków 2003.

Plessis Alain *La Banque de France, une des grandes institutions napoléoniennes,* „Revue du Souvenir Napoléonien", no. 430, 2000, pp. 35–43.

Plessis Alain *La politique de la Banque de France de 1851 à 1870,* Librairie Droz, Genève 1985.

Poisson Georges *Le Comte de Chambord. Henri V,* Pygmalion, Paris 2009.

Popowicz Kamil *Saint-Simon i saint-simoniści – od rewolucji do kolonizacji. Historia pewnej religii (1803–1870),* Wydawnictwa Uniwersytetu Warszawskiego, Warszawa 2018.

Ptaszyk Marian *Liceum Warszawskie. 1804–1831,* Biblioteka Uniwersytecka w Toruniu, Toruń 2020.

Pugacewicz Iwona H. *Batignolles 1842–1874. Edukacja Wielkiej Emigracji,* Wyd. ASPRA, Warszawa 2017.

Rambaud Jules *L'Oeuvre économique de L. Wolowski,* L. Larose & Forcel Libraires Editeurs, Paris 1882.

Raphaël Paul *La loi du 31 mai 1850,* „Revue d'histoire moderne et contemporaine", vol. 13, no. 3, 1909, pp. 277–304; vol. 14, no. 3, 1910, pp. 44–79 i 297–331.

Ravel d'Esclapon de Thibault *Désiré Dalloz – Vivre le droit,* Dalloz, Paris 2019.

Redish Angela *The Persistence of Bimetallism in Nineteenth-Century France,* "The Economic History Review", vol. 48, no. 4, 1995, pp. 717–736.

Rémond René *La Droite en France de la première Restauration à la Ve République*, Aubier Paris 1963.

Rezler Marek *Wielkopolska Wiosna Ludów 1848*, Wyd. ABOS, Poznań 1993.

Rials Stéphane *Nouvelle histoire de Paris. De Trochu à Thiers 1870–1873*, Diffusion, Hachette, Paris 1985.

Rochefort Florence *Laïcisation des moeurs et équilibres de genres. Le débat sur la capacité civile de la femme mariée*, „Vingtième Siècle. Revue d'histoire",, no. 3 (87), 2005, pp. 129–141.

Roos Gilbert *Les Juifs de France sous la Monarchie de Juillet*, Honoré Champion, Paris 2007.

Roth François *La guerre de 1870*, Fayard/Pluriel, Paris 2011.

Rougerie Jacques *Paris libre 1871*, Seuil, Paris 2004.

Roulliet Antony *Wolowski. Sa vie et ses travaux*, Guillaumin, Paris 1880.

Rusinowa Izabella *Generał Karol Otto Kniaziewcz*, Wyd. Aspra Pułtusk-Warszawa 2019.

Scholem Gershom *Mistycyzm żydowski i jego główne kierunki*, Warszawa 2020.

Scholem Gershom *Le mouvement sabbataïste en Pologne (troisième et dernier article)*, „Revue de l'histoire des religions", no. 144 (1), 1953, pp. 42–77.

Sęczys Elżbieta (oprac.) *Szlachta wylegitymowana w Królestwie Polskim w latach 1836–1861*, Wydawnictwo DiG, Warszawa 2000.

Séguin Philippe *Louis Napoléon le Grand*, Bernard Grasset, Paris 1990.

Serman William *La Commune de Paris (1871)*, Fayard, Paris 1986.

Skałkowski Tadeusz *Towarzystwa kredytowe ziemskie w ziemiach polskich. Szkic historyczny*, Lwów 1892.

Skórka Line *Un magnat polonais en Touraine: Xavier Branicki*, „ Bulletin de la Société archéologique de Touraine ", vol. XXXIX, 1980, pp. 555–569.

Skowronek Jerzy *Między Hotelem Lambert a karierami rodziny. Papiery rodziny Sienkiewiczów w Bibliotece Polskiej w Paryżu*, „Miscellanea Historico – Archivitica", vol. IV. 1994, pp. 75–94.

Skowronek Jerzy *Adam Jerzy Czartoryski 1770–1861*, Wiedza Powszechna, Warszawa 1994.

Słupska Julia *Ksawery Branicki (1816–1879). Emigracja: polityka i finanse*, Wyd. Neriton, Instytut Historii PAN, Warszawa 2008.

Soboń Marcin *Od wspólnoty charyzmatycznej do grupy interesu: przypadek frankizmu*, „Czasy Nowożytne", no. 16, 2004, pp. 79–124.

Sokolnicki Michel *Les origines de l'émigration polonaise en France 1831–1831*, Alcan, Paris 1910.

Stankiewicz Wacława *Historia myśli ekonomicznej*, Polskie Wydawnictwo Ekonomiczne, Warszawa 2007.

Stoskopf Nicolas *Les patrons du Second Empire. Banquiers et financiers parisiens*, Picard, Paris 2002.

Sudolski Zbigniew *Mickiewicz. Opowieść biograficzna*, Ancher, Warszawa 1995.

Sulima Zygmunt Lucyan (Przyborowski Walery) *Historia Franka i frankistów*, Wyd. Armoryka, Sandomierz 2014.

Syga Teofil, Szenic Stanisław *Maria Szymanowska i jej czasy*, Państwowy Instytut Wydawniczy, Warszawa 1960.

Syski Aleksander *Zakład Św. Kazimierza w Paryżu. Szkic historyczny*, Drukarnia Kurii Biskupiej, Łuck 1936.

Szarota Tomasz *Dyktatura Langiewicza a przystąpienie Białych do powstania*, „Przegląd Historyczny", vol. 54, Warszawa 1963, pp. 270–296.

Szenic Stanisław *Cmentarz powązkowski 1851–1890. Zmarli i ich rodziny*, Państwowy Instytut Wydawniczy, Warszawa 1982.

Szwankowski Eugeniusz *Ulice i place Warszawy*, Państwowe Wydawnictwo Naukowe, Warszawa 1970.

Tańska-Hus Bożena *Dzierżawa rolnicza w Polsce na przestrzeni wieków*, Wydawnictwo Uniwersytetu Przyrodniczego we Wrocławiu, Wrocław 2009.

Texier Nicolas *Louis-Eugène Cavaignac*, [in:] Ebel Edouard (dir.) *Les Ministres de la guerre, 1792–1870*, Presses Universitaires de Rennes, Paris 2018, pp. 375–383.

Todd Olivier *L'Identité économique de la France. Libre-échange et protectionnisme (1814–1851)*, Grasset, Paris 2008.

Tokarz Wacław (red.) *Studia z dziejów Warszawy 1830–1831*, Kasa im. Mianowskiego, Warszawa 1937.

Tokarz Wacław *Sprzysiężenie Wysockiego i Noc Listopadowa*, Państwowy Instytut Wydawniczy, Warszawa 1980.

Tokarz Wacław *Wojna polsko-rosyjska 1830 i 1831*, Oficyna Wydawnicza Volumen, Warszawa 1994.

Tomaszewski Mieczysław *Chopin. Człowiek, dzieło, rezonans*, Polskie Wydawnictwo Muzyczne, Kraków 2005.

Tombs Robert *La Guerre contre Paris 1871*, Aubier, Paris 1997.

Trzciński Andrzej *Składnik informacyjny w epitafiach ze starego cmentarza żydowskiego w Lublinie*, „Rocznik Lubelskiego Towarzystwa Genealogicznego", vol. VIII, 2016 (2017), pp. 129–188.

Trzeciakowski Lech *Otto von Bismarck*, Ossolineum, Wrocław 2009.

Unger Gérard *Histoire du Second Empire*, Perrin, Paris 2018.

Utkin Joanna E. *Potomkowie kupca Wołowskiego – prawnicy, powstańcy w XIX stuleciu*, „Miscellanea Historico- Iuridica", vol. 18, part 2, 2019, pp. 69–90.

Valance Georges *Thiers, bourgeois et révolutionnaire*, Flammarion, Paris 2007.

Van Hoang Thi Hong *La thésaurisation de l'or en France depuis 1914: d'une thésaurisation monétaire à une thésaurisation refuge,* " Revue numismatique ", vol. 168, 2012, pp. 119–134.

Vigier Philippe *La Seconde République*, Presses Universitaires de France, Paris 1967.

Wacholder Ben Zion *Jacob Frank and the Frankists Hebrew Zoharic Letters*, „Hebrew Union College Annual", vol. 53 (1982), pp. 265–293.

Wachowicz Bogusław *Towarzystwo Kredytowe Ziemskie w Królestwie Polskim w okresie powstania listopadowego*, „Annales Universitatis Mariae Curie-Skłodowska", vol. 37, 1983, pp. 61–82.

Walch Jean *Michel Chevalier. Economiste, Saint-Simonien 1806–1879*, J. Vrin, Paris 1975.

Waresquiel Emmanuel de, Yvert Benoit *Histoire de la Restauration 1814–1830. Naissance de la France moderne*, Tempus Perrin, Paris 2002.

Wawro Geoffrey *The Franco – Prussian War. The German Conquest of France 1870–1871*, Cambridge University Press, Cambridge 2003.

Wereszycki Henryk *Hotel Lambert i obóz Białych przed wybuchem powstania styczniowego*, „Przegląd Historyczny" no. 50 (3), 1959, pp. 514–544.

Werner Klaus *Versuch einer Quantifizierung des Frank'schen Gefolges in Offenbach am Main 1788–1818*, „Frankfurter Judaistische Beiträge", Heft 14, Frankfurt am Main, 1986, pp. 153–212.

Werner Wiktor *Historyczność kultury. W poszukiwaniu myślowego fundamentu współczesnej historiografii*, Wydawnictwo Naukowe UAM, Poznań 2009.

Wichrowska Elżbieta Z. *Hipolit Klimaszewski – nieznana karta z dziejów Wielkiej Emigracji*, Veda, Warszawa 2012.

Winiarz Adam *Szkolnictwo Księstwa Warszawskiego i Królestwa Polskiego (1807–1831)*, Wydawnictwo UMCS, Lublin 2002.

Witkowski Wojciech *Aleksander This i Jan Kanty Wołowski, wybitni prawnicy Królestwa Polskiego*, Wydawnictwo UMCS, Lublin 2001.

Wojtkowski Andrzej *Powstanie wielkopolskie roku 1848*, Związek Powstańców Wielkopolskich, Poznań 1938.

Wyczańska Krystyna *Polacy w Komunie Paryskiej 1871 r.*, Wydawnictwo Ministerstwa Obrony Narodowej, Warszawa 1957.

Wyrozumski Jerzy *Towarzystwo Naukowe Krakowskie w 200-lecie założenia (1815–2015)*, Polska Akademia Umiejętności, Kraków 2016.

Yvert Benoit *La Restauration. Les idées et les hommes*, Editions CNRS, Paris 2013.

Zajda Józef *Kopernikowska teoria pieniądza,* „Ruch Prawniczy, Ekonomiczny i Socjologiczny", no. 35, part 3, 1973, pp. 17–40.

Zajewski Władysław (red.) *Powstanie listopadowe 1830–1831. Dzieje wewnętrzne. Militaria. Europa wobec powstania,* Wydawnictwo Naukowe PWN, Warszawa 1980.

Zajewski Władysław *Walki wewnętrzne ugrupowań politycznych w powstaniu listopadowym 1830–1831,* Gdańskie Towarzystwo Naukowe, Gdańsk 1967.

Zaremska Hanna *Żydzi w średniowiecznej Polsce. Gmina krakowska,* Instytut Historii PAN, Warszawa 2011.

Zdrada Jerzy *Wielka Emigracja po Powstaniu Listopadowym,* Krajowa Agencja Wydawnicza, Warszawa 1987.

Zdrada Jerzy *Zmierzch Czartoryskich,* PWN, Warszawa 1969.

Żebrowski Jan *Szkoła polska na Batignolles w Paryżu w służbie polskości i wychowania narodowego (geneza, rozwój, struktura),* „Studia Gdańskie. Wizje i rzeczywistość", no. 10, 2013, pp. 331–350.

Zgórniak Marian *Za Waszą i naszą wolność,* Krajowa Agencja Wydawnicza, Warszawa 1987.

Ziółek Jan *Studia nad myślą polityczną Wielkiej Emigracji. Napoleon I i Napoleon III,* Towarzystwo Naukowe Katolickiego Uniwersytetu Lubelskiego, Lublin 1995.

Ziółek Sebastian *Sejm Królestwa Polskiego w okresie powstania listopadowego 1830–1831,* Wydawnictwo Sejmowe, Warszawa 2007.

Żychowski Marian *Ludwik Mierosławski 1814–1878,* Wydawnictwo Naukowe PWN, Warszawa 1963.

Novels, poetry, dramas:

Flaubert Gustave *Sentimental Education; Or, The History of a Young Man,* M. Walter Dunne, New York, and London, 1904.

Goncourt Edmond and Jules de *Renée Mauperin,* Charpentier, Paris 1864.

Hugo Victor *Cromwell,* Ambroise Dupont et Cie, Paris 1828.

Hugo Victor *Hernani, Hernani, 1830* (translated by Frederick L. Slous), Newton Crossland, New York 1894.

Hugo Victor *Le Dernier Jour d'un condamné,* Gosselin, Paris 1829.

Hugo Victor *Odes et Ballades,* Pélicier, Paris 1822.

Kowalczykowa Alina (wybór i oprac.) *Manifesty romantyzmu 1790–1830. Anglia, Niemcy, Francja,* PWN, Warszawa 1995.

Lamartine Alphonse de *Autumn* (translated by Margaret Junkin), [in:] Southern literary messenger; devoted to every department of literature and the fine arts, University of Michigan: Humanities Text Initiative, Richmond 1851, p. 659.

Musset Alfred de *The Confession of the Child of the Century,* Penguin Books 2013.

Szymanowski Wacław *Ostatnie chwile Kopernika. Obraz dramatyczny*, Drukarnia J. Ungera, Warszawa 1855.

Szymanowski Wacław *Salomon. Dramat z XVI wieku, w trzech aktach*, Drukarnia J. Ungera, Warszawa 1856.

Tokarczuk Olga *The Books of Jacob, or: A Fantastic Journey Across Seven Borders, Five Languages, and Three Major Religions, Not Counting the Minor Sects. Told by the Dead, Supplemented by the Author, Drawing from a Range of Books, and Aided by Imagination, the Which Bein g the Greatest Natural Gift of Any Person. That the Wise Might Have It for a Record, That My Compatriots Reflect, Laypersons Gain Some Understanding, and Melancholy Souls Obtain Some Slight Enjoyment*, Riverhead Books, 2022, translation by Jennifer Croft.

Vigny Alfred de *Poémes*, Pélicier, Paris 1822.

<u>Websites:</u>

Birth, marriage and death certificates of the Wołowski family and other Frankist families:

- https://www.szukajwarchiwach.gov.pl.
- https://metryki.genealodzy.pl
- http://wielcy.pl
- http://www.sejm-wielki.pl
- https://www.familysearch.org

Antonetti Guy, Cardoni Fabien, Oliveira Mathieu, de *Magne (Pierre)*, [in:] *Les ministres des Finances de la Révolution française au Second Empire*, vol. III, *Dictionnaire biographique 1848–1870*, Vincennes, 2007, http://books.openedition.org/igpde/1251 (retrieved 20.05.2023).

Aprile Sylvie, Huard Raymond *Le coup d'État du 2 décembre 1851. Bibliographie*, [in:] „Revue d'histoire du XIXe siècle", no. 22, 2001, http://journals.openedition.org/rh19/252 (retrieved 31.03.2023).

Bajon Kasper *Polski bankier i francuska rewolucja bankowa*, https://www.newsweek.pl/polski-bankier-i-francuska-rewolucja-bankowa/zy0xxps, (retrieved 19.07.2023).

Bordas Jean *Les directeurs généraux des douanes, l'administration et la politique douanière, 1801–1939*, Vincennes 2004, https://books.openedition.org/igpde/13892 (retrieved 14.06.2023).

Boudon Jacques-Olivier *Baudin et la barricade du 3 décembre 1851: histoire et représentation de l'Empire à la République*, [in:] Corbin Alain, Mayeur Jean-Marie (dir.) *La Barricade*, Paris 1997, https://books.openedition.org/psorbonne/1182 (retrieved 29.03.2023).

Bourillon Florence *La loi du 13 avril 1850 ou lorsque la Seconde République invente le logement insalubre*, "Revue d'histoire du XIXe siècle " no. 20/21, 2000, http://journals.openedition.org/rh19/212 (retrieved 25.03.2023).

Constitution de 1848, IIe République: https://www.conseil-constitutionnel.fr/les-constitutions-dans-l-histoire/constitution-de-1848-iie-republique, (retrieved 11.03.2023).

Constitution de 1852, Second Empire : http://www.conseil-constitutionnel.fr/conseil-constitutionnel/francais/la-constitution/les-constitutions-de-la-france/constitution-de-1852-second-empire.5107.html (retrieved 01.08.2023).

Corbin Alain, Mayeur Jean-Marie (dir.) *Les immortels du Sénat, 1875–1918 : Les cent seize inamovibles de la Troisième République*, Publications de la Sorbonne, Paris :1995. Online : http://books.openedition.org/psorbonne/67972 (retrieved 02.06.2023).

Dubnov S.M., Rosenthal Herman *Frank Jacob and the Frankists*, [in:] *Jewish Encyclopedia*, https://www.jewishencyclopedia.com/articles/6279-frank-jacob-and-the-frankists (retrieved 18.03.2022).

Hass Ludwik *Uzupełnienie do: S. Małachowski-Łempicki Wykaz polskich lóż wolnomularskich oraz ich członków w latach 1738–1821*, https://docplayer.pl/5754739-Stanislaw-malachowski-lempicki-wykaz-polskich-los-wolnomularskich-oraz-ich-czlonkow-w-latach-1738-1821-poprzedzony.html.

Hugo Victor, *Grands discours parlementaires. Victor Hugo, 15 septembre 1848*, https://www2.assemblee-nationale.fr/decouvrir-l-assemblee/histoire/grands-discours-parlementaires/victor-hugo-15-septembre-1848 (retrieved 11.03.2023).

Marchand Bernard *Le financement des travaux d'Haussmann: un exemple pour les pays émergents?* 2011, https://halshs.archives-ouvertes.fr/halshs-00583457/document (retrieved 06.04.2023).

Minakowski Marek Jerzy *Frankiści z Offenbachu i Warszawy*, https://minakowski.pl/frankisci-z-offenbachu-i-warszawy/ (retrieved 17.05.2022).

Monier Frédéric, Portalez Christophe *Une norme démocratique ?: L'indemnité des élus en débats, de la Révolution française à la Grande Guerre*. 2019, https://shs.hal.science/halshs-02404207/document (retrieved 31.07.2023).

Plessis Alain *L'impôt des français au xixe siècle, replacé dans une perspective européenne*, [in:] Lévy- Leboyer Maurice, Lescure Michel et Plessis Alain (dir.) *L'Impôt en France au XIXe et XXe siècles*, Vincennes 2006 https://books.openedition.org/igpde/10121, (retrieved 12.11.2022).

Plessis Alain *Le franc au XIXe siècle*, [in:] *D'or et d'argent: La monnaie en France du Moyen Age à nos jours*, Vincennes, 2005, http://books.openedition.org/igpde/10568 (retrieved 23.06.2023).

Raybaut Alain Mo*ney and banking in the French Liberal School: Wolowski and the debates on banking regulation in the 1860s*. (https://shs.hal.science/halshs-03504232/document, (retrieved 26.06.2023).

Rothbard Murray *Gustave de Molinari – pierwszy anarchokapitalista*, https://mises.pl/storage/files/articles/2020/11/rothbard-gustave-de-molinari-pierwszy-anarchokapitalista.pdf (retrieved 27.06.2023).

Rudelle Odile *Mars 1875, Janvier 1879 : quelle république ?*, [in:] *La république absolue : 1870–1889*, Publications de la Sorbonne, Paris, 1982, online : http://books.openedition.org/psorbonne/71612 (retrieved 08.06.2023).

Scholem Gershom *Shabtai Zvi (1626–1676) The central figure of Shabbateanism, the messianic movement called after him*, http://www.radicaltorahthought.com/BioZvi_Frank.htm (retrieved 23.03.2022).

Silvant Claire *L'école libérale française et la question du bimétallisme (1860–1885). Enjeux économiques et politiques de la controverse*, „ Oeconomia. Hitory, methodology, philosphy ", no. 2–3, 2012, online : https://journals.openedition.org/oeconomia/1314 (retrieved 23.06.2023).

Simon Jules *Notice historique sur la vie et les travaux de M. Michel Chevalier*, 1889, https://www.academie-francaise.fr/notice-historique-sur-la-vie-et-les-travaux-de-m-michel-chevalier (retrieved 26.06.2023).

Tocqueville Alexis de, *Grands discours parlementaires. Alexis de Tocqueville, 27 janvier 1848*, https://www2.assemblee-nationale.fr/decouvrir-l-assemblee/histoire/grands-discours-parlementaires/alexis-de-tocqueville-27-janvier-1848 (retrieved 04.03.2023).

Warszawskie zabytkowe pomniki nagrobne https://cmentarze.um.warszawa.pl/pomnik.aspx?pom_id=2366 (retrieved 09.11.2023).

Wołowski Franciszek *Odpowiedź ze strony Franciszka Wołowskiego Dziedzica dóbr Kaski z przyległościami Jaktorów i innemi na skargę restytucyjną Prokuratoryi Jeneralney w imieniu włościan jaktorowskich podaną*, https://polona.pl/item/odpowiedz-ze-strony-franciszka-wolowskiego-dziedzica-dobr-kask-z-przyleglosciami,NjY4NDMwNTY/.

Index[*]

[*] The index does not include bibliography pages (305–339)

Polish Studies – Transdisciplinar Perspectives

Edited by Krzysztof Zajas and Jarosław Fazan

Vol. 1 Artur Płaczkiewicz: Miron Białoszewski: Radical Quest beyond Dualisms. 2012.

Vol. 2 Kinga Kosmala: Ryszard Kapuściński: Reportage and Ethics or Fading Tyranny of the Narrative. 2012.

Vol. 3 Michał Nowosielski: Polish Organisations in Germany. Their Present Status and Needs. 2012.

Vol. 4 Krzysztof Zajas: Absent Culture. The Case of Polish Livonia. 2013.

Vol. 5 Magdalena Sitarz: Literature as a Medium for Memory. The Universe of Sholem Asch's Novels. 2013.

Vol. 6 Barbara Przybyszewska-Jarmińska / Lech Sokół (eds.): Poland and Artistic Culture of Western Europe. 14th–20th Century. 2014.

Vol. 7 Katarzyna Fazan / Anna Róża Burzyńska / Marta Bryś (eds.): Tadeusz Kantor Today. Metamorphoses of Death, Memory and Presence. Translated by Anda MacBride. 2014.

Vol. 8 Andrzej Hejmej: Music in Literature. Perspectives of Interdisciplinary Comparative Literature. Translated by Lindsay Davidson. 2014.

Vol. 9 Grzegorz Niziołek: Warlikowski: Extra Ecclesiam. Translated by Soren Gauger. 2015.

Vol. 10 Ryszard Koziołek: Sienkiewicz´s Bodies. Studies of Gender and Violence. Translated by David Malcolm. 2015.

Vol. 11 Wojciech Tygielski: Italians in Early Modern Poland. The Lost Opportunity for Modernization? Translated by Katarzyna Popowicz. 2015.

Vol. 12 Dariusz Jarosz / Maria Pasztor: Polish-French Relations, 1944-1989. Translated by Alex Shannon. 2015.

Vol. 13 Urszula Augustyniak: History of the Polish–Lithuanian Commonwealth. State – Society – Culture. 2015.

Vol. 14 Piotr Sobolczyk: Polish Queer Modernism. 2015.

Vol. 15 Jacek Soszyński / Agnieszka Chamera-Nowak (eds.): Book versus Power. Studies in the Relations between Politics and Culture in Polish History. Editorial assistance by Dan Embree. Translated by Jacek Soszyński 2015.

Vol. 16 Wojciech Kriegseisen: Between State and Church. Confessional Relations from Reformation to Enlightenment: Poland – Lithuania – Germany – Netherlands. Translated by Bartosz Wójcik and copy-edited by Alex Shannon. 2016.

Vol. 17 Urszula Sowina: Water, Towns and People. Polish Lands against a European Background until the Mid-16th Century. Translated by Justyna Woldańska. 2016.

Vol. 18 Grzegorz Krzywiec: Chauvinism, Polish Style. The Case of Roman Dmowski (Beginnings: 1886-1905). Translated by Jarosław Garliński. 2016.

Vol. 19 Andrzej Sakson: Von Memel bis Allenstein. Die heutigen Bewohner des ehemaligen Ostpreußens: Memelland, Kaliningrader Gebiet, Ermland und Masuren. Übersetzt von Marek Drewnowski. 2016.

Vol. 20 Antoni Mączak: Unequal Friendship. The Patron-Client Relationship in Historical Perspective. Translated by Alex Shannon. 2017.

Vol. 21 Olga Szmidt / Katarzyna Trzeciak (eds.): Face in Trouble – From Physiognomics to Facebook. Copy-edited by Soren Gauger. 2017.

Vol. 22 Alina Cala: Jew. The Eternal Enemy? The History of Antisemitism in Poland. 2019.

Vol. 23 Agata Brajerska-Mazur / Edyta Chlebowska (eds.): On Cyprian Norwid. Studies and Essays. Vol. 1: Syntheses. 2019.

Vol. 24 Beata Nowacka / Zygmunt Ziątek: Ryszard Kapuściński. Biographie d'un écrivain. 2019.

Vol. 25 Stanisław Bylina: Religiousness in the Late Middle Ages. Christianity and Traditional Culture in Central and Eastern Europe in the Fourteenth and Fifteenth Centuries. 2019.

Vol. 26 Igor Kąkolewski / Christian Lübke / Przemysław Urbańczyk (eds.): The Dawning of Christianity in Poland and across Central and Eastern Europe. History and the Politics of Memory. 2019.

Vol. 27 Bogumił Szady: The Geography of Religious and Confessional Structures in the Crown of the Polish Kingdom in the Second Half of the Eighteenth Century. 2019.

Vol. 28 Ewa Masłowska: Mediating the Otherworld in Polish Folklore. A Cognitive Linguistic Perspective. 2019.

Vol. 29 Adam Andrzej Kucharski: Placing Poland at the heart of Irishness. Irish political elites in relation to Poland and the Poles in the first half of the nineteenth century. 2020.

Vol. 30 Jolanta Sikorska-Kulesza: The Tolerated Evil. Prostitution in Poland of 19th Century. 2020.

Vol. 31 Żaneta Nalewajk: Leśmian Internationally: Contextual Relations. A Comparative Study. 2020.

Vol 32 Anna Machcewicz: Civility in Uncivil Times. Kazimierz Moczarski's Quiet Battle for Truth, from the Polish Underground to Stalinist Prison. 2020.

Vol. 33 Bartosz Kaliski: Messengers of the Free Word. Paris – Prague – Warsaw, 1968–1971. 2020.

Vol. 34 Dorota Litwin-Lewandowska: For the Polish Raison d'État in Austria. Poles in the Political Life of Austria in the Dual Monarchy Period (1867-1818). 2020.

Vol. 35 Marek Kornat: Poland and the Origins of the Second World War. A Study in Diplomatic History (1938–1939). 2020.

Vol. 36 Barbara Klich-Kluczewska: Family, Taboo and Communism in Poland, 1956-1989. 2021.

Vol. 37 Agata Brajerska-Mazur / Edyta Chlebowska (eds.): On Cyprian Norwid. Studies and Essays. Vol. 2. Aspects. 2021.

Vol. 38 Justyna Straczuk: The Graveyard and the Table. The Catholic-Orthodox Borderland in Poland and Belarus. 2021.

Vol. 39 Marta Wojtkowska-Maksymik / Magdalena Zawisławska (eds.): Studies in Polish Language and Literature. 2022.

Vol. 40 Joanna Gierowska-Kałłaur: The Civic Management of Eastern Territories (1919–1920). The Reasons for the Failure of Piłsudski's Federation Idea. 2022.

Vol. 41 Agata Brajerska-Mazur / Edyta Chlebowska (eds.): On Cyprian Norwid. Studies and Essays. Vol. 3. Interpretations. 2022.

Vol. 42 Maciej Junkiert / Krzysztof Trybuś / Michael Düring / Rebekka Wilpert (eds.): Polen und Deutsche im Angesicht der revolutionären Umwälzungen. 2023.

Vol. 43 Agata Brajerska-Mazur / Edyta Chlebowska (eds.): On Cyprian Norwid. Studies and Essays. Vol. 4. Contexts. 2023.

Vol. 44 Magdalena Śniedziewska: Seventeenth-Century Dutch Painting and Modern Literature. 2024.

Vol. 45 Rafał Dobek: Louis Wolowski (1810-1876). Polish insurgent, French politician, Banker and Economist. 2024.

www.peterlang.com

www.ingramcontent.com/pod-product-compliance
Ingram Content Group UK Ltd.
Pitfield, Milton Keynes, MK11 3LW, UK
UKHW041825100926
8556IPUK00002B/23

9 783631 910948